GW01452765

YADA YAHOWAH

BARE'SYTH

VOLUME ONE

BEGINNING

CRAIG WINN

Craig Winn. *Bare'syth*: *Beginning*.

1st edition. *www.yadayah.com*, 2003.

2nd (revised) edition. *www.yadayah.com*, 2005.

3rd (revised) edition. *www.yadayah.com*, 2006.

4th (revised) edition. *www.yadayah.com*, 2008.

5th (revised) edition. *www.yadayah.com*, 2010.

6th (revised) edition. *www.yadayah.com* and Claitor's Publishing Division, 2012.

7th edition. *www.yadayah.com* and Claitor's Publishing Division, 2013.

8th (revised) edition. *www.yadayah.com* and Amazon, 2017.

9th (revised) edition. *www.yadayah.com* and Amazon, 2020.

10th (revised) edition. *www.yadayah.com* and Amazon, 2023.

11th (revised) edition. *www.yadayah.com*, Amazon, BookVault, and Apple, 2024.

Copyright © Craig Winn 2003-2024

Copyright Statement - *About Us - (www.yadayah.com)*

Ver. 20241121

About the Author…

Twenty-three years ago, Craig Winn was an entrepreneur. The turbulent story of his last adventure is shared in his first book, *In The Company*. It is an entertaining read, providing an eyewitness account into the culture of a private and then public company.

After the Islamic suicide bombings of 9.11.01, Craig met with al Qaeda and wrote *Tea with Terrorists* to explain – *Who they are, Why they kill, and What will stop them*. His most widely read book, *Prophet of Doom – Islam's Terrorist Dogma in Muhammad's Own Words* has now been updated and substantially expanded, becoming *God Damn Religion* after witnessing the sadistic savagery of Muslims on 10.07.23 in Israel. The resulting assessment of Islam is irrefutable because the deplorable nature of this death cult was revealed by reordering the *Quran* chronologically and setting it into the context of Muhammad's life using the earliest and most credible *Hadith*, notably Al-Tabari's *Tarikh* | History and Ibn Ishaq's *Sirat Rasul Allah* | Life of Allah's Messenger. Also, by citing the Torah and Prophets, he has conclusively demonstrated that Allah was invented in the 6th century CE and is not God, much less, Yahowah, the God of Abraham and Moses. If you want to know why fundamentalist Muslims commit 90% of the world's most heinous terrorist acts, these 5 volumes will answer your questions.

In his quest to resolve a puzzling prophetic anomaly, Craig began translating the text of the Dead Sea Scrolls. That endeavor led to the 3-volume series providing *An Introduction to God*, the 8 volumes of *Yada Yahowah*, the 5 books encouraging *Observations,* 3 exploring *Babel*, 5 for *Questioning Paul*, now *Twistianity*, and then to the 3 volumes devoted to *Coming Home*. Throughout, Mr. Winn has been committed to providing amplified translations, which are not only more accurate and complete, they are readily verified. As a result, he has been afforded thousands of unique insights into the words Yahowah inspired, many of which are unheralded and profound.

Beyond his books, Craig Winn has been interviewed as an expert on religion, politics, and current events on over 5,000 talk radio programs and has hosted 5,000 more, leaving a vast quantity of archived shows from Shattering Myths to Yada Yah Radio. He currently produces a live podcast every Friday evening, where he discusses insights gleaned from his translations.

Mr. Winn is not a theologian, nor is he associated with any religious or political institution. He does not accept donations or receive financial backing from anyone. Everything he has written is shared freely online. Even his 35 printed books are offered without royalty.

Craig has devoted his life to exploring Yahowah's revelations. He enjoys God's company and is enriched by the experience. If you have an open mind and a desire to learn, you will enjoy his translations and insights.

He encourages readers to share his translations and resulting conclusions, albeit with two important caveats: 1) You may not use them to promote any religious, political, or conspiratorial agenda. And 2) You may not use them to incite or engage in a violent act. When it comes to exposing errant and counterproductive ideas, wield words wisely.

You may contact Craig at YadaYah.com. He enjoys constructive criticism and will engage with readers. But be forewarned: he is immune to religious idiocy and will not respond to threats or taunts. The YadaYah.com site provides links to his books, to Yada Yah Radio, to many of his audio archives, as well as to friends and forums.

Lastly, Craig has a bias and an agenda. He knows and respects Yahowah, and he has devoted his life to advancing God's primary objective: which is to call His people home.

BARE'SYTH
BEGINNING

Table of Contents:

Prelude

A Conversation with God...

We are embarking on life's greatest adventure. It will take us to a place few have experienced, which is surprising considering the unfathomable riches we will encounter along the way. Our path is so far removed from the road mankind has become accustomed to traveling, for all but a score of the past 2,500 years, no one, not a single solitary soul, has attempted this voyage through words, places, and time.

By continuing, we will meet God. Evidence and reason will lead us to Him. We will come to know Yahowah, appreciate what He is offering, and understand exactly what He expects from us in return. We are headed to the seventh dimension, well past the observable constraints of Euclidean space.

Along the way, should you accept His offer, you will become immortal. Our souls will be perfected. We will be adopted into our Heavenly Father's Family. We will be enriched, enlightened, and empowered, liberated from the control and influence of man and the constraints of the physical realm. Ultimately, you will know the truth – and it will set you free.

While the rewards are extraordinary, there is no fee. Our journey to Heaven will cost you nothing. Even the time we invest along the way will be returned.

That is not to say this will be easy or that we will not be asked to relinquish things many hold dear. Religion and politics are notable examples. These human contrivances preclude honest investigation and impede our progress.

They confuse our thinking and distort our perspective, making understanding difficult, if not impossible.

Although it is the antithesis of what we have been led to believe, God hates religion. His foremost goal is to liberate us from the oppressive nature of its propensity to mislead and confuse, to subjugate and control. Rather than bringing the faithful to God, religion is the most pervasive obstacle blocking the path.

As your guide to the Promised Land, you should know that I am not a prophet – although the prophets spoke of me. The evidence is prolific and irrefutable because God wants you to consider what I have discovered by translating His Towrah, Prophets, and Psalms.

Should that not seem credible at this juncture, do not be concerned. Everything written upon these pages was ascertained by closely examining and carefully considering Yahowah's published and public witness to humankind – albeit with a worthy assist from the *Ruwach Qodesh* | Set-Apart Spirit. I share this because the textual basis for these translations and resulting insights are readily available in the Towrah, Prophets, and Psalms. They collectively provide the underlying text supporting everything you are going to read. And this means that you are in the position to validate every word and insight.

Over these past twenty-two years, I have discovered and published far more than most scholars, but I am not a theologian. I am anti-religious and apolitical. As a devoted student and teacher, I am opposed to the errant approach of academia. I am not among those who claim to be a Messiah or the Son of God – although I know who was afforded these titles. I do not seek fame, fortune, or a following. I eschew accolades, and I am immune to threats.

Other than your company and curiosity, I want nothing from you. This is a labor of love. I do not profit monetarily from these books or radio programs. Even your response is entirely up to you.

Twenty-two years ago, when I hesitantly and naïvely embarked on this adventure with Yahowah, I did not know His name. I had previously been religious, but because of the irrational nature of the Christian faith, I had discarded it and become an agnostic. Although it was obvious that God wanted me to do as I have done, I have long considered myself unqualified and irrelevant. As a consequence, I wrote anonymously under the pen name Yada for well over a decade.

Looking back over this journey, and by comparing myself to others Yahowah has chosen to work alongside, I realize that it was largely because I was once political and religious, and had rejected both, that made my candidacy appealing. When God spoke out against these institutions, His concerns resonated within my soul. But more than anything else, the reason we have worked together so successfully over the years is because, when others were not interested in knowing the truth, I was willing to go where His words led – no matter the cost or consequence.

While that may have been enough considering the dearth of qualified candidates and complete void of responsive individuals, especially among the Chosen People, I share something with Yahowah's beloved, *Dowd* | David, which God likely found serviceable – something He will also value in you. I prize evidence and reason over opinions or beliefs. And as was the case with the psalmist, I understand the importance of context in forming logical conclusions. I prefer this more thoughtful approach to the ill-conceived and half-baked notions of believers which result in foreseeable disasters for misguided individuals, institutions, and nations.

Like Yah's Chosen One, I love knowing and live to understand. I thrive on the discoveries which can be gleaned by making informed connections, especially given the opportunity to share the ensuing insights. As a result of having invested ten hours a day, six days a week, over the past twenty-two years translating Yahowah's *Towrah* | Teaching, His *Naby'* | Prophets, and *Mizmowr* | Psalms, you will find a considerably more complete and accurate presentation. To accomplish this, we will explore the Dead Sea Scrolls to ascertain the truth from the most credible text. In the process, we will learn if God can be known rather than believed.

Along with these amplified translations, you will encounter commentary which is offered to broaden our understanding of the words God inspired His prophets to scribe for our benefit. As a result of this study, you will be exposed to many hundreds of profound insights regarding Yahowah – most of which are presented here for the first time. Many are gems as valuable as life itself.

This is Yahowah's story, in His words, the way He wants it to be told from beginning to end. Therefore, it is paramount for us to recognize that Yahowah is our Creator's one and only name – now and forever. Comprised of four vowels, it is pronounced YaHoWaH. His name, by His own declaration, is based upon the Hebrew verb *hayah*, which means "to exist." With it, God answers our most fundamental questions: is there a God and if so, who is He?

The proper pronunciation of YaHoWaH, a name which was written 7,000 times by the hands of the prophets He inspired, is further clarified by His *Towrah* | Teaching and Guidance. This exceedingly well-known title leaves only the Yowd which is incontrovertible in its pronunciation, to vocalize independently. Therefore, between *hayah* and *towrah*, the mystery is solved, making an accurate transliteration of YHWH indispensable and irrefutable.

This is so straightforward and simple, those who would claim that God's name cannot be pronounced are either inexcusably ignorant or willfully dishonest. And based upon Yahowah's testimony, those who would suggest that God does not care what you call Him would be wrong.

Nothing is more essential to our survival. If you do not know Yahowah's name, you do not know Him. And if you do not know Him, He does not know you. His name not only properly identifies Him, but it also completely dissociates God from every religion – all of which call Him everything but Yahowah.

Let's be clear, contrary to the most popular beliefs, Jesus is not God nor is Allah. Shiva is not God either, nor is HaShem or the Lord. Over five billion people are currently misled – most, deliberately.

The Christian New Testament, the Jewish Talmud, and the Islamic Quran are strictly human endeavors. They are inaccurate and counterproductive. The Apostle Paul, Rabbi Akiba, and the Messenger Muhammad were deplorable, tragically misguided megalomaniacs. These men should be exposed and condemned, not venerated. And we will do so.

Now that I have your attention, and now that you know we are not here to be politically correct, to pretend, or to garner popular support, let's move on to the verb which precedes Yahowah's name in our title: *Yada Yahowah*. *Yada'* means: "to know in a relational sense, to recognize, to acknowledge, and to understand." Therefore, *Yada Yahowah* was written to "*yada'* – know" Yahowah as He revealed Himself to humankind.

Using evidence and reason, we will prove beyond any doubt that it is possible to actually *yada'* Yahowah. No faith will be required. Believing will become a liability.

In a world awash in the stench of religion, where God is mischaracterized, Yahowah proves His existence beyond any doubt throughout His Towrah and Prophets. In the process, He conclusively demonstrates that He authored the testimony we are going to consider. He did this in the best possible way – especially considering that His prime objective is for us to get to know Him so that we can choose to develop a personal, family-oriented relationship with Him. This goal necessitates freewill. And that means Yahowah cannot make the choice to ignore Him impossible, which omnipresence and undeniable proof of His existence would do.

Since you are likely wondering how Yahowah conclusively demonstrated that He authored the testimony known as the Torah, Prophets, and Psalms, while at the same time proving that His witness can be trusted, the answer to both is prophecy. And that is why this book of books will focus on God's predictive statements.

By accurately reporting in our past what will happen in our future, and by committing these specific prognostications to writing centuries prior to their fulfillment, Yahowah demonstrated that He is unconstrained by time. As is the case with the eternal nature of light, God is capable of experiencing the past and future as if they were the present. Therefore, since He has already witnessed that which has yet to occur in the ordinary flow of time, God is not predicting what might happen; He is instead reporting on what He has already seen.

If Yahowah got so much as one very specific and highly improbable prophecy right, we would be foolish to ignore what He had to say. But rather than one prediction, He committed thousands of these revelations to writing – all of which were memorialized in the Towrah, Prophets, and Psalms, with most affirmed throughout the Dead Sea Scrolls.

The ongoing chance fulfillment of these specific and highly unlikely predictions is less likely than winning a million-to-one lottery grand prize with a single ticket a thousand times in a row. Yahowah is so confident regarding His predictions, He says that we are free to reject Him should we find a single error.

Accordingly, while we will focus on God's predictive testimony, do not assume that prophecy will monopolize our time. I say this because with every prediction Yahowah teaches us something important, often profound. And since these instructions are coming from God, the guidance He is providing, along with His prophetic revelations, becomes vastly more important than the fact He can reliably foretell our future.

Speaking of time, one of the more intriguing nuances of Hebrew, the language of revelation, is that there are no past, present, or future tenses. Therefore, as is the case with the inherent properties of light, Hebrew verbs are unrestrained in time. In this way, the language itself explains the method behind such prophecies.

Considering the flow of time, Yahowah's prophets often look back to a period prior to recorded history, presenting the distant past with the same level of accuracy and detail as the present and future. But that is not all that can be uniquely derived from this remarkable language. You will soon discover that Hebrew verbs feature a relational stem, and many are written in a volitional mood. This means that a connection is being developed between the subject and object of each discussion and that the message being conveyed is subject to freewill.

These are some of the elements which work in concert to give Yahowah's revelation greater authenticity. God made these statements to demonstrate His existence and prove His authorship so that we might come to trust His testimony.

His message to us was revealed to present the conditions and benefits associated with His Covenant. Throughout His *Towrah* | Teaching and *Naby'* | Prophets, Yahowah reveals who He is, what He wants, and what He is willing to offer us in return for our respect and appreciation.

These things known, please do not assume that this is a religious book. It is not. The God of the Towrah, Prophets, and Psalms (collectively and known as the "Old Testament") is anti-religious. His animosity toward Judaism, Christianity, Islam, and Socialist Secular Humanism is extreme and unambiguous. More than anything man conceived, God hates religion most of all – every religion without exception. Walking away from these corrupt human institutions is the lone prerequisite for participating in the Covenant relationship. This is perhaps the greatest of all ironies.

As an interesting aside, if you are an agnostic, God's complete disassociation from religion may eliminate most of your objections to Him. You will quickly discover that the idiocy you attribute to mankind's belief in the gods of their own making is invalid, because it has nothing in common with Yahowah's witness. In fact, most of those who have benefited from the testimony which is set out before you were formerly agnostics. It is much easier for someone who is open-minded to examine evidence logically than it is for those plagued by religious beliefs. And ultimately, the case Yahowah makes on His behalf is rationally irrefutable.

It all comes down to this: humans are complex creatures and often malfunction. The Towrah is our Operator's Manual.

𐤉𐤅𐤄𐤉

Composition and Methodology

Getting it Right...

Yada Yahowah will begin where God began, by examining what occurred during the formation of the universe. By carefully observing the Towrah testimony we will come to better appreciate the prophetic, spiritual, and scientific implications associated with the creation account and life on our planet. In so doing, we will prove that there are no material disparities between science and the Divine Writ.

We will consider the conditions in 'Eden, even locate the Garden geographically. Here our focus will be on the prophetic implications of life with God and how we will soon return to where we began.

As it relates to the Protective Enclosure of Great Joy, we will consider why Satan was allowed into the Garden, and then contemplate how he corrupted Yahowah's testimony once inside. In the process, we will learn a great deal about the underpinnings of religion.

Moving on, we will turn our attention to the flood, pondering its implications from a prophetic, spiritual, and scientific perspective. What many have dismissed as a myth will be proven as fact. In the process, we will be introduced to the benefits of listening to Yahowah and then acting upon His advice.

This will lead us to the heart of the purpose of the Towrah – to 'Abram who became 'Abraham – and to the formation of the Covenant. Yahowah's depiction of this relationship is so essential the discussion underlying the establishment of the Covenant is featured in almost every book in this series. Specifically, we will deduce from this discussion the five instructive conditions and five marvelous benefits awaiting those who accept Yahowah's terms.

Each benefit is provided through the fulfillment of the *Miqra'ey* | Invitations to Be Called Out and Meet with God. An anathema and enigma to the faithful adherents of Christianity, Judaism, Islam, as well as Secular Humanism, these seven annual appointments with Yahowah serve as the narrow, unpopular, and restrictive way to become part of our Heavenly Father's Family and to live with Him in His Home.

It is by responding favorably to Yahowah's Invitations, and capitalizing upon their intent, that we are allowed to participate in the "*Beryth* – Covenant" with Him. There is no other path to Heaven, no other means to salvation.

Therefore, we will devote three volumes of *Yada Yahowah* to the *Miqra'ey* | Invitations to Be Called Out and Meet. By carefully observing the *Mow'edym* | Eternal Witnesses to the Restoring Testimony, we will become aware of God's most sweeping prophecies throughout time. We will not only analyze what occurred during the three most important days in human history – *Pesach* | Passover, *Matsah* | UnYeasted Bread, and *Bikuwrym* | Firstborn Children in 33 CE (year 4,000 Yah), we will ascertain the timing and consequence of the last four: *Shabuw'ah* | Sevens, *Taruw'ah* | Trumpets, *Kipurym* | Reconciliations, and *Sukah* | Shelters. We will share the proper approach to observing Yahowah's Festival Feasts and, in so doing, convey God's redemptive plan.

Speaking of the *Miqra'ey* | Invitations to Be Called Out and Meet, we will closely examine why *Dowd* | David wrote, "My God, my God, why have you forsaken me?" at the inception of his prophetic depiction of himself enduring the torturous effects of Roman crucifixion. We will also explain why we have concluded that it was *Dowd* | David as *Gabry'el* | God's Most Capable and Competent Man who told Daniel not only what he would accomplish by fulfilling the *Mow'edym*, but also precisely when he would enter *Yaruwshalaim* | Jerusalem as the Passover Lamb in year 4000 Yah / 33 CE.

The realization that Yahowah fulfilled the first three Miqra'ey – Pesach and Matsah leading to Bikuwrym – with His Son, Dowd, is profoundly important. And not only is it essential to our salvation, the most courageous and compassionate act in human history has been missed by everyone for thousands of years. Nonetheless, this reality is affirmed countless times throughout Yahowah's prophetic testimony, to the point that it is irrefutable. And yet, it is overtly denied by the founders and advocates of Judaism, Christianity, and Islam.

Beyond this profound truth, *Dowd* | David, as the Son of God, the Messiah, and returning King, made the Miqra'ey Qatsyr and Laqat of Shabuw'ah and Taruw'ah possible and he is the one who will fulfill Yowm Kipurym on behalf of Sukah in year 6,000 Yah – beginning at sunset, October 2nd, 2033. So should the testimony regarding how Father and Son redeemed the children of the *Beryth* | Covenant and will soon reconcile the relationship with *Yisra'el* | Individuals who Engage and Endure with God be of great interest to you, consider jumping ahead in this study of Yahowah's Word to the *Coming Home* series which explicitly deals with it.

Some may ask, what about the thirteen principles of Judaism? Why speak of "God's unity" when His identity is kept from the faithful? How can God have dined with 'Abraham and Moseh if He was incorporeal? Were the column of fire by night and the pillar of clouds by day during the Exodus imaginary? Why state that "God alone should be the object of worship" when Yahowah clearly detests the idea of being worshiped? What is the thinking behind "God's law having been given to Moseh" when Towrah means "Guidance and Teaching," not "Law," and the Talmud takes precedence over it in Judaism? Why speak of the "resurrection of the dead" when there is no means within Judaism to ascertain the fate of a soul? Why speak of a nameless "coming of the Jewish Messiah" when the Mashyach has not only been here twice previously, but he was also prophet and lyricist, Shepherd and Lamb, Messiah and King?

Clearly, neither religious Jews nor Christians will find God's answers compatible with their sensibilities. Most will reject His approach outright in preference for Paul's, Maimonides', or Akiba's arguments. And that is why God condemns religion, and so we offer a foreshadowing of the adversarial roles of religious, political, and geographic Babylon.

Unique to *Yada Yahowah* is the riveting comparison between *Howsha's* | Hosea's *Yisra'el* | Israel and today's troubled world. Through it, Yahowah reveals that observing His Towrah is central and essential to developing a relationship with Him. He emphatically states that ignorance is disastrous.

Especially fascinating, by studying the prophetic pronouncements chronicled in Howsha', we will discover something very few people have considered: the overwhelming preponderance of human souls will simply cease to exist, not going to heaven or hell. We will also find affirmation of God's timeline – of humankind's six-thousand-year journey from the Garden and then back to 'Eden.

While the concluding volume of *Yada Yahowah* will describe the evolution of the most debilitating beasts man will encounter along the way, from Babylon to Persia, from Persia to Greece, from Greece to Rome, and from Imperial

Rome to Roman Catholicism, the essence of what constitutes *Babel* | Confusion, known as Babylon, will not be pursued until *Observations*. There we will find ample evidence revealing the root cause of religion and demonstrate why God hates it.

We will discover that "*babel* – intermixing" is the method behind Satan's madness. The Devil has literally managed to "*babel* – confuse" the preponderance of people so thoroughly, they unwittingly worship him as if he were God. Satan commingles his objectives with snippets of Yahowah's testimony – always out-of-context, twisted, misappropriated, and misconstrued.

As our understanding grows, we will come to better appreciate the reasons why Yahowah asks us to walk away from controlling human schemes before trying to approach Him. Many hundreds of God's most anti-religious and anti-political statements will be scrutinized in *Yada Yahowah* to comprehensively demonstrate that Babylon is symbolic of the means Satan uses to beguile humankind into bowing down to him as the Lord.

Even after all of this time, many of the most riveting prophecies are still waiting to be translated, making *Yada Yahowah*, *Observations*, and *Coming Home* works in progress. Eventually, we hope to present almost everything which can be known about the Last Days on Earth. Witnessing the fulfillment of Yahowah's prophetic testimony as it unfolds before our eyes is both reassuring and motivating.

As we pursue this mission, our goal remains to make certain that *Yahuwdym* | Jews primarily, and *Gowym* | Gentiles secondarily, are equipped with ample and irrefutable evidence to reject the ways of man and come to trust and rely upon Yah. Doing so continues to constitute a life well spent.

Should you come to share my passion to know the truth, should you be able to endure the level of detail and analysis required to understand what Yahowah is seeking to achieve, and should you be willing to invest the time needed to examine the connections and associations God has drawn, contemplating the symbols and metaphors which permeate His every thought, you will come to *"yada'* – know" Yahowah. That is a promise. Should you be able to open your mind, alter your perspective, and change your thinking, you will come to know God as He revealed Himself. And that is His guarantee.

What is more, you will be properly prepared to capitalize upon Yahowah's Covenant Relationship, ultimately traveling to the seventh dimension in the process. There is nothing better in life or the universe.

This progression of things, of coming to know Yahowah first, capitalizing upon His Covenant Relationship second, and then relying upon His means of liberation and salvation, are among the many things the religious get wrong. They never come to know God as He revealed Himself in the Towrah, Prophets, and Psalms. Their religion focuses instead on what they must do to be seen as good so that they can be saved.

And even that is a bone of contention because Yahowah has very little interest in us trying to be good. Even the best will not find salvation. Instead, God wants us to be right. Being correct rather than good is what distinguished Dowd above all others. And since this is an open-book test, with a little help along the way, you will soon be following in Dowd's footsteps.

Speaking of being right, as a direct result of reading *Yada Yahowah, An Introduction to God, Observations,* or *Coming Home,* you will become aware of the one surprising prerequisite, and then encounter the four requirements associated with the Covenant relationship, in conjunction with its amazing array of benefits. Coming to understand and embrace these things is absolutely vital to the health and wellbeing of your soul.

As we turn the pages of the Towrah we find Yahowah not only explaining His name, but also revealing how He wants us to view Him, and how He wants us to live our lives, scribing His perspective in stone. Therefore, we will carefully examine the words Yahowah personally etched on those two tablets. I dare say you will be shocked by how different God's revelation is from man's popular renditions of the "Ten Commandments."

As we embark on this journey, we will scrutinize the terminology Yahowah revealed under an etymological microscope, amplifying His every word, so that we learn as much as possible. During our voyage through terms and time, the overall portrait God has painted will be brilliantly illuminated.

All the while, we will focus on prophecy because precise predictions which consistently materialize as written serve as the means Yahowah uses to prove that we are searching in the proper place for answers. Through them, God not only proves His existence, but He also demonstrates beyond any reasonable doubt that He inspired His testimony. He did so because He wants us to know Him, to choose to engage in a relationship with Him, and to understand the path He has provided Home.

And yet, with all of this before us, finding God in the Towrah is so contrary to the teachings of the Jewish, Christian, and Islamic religions, most will simply reject this possibility, choosing instead to cling to the misguided tenets of their faith. For the religious, God's Word remains insufficient to free them from their beliefs. In fact, the onslaught of irrefutable evidence and unassailable logic which God provides continues to be squandered on those beguiled by man's religious schemes.

Jews disregard Moseh's (Moses') eye-opening proclamations in the Towrah in favor of their Talmud's mind-numbing rabbinical arguments. Christians replaced everything God has to say with the idiocy of Paul and pals who thought it would be fun to demean God's Son in favor of their Dionysian myth, "Jesus." And Muslims disregard the fact that Muhammad's Quran is the antithesis of Yahowah's Towrah, even though Allah's most basic claim is that his book confirms that which it constantly contradicts. Sadly, most of those seeking God will be precluded from finding Him as a consequence of the ignorant and illogical nature of their faith.

A thorough investigation of the evidence pertaining to mankind's presence in the universe, and to an accurate understanding of God, leads to an inescapable conclusion: the words Yahowah inspired – His Towrah, Prophets, and Psalms – comprise the world's only rational candidate for Divine inspiration. I do not expect you to concur with me, or Him, in this regard, seeing as you are less than twenty pages into this process, but I have no doubt that, somewhere along this journey, if you are intellectually honest, you will render a similar verdict. Frankly, the case Yahowah makes on behalf of His revelation is so compelling I am amazed most people continue to stumble in the dark.

You can be assured that we will travel along a completely reliable path to God – the very one Yahowah, Himself, provided. And when we reach our destination, we will know exactly what we can expect from Him – and we will not be disappointed. We will even find Father and Son waiting for us with open arms.

We have a lot of ground to cover. In order to understand what Yahowah had to say about Himself, His Son, and their relationship with us, many religious myths will have to be shattered, and new, fertile ground will need to be plowed. In the pages which follow, we will pull the weeds of heresy. We will lay fallow false terminology, replacing it with God's testimony.

We will cultivate an appreciation for God's Word. In so doing, we will reveal the names and titles our Creator selected. We will determine the proper recipient for each – something you may find shocking initially but ultimately reassuring. We will also expose the sordid history of religious texts and Bible translations. The truth in this regard may be difficult for many to accept even though the evidence is incontrovertible.

Throughout the 8 volumes of *Yada' Yahowah*, and in each of the collections which follow, including 3 volumes of *An Introduction to God*, 5 of *Observations*, 3 of *Coming Home*, 3 of *Babel*, 5 of *Twistianity*, and the 5 volumes of *God Damn Religion*, we will prevail by relying upon Yah. We will commence with His Towrah Guidance and Teaching. By diligently composing and systematically analyzing amplified translations, then thoughtfully considering each word, we will find ourselves probing the implications of Creation, contemplating the instructive conditions of the Covenant, and observing Yahowah's seven Invitations to be Called Out and Meet. Along the way, we will evaluate God's most sweeping prophecies so that we know where we have been and understand exactly where we are going.

We will come to realize that one man means more to us and to God than all others. His name is *Dowd* | David. He is the *Mashyach* | Messiah, the *Melek* | King, the Shepherd, Chosen One, Hand of God, Son of God, Firstborn, and Passover Lamb. Dowd is the central figure in God's ongoing relationship with man and our Savior.

Turning our attention to the words which comprise the Word of God, we will assess the oldest Hebrew manuscripts using the most reputable lexicons. And in order to provide the proper perspective from which to view

God's testimony, we will review the legacy of the underlying texts demonstrating what was, and was not, inspired and trustworthy.

We will scrutinize the sordid history of translations and reveal the truth about the texts so many have been fooled into believing "inerrant" when they are hopelessly unreliable. We will deploy every tool at our disposal to scrutinize the witnesses whom Yahowah proves are trustworthy.

Since it is foundational, since it provides the proper perspective from which to understand Yahowah's Word, His Name, His Covenant, His Teaching, His Instructions, and His Way, once we have drained the religious swamp of its corruptions, our journey of discovery will commence with a systematic review of what the Towrah has to say about itself. In the process, we will determine that *Towrah* / Torah does not mean "Law" and that there is no Hebrew word for "obey."

Be forewarned, our devotion to the terms Yahowah inspired will be comprehensive. God did not intend for us to divide His instructions into testaments, chapters, or verses, much less hide them behind Talmud*s*. It is counterproductive to take snippets of His teaching out of context. Therefore, we will be methodical and thorough in our observations, closely examining and carefully considering the guidance Yahowah has thoughtfully provided.

In the order of things, Yahowah etched the Ten Statements in stone 586 years after He established His Covenant. We will follow His example and consider the sweeping three-statement introduction and seven instructions because the ultimate destination of our souls relies upon them. To understand what He had to say to us, we will open the second book of the Torah to *Shemowth* | Names, where we will find Yahowah not only explaining

His name, but also revealing how He wants us to view Him, to interact with Him, and to live our lives.

While you may think that you know what God wrote on these tablets, I am fairly certain many will be astonished to learn that God's mercy isn't for everyone, even for most, but instead "for thousands." This represents less than one in a million souls. This realization, in and of itself, disqualifies every religion, as their adherents are in the millions and billions.

Moreover, the fortunate beneficiaries of Yahowah's fortuitous gift will receive it, not through faith or grace, nor through strict obedience to an exhaustive set of laws, but instead by trusting in that which can be proven. As is the case with most everything Yahowah revealed, the message He wrote is profoundly different than man's perverse revisions of the "Ten Commandments" plastered on church, synagogue, and courthouse walls.

𐤟𐤉𐤄𐤅𐤄𐤟

It would be disingenuous and disrespectful of us to seek salvation before coming to know our Savior. Who are we to tell God what we want from Him before we even bother to consider what He expects from us? Praying to God before even listening to Him is disrespectful, selfish, and rude.

It should be obvious. Yahowah is considerably smarter and more capable than His creation. Since it follows that we will gain far more listening to His advice than offering our own, why do the faithful prefer prayer over reading the Towrah?

By avoiding the only sensible approach, religions have conjured up a cadre of ridiculous notions – none of which will prevail. They are all ludicrous. It matters not if they propose adherence to rabbinic laws, faith in the gospel of grace, institutional vows and conversions, jihad, political correctness, or multiculturalism. All of this leads to the same place – the death and destruction of one's soul.

While there are countless gods that have been created in the likeness of the men promoting them, including Bel, Ba'al, Ra, Zeus, Apollo, Dionysus, HaShem, the Lord, Jesus, and Allah, individually and collectively they are worse than worthless. Clerics with their caricatures in hand, contrive scriptures which focus upon what one has to agree upon, ally with, support, fight for, pay homage to, do, or believe in to be saved from the specter of death. And yet, what on earth prompts the faithful to believe that God wants to accept someone into His Home who wouldn't even recognize Him if they were invited inside?

Sadly, most of those seeking God will be precluded from finding Him as a direct result of their religious and political indoctrination. That is because beliefs are actually a substitute for knowlege, and knowing renders faith invalid and obsolete. Rather than deal with the truth, those who are overtly religious, political, or conspiratorial will invariably accept human counterfeits, corruptions, justifications, and interpretations over the Word of God.

But what words did God actually authorize, endorse, and inspire? Is there a way we can know for certain that the Towrah, Prophets, and Psalms are factual and reliable and that the letters which comprise the New Testament are not? Turns out, Yahowah provided us with a very specific test in *Dabarym* | Deuteronomy that He wants us to use to conclusively demonstrate that He did not inspire Enoch, Jubilees, Maccabees, the Gospels, Acts, any of Paul's Epistles, the Talmud, Zohar, Book of Mormon, or the Quran. His test requires consistency and accuracy throughout the whole of time. It is specific in saying that every pronouncement, whether historic or prophetic, must be one hundred percent accurate – even in the details.

Beyond God's detailed and specific test, after having dedicated myself to addressing this question, I have come to realize that once you achieve the proper perspective and stand on the right foundation, the process of affirming what Yahowah inspired is not difficult. Not only is He consistent in His message and style, but His testimony is also filled with so many profoundly revealing insights, and so many prophetic references, collectively they prove Divine inspiration. And by contrast, the works of man are conflicting, contradictory, historically invalid, and sorely lacking. We will find this irrefutably so in the first half of Daniel and throughout Ezekiel. The same is true with the books of Enoch and Esther, Job and Jonah – and, of course, the entirety of the Christian New Testament and Quran.

As evidence of God's position on this issue, please consider the following introduction to an amplified translation:

"**Yahowah's** (*Yahowah* – the proper pronunciation of YaHoWaH, our *'elowah* – God as directed in His *ToWRaH* – teaching regarding His *HaYaH* existence and our *ShaLoWM* – restoration) **Towrah** (*Towrah* – source of instructions, teaching, directions, and guidance) **is complete and entirely perfect** (*tamym* – without defect, lacking nothing, correct, sound, genuine, right, helpful, healing, beneficial, and true)**, returning, restoring, and transforming** (*shuwb* – turning around, bringing back, changing, and renewing) **the soul** (*nepesh* – our consciousness).

Yahowah's (*Yahowah* – written as directed by His *towrah* – teaching regarding His *hayah* – existence) **testimony** (*'eduwth* – enduring witness) **is trustworthy and reliable** (*'aman* – verifiable and true, confirming and supportive, dependable and establishing), **making understanding and obtaining wisdom** (*chakam* – educating and enlightening to the point of comprehension)

simple for the open-minded (*pethy* – open and straightforward for the willing and inclined).**"** (Psalm 19:7)

Since many are just now becoming accustomed to witnessing Yahowah's personal and proper name in print, let's reconsider its pronunciation. Many have heard and read that Jews and/or Christians have "too much respect for it" to write it or that "no one actually knows how to pronounce it because it was written using four consonants." Yet none of this is true.

The religious despise Yahowah's name, from Orthodox Jews to Roman Catholics, from Muslims to Secular Humanists. Their disdain is so great, the pope has actually banned its use, and the last time Jewish clerics were empowered, they killed anyone who said it.

God's name consists of four letters, which are all vowels and all of which are among the standard twenty-two characters which comprise the Hebrew alphabet. Also interesting, especially relative to these characters, they were scribed in the ancient paleo-Hebrew script, which represents mankind's oldest phonetic alphabet. Our word "alphabet" is derived from a transliteration of the first two Hebrew letters: Aleph and Beyth.

Using these twenty-two characters, five of which are vowels (representing the open-mouth sounds in a language as opposed to the more closed-mouth pronunciation of consonants), we can pronounce all 8,000 words, titles, and names which appear in the Towrah, Prophets, and Psalms – without exception. The notion that one name using these same letters is unpronounceable is preposterous.

The first Hebrew letter in Yahowah's name, the Yowd ('), is pronounced similarly to the y or i in English. *Yisra'el*, which we transliterate as "Israel," is a prime example. *Yasha'yah*, which is transliterated as "Isaiah," is another case in point. No one questions the proper pronunciation of *yada'* either.

Moving to the next letter in God's name, some 99.9% of the time the Hebrew letter Hey (ה) appears in a word, it is pronounced "ah," as is the case with the verb upon which Yahowah's name is based: "*hayah* – to exist." Towrah, which is commonly transliterated "Torah," is another classic example, as is *'elowah*, the Hebrew word for "Almighty God."

That leaves us with a single challenge – the Hebrew letter Wah (ו). But it is hardly a mystery. Four of the best-known Hebrew words all contain a Wah: *Towrah*, *Shalowm*, *'Elowah*, and *Gowym*. In every case, the Wah is pronounced as an "o" in English.

In English, the *lingua franca* of the world, the Wah's legacy is reflected in words like own, owl, owe, and growth. Or consider allow, bow, brow, brown, clown, crown, cow, down, dowry, empower, fowl, flower, frown, grow, growth, grown, growl, how, know, low, mow, now, pow, row, sow, shower, tow, town, towel, vow, ow, or wow. The evidence is overwhelming.

Therefore, even with a cursory review of the language, it becomes obvious that God's name, יהוה (reading right to left) – YHWH, is pronounced: Y-aH-oW-aH. The only mystery is why something this important has been hidden for so long and why so many who actually know better have lied.

Focusing upon the statement *Dowd* | David was inspired to compose in his *Mizmowr* | Psalm, we discover that the "means to understanding," even "to wisdom," as well as "to the restoration of our soul," is "to trust Yahowah's testimony." At the time this was written, it was found exclusively in the Torah, which later developed into the Prophets and Psalms.

By the time we have reached the conclusion of *Yada Yahowah* and have moved on to *An Introduction to God*, *Observations*, and *Coming Home*, even *Babel*, *Twistianity*, and *God Damn Religion*, you will become acquainted with many things, including the challenges inherent in translation, the history and corruption of the textual witness, even the emergence of counterfeit names, words, titles, and rituals. But more than this, you will be given a window into the mind of God, and come, perhaps for the first time, to understand His nature, His purpose, His offer, His timing, and His plan – especially as it pertains to the development of the Covenant. It is a personal and familial relationship where we are invited to walk with, to talk with, and to be upright in the presence of God Himself. In these pages, you will discover the extraordinary means Yahowah deployed so that we might camp out with Him and explore the universe for all eternity.

While Yahowah stated that "enlightenment and comprehension" would be "simple for those who are open" to His *Towrah* | Guidance, Teaching, and Instructions, that will not come easy to those whose minds have been closed by religious, political, patriotic, or conspiratorial beliefs. Faith, and/or conviction in man's musings repels evidence and reason. And yet, your relationship with God is predicated upon correctly understanding His testimony. I hope that you are up for this challenge.

Recognizing that three out of every four people living today, some six billion Christians, Muslims, Hindus, and Secular Humanists, are conditioned to believe that the Torah is no longer pertinent because it is superseded by more modern approaches to life, I'd be remiss if I didn't encourage you to contemplate the ramifications of what was just revealed. By stating that "Yahowah's Towrah is complete and perfect, lacking nothing," that "the Towrah" is responsible for "restoring and transforming the soul," and by saying that "Yahowah's…testimony is trustworthy and reliable," especially "easy to understand," God undermined the foundations of Christianity, Judaism, and Islam with a single stroke.

Through His Son, God contradicted the messages delivered by the "Apostle Paul" (that the Towrah was obsolete and cannot save), by Rabbi Akiba (that rabbis must interpret the Towrah using their Oral Law), and by the 'Prophet Muhammad' (that the Quran is God's first, last, and perfect revelation). The very God all three of these men used to justify their authority, the God they all claimed to speak on behalf of, effectively told us that they could not be trusted.

This is an astonishing observation, so let's linger here a moment longer. Paul, who appears to be the first to speak of himself and others as rabbis, wrote Galatians and Romans (his first and sixth letters) for the express purpose of convincing his audience that "the Torah was now obsolete, that the Torah was a cruel taskmaster which enslaved, that the 'Law' was of the flesh, that Yahowah's instructions should be ignored, and that this Torah never had the power to save anyone." The fact that Father and Son, Yahowah and Dowd, said and did otherwise was no issue for Paul because he defamed and renamed both, burying their testimony beneath his own.

It was upon Paul's letters, and the likes of Matthew, Mark, and Luke whom he inspired, that the religion of Christianity was conceived. Yet based upon this statement from Yahowah (and many others like it), the Christian New Testament is proven invalid. And without Paul's letters, and the books his devotees authored, there would be no New Testament, no "Gospel of Grace," and no "salvation by faith." Simply stated: Christianity dies with Paul – a man whose doctrine God just refuted.

It is no better for religious Jews. They not only refused to accept Dowd as the Passover Lamb, thereby nullifying his sacrifice, they augmented and replaced the book that was deemed complete and perfect with two Talmuds, the Mishnah, and Zohar.

I am not sharing this with you to make you angry but in hopes that Jewish and Christian readers might be able to cleanse their mental slate, or at least realize that it may require some scrubbing. And that is because the only informed and rational conclusion which can be drawn from this passage is that Paul's letters and Akiba's arguments were neither inspired nor reliable.

"Yahowah's Towrah" is comprised of our Creator's "prescriptions for living," His "authorized instructions and directions." It "lacks nothing," which would include the means to find the truth and restore our relationship with Him. Based upon the Psalm, God's Word is unchanged from beginning to end. Especially relevant in this regard is the fact that the purpose of Yahowah's Towrah is to "restore and transform our soul" so that we can "return" Home. This makes the Towrah the eternal path to God – something which ought to have been obvious since *towrah* means "to guide and direct."

In due time, we shall discover that the Way to God is presented in the heart of the Towrah. This path Home is comprised of a seven-step plan whereby Yahowah, with Dowd's assistance, provided the means to eternal life through the promises contained in the seven "*Mow'ed Miqra'ey* – Called-Out Assembly Meetings." Our journey to heaven begins with "*Pesach* – Passover," the Doorway to Life, and culminates with "*Sukah* – Shelters," our invitation to Camp Out with our Heavenly Father for all eternity.

I realize that this view is unpopular, but ought not God's position on this issue matter more than humankind's – no matter how many religious people say otherwise? Simply stated, if God used prophecy to prove that He exists and that He inspired the Torah, Prophets, and Psalms, as this book will affirm, then who are we to contradict Him?

While this lone statement from Dowd, assuredly the most important man who ever lived, serves as a wholesale repudiation of Pauline Doctrine and thus of Christianity, it was not the only religion impaled by Yahowah's Word – just the first. Rabbi Akiba's Rabbinic and Pharisaic Judaism, which is the surviving form of the religion codified by Maimonides and practiced today, was predicated on the notion that the pronunciation of God's name was unknown, that it should never be spoken, that His Torah was not complete, which necessitated their Oral Law, and that they, not He, controlled the fate of Jewish souls. They professed that the only way to understand their nameless god's "rules" was to rely upon their explanations.

Therefore, while religious Jews claim that they are "observing the Torah," in actuality, based upon the countless conflicts between Yahowah's Torah and Rabbinic Oral Law, religious Jews have been "*halakhah* – walking" away from Yahowah, His Torah, and His Covenant, for centuries.

Muhammad's rhythmic recital, better known as the Quran (based upon the Hebrew word *qara'* – to read and recite), repetitively claims to have "confirmed the *Tawrat* (an errant transliteration of *towrah*), the *Zabur* (a reference to the Davidic Psalms from a perversion of the Hebrew *zamir*, meaning "song"), and the *Injeel* (a corruption of the Greek *euangelion*)" – all written in "perfect Arabic." And yet, the Arabic alphabet is actually comprised of Hebrew letters and all of the Quran's most important words are of Hebrew origin. And it is those words which have been twisted to convey a message opposite of the one communicated in this Psalm. As such, whether or not God's Towrah is reliable, Islam is not, because something which consistently contradicts that which it claims was inspired by God cannot be true.

Therefore, the Torah, which is claimed by three faiths, destroys the credibility of these religions with a single stroke. And perhaps, this is the greatest irony of all.

ฬYฬ⅃

Now for a word of warning: each volume of *Yada Yahowah* is longer than most books, and vastly more detailed, as are the longer and more challenging series that follow it. God is much smarter than we are, and His writing style is brilliantly majestic. He has woven a marvelous plot, one in which every detail is included for a reason, and one in which passages communicate on several levels simultaneously.

I have been asked many hundreds, perhaps even thousands, of times, to simplify and shorten *Yada Yahowah* – and yet, each iteration I compose becomes longer and more insightful. The more I learn and the deeper the understanding, the better it becomes from my perspective – and I think from God's. While it is all stimulating and satisfying, it is never enough. I want to continue learning and growing forever.

However, for those who do not share my enthusiasm, I have endeavored to condense this twenty-thousand-page study of divine revelation into a hundred-page introductory book. Focused upon the Ten Statements Yahowah wrote with His own hand, it is entitled, *Written in Stone*. And even then, it will require a reader's undivided attention.

Yahowah does not want any of this to be overly simplified, such that an insincere individual can sneak into Heaven with the least amount of effort. It is the wrong attitude and approach. It would also set up future conflicts in Heaven which would be uncomfortable for those who are more genuine in their quest to know God. Therefore, I cannot and I will not abridge my commentary on the text.

While *Yada Yahowah* is among the best-researched and most accurate presentations of Yahowah's Word, and while the many unique insights contained within it are especially relevant and revealing, it will always be little more than a pale reflection of the truth manifested in God's own testimony. The overall scope of the redeeming and affirming revelations contained within Yahowah's Word exceeds my grasp by many magnitudes – and I'm constantly learning. This means that what I wrote yesterday isn't as astute as what I can share today.

So, since my best efforts to till the depths of His testimony fall short of finding everything He provided, at the very least, I owe it to you and to God to convey as much of His revelation as I am capable of understanding. Fortunately, in spite of my deficiencies, the richness of Yahowah's revelation is more than sufficient for you to know God, to appreciate the benefits of His Covenant, and to rely upon Him. That is, so long as you are willing to open your mind, walk away from religious and political affiliations, and invest the time.

The evidence affirms that Yahowah's testimony was as inerrant as words allow when it was revealed in Ancient Hebrew to Moseh and to the Children of Yisra'el. But God makes no claim that human translations are inerrant because He knows that it is impossible. While language is mankind's most important tool, it is an imprecise one – especially apart from Hebrew, the language God, Himself, authored.

No language translates perfectly from one dialect to another. And while we grapple with these issues, the biggest problem with translations is that the most popular "Bibles" bear little resemblance to the oldest manuscripts. As a rough rule of thumb, at least with regard to the Torah, Prophets, and Psalms, I have found that the oldest manuscripts (those found in Qumran dating from the 1st, 2nd, and 3rd centuries BCE and 1st century CE) differ from the more recent ones that serve as the basis of our translations (the oldest Masoretic Text dates to the 11th century CE) by one word in fifteen prior to diacritical markings – and most of these differences are fairly minor. The Masoretes' scheme of diacritical markings for "vowel pointing" alters the text by a similar degree.

However, when we examine man's attempts at translation, the problem is much worse. When communicating important concepts, one word in five is errantly conveyed, and yet, another one in five is so inadequately presented that much of the meaning is lost. In other words, less than fifty percent of what was derived from the Hebrew text is reliably presented in English Bible translations.

By way of example, God asked His prophets to scribe His name – Yahowah – 7,000 times in His testimony. That is an average of seven times per page when His message is formatted in a standard fashion. But on each occurrence, religious men elected to copyedit the Author, replacing His name with a title of their own choosing – one associated with the Lord, better known as Satan.

But that's comparatively great news. With access to the Dead Sea Scrolls, with the capacity to look beyond the Masoretes' vowel-pointing scheme, with access to a score of lexicons, with the ability to examine the etymological roots of each word, by thoughtfully considering the pictures painted by the earliest Hebrew alphabet, and with amplification, Yahowah's testimony can be rendered with ninety-nine percent accuracy. It will take a patient, diligent, and systematic approach, but considering the Source, it is worth the effort.

With all of these tools at our disposal, the Masoretic Text, the Dead Sea Scrolls, copious lexicons, and the pictures drawn by the original letters, we can turn back the pages of time and observe the words as Yahowah intended them to be seen. And with these tools, you are empowered to validate or challenge my conclusions. With a little effort, you will gain a working knowledge of the most revealing Hebrew words along with an understanding of the language's relational stems, volitional moods, and descriptive conjugations.

The Greek text comprising the Christian New Testament is another story altogether. The oldest extant manuscripts, representing codices dating to the 2nd through early 4th century CE, differ so substantially from one another and so overwhelmingly from the mid-4th century manuscripts fabricated by the Roman Catholic Church, like the *Codexes Sinaiticus* and *Vaticanus*, that there is no hope of accurately reconstructing the overwhelming preponderance of that text.

Philip Comfort, the world's leading authority on this subject, wrote the following indictment in his "Introduction" to the *Text of the Earliest New Testament Greek Manuscripts:* "This book provides transcriptions of sixty-nine of the earliest New Testament manuscripts.... All of the manuscripts are dated from the early second century to the beginning of the fourth (A.D. 100 – 300). We chose A.D. 300 as our *terminus da quem* because New Testament manuscript production changed radically after the persecution under Diocletian (A.D. 303 – 305) and especially after Constantine declared Christianity to be a legal religion in the empire."

As obvious as it has become that the text of the Christian New Testament (CNT) is nearly worthless, errant in its inception and careless in its transmission, most people are so blinded by their faith that they continue to believe its beguiling words. They have no idea what they are missing, having traded the truth for a lie. There is, however, some value to the CNT because we can use it to expose and condemn the authors, demonstrating how the anti-Semitic rants and senseless fairytales were comprised. In other words, we will refer to the CNT to prove that it is false.

With Yahowah, it is a completely different experience, because every word is revealing, telling a consistent story. For example, "Jew" is actually Yahuwd and means "Related to Yah and Beloved of Yah." "Israel" is a transliteration of Yisra'el, which means "Individuals who Engage and Endure with God." "Isaiah," the most prolific of the prophets, is based upon Yasha'yah, which can be translated: "Liberation and Salvation Are from Yah." "David" is actually written Dowd and means "Beloved." "Moses" is from Moseh, meaning "To Draw Out."

And on and on it goes, with a lost lesson encapsulated in every anglicized name. In fact, as we shall discover, there are 260 names and titles which are based on Yahowah's name found throughout the Torah, Prophets, and Psalms. Collectively, these affirm aspects of God's character and purpose no less than ten thousand times.

In this regard, it is interesting to note that, second only to Yahowah's name, *Dowd* | David is the next most prevalent, appearing over 1000 times. By comparison, the Christian fixation on "Jesus" is negated by the fact that it is not found in a single prophecy – which is why Christians must rob Dowd to contrive the myth of Jesus. Then moving on to the next name in the order of importance after Yahowah and Dowd, we find that Moseh is the third most-cited moniker.

The same is true with many of the words Yahowah selected. Men have changed them. "Holy" is a misrepresentation of *qodesh*, meaning "set apart." It is one of the most oft-repeated and revealing concepts – one applied to Yah's Spirit and to His Son, Dowd, to Yisra'el and Yahuwdym, to the Sabbath and to the Temple, to the Covenant and to the seven Invitations to Be Called Out and Meet with God.

Towrah, as we have mentioned, means "guidance and teaching, instruction and direction," not law. The correct definition is subject to freewill and is liberating, while man's corruption must be obeyed and is limiting.

Speaking of "obey," the concept does not exist in the Hebrew language. The term typically misrepresented as such is *shama'* and it means "listen." Likewise, *shamar* is often rendered as "keep" when it actually means "observe."

If we want to know what God said, we need to ignore these faulty renditions and translate His words accurately. And we should not make up words and wrongly attribute them to God. There is no reference to a church or to faith, to rabbis or being kosher, or even to something called a Bible.

The concept of an Old and a New Testament was developed by Paul to discredit the Towrah and then popularized by Marcion, an anti-Semitic Christian, who shaped and promoted the new religion Paul had conceived. According to Yahowah, there is one Covenant that He will renew upon His return by integrating His Towrah.

Moreover, the term "Covenant" is from *beryth*, which speaks of "a family-oriented relationship." I say that because *beryth* is based upon *beyth*, meaning "family and home," further defining the kind of relationship Yahowah is interested in establishing.

𐤉𐤄𐤅𐤄

At their best, translations are a compromise between attempts at word-for-word literalism and thought-for-thought interpolations. Either way, much of the intended message is lost or misrepresented for the sake of readability, brevity, or familiarity. Alternatively, we will dig for the truth.

The keywords in most passages will be amplified from the original language. Amplification is a process whereby many words are used to properly convey the full meaning and nuances of the original term as known and used in its time, context, and culture. If a Hebrew word requires a paragraph to adequately communicate its implications, you will find the required background, etymology, verbal roots, and shadings.

And when it is vital to our full understanding, we will explore the additional insights which can be deduced by analyzing the stems, conjugations, and moods. In other words, we are going to scratch well below the surface. This will require you to read some passages several times to fully appreciate what Yahowah is saying. But if we are to err, let us do it on the side of providing too much information rather than too little.

When it comes to translations, my goal is to accurately communicate the totality of the message Yahowah intended as honestly and forthrightly as possible. But that does not necessarily make the translations hyperliteral because the grammar and sentence structure in Hebrew are different from that of English. Like most ancient languages, there were no capitalization, punctuation, or quotation marks in Ancient Hebrew. Therefore, the moment we apply English grammar rules we begin making some reasoned accommodations.

Second, conjunctions (and, but, so, yet, nor, or, for) in Hebrew are usually attached to a noun or verb, as opposed to being rendered independently. This is also the case with articles (a, an, the), prepositions (in, by, with, of, on, to, from), and especially personal pronouns (I, me, we, us, you, she, he, they, them). In English, we will naturally separate all of these into individual figures of speech.

In this regard, you will notice that the transliterated sound of each Hebrew word set within the parenthetical was written without reference to conjunctions, articles, prepositions, or pronouns. Had I done otherwise, you would not have been able to verify the meaning of the Hebrew words for yourself. While you can look up *qara'* or *dabar* in any Hebrew lexicon, you will not find the prefixed and suffixed forms, such as *wyqara'* or *wydabar*.

The reason that I have taken the time to convey the Hebrew basis of each sentence is because verification is an essential component of discovery. Questioning leads to understanding. By presenting the Hebrew for your consideration, your search for answers is facilitated. On this topic, you will find that I routinely reveal the source of the transliterated vowel sounds in words with the Hebrew letters Aleph (א) and Ayin (ע) by way of apostrophes – such as *'el* | God or *'ayn* | eye.

This brings us to a third opportunity: completeness. Let's consider *qara'*, for example. It forms the basis of *Miqra'* (the plural being *Miqra'ey*), and is most often translated as "called out," but it also means "to summon, to invite, to recite, and to read, to proclaim and to pronounce." Even more than this, *qara'* speaks of "being welcomed into someone's company and meeting with them." Therefore, depending upon the context, *qara'* could be rendered in many different ways, most of which might apply.

The fourth challenge to providing an accurate and complete translation is symbolism. For example, *'ohel* is the Hebrew word for "tent." But if this is all you read, you would miss the fact that *'ohel* is also a "covering, a home, a shelter, and a protected place suited for living." These symbolic implications are just the beginning. *'Ohel* is based upon, and in the text is written identically to, *'ahal*, which means "to shine brightly, clearly reflecting light."

Like so many Hebrew concepts, there are both physical and spiritual dimensions associated with the word. Therefore, rather than depicting a nondescript "tent," the *'ohel* / *'ahal* often represents a "protective enclosure of radiant light," a "shining shelter," a "covering which is conducive to life," and a "home" which is associated with Yahowah Himself by way of His Covenant. As such, this "radiant shelter" is symbolic of the Set-Apart Spirit's Garment of Light, which makes us appear perfect in God's eyes and enables us to enter His presence and camp out with Him on the *Miqra'* of *Sukah* – Shelters.

This leads us to the fifth consideration, where we have the opportunity to consider each reasonable vocalization of each word. The diacritical markings, or vowel points in the Masoretic Text, are the product of rabbinical interpretation. This was highlighted by our discussion of *'ohel* versus *'ahal,* where the meanings were different, albeit complementary. In that vocalization influences almost every word in the text, it is important that we are aware that the rabbinical choices were often reasonable, but at times arbitrary, and sometimes purposefully misleading.

While we are on the subject of vocalization, there is but one non-negotiable rule: names and titles must always be transliterated (replicating the same sounds in the new alphabet) while words must be consistently translated (conveying the meaning in the other language). The pronunciation of names of Pharaoh Ramses, Genghis Khan, Der Fuehrer Adolf Hitler, and Islamic Jihadist Osama bin Laden do not change from one language to another. Similarly, the name and title Mashyach and Melek Dowd should never be altered, much less substituted for something of man's choosing.

Sixth, word order in Hebrew is less significant than it is in English, and it is often reversed. Rather than write "Yahowah's Torah," or "Set-Apart Spirit," the text reads "*towrah yahowah*" and "*ruwach qodesh*." Further, verbs do not always sit in the middle of the action, as is required in English, between subject and object. Therefore, in the transition from Hebrew to English, one cannot slavishly follow the word order of the original language.

Our seventh challenge to a proper translation is a surprise to almost everyone. Ancient and Paleo-Hebrew exist as an aspectual language, meaning that the same form of a verb can be translated as past, present, or future tense. Hebrew verbs are inclusive with regard to time. While we can often deduce the intended tense based on the context of a discussion, the realization that the message itself was not limited to a certain period of time makes everything God revealed applicable to everyone throughout time. Yahowah's Word, like Yahowah Himself, is always true, regardless of time or place.

In this regard, Hebrew verbs are akin to light, where on a photon the past, present, and future exist simultaneously. And since Yahowah equates Himself to light, it means that He can also see the past and future simultaneously. This, then, explains how Yahowah gets every prophecy correct. He has witnessed our future in our past, and then revealed what He has seen, committing it to writing in a language that reflects His nature.

The eighth issue which must be resolved when providing a complete and accurate translation lies in determining when enough is enough. The more completely each word is defined, the more nuances and shadings which are conveyed, and the more difficult each sentence becomes to read and comprehend. After a while, it can become information overload. So, when the number of relevant insights exceeds our ability to process them within the context of a sentence and still retain the flow and substance of each discussion, it is best to color Yah's linguistic palette in subsequent paragraphs. Recognizing the difficulty of processing such an enormous amount of new information, I will endeavor to introduce passages in such a way that you are grounded within the relevant context.

Toward this end, the floodgates of understanding are opened by the unique nature of Hebrew stems, conjugations, and moods. But there is no succinct way to communicate their contribution in English. A stem can necessitate a literal interpretation or might demonstrate a causal relationship. A conjugation can be used to reveal the continuous and unfolding nature of something, or just the opposite, that something has been, or will be, completely accomplished. The moods all convey volition, which is to say that they express a desire which is subject to freewill. Therefore, while these ideas are all germane to our relationship with God, they cannot be expressed in English as fluently as they are conveyed in Hebrew. But to ignore them, as almost every English Bible translation does, is to shortchange the message.

The ninth consideration is also surprising. Many of the best lexicons were published by the very institutions which have brought us such horribly errant translations. And while lexicons, interlinears, and dictionaries bearing titles such as the *New American Standard Hebrew-Aramaic and Greek Dictionaries* and *The ESV English-Hebrew Reverse Interlinear Old Testament* often provide the best window into the etymology of the Hebrew words themselves, if their definitions are correct, their translations are not. Moreover, a lexicon like *Strong's*, while valuable for searching roots and providing accurate transliterations, will consistently seek to justify whatever is found in the *King James Version*, no matter how ridiculous.

Along these lines, a dependence on one, or even two lexicons, dictionaries, or interlinears will produce unreliable results, as they are individually filled with errors. Many hundreds of their definitions were religiously inspired, and they are not the result of scholastic etymology. The *Brown-Driver-Briggs Hebrew and English Lexicon* uses Arabic to define Hebrew terms, not recognizing that written Hebrew existed 2,500 years before the first Arabic word was penned. And the *Gesenius Hebrew-Chaldee Lexicon to the Old Testament* is filled with theological opinions, most of which are invalid. Moreover, every Hebrew lexicon and interlinear is synced with the Masoretic Text and their vocalizations, which are often wrong.

The tenth opportunity is unlike the others. An accurate translation of Yahowah's testimony is so radically different from what is found in popular English Bibles (all of which profess to be "the word of God"), the translations I have composed for *Yada Yahowah*, *An Introduction to God*, *Observations*, *Coming Home*, and even *Babel* and *Twistianity* may be hard for many people to accept. How is it, some will ask, that an individual without professed qualifications could be right, and every other translation be wrong?

The answer is typical: motivation. If English Bibles were to differ from what Christians or Jews have become comfortable hearing, sales would decline. So, rather than losing money publishing new translations of the oldest manuscripts, the NKJV, NASB, NIV, and NLT provide modest revisions of their own previous translations which were simply stylistic interpretations of the *King James Version*. And even it was a revision five times over of a translation of the Latin Vulgate, which served as an amalgamation of Old Latin texts based upon the Greek *Septuagint*, a highly unreliable translation of the Hebrew text. With each subsequent translation, from Hebrew to Greek to Latin to English, the message became confused and corrupted and ever the more distanced from the original.

From this point forward, all subsequent translations became nothing more than politically or financially inspired revisions. Specifically, the *King James Version* (circa 1611 – originally with Apocrypha) was a modest modification of the *Bishops' Bible* (circa 1568), which was a revision of the *Great Bible* (circa 1560), which amended the *Coverdale Bible* (circa 1535), which was a revision of John Wycliffe's translation of the Latin Vulgate, which was a blend of disparate Old Latin texts, which were translations of widely variant renditions of the Greek *Septuagint,* which were uninspired religious translations of Hebrew scrolls that had been carted off to Egypt.

The bottom line in marketing, and especially publishing religious texts, is familiarity sells. As a result, every popular modern Bible translation is similar to every other popular Bible translation, because had they not been similar, they would not have become popular. Their familiarity should not be surprising. Bible translations are all style over substance. And their authors have no compunction against changing God's testimony to suit their faith – or pocketbooks.

While it has not occurred for a long time, early on there were those who sought to dismiss the translations found in *Yada Yahowah* with an uninformed: "I can't believe God would allow His Bible to be corrupted." They were saying, in essence, that the translation they preferred was perfect. And yet, to hold this view, one enormously popular throughout Christendom and in Judaism, where the claim is made that the Talmud and Towrah are "unchanged and infallible," a person has to ignore an ocean of irrefutable evidence to the contrary.

In particular, religious Jews are mercilessly harassed should they not acquiesce to rabbinical infallibility and superiority. For an Orthodox Jew, when it comes to a gowy vs. rabbi, if the argument remains ad hominem, guess who loses even without any attempt to corroborate the translations?

God, Himself, told us that men would pervert His testimony. He even revealed the consequence of such corruption. But, if you choose not to believe Him, as is the case with the religious, what about the evidence?

For this religious myth to be plausible, there could be no divergent parchments among the 215 manuscripts found in the cliffs above Qumran, collectively known as the Dead Sea Scrolls (dating from 350 BCE to 68 CE). And yet, significant differences exist between them – from misspellings to entire lines being either unintentionally omitted or duplicated. Since they differ, inerrancy is a spurious claim.

These issues are magnified exponentially by the time the revelations were taken to Babylon and reemerged in the city of Tiberius under the auspices of the Masoretes with the *Codex Aleppo* circa 900 CE. While it was endorsed by Maimonides (the rabbi who codified Judaism) for its "accuracy," it differs considerably from the *Leningrad Codex* – the second oldest and only complete manuscript – which was copied in Cairo in the 11th century. Within it, we find that *Leningradensis* not only contradicts its own Masoretic apparatus many hundreds of times, but there are also numerous alterations and erasures.

Therefore, the evidence is irrefutable: the Dead Sea Scrolls cannot be considered inerrant because they differ from one another, as is also the case with the earliest editions of the Masoretic Text. Worse for the "it is infallible" crowd, as we have already attested, the scrolls found in the caves above Qumran and the Masoretic Text differ on average by one word in fifteen.

Some are wont to pin their hopes on the *Septuagint*, but that is a fool's folly. The earliest *Septuagint* manuscript (dating to the 1st century BCE and produced in Egypt) provides an interesting mix of Hebrew and Greek, with names, such as God's, written in Hebrew (using the Ashurit script with Babylonian vocalization according to the Yemenite custom). It is actually closer in content to *Codex Aleppo* than subsequent copies of the *Septuagint*. Also dating to this same period, there are several fragments scribed in the 1st century BCE found in Qumran, covering three books from the Towrah and the Book of Baruch. Other than these, almost every copy of the *Septuagint* dates from the 5th century and beyond. They differ so widely, it is essentially impossible to form a consistent thread between them.

In fact, *Septuagint* copies were so divergent that, in the 3rd century CE, Origen, one of the few early theologians to study Hebrew, was compelled to dedicate most of his life to resolving the conflicts between the copies at his disposal, creating his *Hexapla* (which unfortunately has been lost to time). If God had intervened to keep His testimony from being corrupted, both the *Septuagint* and the Masoretic Text would have mirrored the Dead Sea Scrolls, and yet, this is not what the evidence reveals.

Among the legacy of divergent texts, in addition to the Dead Sea Scrolls, the *Septuagint*, and the Masoretic Text, there is the Syriac *Peshitta* and the Samaritan *Pentateuch*. But between them, differences abound, emphatically disproving the myth that God intervened throughout history to keep "His 'Scriptures' inerrant."

While it can be proven that Yahowah's words in the Towrah, Prophets, and Psalms were inspired, and while much of what they revealed has been preserved in old manuscripts and thus can be known, translations are strictly human affairs. As such, I do not claim that my presentations are perfect, only that they are as accurate and complete as I can render them using the oldest manuscripts and best research tools. For this purpose, I have relied upon:

> *The Dead Seas Scrolls Bible* (to highlight differences between the older scrolls and the Masoretic Text, and not for its translation)
>
> *Enhanced Brown-Driver-Briggs Hebrew and English Lexicon* (which is my favorite because it is the most straightforward, least religious, and most comprehensive)
>
> *The Hebrew & Aramaic Lexicon of the Old Testament*
>
> *Dictionary of Biblical Languages With Semantic Domains: Hebrew*
>
> *Gesenius' Hebrew-Chaldee Lexicon to the Old Testament*
>
> *A Concise Hebrew and Aramaic Lexicon of the Old Testament*
>
> *New American Standard Hebrew-Aramaic and Greek Dictionaries*
>
> *A Biblical Hebrew Reference Grammar*
>
> *The Enhanced Strong's Lexicon* (readily available online and a good source when searching for verbal roots)
>
> *Englishman's Concordance*
>
> *Theological Wordbook of the Old Testament* (often helpful for doing an in-depth study of a word's use throughout the Towrah and Prophets)
>
> *The Complete Word Study Guide of the Old Testament*
>
> *The Theological Dictionary of the Old Testament*
>
> *The ESV English-Hebrew Reverse Interlinear Old Testament* (it's convenient to have one or more

interlinears available to compare sentence structure)

Biblia Hebraica Stuttgartensia; Werkgroep Informatica, Vrije Morphology

The Lexham Hebrew-English Interlinear Bible

Zondervan's Hebrew-English Old Testament Interlinear

Logos Scholar's Platinum Edition Software (my primary tool because it not only includes almost everything in this list, but it is also all electronically linked and thus more readily searchable)

During the initial writing and first nine edit passes through *Yada Yahowah* and in the process of writing *Twistianity*, I deployed a host of Greek resources. Since I use them sparingly now, and since I have found that studying the New Testament is mostly counterproductive, I am hesitant to list them as I had done previously. That said, here is a sampling:

The Text of the Earliest New Testament Greek Manuscripts

Analytical Lexicon of the Greek New Testament

The Complete Word Study Dictionary, New Testament

Dictionary of Biblical Languages With Semantic Domains: Greek

Strong's Exhaustive Concordance of the Bible

The Theological Dictionary of the New Testament

The ESV English-Greek Reverse Interlinear

Nestle-Aland Greek New Testament, with McReynolds English Interlinear

Therefore, in *Yada Yahowah*, *An Introduction to God*, *Observations*, *Coming Home*, and *Babel*, you will find a complete translation of each Hebrew word, as well as the Greek in *Twistianity* or Arabic in *God Damn Religion*, all rendered in accordance with the definitions and synonyms provided by the world's most reputable resources. I almost always have a dozen or more scholastic tomes open, surrounding me on revolving Jeffersonian carousels, and another score of research tools electronically linked to the text via *Logos* interactive software.

It is a lot of information, so recognize that, in the quest to be thorough and accurate, fluidity will suffer. Statements will not roll off the tongue in familiar word patterns. However, there is something far better. If you are willing to invest the time to question, verify, and study the words Yahowah revealed, you will come to know the truth – as God revealed it to us. And I can promise you: He is worth knowing.

However, the substantial difference between the definitions rendered in the lexicons which bear the names of popular Bible translations, and the translations themselves, means that if their word definitions are accurate, their translations are not. And in this way, serious students of God's Word quickly come to appreciate the Achilles' heel of the Bible. If believers questioned the texts they were reading, if they did their homework, they would reject their Bibles, their pastors and their church, their rabbis and their religion.

This is to say that our quest to understand will not be easy. And that, surprisingly, is exactly as Yahowah wants it to be – at least between now and His *Yowm Kipurym* return in 2033 – when He will write His Towrah inside of us. He wants all of us to value knowing Him sufficiently to prioritize this endeavor.

Along these lines, when Yahowah introduces a new term, one that seems to defy normal translation, we will study other related statements to see how He initially deploys the concept. For example, the singular Hebrew noun *zarowa'* is usually translated as "arms," and yet, the Towrah indicates that it means "sacrificial lamb" in addition to "protective shepherd," "leading ram," and "strong arm" of God. As we study this remarkable word, we will learn that there are three *Zarowa'* – two of whom are essential to our wellbeing: Moseh and Dowd, and the other serves as a witness to draw your attention to them.

At other times, we will find that a simple translation is just not possible. In that case, the word will be transliterated in the text and then explained in subsequent paragraphs. *Neshamah,* whose best analog is "conscience," is such a term, one we will examine at the end of the *Chay* | Life chapter. It is one of Yah's greatest gifts – one most people continue to squander.

For your benefit, the genitive case (scrubbed of pronouns and conjunctions) of the actual Hebrew words found in the inspired text are italicized and set inside parentheses. The most generic forms are provided so that you will be able to look them up in Hebrew lexicons. This is also done so that you might gradually become more familiar with God's most commonly used terms.

Since understanding is based upon evidence, and since the best source of information, at least as it relates to the existence of God, is a complete and accurate translation of His testimony, we will undertake a comprehensive evaluation of the words He selected to communicate to us. That is why this book is dedicated to Yahowah's predictions and instructions, not mine – or anyone else's. This is a conversation with God, not with me. All I have attempted to do is provide a handrail, a bit of augmentation, a running commentary, and a contextual framework for considering and connecting His insights so that they are as revealing as possible. Hopefully, this will encourage you to reflect upon the significance of His words.

To maintain a clear distinction between my observations and Yahowah's, **His testimony is printed in a bold font.** Yahowah's words (correctly translated) can be trusted. Mine are only there because I want you to think about His.

I do not purport to have all the answers – but fortunately, I do not have to because He does. And He has told us where to find them. Revealing them, and where to find them, is the intent of His testimony and thus of this book.

While my opinions are mostly irrelevant, I think that it's useful for you to know that I am of the conclusion that Yahowah's Towrah, Prophets, and Psalms were without error, so far as language makes that possible, as the inspired writers put quill to parchment 2,500 to 3,500 years ago. But as time passed, occasional scribal errors, a considerable onslaught of religious gerrymandering which has corrupted the language, and changes in customs conspired to rob us of the message which originally permeated the divine texts.

These problems were multiplied when the Hebrew manuscripts were translated into Greek, then Latin, en route to being rendered in English. And this issue was exacerbated by political and religious agendas – all designed to make the flock easier to control and fleece.

In rendering Yahowah's Word in English as completely and accurately as possible, I have favored the preferred meanings of the Hebrew terms unless a different vocalization of the text or a secondary definition provides a better, more consistent fit considering the context. Etymological roots will be our principal guide as we explore. If a phrase still begs for elucidation, we will consider colloquialism, and will always be attuned to metaphors and especially symbolism.

Hebrew provides a rich linguistic palette – especially for subjects related to human nature and relationships, things Yahowah cares deeply about and about which He had a lot to say. And the language is spiritually revealing. It speaks to mind and soul.

Some say that there may be a deeper, mystical meaning to passages, some esoteric code latent in Gematria and Equidistant Letter Sequences. While there may be merit to these claims, no matter what is buried under the words, their plain meaning, and the mental pictures they provide, is primarily what God intended for us to understand.

Since words comprise the totality of God's testimony, and thus prophecy, and since Yahowah calls Himself "the Word," it is important that we render them correctly. Words are Yahowah's most important symbols. His testimony represents Him, His Word defines Him, and it explains His purpose and plan.

Words are the basis of almost everything: communication, thought, consciousness, relationships, and causality. It is even possible that a communication medium lies at the heart of what we consider matter and energy – the very stuff of creation. We think in words. Without language, virtually nothing can be known and nothing happens. There are no meaningful relationships without words. Written language is considered man's greatest invention and our most important tool. Therefore, when it comes to the Word of God, we will examine His thoughts closely.

𐤉𐤄𐤅𐤄

There are several reasons I have chosen to focus on prophetic statements – regardless if they are addressing our immediate future or distant past. These passages not only provide assurance of Divine inspiration, proving that Yahowah authored these words, but they also provide us with a framework of time itself. Only a Spirit who exists beyond the constraints of time can know what occurred before there were men to write it down and what will happen before it transpires. When events play out precisely as He said they would, historical reality demonstrates that His revelation is trustworthy and true. Faith is replaced by logic, probability, and reason. For example, during this study, I have grown from believing God exists to *yada'* Yahowah – to knowing Him. Hopefully, you will too.

Proving that His Word is reliable, and thus worthy of our consideration, is one of three ways our Creator uses prophecy. He also uses it to reveal His nature, His plan, and His instructions. Most every prediction is designed to "*towrah* – teach" us something. That is why we will dissect fulfilled prophecies, not only to validate their veracity but to better understand Yahowah's plan.

Then we will examine yet *un*fulfilled prophecies, not only to understand what lies in our future, but more importantly, so that we may be prepared to help others deal with what is coming. All along the way, we will analyze the profound lessons attached to God's prophetic proclamations so that more souls will *Yada Yah* and be inclined to enjoy an honest and open conversation with God.

The third purpose of divine prediction is to let us know how the whole story fits together from 'Adam to the Time of Ya'aqob's Troubles, from the first family to the eternal one. Prophecy provides us with the skeleton upon which to flesh out the body of information Yahowah has given us regarding our redemption – past, present, and future. There is virtually nothing of consequence that can be effectively understood without tying prediction to fulfillment and dress rehearsal to final enactment. The Covenant is affirmed by its subsequent fulfillments, just as the Towrah defines the Passover Lamb's purpose while explaining Dowd's sacrifice. It is all one unified message.

Therefore, our only textbook in this voyage of discovery will be Yahowah's Testimony. Outside sources will only be consulted when they are necessary to appreciate the historical or scientific implications of a passage.

Beginning at the beginning, you will soon discover that *Bare'syth* / In the Beginning / Genesis lies at the intersection of prophecy, history, and science. It tells three stories at one time, all designed to reveal God's purpose and plan. Yahowah's opening salvo provides the framework upon which all significant prophetic events are fulfilled. It is scientifically accurate, right down to the specifics, providing a precise accounting of events over the course of six days from the perspective of the Creator. It even provides us with an overview of mankind's history—past, present, and future. More important still, each verse is laden with guidance and essential insights for continued and better living.

In this regard, the Towrah quickly dispels the misconception that the Earth is 6,000 years old – a myth that is held by some 40% Christians. As a result, the debate between science and creation should never have existed. The initial chapters of *Yada Yahowah* demonstrate that *both* are correct. The universe is just shy of 15 billion years old, and it took God exactly six days to create it. The evidence that both answers are correct is, as we shall see, irrefutable.

It should be apparent that *Yada Yahowah* is not going to shy away from controversy in order to win friends and influence people. You will find its commentary as blunt as God's Word.

In fact, if one passage seems to contradict another, we will examine both without reservation. We will trust God to resolve the perceived inconsistency. When Yahowah says something that is contrary to established religious teaching, which is frequent, we will pause long enough to evaluate a sufficient quantity of related passages to understand what is actually being revealed. And if what we find undermines the teachings and credibility of religious and political institutions, so be it. I do not belong to any organization, and I am not advocating for any human institution. My only concern is properly reporting what Yahowah has to say so that His people come to know Him.

We are going to give God the credit He deserves. If He is providing multiple insights in a single account, we will examine all of them (at least as many of them as our minds can grasp). When God decides to ascribe teaching to His predictions, as He most often does, we will contemplate His advice. When God broaches a new subject in a prediction, we are going to follow His lead and study related passages to better appreciate His prescriptions.

That leads us to another delightful challenge, one that has caused these volumes to expand in length and complexity. We will not rest until we understand the essential lessons He is teaching. Consider this example: a score of verses says that some souls, upon death, will experience eternal life in the company of God. Half that number says that some souls will end up in She'owl, where they will experience perpetual anguish. Yet hundreds of passages reveal that most souls will simply cease to exist. When they die, their soul dissipates to nothingness. How can this be?

Pastors, priests, and imams all teach that there are only two eternal destinations: heaven or hell. Yet eternal anguish is a completely different result than death and destruction. Therefore, for Yahowah's witness to be trustworthy (and for God to be lovable), there must be three options – eternal life with God, eternal separation from Him, and the option to fritter away one's soul, wastefully squandering it. This is one of many profound insights that you will find in these pages and perhaps nowhere else.

The same is true with the concept of worship. There are a score of verses which seem to suggest (at least prior to an accurate rendering of the words) that God wants to be worshiped and hundreds that say otherwise – that He wants us on our feet, not on our knees. The truth in this regard is essential to our understanding of the Covenant where we are asked to walk with God, which is to be upright with Him.

This perspective lies at the heart of the debate between Yahowah wanting to enjoy a familial relationship with us as opposed to imposing a submissive religion. While it seems to escape the grasp of the religious, a god who would create an inferior being to worship him would be chronically insecure and not worth knowing.

Similarly, our translations tell us that God wants to be feared, and yet, in *Yasha'yah* / Freedom and Salvation Are from Yahowah / Isaiah, Yahowah states that "the fear of God is a manmade tradition." Moreover, one cannot love that which they fear. Therefore, fear cannot be the right answer.

Rabbis have made a religion out of ceremonial prayer and Christians are told to pray without ceasing. And yet, God never once asks us to pray to Him, preferring that we listen before we speak. Each time we find the inverse lurking in the passages of a typical Bible, the deception is predicated upon a textual misrepresentation.

Statements within the CNT say that we cannot know the timing of things, such as the date God will return. Yet the Towrah begins by detailing Yahowah's chronology and timeline, something Yasha'yah's prophetic portraits amplify and affirm. If prophetic timing is unknowable, why did God provide a specific timeline and a thousand revealing clues?

I suspect that my willingness to date Yahowah's prophetic fulfillments – past, present, and future – will be one of the most contentious aspects of *Yada Yahowah* – at least for former Christians. Rabbis have long suspected that what I am going to share is right – although their timeline was convoluted by Maimonides.

As we make our way through Yahowah's testimony, He will tell us, so I will tell you exactly when God is going to fulfill His remaining prophecies. All I had to do was consider the evidence and then connect the data.

Another point of contention may arise because I am opposed to quoting or commenting on any statement out of context. If you write to me and ask how one declaration or another fits within the universal truths contained in the whole, I am likely to encourage you to read the rest of the book because it is likely explained elsewhere. Moreover, the practice of referencing isolated phrases leads to false assumptions which in turn lead to incomplete and errant thinking.

Misappropriating statements is what led to the doctrines of heaven *or* hell, to the three persons of the Trinity, to Replacement Theology, to the impossible notion that "Jesus" is completely God and completely man, to the diminished relevance of the Towrah, to Sunday worship, and to disputes over the timing and existence of the harvest of souls errantly known to many as "the rapture." While an erroneous theological position can appear to be supported with isolated verses, for a conclusion to be valid, no passage should be able to refute it.

The combination of taking statements out of context and then misrepresenting Yahowah's intent is what has led to the horrible deceptions known as Jews for Jesus, Messianics, Yahwehists, the Hebrew Roots Movement, and the myth of Black Hebrew Israelites. They have all created beguiling religions through twisting God's intent to support their lies.

𐤋𐤉𐤄𐤅𐤄

I translated and wrote for over a decade before I ascribed my name to this mission. This is largely because I had thought that my only qualification for compiling this witness to expose deception and proclaim the truth was my willingness to engage when Yahowah asked. And while I am now aware that there is much more, should that not be sufficient for you, if you are more interested in the messenger than the message, if you are impressed with accomplishments and credentials, find a book written by someone in the religious or political establishment. Such authors will gladly exchange your money for confirmation of what you have already been led to believe.

So now you know: these volumes are not religious – and are in fact, anti-religious. This message does not portend to be popular, either. One of the more limiting factors in this regard will be the unfamiliar vocabulary provided throughout these books. I avoid many of the terms you are accustomed to hearing, even though using them would attract a much larger audience. God does not combat deception with lies, nor shall I.

Therefore, in the closing pages of the Prelude, I'm going to share a truncated portion of something found in *An Introduction to God* to demonstrate why each of the following names, titles, and words are inappropriate: Lord, Jesus, Christ, Christian, Bible, Old Testament, New

Testament, Gospel, Grace, Church, and Cross. And in their place, I am going to present Yahowah's preferences. I am doing so, not for the benefit of Christians, but instead to negate the religious claims of those who have taken so much from God's people.

It is vital that the Chosen People have the opportunity to know that religions, all of which God detests, abused and deceived them, preying upon their devotion. God wants us to stop trusting clerics so that we might choose to rely on Him. Therefore, providing readers with reasons to jettison their associations with political and religious institutions is consistent with Yahowah's instructions. Further, there is a lesson in every human deception and vital insights in every divine revelation.

In this light, I have often been accused of being overly zealous regarding terminology. But this is the only rational option available to us. If we see the Torah, Prophets, and Psalms as being from God, then every word was inspired and chosen by Yahowah. Changing His words to suit us is then arrogant, misguided, and counterproductive.

Therefore, throughout *Yada Yahowah* you will find Yahowah's name properly written, even though it may be unfamiliar to you, in each of the 7,000 places He cites it in the Torah, Prophets, and Psalms. I will not use "LORD" in reference to God because "lord" is synonymous with Ba'al, which is Satan's title. It describes the Adversary's ambition, which is to be seen as superior to God, to lord over men, and to control the messages pontificated by clerics and kings so that the masses submit to him. The nature and ambitions of a lord are the antitheses of a father.

God's aversion to being called "the Lord" is why Yahowah revealed that upon His return, on the Day of Reconciliations when the Covenant is finally renewed, He will never again tolerate its use. In context, God's prophetic proclamation is integrated into a larger discussion focused upon His hatred of religion and religious holidays – especially those conceived by *Yahuwdym* | Jews and celebrated in association with *Yisra'el* | Israel.

"'**And it shall be** (*wa hayah* – it will exist) **in** (*ba* – at and on) **that day** (*ha yowm ha huw'* – His specific and unique day (addressing His return on the Day of Reconciliations)),' **prophetically declares** (*ne'um* – reveals and promises in advance of it occurring) **Yahowah** (*Yahowah* – the proper pronunciation of YaHoWaH, our *'elowah* – God as directed in His *ToWRaH* – teaching regarding His *HaYaH* – existence and our *ShaLoWM* – restoration), **'you will call out to** (*qara'* – you will actually and consistently refer to, summon or invite, encounter or meet with (qal imperfect)) **Me as an individual** (*'ysh 'any* – as my husband and spouse, with Me existing in your presence; from *'enowsh* – mortal man, a person who dies who is *'anash* – weak, wicked, and woeful, incurable and desperate, in the guise of *'enash* – a human being), **and therefore** (*wa* – but), **you will not call out** (*lo' qara'* – you will not ever again throughout time, actually summon or read aloud (qal imperfect)) **to Me as** (*la 'any* – to approach and come near Me, addressing Me as) **"my Lord"** (*ba'al 'any* – my Master, the one who owns and possesses me, the one who controls me) **ever again** (*'owd* – any longer throughout time, now and forevermore). (*Howsha'* / Hosea 2:16)

In addition (*wa*), **I will remove** (*suwr* – I will reject and abolish, separating Myself from, renounce and repudiate, getting rid of) **that which is associated with** (*'eth* – accordingly as a result) **the Lords'** (*ha Ba'alym* – the masters' and controllers', the political rulers' and religious leaders', the false gods' and those who possess others) **names** (*shem* – designations and reputations) **out of** (*min* – from) **her mouth** (*peh hy'* – speaking of the lips and language of Yisra'el).

Then (*wa*), **they shall not be remembered, recalled, or mentioned** (*lo' zakar* – they shall not be proclaimed or be brought to mind) **by** (*ba*) **their name** (*shem hem* – their designation, reputation, or renown) **any longer** (*'owd* – ever again).'" (Howsha' / Salvation / Hosea 2:17)

Throughout the Towrah and Prophets, *Ba'al* is the name and title ascribed to the Adversary, particularly when Satan is being worshiped as if he were a god. Humankind has elevated him to this lofty position in almost every religion. The Lord is god in Christianity, Judaism, and Islam. He wants to be worshiped and feared. He seeks submission and obedience. He insists that his subjects bow down before him and lift him up in praise. He seeks to possess and control humankind. The Lord is the antithesis of Yahowah.

And as such, Yahowah despises being called "the Lord." Those who know and love Him never refer to Him by that name or title. And that is why, when only His Family remains, Yahowah will never have to hear this offensive religious and political designation ever again.

However, *ba'al* is not the only Hebrew title for "Lord." There is another. It is *'adown* (אָדוֹן). In the custom of this period when *'adown* was spoken, it was often akin to us calling an older person "sir." It was simply a sign of respect and good manners. Unlike *ba'al*, *'adown* conveyed far less of the "lord and master" implications.

And yet even then, *'adown* was used on occasion to describe ambitious and covetous men with lofty positions in politics and religion, as well as conniving merchants and belligerent military leaders who schemed to "lord over" the masses as their "master."

The problem is that this arrogant and oppressive human title was pointed to read *'adonai* or *'adonay* | my Lord, and then used by rabbis to replace Yahowah's name all seven thousand times YHWH appears in the Towrah,

Prophets, and Psalms. And there is no crime in all of human history more egregious than this one.

There is more to the story. The commonly contracted form אדן in the Torah, Prophets, and Psalms, can be pointed to read 'eden (אֶדֶן), 'edon, or 'adon. These vocalizations describe an "upright pillar rising up from an established foundation." Spelled identically in the text, these renditions of the same word are used to depict the strong and reliable nature of the "'eden – foundation" upon which the "cornerstone is laid," thereby serving as a reference to Dowd being the cornerstone of Yahowah's Tabernacle. 'Eden, which is more accurately transliterated 'edon, in that it is contracted from 'edown, emphasizes something which is "firm, strong, and solidly reliable," as in a "well designed and constructed foundation." And these are all very positive, Godly depictions, which are due thoughtful consideration.

In the Towrah, 'eden / 'edon is also used to portray the "base into which tent pegs were inserted to hold the upright pillar" of the Tent of the Witness. This structure, which is symbolic of Yahowah's Home and of Divine protection, was enlarged and held erect by the upright pillar, which is symbolic of Yahowah standing up for us when we need Him most.

The Hebrew letters אדן vocalized 'eden and 'edon are found fifty-seven times in the Tanakh, with all but the two instances describing an aspect of the Tabernacle of the Witness. In the Towrah, which teaches us how to properly observe Yahowah's instructions, every time 'eden / 'edon appears it depicts the upright pillar placed in the center of Yahowah's home on Earth to raise it and to enlarge and secure it.

Once the Torah, Prophets, and Psalms are scrubbed of the most obvious Masoretic copyedits – especially that of writing 'adony above YHWH some 6,873 times, a comprehensive review of the Dead Sea Scrolls reveals 127 places where religious rabbis simply erased Yahowah's name and scribed 'adony in its place. Once these are removed, the context dictates that the first-person singular suffixed variation of אדן, which is יאדן, should have been vocalized 'edowny and translated as "my Upright Pillar," "my Upright One," or "my Foundation," each of the 307 times it appears in conversations directed at Yahowah.

As evidence that 'adown is descriptive of men, not God, it shares the same root as 'adam, the Hebrew word for "man." Further, all 335 times 'adon appears in the Tanakh, it applies to politically or religiously empowered men, with two-thirds of these translated as "lord," and one-third rendered as "master." *Strong's* defines 'adown and its contracted form, 'adon, as "a reference to men" who are "owners, strong lords, and masters." They suggest that it may be derived from an unused root meaning "to rule." As such, it also describes the Adversary's ambition: to be called Lord by men, to rule over them and to be their master, to control, intimidate, and overpower men—to own their souls.

Therefore, it is completely appropriate to attribute the Towrah's own definition of 'eden / 'edon to Yahowah. He is the "Upright One," the "Foundation," and the "Upright Pillar of the Tabernacle." He stood up for us so that we could stand with Him. However, it is not appropriate to associate Satan's ambitions, name, or title with God. Our Heavenly Father is not our "Lord." His Covenant is based upon an entirely different kind of relationship. Lord is inconsistent with both freewill and family.

Now that God has affirmed that He does not like being referred to as the "Lord," and now that you understand why, let's consider His name, and whether we can and should pronounce it. The most telling passage in this regard is found in the book Yahowah entitled *Shemowth* | Names. You may know it as "Exodus."

"He said (*wa 'amar* – He (Yahowah) actually declared and promised with ongoing implications (qal imperfect)), 'Indeed (*ky* – emphasizing the rationale behind this statement while affirming that it is truthful and reliable), I am and always will be (*hayah* – I actually exist and will continually be (qal imperfect – a literal interpretation of an actual relationship with ongoing consequences throughout time)) with you (*'im 'atah* – associated with you, in a relationship with you, interacting with you and experienced through you).

And (*wa* – therefore) this is (*zeh* – with regard to this specific discussion) on your behalf (*la 'atah* – for you to approach and draw near) the sign (*ha 'owth* – the means to communicate an oath or promise, often by way of a supernatural signal, distinguishing mark, miraculous indication, ensign, banner or standard which serves as proof) that I, absolutely (*ky 'anoky* – that indeed, truthfully and reliably), have sent you (*shalach 'atah* – have dispatched you, encouraging you to go at this moment in time (qal perfect)): when you come out (*ba yatsa' 'atah* – in conjunction with you being brought out (hifil infinitive – God is telling Moseh that He will be enabling him such that Moseh becomes an extension of God for this purpose while as a verbal, or actionable, noun, yatsa' becomes descriptive of the mission)) with (*'eth* – along with and among) the family (*ha 'am* – the people, all of whom are closely related) from the Crucibles of Oppression in Egypt (*min Mitsraym* – of extremely hostile conditions and subjugation, a smelting furnace of anguish, distress, hardship, and trouble; from *metsar* – suffering, torment, and torture, privation, adversity, and poverty, anxiety and misfortune and *matsowr* – to be besieged and confined, bound and contained), it is My desire that you will actually and continually work (*'abad 'eth* – you will genuinely engage to accomplish the mission I have chosen, laboring and serving in this capacity with literal and ongoing implications which reflect My will (qal imperfect paragogic nun – literal interpretation with ongoing effort and consequences conveying first-person volition)) **together with the Almighty** (*'eth ha 'elohym* – alongside, in conjunction and in accord with God) **upon this very mountain** (*'al ha har ha zeh* – on this specific mount, mountain range, and elevated ridge line)." (*Shemowth* / Names / Exodus 3:12)

What a marvelous introduction. Yahowah promised Moseh that He would always be with him. In the qal stem and imperfect conjugation, *hayah* expresses a state of existence which is literal and genuine, continual and consistent. In this case, and so many others, we can learn a great deal from the unique nature of Hebrew grammar.

There are many words for "sign" including *'owth*. The thing that makes this one special is that it carries with it the connotation that it is "being displayed to communicate an oath or promise, often by way of a miraculous or supernatural means to prove something which is important." While this *'owth* was for this day, as we progress through Yahowah's revelation, we will encounter another sign, called a *nes*, which is for our day.

Speaking of the Sign, the most readily accessible lexicon, *Strong's*, translates the letters, Nun Samech, *nec*. However, there is no "c" in the Hebrew alphabet, only a "ch." That said, it is easy for readers to copy and paste "nec" into a search engine and validate these translations. Yet, the proper pronunciation is more accurately achieved through *nes* which rhymes with "case." More importantly, correctly pronouncing these Hebrew words is considerably less important than correctly conveying their meaning.

It is interesting that Yahowah would choose to rescue His people from Egypt and convey His Towrah alongside an eighty-year-old shepherd, a criminal by man's standards, with an acknowledged speech impediment. But the reasons were many, including the fact that Moseh had rejected and walked away from the political, religious, military, and economic establishment of what was then the world's most powerful nation.

Speaking of that nation, even today Egyptians call their country Misr. It is from the Hebrew *Mitsraym*, the plural of *Mitsra*. The name is based upon *metsar* and *matsowr*. Its meaning is essential to understanding what God was offering to free His people – then and now. Egypt, by definition, symbolized "a crucible of the worst of human religious, political, economic, and military oppression." It was a place of "subjugation, a smelting furnace of anguish and hardship, a place of suffering, torment, and torture, of extreme poverty, anxiety and misfortune," where the Children of Yisra'el "were besieged and confined, bound and contained."

It was a condition the Yisra'elites would find themselves in again when fighting off the Philistines and Amalekites, the Assyrians and Babylonians, the Greeks and Romans, the Roman Catholic Church and the Muslims, then Europeans, and especially Germans. And it will be from a similar situation when politics, religion, conspiracy, and racism collude once again to blame and abuse God's people, that Yahowah is offering to save them as the grains of sand run out of the hourglass of man's dominion over the Earth.

This book, and those which preceded and follow it, were written expressly for this purpose: Yahowah wants His people to know what is coming so that we can look to the past to better appreciate what He is offering and expects in return. In a world that will soon be devoid of civility and opportunity, a world without peace or prosperity, lacking liberty and justice, there will be one way out. Yahowah is calling His people home.

Most translators render *'abad* as "serve" and then completely ignore *'eth*, meaning "with," even though *'abad*'s primary meaning is "work" and *'eth* is essential to establishing the nature of Yahowah's relationship with this, and every man He has engaged since this time. Yahowah chooses to work with, alongside, and through humankind. It is the purpose of creation. He values "*'abad* – work" and our "*'eth* – company."

There is even more to this story. *'Abad* was scribed using the qal stem, imperfect conjugation, and paragogic nun mood. As such, "work" was expressed such that it should be literally and relationally interpreted and seen as an ongoing effort with unfolding consequences throughout time. And if that were not sufficiently insightful considering the mission, which is to liberate God's People and reveal His Towrah Guidance, it was written with a concluding nun. This ascribes the cohortative mood, conveying first-person volition. In this case, it means that this mission was of Yahowah's choosing, that it was His will to work with Moseh in this way and for this purpose.

"Upon this mountain" is also insightful. This is Mount Choreb where the Towrah was revealed. In other words, Yahowah first met with Moseh in the exact place He would return with him, along with His people, to convey His Instruction and Guidance to mankind. God has a habit of sharing stories that come full circle, taking us back to the place we began. For example, Yahowah commenced His relationship with 'Adam in the Garden of 'Eden and He will soon be restoring the entire Earth to similar conditions so that He can return us to this place.

Evidently, I am more impressed with the nuances of Yahowah's statement than was Moseh, because rather than engaging God in conversation about it, Moseh asked the following question…

"**And** (*wa* – so then) **Moseh** (*Mosheh* – the one who draws us away from human oppression and divine judgment) **said** (*'amar* – asked and stated) **to God** (*'el*), **the Almighty** (*ha 'elohym* – the Mighty One),

'**Now look, if** (*hineh* – behold, look here, and note if) **I** (*'anky*) **go** (*bow'* – I return and come) **to** (*'el*) **the Children** (*beny* – sons) **of Yisra'el** (*Yisra'el* – a compound of *'ysh* – individuals, who *sarah* – strive and contend with, engage and endure with, are set free and are empowered by *'el* – God), **and I say to them** (*wa 'amar la hem* – I speak to approach them, talking while drawing near to them), "**God** (*'elohym* – the Almighty) **of your fathers** (*'ab 'atem* – of your forefathers) **has sent me out** (*shalach 'any* – has extended Himself to dispatch me at this moment in time (qal perfect – actually sending me to complete a finite action)) **to you** (*'el 'atem* – on your behalf), **and they ask** (*wa 'amar la 'any* – they pose this question regarding my approach), '**What is** (*mah*) **His personal and proper name** (*shem huw'* – His designation),' what (*mah* – an interrogative indicating a question, especially what and who) **shall I say** (*'amar* – answer will I convey) **to them** (*'el hem* – on their behalf)?"''' (*Shemowth* / Names / Exodus 3:13)

Names are important, but none was ever this important. And so, while God would give Moseh a direct answer, He did not do so initially. And that is because there is a bigger difference, between Ba'al, Bel, Bat, Marduk, Amun Ra, Amon, Aten, Amenhotep, Astarte, Ishtar, Ma'at, Neith, Re, Horus, Seth, Isis, Osiris, Nun, Hathor, Hapi, Heka, Thoth, Sobek, *et al*, and Yahowah, than just a name. They were many, but Yahowah is real. He actually exists. Therefore, by revealing the basis of His name first, Yahowah answered the most important question we can ask: yes, there really is a God.

Jews have always been smart, and Moseh knew that they would be sufficiently intelligent to inquire about the name of God. It's a shame that over the millennia Jews, and almost everyone else, are no longer interested in knowing the most important name in the universe.

"Then (*wa* – and so), **God** (*'elohym* – the Almighty) **said** (*'amar* – answered and promised, expressing (qal imperfect – literally with ongoing implications)) **to** (*'el*) **Moseh** (*Mosheh* – One who Draws Out; from *mashah* – to draw out), *"Ehayah 'asher 'ehayah* | **I Am Who I Am."'** (*Shemowth* / Names / Exodus 3:14) In His response, God conveyed: "I Exist." "I was, I am, and I always will be." "I am exactly who I say I am."

'Asher not only played a starring role in Yahowah's introduction to Moseh and subsequent reunification with His people, but it is also the word which brought me to Yahowah's words and thus us together – to this very place. It means so much more than "who," found in English Bible translations.

While writing *Tea with Terrorists* following my meeting with al-Qaeda in 2001, I found myself trying to distinguish the absurdity of the Quran from the integrity of the Torah. Realizing that there were no accurate prophecies in the Quran and a multitude of mistakes, I turned to some of the more interesting predictions found in the Prophets. This led to a passage in *Shamuw'el* / 2 Samuel 7 which we will translate many times in *Observations* and *Coming Home* as we grow in understanding. While doing so, I learned that *'asher*, as one of the pivotal terms within that prophecy, describes "a connection or affiliation" and conveys "a beneficial relationship and a joyous association" in addition to "revealing the correct, albeit narrow and restrictive, path to walk to get the most out of life." It addresses the idea of "being elevated in status and attitude, becoming happy as a result of being properly guided." To be *'asher* is to "be transformed and encouraged, to be changed as a result of speaking well of another as a result of their teaching."

All of these things can be thoughtfully applied to Yahowah's introduction to His name in *Shemowth* / Exodus 3:14. And if it were not for the universal failure of English Bible translators to render the word accurately in 2 Samuel 7, I do not know if I would have questioned existing translations sufficiently to justify the twenty-two years I have now devoted to correctly presenting God's testimony. Therefore, the word Yahowah chose to introduce Himself to us through Moseh is the same word that served to introduce Him to me. *'Asher*, as the word implies, brought us together and revealed the proper path to walk to get the most out of life.

'Ehayah is the first-person singular of *hayah*, meaning: "I exist, I am, I was, I will be." *'Asher*, as I've just shared, denotes a "relationship, an association, or linkage," and is often translated as "with, who, which, what, where, or when." *'Asher* is also "the way and a blessing and benefit." So, by using these words, Yahowah told us: 1) He exists, 2) that our continued existence is predicated upon His blessing, 3) that relationships are beneficial and of vital interest to us, and 4) how to pronounce His name (Yahowah is based upon *hayah*).

"And then (*wa*)**, He said** (*'amar* – He shared)**, 'So, this is what** (*koh*) **you should say** (*'amar* – you should answer (scribed in the qal stem, affirming the reliability of this advice, and in the imperfect conjugation, telling us that this pronouncement would have ongoing consequences)) **to** (*la* – to approach and on behalf of) **the Children** (*ben* – the sons) **of Yisra'el** (*yisra'el* – those who engage and endure with God)**,

"I Am** (*'ehayah* – first-person singular of *hayah*, meaning I exist (in the qal stem, imperfect conjugation, affirming the reliability and ongoing consequences of His existence on our existence))**, He has sent me** (*shalach 'any* – He has reached out and extended Himself to actually dispatch me (in the qal perfect, telling us that this act of

God was complete and would not need to be repeated)) **to you** (*'el 'atah* – on your behalf).""" (*Shemowth* / Names / Exodus 3:14)

There may be no more profound a statement, no more important a mission, and no higher authority. The source of our existence, the one God who actually exists, was going to go from Arabia to the Nile Delta with an eighty-year-old shepherd to rescue His wayward and enslaved children from Egypt – the most oppressive religious, political, and military power man had yet conceived.

Those who promote the myth that God's name is not known, that it is not important, and that it cannot and should not be pronounced can stop reading at this point. But God was not finished speaking…

"And (*wa* – in addition), **God** (*'elohym* – the Almighty), **furthermore** (*'owd* – besides this and also, beyond this), **said** (*'amar* – declared, clearly and unequivocally stated (qal imperfect)) **to** (*'el*) **Moseh** (*Mosheh* – from *mashah*, the one who would draw us away from human oppression), **'This is what** (*koh*) **you should say** (*'amar* – promise and declare (also scribed in the qal imperfect)) **to** (*'el*) **the Children of Yisra'el** (*beny yisra'el* – the descendants, offspring, and sons who strive, contend, and struggle with, in addition to those who engage, persist, and endure with, and are set free by God),

"Yahowah (*Yahowah* – written as directed by His *towrah* – teaching regarding His *hayah* – existence), **God** (*'elohym*) **of your fathers** (*'ab*), **God** (*'elohym*) **of 'Abraham** (*'Abraham* – Loving, Enriching, and Merciful Father), **God** (*'elohym*) **of Yitschaq** (*Yitschaq* – Laughter), **and God** (*'elohym*) **of Ya'aqob** (*Ya'aqob* – One who Embeds His Heels), **He sent me** (*shalach 'any* – He has reached out and extended Himself to actually dispatch me (in the qal perfect, revealing that God was offering to do this for them there and then, but would not be making a habit of it)) **to you** (*'el 'atem*)."

This is (*zeh*) **My name** (*shem 'any* – My personal and proper designation (scribed in the singular construct form, making Yahowah inseparable from His one and only *shem* – name)) **forever** (*la 'owlam* – for all time and into eternity, everlasting and eternal).

And (*wa*) **this is** (*zeh*) **My way of being known and remembered** (*zekar 'any* – My status and renown, My way of being mentioned and recalled, My commemoration and memorial, My inheritance right, symbol, sign, and signature) **for** (*la* – throughout) **all places, times, and generations** (*dowr dowr*).'" (*Shemowth* / Names / Exodus 3:15)

Considering how clear and direct Yahowah was with this announcement, how does anyone justify calling God "Lord" or "HaShem?" God said as clearly as words allow: "My name is Yahowah. That is the way I want to be recalled, the way I want to be known, and the way I want to be remembered. Yahowah is My signature. Tell those who want to live with Me, those who want to be saved by Me, that Yahowah has sent you." Know it, say it, remember it.

Now that we see God destroying the myth that He has many names, some of which are too sacred to utter, what about the myth that no one knows how to pronounce the "Tetragrammaton," or "four consonants," which comprise His signature? The answer is also straightforward and direct.

Therefore, I was not the first to determine that Yahowah's name is comprised of vowels, not consonants. Flavius Josephus, the most famous of all Jewish historians, wrote in the 1st century CE, in his *The War of the Jews*, Book 5.5.7: "...the set-apart name, it consists of four vowels."

Weingreen, a noted scholar in Hebrew grammar, subsequently stated in 1959 for Oxford University Press: "Long before the introduction of vowel signs, it was felt that the main vowel sounds should be indicated in writing, and so the three letters Wah (ו), Hey (ה), and Yowd (י) were used to represent long vowels."

The easiest way to dispense with the "consonant" myth is to examine the many thousands of words which contain the letters Wah (ו), Hey (ה), and Yowd (י) and consider how they are pronounced. Almost invariably, the Wah (Y - ו), conveys the vowel sounds "o," "oo," or "u." In this regard, it is similar to the vowel form of the English W, which is pronounced "double u." The Hey (ℓ - ה) is pronounced "ah" and, to a significantly lesser degree, "eh." The Yowd (ﬦ - י) communicates an "i" sound, and is otherwise similar to the vocalization of the vowel form of the English Y.

In reality, these three vowels, in conjunction with the Hebrew Aleph (ℓ - א) and Ayin (⌀ - ע), made it possible to pronounce every Hebrew word several millennia before the Sheva System was developed, or vowel points were introduced, by the Masoretes.

With this in mind, let's consider the vowels which comprise Yahowah's name as they appear elsewhere in the lexicon. Among the most familiar Hebrew words beginning with a Yowd (י) is *"yada' (יָדַע),"* meaning "to know." You often hear it repeated: *"yada, yada, yada."* Indirectly, we know the Yowd sound from Israel, which is a transliteration of Yisra'el. It is the source of the vowel in: Isaiah (Yasha'yah), Messiah (Mashyach), Zechariah (Zakaryah), Hezekiah (Chiziqyah), Nehemiah (Nachemyah), and Moriah (Mowryah).

Those who have sung "kumbaya (*quwmbayah* (stand with Yah))" or "hallelujah (*halaluyah* (radiate Yah's light))" know this Yowd (י) sound all too well. The letter provides the vowel sound for the common Hebrew words *yad* – hand, *yadah* – to acknowledge, *yatab* – good, and *yahad* – united.

There are literally thousands of Hebrew words where the Yowd (י) is pronounced just like the Y/y is in English words: "yes, yet, yarn, yaw, yea, year, yearn, you, young, or yolk. And just like Hebrew, in English, the letter Y is often a vowel. Consider: "myth, hymn, my, fly, and cry." In fact, according to the Oxford Dictionary, "the letter Y is more often used as a vowel than a consonant. And in this role, it is often interchangeable with the letter I/i." This similarity to Hebrew is not a coincidence, because Hebrew served as the world's first actual alphabet – a word derived from a transliteration of the first two letters of the Hebrew alphabet: Aleph and Beyth.

The second and fourth letter in Yahowah's name is the Hebrew Hey (ה). I was curious as to how Yahowah could be based upon *hayah* (היה) and yet, in spite of this being so, often rendered as "Yahweh," where the first Hey is presented correctly but the second is changed to "eh." So, I examined every Hebrew word with the letter ה – paying special attention to those concluding with Hey. What I discovered is that, just like *hayah*, *'elowah*, and *towrah*, the Hebrew ה is almost invariably pronounced "ah." In fact, the ratio of "ah" to "eh" in Hebrew words is nearly one hundred to one. Therefore, in *hayah*, Yahowah told us how to pronounce all but one letter of His name.

One of the best-known Hebrew words is particularly helpful: "*towrah* – Torah," meaning "Teaching." It demonstrates how to properly pronounce the Hebrew Wah (ו) accurately. This title for "instruction, teaching, direction, and guidance" is written TWRH (right to left as: תּוֹרָה), where the "o" sound is derived from the Wah ו.

If that were not enough, the most oft-repeated Hebrew word over the last one hundred generations is "*shalowm*

(שָׁלֹום) – peace," where once again, we are greeted with the means to properly enunciate the Hebrew Wah ו. And I suppose Zion and Zionist would be almost as well-known. The Hebrew word is spelled *tsyown*, once again providing a consistent answer.

Other familiar Hebrew words which are pronounced similarly include: *gowym* – Gentiles, *yowm* – day, *'adown* – master, *'owy* – alas, *'owr* – light, *'owth* – sign, *qowl* – voice, *towb* – good, *'acharown* – last, and of course *'elowah* – God, in addition to the names Aaron, Jonah, Moriah, Zion, and Jerusalem from 'Aharown, Yownah, Mowryah, Tsyown, and Yaruwshalaim.

Therefore, in the definitive statement " *'elowah hayah ba ha towrah bow' shalowm* – God exists in the Torah to bring reconciliation," all of our questions are answered. Getting Yahowah's name right was so straightforward and easy, it is shocking that I was the first to transliterate it correctly. YHWH is Y·aH·oW·aH. Mystery solved.

There is even more we can learn about this magnificent name. In Ancient Hebrew, the first letter of Yahowah's name was conveyed using a pictographic depiction of an open hand ⼿ reaching down and out to us. This hand symbolized the power and authority to do whatever work was required. Even today, *yad* means "hand" in Hebrew, and metaphorically, it still represents the idea of "engaging and doing" something beneficial. With Yah, the ⼿ reveals His willingness to reach down to lift us up, to extend Himself and reach out to us with an open hand, hoping that we will grasp hold.

The second and fourth letters in Yahowah's name were drawn as a person standing and reaching up while pointing to the heavens ⼌. In Ancient Hebrew it conveyed the importance of observing what God has revealed, of becoming aware of Him, and of reaching up to Him for help. Affirming this, the Hebrew word *hey* still means "behold" in addition to "pay attention." The individuals depicted are standing upright, walking to and with God. They are not shown bowing down in worship.

It is interesting to note that there are five hands depicted in Yahowah's name – 𐤉𐤄𐤅𐤄 – just as there are five conditions associated with His Covenant which we must accept if we want to engage in a relationship with Him. Just like our hand which is comprised of a thumb and four fingers, there is one prerequisite associated with our participation in the Covenant and then four subsequent requirements. Therefore, Yahowah is telling us that while He is offering to do the work, we control our destiny by our response to Him.

The third letter in YHWH provides a pictographic representation of a tent peg or stake 𐤅. These were used to secure a shelter and to enlarge it. And as such, the preposition *wa* communicates the ideas of adding to and increasing something by making a connection.

Bringing this all together, we discover that Yahowah is reaching down and out to those who observe His revelation and embracing those who reach up to Him for help. His is an open hand, ready and willing to grasp hold of those seeking to be added to His Family. They will be sheltered and become secure. They will live forever with God in His Home. Will you join them?

𐤉𐤄𐤅𐤄

Audience Appeal and Appraisal

Keeping it Real…

I have long wondered why so few have studied the Towrah and Prophets with the intent of coming to know its Author. I find it surprising, not only because it is the most credible and well-preserved ancient text, but also because the inspiration behind it is so interesting.

It is also perplexing how few have closely examined the underlying scriptures of the Assyrian, Babylonian, Egyptian, Canaanite, Greek, or Roman religions to see how they were integrated into Judaism, Christianity, Islam, Mormonism, and Socialist Secular Humanism – especially considering the multitudes that have been beguiled by them. The fact that these belief systems are rife with regurgitated paganism and that they are all flawed to the point of being irrational, is lost on the vast preponderance of people. And I suspect that the principal reason they avoid scrutiny is because they have managed to usurp the credibility of the Towrah and Prophets – a remarkable feat considering the fact that its inspiration is vehemently opposed to those religions.

As a result, I find it inexplicable that something as credible as the Towrah, Naby', wa Mizmowr of Yahowah would be consistently misconstrued and misappropriated to validate all manner of misconceptions but never used to affirm the truth. Likewise, it is amazing that with man's contradictory and self-promoting fingerprints all over them that there are so few books devoted to discrediting man's most popular religions. And this is not an idle curiosity because the biggest obstacle to overcome when approaching Yahowah's testimony is the removal of religious rubbish that these religions have piled on top of it, impugning it by association.

It will soon become evident that Yahowah proved that His testimony and revelations are valid. His Towrah, Prophets, and Psalms were inspired and remain trustworthy and true, which means that all conflicting paths are invalid. The God who inspired the actual prophets is too merciful to be tolerant of deception – no matter how enticing man's words may seem, nor how clever the counterfeits may appear to the unwary.

At this point it may still be difficult for many to process why I would be so openly critical of all religions, especially the religions of Judeo-Christianity, seeing that this is an introduction to a multi-volume tome dedicated to the revelations of the God most believe was responsible for establishing these doctrines. Why am I insistent on ascribing a name to God? Why do I include Socialist Secular Humanism in the list of human belief systems? Why focus on prophetic verses as this enterprise does? Good questions all—and all questions God Himself will answer early and often.

By reading the *Prelude, Composition and Methodology*, and *Audience Appeal and Appraisal, Prophecy,* and then *Yada Yahowah*, followed by *An Introduction to God, Twistianity, Observations, Babel*, and *Coming Home,* even *God Damn Religion, Tea with Terrorists*, and *In The Company*, you will find that much of what you have been led to believe is not true. Religious founders, clerics, and politicians have deliberately deceived most people, as they once did me. And they have done so to empower and enrich themselves.

It is not that everything they say is a lie; it is that so many lies have been blended with the truth that what's left is akin to Kool-Aid laced with poison. Most guzzle it down because we have been conditioned to evaluate religious claims through the nebulous criterion of faith. And we are taught that it is good to believe, even that we ought to respect the faiths of others.

And yet in actuality, there is nothing more beguiling, destructive, or deadly than half-truths – deceptions which are crafted to seem plausible, making them effective counterfeits. The religions of Judaism and Christianity are prime examples of this strategy. Islam, like its Mormon counterpart, on the other hand, is simply too inane to be credible – regardless of their feeble attempts to usurp the credibility of the Towrah and Prophets.

Speaking of a lack of integrity, we live in an exceptional era, a place and time where so many people have been indoctrinated, by either political correctness, a conspiracy theory, their religion and their politics, or all of the above, that they have become intellectually dysfunctional. As I write these words during a 2023 edit pass through all of my previous books, the world has lost its collective marbles.

While it is worse than the common flu, it is not the virus, called COVID-19, which has upended the sensibilities of man. Instead, it is the moronic manner politicians and the media have responded to it. They have deprived almost everyone of their liberty and livelihoods, destroying the world's economies and currencies – leaving people dependent upon unethical and inept authoritarians. We have come within a breath of worldwide government domination over everyone's lives. And yet, most are giving up their freedoms willingly.

If that was not bad enough, an out-of-control Minneapolis cop restrained and ultimately killed an intoxicated thief and counterfeiter after he attempted to elude arrest, and riotous protests broke out around the globe. The Black Lives Matter cult justified looting and arson, chanting "no justice, no peace," predicated upon the false assumption that Caucasians are generally racists who unfairly target blacks and murder them. Not only was that assumption an inversion of reality, but even if it were true, it would not justify far worse behavior on the part of many of the protesters.

Thousands have lashed out like animals – beating innocent individuals and robbing them. Further, when it is pointed out that even though blacks represent less than 13% of the US population, 93% of black murders are perpetrated by other blacks, those who hear such facts get offended and condemn the presenter. Worse, the overwhelming majority of people sympathize with this wholly misinformed and delusional conspiracy which seeks to blame others for their own problems. And when that occurs, anti-Semitism is seldom far behind. Blaming and condemning Jews has become an increasingly prevalent part of this socialist agenda.

It is true that police are far too aggressive and that because many are former military, they have a belligerent, shoot-first approach in imposing their superiority over those they are apprehending. The US Justice Department is irrecoverably corrupt – with countless innocent men and women being convicted based upon false testimony. But the problem is not racism. The underlying issue is that we have lost the capacity to think rationally and respond appropriately. The issue is character and culture, not racism or ethnicity.

And that is why the deceptions which underlie Black Lives Matter and the counterproductive responses to COVID-19 have become so popular. No one is thinking. We are witnessing the ultimate demise of freedom and free enterprise, of individual viability and accountability, of evidence and reason – and no one seems to care. The more power is concentrated, and the less it is distributed and democratized, the worse the human experience, with the world becoming more gang-like, perverted, and corrupt, vicious and deadly.

Anticipating your willingness, let's clean our mental slates so that we are properly prepared for what we are about to read. To begin, recognize that it is absolutely impossible for the religions of Christianity (Roman Catholic, Orthodox [Greek, Eastern, Russian, or Copt], Protestant, or Evangelical), Judaism (Conservative, Orthodox, or Reform), Islam (Sunni or Shi'a), or Mormonism to be valid. Each of these religions claims that the Torah is the inspired word of God, and each draws its authority from it. And yet, they deliberately conceal, change, convolute, contradict, criticize, curtail, and counterfeit (in hundreds of ways) the very testimony they claim was inspired, and upon which they claim to be based.

Therefore, if Yahowah's testimony is true, they are false, based solely upon their variations from God's actual revelation. But if Yahowah's testimony is untrustworthy, then they are also unreliable because they all claim to represent what would then be a deceitful deity – a reality which destroys their authority and credibility.

It is thus impossible to be an informed and rational Catholic, Christian, Muslim, Mormon, or Orthodox Jew. It is foolish to trust these human religious schemes – no matter how they make you feel or how popular they have become.

If what Yahowah says is true, there is only one God, He has but one name, He wants only one thing, and there is just one way to Him. If what Yahowah says is true, nothing is more important than closely observing and carefully considering what He revealed. And if God lied, if men wrote the texts we are going to scrutinize, then, even if there is a God, He is unknowable.

The verdict you will ultimately be able to render on what is true and what is not, on what leads to life or to death, will be based upon considerably more accurate and complete information than has been made available to you previously. Together, we are going to scrutinize the oldest Hebrew manuscripts of Yahowah's Towrah and Prophets. I will translate and amplify God's revelations for you, just as I did with Psalm 19:7 in the previous chapter, using the most effective tools.

As we journey down this road, we will discover what God wants us to know about His nature, our purpose, and His plans, even His timeline. And in the process of closely examining His revelation, we will uncover something profound, perhaps even surprising: Yahowah wants us to enjoy an engaged yet relaxed, personal, conversational, and familial relationship with Him. He wants to adopt us. God does not want us to fear Him, to bow down to Him, or even to worship Him. He despises religions – all of them. He adores relationships and will sacrifice everything (save His integrity) to achieve them.

Yahowah's every word is a story in itself, and collectively, they serve to flesh out the who, what, where, when, and how of the relationship our Heavenly Father seeks to develop with each of us. But beyond this, what Yahowah has to say is so contrary to most of the things we have all been taught, you will have to spend as much time unlearning as you do learning, especially if you want to know God as He revealed Himself to us.

To appreciate how everything relates to the ongoing story of our purpose and of our redemption, to understand how the provision Yahowah has delineated leads to the establishment of an eternal Family, will require considerable time and an open mind. Your willingness in this regard will most likely determine the fate of your soul, as well as those you love. I do not say these things because I have the market cornered on truth, but because I have come to recognize that religious writers lead people away from what is true, and therefore, away from Yahowah.

The reason religious scholars, rabbis, pastors, and priests deceive is because their foundation is faulty. They not only base their revelations on grotesquely errant translations of the prophets, and on things which were not inspired like Paul's letters, the Talmud, and the Quran, they embody the traditional religious milieu – a caustic brew based more upon Babylon than upon God's Word. They do so to be accepted, and because it is good for business.

To know Yahowah, and to understand His offer, requires three things: a change in attitude, a different perspective, and judgmental thinking. Attitudinally, you are going to have to want to know Yahowah to the extent that you are willing to invest the time required to diligently observe His testimony. This is not unlike communicating extensively with someone and getting to know him or her before you choose to marry them.

Additionally, you are going to have to be willing to risk saying goodbye to people, institutions, and ideas you have held dear. Walking away from religion, national politics and patriotism, a reliance upon one's military, an affinity for economic schemes, social customs, and family traditions, as well as conspiracy theories is God's unequivocal prerequisite for engaging in a relationship with Him.

Your perspective will have to change so that you view Yahowah, the Covenant relationship He solicits, and the redemptive plan He facilitated from the vantage point He provided and established – and thus from the Towrah's perspective. God's book was designed to be read from beginning to end, starting with *"Bare'syth* – In the Beginning,"* and then continuing through the Torah, Psalms, and Prophets to the final prophet, *Malaky* | Malachi. And yet, most Christians, unaware of God's story, and the foundation and perspective it provides, read Paul's letters instead. Jews prefer the Talmud, never so much as realizing that it is inconsistent with the Towrah.

To recognize this, to properly distinguish between right and wrong, to discriminate between truth and fiction, you will have to become judgmental. God wants us all to think rationally, morally, decisively, and correctly, such that we exercise our conscience – something the politically correct mantra has dictated we dare not do.

That is extremely difficult for most people because it often means distancing oneself from friends and family, from social customs and religious holidays, and abandoning their primary perspective of the world around them. The truth will prompt consternation over the fate of loved ones, while at the same time undermining the basic tenets of each individual's religious and political beliefs.

So be forewarned: the truth will remain unpopular. It will cause considerable consternation among those without the good sense to embrace it. I know this all too well because I have experienced it. I lost access to my son and granddaughter over it. I got divorced because of it. I have received a thousand letters condemning me, many threatening to kill me. I know it as well because Yahowah told us that this would occur. And yet, I would have it no other way. This is the best decision I have ever made. It will be for you as well. It has been for all of us who have embraced Yahowah and His Covenant.

But the fact remains, the vast preponderance of people are too insecure to tolerate anyone questioning their faith. For most, especially Christians, faith has become synonymous with religion. For them, belief is all that matters. Anyone who questions it is quickly slandered and discarded. And for Jews, a relationship with Yah necessitates invalidating cultural traditions and thus a sense of community. For Muslims, they risk being murdered by their own family for choosing Yahowah over Allah. So, the stakes are high.

And yet, with God, even the most benign of religions is counterproductive. Faith is nothing more than belief in the unknown – a religious substitute for the evidence the faithful lack. It is therefore, by definition, ignorant and irrational to "believe in God," when God can be known.

Worse, most religions worship a false god. They squander their lives chasing after myths man has made.

In opposition to faith and belief, Yahowah wants to be acknowledged for who He actually is, to be understood, to be trusted, and to be relied upon. This is the reason He encourages us to closely and carefully observe His Towrah. It is why He revealed it, and why He filled it with prophetic proclamations.

𐤉𐤄𐤅𐤄

No less than three of the four so-called Christian "Gospels" were hearsay and should have been considered inadmissible as evidence. Matthew was composed three generations after the events it purports to reveal. Further, Matthew plagiarized 90% of Mark's 660 statements and 50% of Luke's – neither of which were remotely accurate. It is so devastating to Christianity's credibility that neither Mark, Luke, nor Matthew were eyewitnesses to anything they reported that it's a miracle anyone believes them.

It is obvious that the first "Gospel" was written by "Mark" because "Matthew" and "Luke" are based upon it. It is unlikely that "Mark" was ever in Judaea, much less Jerusalem. Of him, Eusebius wrote: "Marcus, who had been Petra's interpreter, wrote down…all that he remembered of Iesous' sayings and doings. For he had not heard Iesous or been one of his followers, but later, he was one of Petra's followers." Origen, Tertullian, and Clement concurred, writing at the end of the 2nd century that

"Marcus compiled his account from Petra's speeches in Roma." That is not the way Yahowah communicated to us through Moseh, Dowd, Yasha'yah, or any other of His prophets.

Beyond this unpopular reality, we must also deal with Paul's alliance with Satan. His fourteen letters along with the two books composed by Luke, his associate, completely undermine the Christian New Testament such that it is actually adversarial and counterproductive. This dismissal of Paul, and assessment of his veracity, is explained in *Twistianity*. In it, Paul's letters are compared to God's Word so that you will be equipped to make an informed decision. You are also encouraged to read *Observations* and *Coming Home* because, in both, you will find Yahowah excoriating this man by name and reputation, calling him the Plague of Death, the Father of Lies, and the Son of Evil.

The simple truth is: God did not replace Judaism with Christianity, Jews with Gentiles, or Israel with the Church. He has consistently described and facilitated the relationship He originally established with 'Abraham, expanded with Ya'aqob, developed through Moseh, and lived with Dowd. His chosen people remain Yisra'el.

Yada Yahowah will not claim that every obfuscation of truth was purposeful, yet each publisher's reluctance to correct their "Bibles" serves as an indictment against them. Moreover, at times the comparison between the oldest manuscripts and today's revisions will leave us with no alternative but to assume that the Christian copyedits were deliberate.

And since these deceptions are willfully and knowingly advanced by pastors, priests, and rabbis, clerics are complicit in the corruption – coconspirators if you will. Hopefully, this realization will lead you to the place Yahowah wants you to be – trusting Him and not men.

While the Greek texts underlying the Christian New Testament are unreliable, inadmissible, and worse, deplorable, the cast of characters responsible for promoting the Masoretic Text are also suspect. In this light, we would be wise to consider the *Codex Aleppo* along with the man who endorsed it. Forty percent of the Codex, scribed during the Abbasid Caliphate, the Islamic state from 750 – 1517 CE, is now missing including most of the Torah. The manuscript was kept for five centuries in the Central Synagogue of Aleppo, Syria until the synagogue was torched by Muslims during anti-Jewish pogrom riots in 1947. It is also telling that the synagogue, which dates to the 10th century BCE, was damaged and then converted into a mosque by the Muslim Mongols in the 13th century CE. It was again destroyed during Tamerlane's subjugation of Aleppo in 1400 CE but was rebuilt as a synagogue in the 15th century. And while the synagogue was restored by American Jews after Muslims burned it following the Holocaust, it stands silent and empty. Jews are prohibited from going inside.

It gained considerable renown when Rabbi Moshe ben Maimon (whose acronym forms Rambam), now known as Maimonides, sanctioned it. The man is central to our story because he is responsible for codifying the religion of Judaism as it is practiced today. And therefore, the Rambam has separated as many generations of Jews from Yahowah as Rabbi Akiba. The religion could not have picked two more nefarious fellows had that been the objective.

The Rambam was born in Cordoba, Spain in the Berber Muslim-ruled Almoravid Empire – shortly after the Moorish influence subsided. In his youth, he was a student of Islam – which speaks poorly of his judgment. He also studied the Greek philosophers, which is troubling because their Gnostic religious philosophy was not only universally errant, he allowed it to influence his conception of Judaism

– just as Paul brought it into Christianity. The Rambam was also a mystic and promoted the precursor to Kabbalah. Strike three.

Maimonides actually converted to Islam when the Almoravids conquered Cordoba in 1148 CE. They abolished the horrific dhimmi status of Jews (the condition whereby non-Muslims exist in a humiliating state with no rights, while required to pay Muslims the debilitating jizya tax). And while ending something that dehumanizing might sound compassionate, it was actually murderous. The only option for Jews became to convert to Islam, die by being beheaded, or flee leaving everything behind for the Muslims.

Further degrading, the Jews who converted were forced to wear distinguishing clothing to degrade their status based solely on race. As a result, they were publicly humiliated, subjugated, and abused. This would become a foreshadowing of what would befall Jews throughout Europe during the rise of the Third Reich. It makes Maimonides' affinity for this evil, anti-Semitic religion all the more troubling.

After his conversion to Islam, Maimonides roamed Southern Spain for a decade. However, a rival in Egypt had the Rambam's conversion ruled un-Islamic, giving him the option of exile or death. He chose a life in Fez, Morocco, which was the site of unimaginable carnage. As a symbol of its violent past, the red Fez (which means pickaxe), worn by Muslims and Freemasons alike, is symbolic of a time when the first Muslims murdered so many people in this place, the Islamic jihadists dipped their hats in rivers of blood. And the slaughter would continue, with Muslims savagely murdering over six thousand Jewish men during the Fez Massacre in 1033 CE, stealing their property and possessions, while enslaving the Jewish women to serve their carnal desires, all prior to the Rambam's arrival.

It was in the lingering anti-Semitic stench of this festering cesspool of Islamic culture that Rabbi Maimonides composed his acclaimed commentary on the Mishnah in 1167 CE. A year later, this twisted religious charlatan passed through Judea before doubling back and choosing to serve the Fatimid Caliphate in Egypt in 1168. His cult of personality grew when he confiscated money from a Jewish community besieged in Lower Egypt so that he could bribe Crusaders to turn the Jews they captured in Jerusalem over to him. So much for being a student of the Towrah (Yahowah is overtly opposed to receiving or paying bribes).

The man who had just violated the Towrah's Teaching, not only hailed what he had accomplished with other people's money as a "triumph," he immediately sought to increase his fortunes. Seeking to parlay some of the funds he had taken from his fellow Jews in rabbinic fashion, he financed his brother, David, and sent him off to trade with the Sudanese. Finding their merchandise to be of lesser quality than Maimonides had imagined, David sailed on toward India in search of a greater fortune – drowning en route.

Of David and this sordid enterprise, Maimonides would write in the Cairo Genizah: "The greatest misfortune that has befallen me during my entire life – worse than anything else – was the demise of the saint, may his memory be blessed, who drowned in the Indian sea, carrying much money belonging to me, to him, and to others, and left with me a little daughter and a widow. On the day I received that terrible news I fell ill and remained in bed for about a year, suffering from a sore boil, fever, and depression, and was almost given up. About eight years have passed, but I am still mourning and unable to accept consolation. And how should I console myself? He grew up on my knees, he was my brother, he was my student."

I will leave you to ponder all of the missteps in his obituary so that we can move past his failure as a banker to Maimonides' political career. During this time, he gained supreme power over Jews in Egypt only to lose it, and then gain it back again after excommunicating his rival.

It was then, still short on money, that the Rambam started working as a doctor. He would receive a court appointment to serve as the physician to the Grand Vizier al-Qadi al Fadil, then to Sultan Saladin. Yes, that Saladin – the Kurdish warrior who became the first Islamic sultan of Egypt and Syria, and who, after murdering his way to power, became Islam's champion. He would lead the vicious military campaign against the Crusaders. It was Saladin who solidified Islamic rule over Judea, Syria, and Iraq. He called for all Muslims around the world to rise in Jihad, a Holy War, against Christians.

If we are to be known by the company we keep, Maimonides was as disreputable for his association with Saladin as was Akiba for his promotion of Simon bar Kokhba. It is hard to imagine two people whose choices have had a more detrimental influence on Jews. And yet, it is these men who Jews revere, respect, and admire most. It is to them that they listen without questioning. And it is these men who have written their scriptures. It is truly astonishing that Jews have plagued themselves over the centuries believing such disreputable individuals.

And it only got worse. The Rambam became so consumed with his medical practice that he would routinely, by his own admission, ignore the Shabat. After spending the day in the palace attending to Saladin, he would return to heal Jews and Gentiles in the antechambers until sunset. How is it, then, this man who ignored Yahowah's *Towrah* | Instructions became the author of the most influential treatises on *Halakhah* | Rabbinic Law? After all, it is in his Mishnah (tractate Talmud Sanhedrin, chapter 10, the introduction to Perek Chelek) that his

"Thirteen Fundamental Principles" of the Jewish faith preside – eight of which are wrong.

But that should not be surprising since he was guilty of *babel* | commingling his affinity for Islamic principles, Greek philosophy, and the Babylonian Talmud. He was also an adherent of apophatic theology, where his nameless god was described using only negative attributes. He would even write of "necessary beliefs" which were "conducive to improving social order." He would actually negate the Towrah's presentation of Yahowah's growing animosity in response to His people's tendency to be religious by saying that God was incapable of anger and that this false perception was perpetrated, necessary, and justified to encourage good behavior.

If that were not enough to bury this man's credibility in the swamp of his own making, there is considerable evidence that Maimonides plagiarized much of his work. He stole it from Kaifeng Jews, who, as descendants of Persian merchants, had settled in China. They not only preceded him, but their teachings found their way to the Middle East by way of the Mongols, leaving no opportunity for the Rambam to travel back in time to them.

There appears to be a reason the Spirit has encouraged me to write about this man. No one has been more influential among *Yahuwdym* | Jews – the target audience for everything I have written on behalf of Yahowah. It appears that God wants His people to know their options.

As a Jew, you can continue to believe the man who once served the Islamic religion and has been the source of such pain, or you can consider what the man who excoriated that religion in *God Damn Religion* has to share. You can believe the man who rose to power by fleecing your people so that he could bribe Crusaders, siphoning off money to finance his own aspirations, or the one who has invested the money he made as a merchant into translating

Yahowah's testimony so that he could share the result freely. Are you going to continue to have your life influenced by the man who commingled the worst of Islam, Gnosticism, and the Talmud into a religion in defiance of Yahowah, presenting Him using negative attributes, or will you consider the translations, commentary, conclusions, and insights of one who has steadfastly sought to expose and condemn all religions and political philosophies so that you might be open to the Word of God?

You will discover that Yahowah's prophets had a great deal to say about the alternative to the Rambam. God refers to him as the *choter* | stem and *nakry* | observant foreigner, and to the message he is providing on behalf of His people as the *nes* | banner. For His people to hear His call for them to come home, for them to return to Him, they must not only reject the likes of Maimonides but also come to accept Yahowah. And while I wish that there were hundreds of options available for you to do just that, all much better than this, there are not. And thus, this is a referendum. The most acclaimed of Jews is leading you in one direction, one that has turned out very poorly, while a Gentile, an observant foreigner, is offering to lead you back to the Promised Land by sharing the Word of God.

Pause now and contemplate your options.

Yahowah has also provided the *nes* | banner for the gowym who have disassociated from religion and politics as I have done. And now to help others, let's return to the Christian myth of "Godly protection" and "inerrancy." The sixty-nine pre-Constantine codices which have now been unearthed differ substantially among themselves. This variance then becomes irresolvable as the 2nd-through-early-4th-century textual witnesses are compared to those scribed in the wake of Catholicism's emergence in the 4th century with their augmentative and divergent *Codex Sinaiticus* and *Codex Vaticanus*. And yet, the biggest discrepancy of all exists between these manuscripts and the

Textus Receptus – which was acclaimed as being "without error" by the religious community in the 16th century.

The known disagreements between the Textus Receptus and older codices have now been shown to exceed 300,000 in a 182,000-word text. Further, for the "always accurate" myth to be valid, the Textus Receptus would be word-for-word identical to the more scholarly and modern textual blend known as the Nestle-Aland, but they differ almost as much as they agree. And these inconsistencies still do not take into consideration a myriad of religious copyedits or countless invalid translation choices. In reality, the original hearsay autographs were akin to the myths associated with Dionysus and Odysseus.

For Christians who are still murmuring: "I can't believe God would allow anyone to corrupt His message," for this leap of faith to be grounded in something remotely credible, at some point you will have to deal with the fact that the 16th-century Textus Receptus and the 20th-century Nestle-Aland differ materially, and both are overwhelmingly divergent from the now extant 1st-through-3rd-century manuscripts of the very text they purport to present. So, if your current "Bible" is accurate by happenstance of fate, it means that every prior witness to the text was inaccurate. But let's be clear: even if the thousands of textual incongruities suddenly disappeared, the text of the CNT remains false because it continually contradicts and misappropriates the testimony of the God it claims to represent. This is not logically possible.

Keeping it real, was the Christian God unable or unwilling to protect His message from human corruption? The notion that "God would not allow anyone to corrupt His message" requires complete ignorance of the textual evidence to the contrary. It requires faith in that which is not true, completely undermining the value of religious belief.

Then we must face the issue of Roman Catholicism, and Jerome's Latin Vulgate, which served as the only "Bible" for most of the world for over one thousand years. As a blend of divergent Old Latin manuscripts which were free translations of wildly divergent copies of the *Septuagint*, which were themselves imprecise translations of the Hebrew text, the Vulgate is predictably in substantial conflict with the five-centuries-older Qumran parchments. Yet inexplicably, it is eerily similar to today's most popular English translations, which cast a dark shadow on their validity.

Equally damaging, for over one thousand years, no one outside of Roman Catholic clerics could read the official Latin text, effectively preventing any layperson from knowing God's Word, even if it had been preserved without corruption. The Roman Catholic Church, by way of their marriage of cleric and king, made it a crime punishable by death to own a translation of the Vulgate. And to make matters worse, in the rare case that someone would attempt a translation into a language which could be read and understood by those outside the Church's hierarchy, as was the case with John Wycliffe in 1384, the perpetrator and their product were labeled heretical and burned.

Simply stated: none of these variations or eventualities would have been possible if God had intervened and refused to allow the CNT to be corrupted by man. So, since He obviously allowed it, isn't it incumbent upon us to not only come to understand why He did so, but also to strive to discover what He actually revealed? And this is especially important for Jews to understand because nothing has been more hostile to them than Christianity – well, it and the other religion it spawned with a competitive false Messiah: Judaism.

Considering, therefore, the complexity of these many challenges, we will not rely upon the Latin Vulgate, KJV,

NKJV, ASB, NASB, IV, NIV, NLT, or any other popular Bible. All English translations vary from poor to horrible and are not worth recommending. Even those with the good sense to write God's name back into the text do very little to correct the message Yahowah is revealing.

In that one of the biggest obstacles to knowing the truth about God is the inaccuracy of today's Bible translations, I would like to linger here a bit longer, even at the risk of being repetitive. The *King James Bible* is nothing more than a politically inspired revision five times over of those texts. The *Geneva Bible*, which had become popular at the time, used marginal notes to highlight passages which demonstrated that God had not anointed any king with the right to rule. Since this was contrary to the claims made by all kings, including King Iames (as he was known at the time), it became politically expedient to pen a new Bible, whereby the marginal notes were removed, the translations tweaked to please the king, and the thirteenth chapter of Paul's letter to the Romans was recast to reclaim the Divine Sanction. So, Iames hired the era's most acclaimed secular humanist, Rosicrucian, and occultist, Sir Francis Bacon, to create a more accommodating rendition of Catholicism's Vulgate.

Until quite recently, the Textus Receptus was touted as the foundation of all English translations of the Greek text known as "the Christian New Testament." And yet, it was little more than an intellectual fraud and financial hoax. In October of 1515 CE, a Dutch secular humanist, who was also a Catholic priest, Desiderius Erasmus, and Johann Froben, a publisher of low repute, took five months to mark up, adding and taking away from a flawed 12th-century Medieval Greek manuscript, and they set type directly from those arbitrary scribbles. Then in places where their manuscript was void, they filled in the blanks by translating portions of the Latin Vulgate back into Greek.

Equally reprehensible, when Roman Catholic clerics protested that some of their pet passages weren't included, to quiet their critics, Erasmus and Froben added them without any legitimate basis. Such an example is the aforementioned story of "Jesus and the adulterous woman" recounted in the Gospel of John 8:1-11, whereby the "one without sin" was told "to cast the first stone." This is one of the most famous and often quoted New Testament abstracts, and yet, it is false. As we know, it did not occur. The alleged discussion, which if true, would have the Messiah disavowing the Towrah – which is why it was added, though it is not found in any manuscript prior to the 8th century CE. Similarly, you will not find the ending of Mark, chapter 16 verses 9-20, in any pre-Constantine manuscript, nor even in the 4th-century *Codex Sinaiticus* or *Codex Vaticanus* – when it was added by the Roman Catholic Church.

In the absence of a viable competitor, Erasmus' and Froben's scholastic and financial fraud was said to be "a text received by all in which we have nothing changed or corrupted." This myth was thus rendered: "the Textus Receptus." And while the evidence is overwhelming that the *King James Bible*, first printed in 1611, was actually a revision of prior English translations of the Latin Vulgate, whose authors attributed their text to this very same and highly flawed Textus Receptus. The KJV then became so popular no English translation has yet been offered which dares to correct its familiar phrasing, especially of the most memorable passages.

It was not until 1707 that the Textus Receptus was challenged – effectively undermining the basis of the Reformation and Protestantism. John Mill, a fellow of Queens College in Oxford, invested 30 years comparing the Textus Receptus to some one hundred much older Greek manuscripts. In so doing, he documented 30,000 variations between them. And even this was just a rash on a donkey's posterior. Known variations between the oldest manuscripts of the Greek text, and those which publishers now claim serve as the basis for their translations, may actually exceed 300,000.

Even though some accommodations were made in the later *Westcott and Hort* (1881) and *Nestle-Aland Greek New Testament* (1898 (also known as *Novum Testamentum Graece*)), both texts, while differing substantially from the Textus Receptus, remain more in sync with it than with the earliest extant (and recently discovered and published) Greek manuscripts from the 2nd through 3rd centuries CE. So, while Christian pastors hold up their favorite English translation of the "Bible" and proclaim that it is "the inerrant word of God," factually, the book they are touting isn't even remotely consistent with the earliest witnesses.

And to these embarrassing realizations, to be honest with our God, it is long past time that we come to acknowledge that the Christian New Testament was rotten long before the first scribe took his liberties with it. The Gospel According to Matthew is plagiarized, as is much of Luke – which is deliberately mythological. Neither, of course, were eyewitnesses, which begs the question: if miraculous words and deeds were spoken by "Jesus," why didn't anyone bother to write about it as it was occurring? Or ask yourself this: if "Jesus" said and did such marvelous things in God's name, why didn't he write anything down as had every prophet and witness before him?

Beyond the anti-Semitic cesspool of the Gospels, Paul's fourteen letters are all poison, literally inspired by Satan, who Paul admits controlled him. Peter's claims were no less inaccurate, particularly with regard to robbing Dowd to create the myth of Jesus. And Revelation cites Ezekiel throughout – a book which serves as an autobiographical account of *ha Satan's* ambition.

There is a complete dearth of credibility associated with the instigation and perpetuation of the CNT. Billions of Gentiles have been played for fools and tens of millions of Jews have been horrifically dehumanized and demonized as a result. More than any others, these reasons are why the eight volumes of *Babel* and *Twistianity* were written.

ᛩᚤᛩᛃ

In *Composition and Methodology*, we sought to understand the most important name in the universe – Yahowah. Now, let's turn our attention to one which was integrated into earlier versions of these writings: Yahowsha'. In the years before I came to realize that Dowd, in his second of three lives, volunteered to fulfill the first three Miqra'ey, I used "Yahowsha'" as a mission statement to depict what Father and Son had achieved. *Yahowsha'*, which means Yahowah Delivers, Liberates, and Saves, was consistent with God's overall intent and is indicative of the benefits associated with the *Beryth* and *Mow'edym*. Its pronunciation and derivation were based upon terminology Yahowah and Dowd used throughout their witness, making Yahowsha' an apt job description.

It does not, however, work as a name, and ultimately, that is how I used it. Therefore, I'm systematically removing this nomenclature from *Yada Yahowah* so that credit is more adroitly afforded the actual Messiah, Son of God, and Passover Lamb – *Dowd* | David.

My awakening to this reality occurred when expanding *Coming Home* into a third volume. When translating *Mizmowr* / Psalms, I read that Yahowah and Dowd were in one accord, both recognizing that it would be best for everyone, including Father and Son, if the Messiah was afforded the opportunity to fulfill the seven

Miqra'ey, beginning with Pesach, Matsah, and Bikuwrym. And once my eyes were opened to their motivations and conversations, the evidence supporting this realization was abundantly evident. There was a reason that every prophecy pertaining to the fulfillment of the Miqra'ey included either Dowd's name, his titles, or both. And that is because he fulfilled them. The best explanation of why Dowd wrote in first person about what he would endure, including crucifixion, is because he was there.

Peter, Paul, Luke, Mark, and Matthew had to pilfer every prophecy pertaining to Dowd to prop up their mythical misnomer, Jesus, because there is no mention of anyone else apart from Dowd serving in this manner. And this begs the question: if I could prove this, why didn't God's people do so in the 1st and 2nd centuries CE? Had they done so, Christianity would have been stillborn without any justification for "Jesus" being the Messiah or Son of God. Further, there would be no reason for Akiba to promote the false Messiah bar Kokhba. And without this false messianic star, there would have been no enslaving of Jews, no Diaspora, no renaming of the land, no Roman Catholic subjugation, no Jewish ghettos or shtetls, and no Holocaust.

If it was possible for a single gowy to ascertain and demonstrate this over the course of 22 years, where have the hundreds of thousands of rabbis been these past 2,000 years? Quite literally, the disposition and salvation of the Jewish people hang in the balance, and yet, every effort was made to conceal the truth. The fact that Dowd is and remains Yahowah's Son and Messiah, the Passover Lamb and returning King, invalidates the musings of Maimonides, Akiba, and every Talmud-contributing rabbi thereafter. So, rather than serve Jews by telling them the truth, they choose to remain in control by perpetuating lies.

Should you be on the fence in this regard, unsure if you should accept what I've discovered by translating

Yahowah's and Dowd's testimony or believe the machinations of Jewish sages and Catholic priests who contradict both, please pull the opening volume of *Coming Home, A Voice*, from the YadaYah.com bookshelf and read what was written in the 89th Mizmowr.

As for Christians who are played for fools, ignorantly and irrationally believing that someone named "Jesus Christ" lived in the 1st century and that he was the Son of God, the Messiah, and your Savior, wake up because it was all a result of robbing "David" of his achievements and accolades. I would recommend reading *Twistianity* before it is too late.

Not only was the name "Jesus" invented in the 17th century CE, but the "Christ" nomenclature also is not Hebrew. The closest analog to "Jesus" is Gesus, who was the Son of God in the Celtic religion where the chief deity was known as the "Horned One." And Christ is from the Greek adjective *christos*, whose root is *chrio*, and speaks of the application of drugs.

Since there is no mention of "Jesus" or "Christ" in any prophecy, nor any evidence that a person by this name and title existed, there is no basis for Christian or Christianity, Christmas or Easter, crosses or churches. There was no bodily resurrection, and the myth is not returning. And most important of all, there is no Divine sanction for a New Testament or for the Replacement Theology which serve as the basis of this religion.

The evidence to support these conclusions is conspicuous and readily verifiable, and yet, blind to it, one out of every three souls is plagued by these deceptions. And if that were not bad enough for them, their religion has so abused *Yahuwdym* | Jews over the millennia, Yahowah is committed to ridding the world of every soul infected by this disease. It is little wonder why Christians do not like Him.

There was, however, a soul reborn to a woman in 2 BCE who would come to serve as the Passover Lamb – as Dowd, himself, had prophesied. There was nothing about his physical manifestation at this time which would have caused anyone to pay attention to him – even though he was the most important person who ever lived. Specifically identified by name in every prophecy, the people should have recognized him as *Dowd* | David – their Messiah and King. The fact is, when speaking with Daniel 600 years earlier, he had revealed the exact day he would enter Jerusalem as the *Pesach 'Ayil* | Passover Lamb.

What is particularly interesting regarding all of this is that Dowd, the prophetic eyewitness to what he would endure, is the Son of God and Messiah. The most acclaimed Yahuwd of all is *ha Mashyach* Yahuwdym seek. And yet, most Yisra'elites continue to squander their lives by not recognizing the role he played in their redemption and reconciliation.

The implications of these irrefutable conclusions are earth-shattering and life-changing. Therefore, I am going to ask Yahowah's target audience, *Yahuwdym* | Jews, to endure a level of detail on this excoriating exposé which they might otherwise see as pertaining to Gentiles and not to themselves. The religion which grew out of these lies has not only sought to confiscate every promise Yahowah made to His people, the faithful have been the most abusive toward them. There are few things more liberating for the Chosen People than knowing that their historic adversary is without justification. The Christian Jesus they have falsely been blamed for killing will no longer haunt them. And since there are two and a half billion Christians, it is long past time someone told them the truth.

As I have attested, the name "Jesus" cannot be found anywhere in God's Word. There is no J in the Hebrew alphabet – nor one in Greek or Latin. The letter was not invented until the mid-16th century, precluding anyone named "Jesus" from existing prior to that time.

The first English book to make a distinction between the "I" and "J" was published in 1634. Therein the new letter débuted on words loaned from other languages, specifically Hallelujah (instead of *halaluyah*, meaning: radiate Yahowah's brilliant light). For those who relish dates, you may have noticed that 1634 is twenty-three years after the first edition, of what was then called the *"King Iames Bible,"* was printed in 1611. In it, the publishers introduced "Iesous."

Again, as affirmed, not only is "Jesus" a 17th-century forgery, but this name is also most closely allied linguistically with "Gesus" (pronounced "Jesus"), the savior of the Druid religion (still practiced throughout England) wherein the "Horned One" is considered god. This is highly incriminating.

There is a plethora of Christian (a title we will refute momentarily) apologists who errantly claim that "Jesus" was a transliteration of the Greek Iesou, Iesous, and Iesoun. The problem with that theory is four-fold. Dowd wasn't Greek; He was Hebrew from the tribe of Yahuwdah. The Greek Iota is pronounced like the English I, rather than the come-lately J. The "u," "us," and "un" endings were derivatives of Greek grammar and gender rules without a counterpart in Hebrew or English.

Beyond these issues, you will not find Iesou, Iesous, or Iesoun written on any page of any 1st- 2nd- 3rd- or even early 4th-century Greek manuscript of the so-called "Christian New Testament." Placeholders were universally deployed (without exception) by the scribes. Simply stated: it is impossible to justify the use of "Jesus." And it is wrong.

There are many misguided Messianic Jews, countless rabbis, and otherwise misinformed pseudo-intellectuals who favor Yeshu or Yeshua, neither of which were written in the Towrah, Prophets, or Psalms. At least the mission designation I proposed, *Yahowsha'* | Yahowah Delivers and Saves, has a precedent in Yahowsha' ben Nuwn – Moseh's successor. Their variation has none.

The earliest undisputed extant occurrence of Yeshu is found in five brief anecdotes in the Babylonian Talmud (a collection of rabbinical discussions constituting Jewish Oral Law circa 500 CE). Yeshu is cited as the teacher of a heretic (in Chullin 2:22-24, Avodah Zarah 16-17), as a sorcerer scheduled to be stoned on the eve of Passover (in Sanhedrin 43a), as a son who burns his food in public (in Sanhedrin 103a), as an idolatrous former rabbinical student (in Sanhedrin 107b), and as the spirit of a foreigner who is an enemy of Israel (in Gittin 56b and 57a). (Sounds a lot like Paul.)

Yeshu is also used in the rabbinical Tannaim and Amoraim as a replacement for Manasseh's name. He was Hezekiah's only son. At twelve, upon assuming the throne, he instituted pagan worship in direct opposition to his father (Sanhedrin 103s and Berakhot 17b).

The earliest explicit explanation of the rabbinical term "Yeshu" is found in the medieval Toldoth Yeshu narratives which reveal: "Yeshu was an acronym for the curse *'yimmach shemo wezikhro,'* which means: "may his name and memory be obliterated." Considering the fact that Dowd served as the Passover Lamb, these perceptions have certainly drawn Yahowah's ire. Little wonder rabbis have written Yahowah out of their lives.

If that was not sufficiently sobering, if that is insufficient to make you scream every time you read or hear "Yeshu" or its clones, "Yehshu" and "Yehshua," then you don't know Yahowah very well. And that is a serious problem because Yahowah is God and Dowd is His beloved Son.

Thanks to what Christians and Jews have done to upend the truth, "Jesus" is worshiped as if he were God and Dowd is not credited with being the Pesach *'Ayil* | Lamb. All the while Yahowah remains unknown – obscured by both goddamn religions.

Moving on to the next religious deception, "Christ" is wrong in every possible way. There was no "Jesus" and "Christ" was not Dowd's last name or title. Moreover, without the definite article, "Christ Jesus" would also be wrong – even if there were actually a person named Jesus or if he were *the* Messiah.

As we dig deeper, what we discover is that Classical Greek authors used *chrio*, the basis of "*Christos* – Christ," to describe the "application of drugs." A legacy of this reality is the international symbol for medicines and the stores in which they are sold—Rx—from the Greek Rho Chi, the first two letters in *chrio*. This would make "Christ" and "Christians" "drugged."

Those who may protest that "Christ" is simply a transliteration of Christos, Christou, Christo, or Christon are unaware that there is only one occasion in the whole of the Greek text prior to the mid-4th century where any variation of *chrio* was actually written – and it does not apply to Dowd. Every reference to this misappropriated title was written using the Placeholders ΧΣ, ΧΥ, ΧΩ, and ΧΝ.

The only time we find a derivative of *chrio* in the CNT is when a heavenly messenger is allegedly speaking to *Yahowchanan* | John during his Revelation. The unsupported encounter serves to toy with the Laodicean Assembly (perhaps representing Protestant Christians living in today's Western Democracies) in the seventh supposed letter. To appreciate the point he was attributed to making, realize that the Laodiceans at the time were wealthy and self-reliant. They made a fortune promoting their own brand of ointment for the ears and eyes known as "Phrygian powder" under the symbol "Rx." Referencing their healthcare system, the alleged spiritual messenger admonished: "I advise that you...rub (*eg-chrio* – smear) your eyes with medicinal cake (*kollourion* – a drug preparation for ailing eyes) in order that you might see." (Revelation 3:18) Therefore, in this, the singular reference to *chrio*, the root of *christo*, in the totality of the pre-Constantine Greek manuscripts of the so-called "Christian New Testament," the word was used to describe the application of drugs.

To further indict "Christ" and "Christian," even if the revisionist definition of *chriso* could be interpreted as "anointed," and if this were intended, that connotation still depicts the "application of a medicinal ointment or drug." And should we ignorantly and inadvisably jettison this pharmaceutical baggage, we would be left with other insurmountable problems associated with "Christ" as a Greek rather than a Hebrew concept. Should Christians want to name their gods using Greek nomenclature, they cannot at the same time claim an affinity with Yahowah, His people and prophets. For example, every reference to what I'm doing for Yahowah, Dowd, and Yahuwdym was scribed in Hebrew using terms such as *Choter*, *Nakry*, *Basar*, *Zarowa'*, and *Mal'ak*, even *Tsuwr*, but never *Petra* which is the closest Greek analog of the meaning Craig conveys in Celtic.

The Torah, Prophets, and Psalms afford the title *Mashyach* | Messiah to Dowd, never "Jesus." In the only passage prophetic of a coming *Mashyach*, we find Dowd, under the title *Gabry'el* | God's Most Competent and Courageous Man telling Daniel what, he, himself, as *ha Mashyach*, would accomplish by fulfilling the seven Mow'ed Miqra'ey. He even told us when he would arrive.

Ha Ma'aseyah | The Anointed Messiah, as a Hebrew title, should be transliterated (presented phonetically) in

cix

Greek and also English, not translated – at least when used as a title. For example, the titles Rabbi, Satan, Imam, Pharaoh, Czar, Caesar, and Pope were all transliterated from their original languages, not translated.

Dowd was not Greek. He did not speak Greek. He did not have a Greek name or a Greek title. So, to infer that he did, by pretending that *Ieosus Christos* | "Jesus Christ" was the Son of God, Messiah, and Savior is grossly inaccurate and deceptive – in addition to being wrong on all accounts.

This would be like transliterating Genghis' "Kahn" title, which means "ruler" in Mongolian, to "Sheik Jinjeus" because we like the letter J, the "eus" ending derived from Greek grammar, and sheik, which has the same meaning in Arabic. Worse, how about rendering Caesar Augustus, "Hairy August" as that is what *caesar* means in English? It is idiotic.

Furthermore, the textual evidence within the spurious CNT affirms that the Placeholders XΣ, XY, XΩ, and XN were not actually based upon Christos, Christou, Christo, or Christon, as those who have an aversion to all things Hebrew would have you believe. Consider this: writing about the great fire which swept through Rome in 64 CE, the Roman historian Tacitus (the classical world's most authoritative voice) in *Annals* XV.44.2-8, revealed:

"All human efforts…and propitiations of the gods, did not banish the sinister belief that the fire was the result of an order [from Nero]. Consequently, to get rid of the report, Nero fastened the guilt and inflicted the most exquisite tortures on a class hated for their abominations, called Chrestucians (*Chrestuaneos*) by the populace. *Chrestus*, from whom the name had its origin, suffered the extreme penalty during the reign of Tiberius at the hands of one of our procurators, Pontius Pilate. And a most mischievous superstition, thus checked for the moment, again broke out not only in Iudaea, the first source of the evil, but even in

Rome, where all things hideous and shameful from every part of the world find their center and become popular.

Accordingly, an arrest was first made of all who pleaded guilty; then, upon their information, an immense multitude was convicted, not so much of the crime of firing the city, as of hatred against mankind. Mockery of every sort was added to their deaths. Covered with the skins of beasts, they were torn by dogs and perished, or were nailed to crosses, or were doomed to the flames and burnt, to serve as a nightly illumination when daylight had expired."

Chrestus and *christos* are completely different words in Greek with highly divergent meanings. The historical term is actually closer to Yahowah's intent because it speaks of someone who is set apart for a noble enterprise. As a result, for a while, I used *Ma'aseyah* | Work of Yah to describe the way the Mow'edym were fulfilled. But once I realized that Dowd, the actual Messiah, served in this role, I dispensed with *Ma'aseyah*.

The *Nestle-Aland 27th Edition Greek New Testament* affirms to the chagrin of Christians that *Chrestus* (χρηστὸς) was scribed in 1 Peter 2:3, not *Christos*. Their references for this include Papyrus 72 and the *Codex Sinaiticus*, the oldest extant witnesses of Peter's letter.

He is purported to have written: "**As a newborn child, true to our real nature** (*logikos* – in a genuine, reasonable, rational, and sensible manner), **earnestly desires and lovingly pursues** (*epipotheo* – long for, showing great affection while yearning for) **the pure and unadulterated** (*adolos* – that which is completely devoid of dishonest intent or deceit and thus is perfect) **milk in order to grow in respect to salvation, since we have experienced** (*geuomai* – partaken and tasted, have been nourished by) **Kurios** (KΣ – from a Divine Placeholder) **as the useful implement and upright servant** (*chrestus* – as a useful tool)." (1 Peter 2:2-3)

The fact that we find *chrestus* written in the *Codex Sinaiticus*, and the Placeholder XPΣ written in P72 in the same place in this passage, we have an early affirmation that the Placeholder was based upon the Greek *chrestus*, not *Christos*. This means that the title the authors of the CNT selected said nothing about their man-god being *ha Mashyach* | Anointed Messiah but, instead, referred to him as a *chrestus* | a useful implement and workable tool.

However, *chrestus* is not a title. Nonetheless, it is better than "drugged. It was used to "depict the good and beneficial work of a moral person." So rather than being "drugged," a *chrestucian* would have been a "useful implement, an upright servant, and a moral person working beneficially as an effective tool."

Since our preference is to use evidence and reason as our guide to the truth, be aware that there are eight partial manuscripts of Daniel in the Dead Sea Scroll collection. These were copied between 125 BCE and 50 CE. It should be noted that all four scrolls containing material from the first eight chapters were initially scribed in Babylonian Hebrew, but they switch to Aramaic in the midst of chapter 2, verse 4, and then revert back to Hebrew at the beginning of the 8th chapter. (Along these lines, it is also interesting to be aware that the longer Roman Catholic version of Daniel, with the Prayer of Azariah, the Song of Three Men, Susanna, and Bel and the Dragon, isn't supported by any Qumran manuscript.)

It is further revealing that the first 6 chapters of Daniel depict the Babylonian mindset Yahowah finds so appalling. They were obviously uninspired. And while the second half of the book contains serious historical anomalies, the inaccuracies are all in Daniel's voice rather than occurring in the witness of the prophets who visited with him – the most important of whom was Dowd.

None of the eight scrolls found in the caves above the Dead Sea provide any witness to the text between Daniel 7:18 and 10:4. And unfortunately, the statements which speak prophetically of Dowd as the Mashyach in Dany'el 9:21 through 9:26, are right in the midst of this void. That means the oldest manuscript attesting to this prophecy was scribed by rabbinical Masoretes in the 11th century CE in the manuscript, known as the *Codex Leningradensis* (dated to 1008 CE and published in 1937).

The result reads...

"While I was continuing to (*wa 'owd 'any*) **converse,** (*dabar*)**, pleading for intercession with the intent of being distinct and different** (*'el taphilah*)**, then** (*wa*) **the individual, this man,** (*ha 'iysh*)**,** *Gabry'el* **| God's Most Confident and Capable, Courageous and Combative Individual** (*wa Gabry'el* – a.k.a., Dowd)**, whom, to reveal the proper path** (*'asher*)**, I had seen** (*ra'ah*) **during the initial prophetic revelation** (*ba ha chazown ba ha tachilah*)**, offering advice while preoccupied with the destruction of existing militaries, maneuvering quickly between battles** (*ya'aph ba ya'aph*)**, reached out to make contact with me** (*naga' 'el 'any*) **around the time of the evening** (*ka 'eth 'ereb*) **offering, the apportionment which is bestowed as a gift** (*minchah*)**.** (*Dany'el 9:21*)

So (*wa*)**, he made the connections to encourage understanding** (*byn*)**. He spoke with me** (*wa dabar 'im 'any*)**, and he said** (*wa 'amar*)**, 'Dany'el** (*Dany'el*)**, now at this time in this sequence of events** (*'atah*)**, I have come forth** (*yatsa'*) **to provide insights and instruction which, if you are circumspect and considerate, will promote** (*la sakal 'atah*) **understanding through discernment** (*bynah*)**.** (*Dany'el 9:22*)

In the beginning, the sickening and wearisome (*ba tachilah*) **matter** (*dabar*) **of your desire for favors and your pleading for mercy** (*tachanuwn 'atah*) **was brought**

up (*yatsa'*). So, I, myself, have come (*wa 'any*) to conspicuously report an informative announcement, making this known (*la nagad*), because (*ky*) you are overly needy (*chamadowth 'atah*). Therefore (*wa*), you will want to consider and understand after a diligent and systematic evaluation (*byn*) of this message (*ba ha dabar*), choosing to make the connections needed to comprehend (*wa byn*) what is being revealed (*ba ha mar'eh*). (*Dany'el* 9:23)

The many promises associated with Shabuw'ah and the Shabat, along with the vows pertaining to the things Seven represents (*shabuwa'ym shib'iym*) are determined and decreed, divided out and planned (*chathak*) on behalf of your people, the extended family (*'al 'am 'atah*), and upon your set-apart city and its distinctly uncommon inhabitants (*wa 'al 'iyr qodesh 'atah*) to bring an end to the religious rebellion, eliminating the revolting communal defiance and contrarian views (*la kalah ha pesha'*), to affix the signature which seals up the guilt associated with having missed the way, precluding ever being wrong again (*wa la chatham chata'owth*), to provide reconciliation for religious error, purging the perverse corruptions and twisted perversions (*wa la kaphar 'awon*), to arrive with and bring that which is eternally right, always correct, forever accurate and honest, thereby attaining everlasting deliverance and vindication (*wa la bow' tsedeq 'owlam*), to provide a personal seal and signature to revelation, confirming and completing these communications (*wa la chatham chazown wa naby'*), and to prophecy (*wa naby'* – to the prophet), while also anointing the Most Set Apart (*wa la mashach qodesh qodesh*). (*Dany'el* 9:24)

Therefore (*wa*), know, because it is beneficial for you to be aware by coming to possess the information required to recognize reality (*yada'*) and gain the insights needed to understand, realizing that the best option is for you to be prudent after learning, succeeding and prospering by being attentive, properly educated, intelligent, and wise, perceiving (*wa sakal*) that from (*min*) the going forth of the word (*mowtsa' dabar*) to return to restore (*shuwb*), reestablishing (*wa la banah*), **Yaruwshalaim** | the Source of Teaching and Guidance on Reconciliation (*Yaruwshalaim*) until the restoring testimony and eternal witness (*'ad*) of the Son of the Sovereign who is conspicuously making this known, and who will provide the leadership and counsel (*nagyd*) as **Mashyach** | the anointed Messiah (*Mashyach*) are seven sevens and thus seven promises and fulfilled vows (*shabuwa'ym shiba'ah*).

Furthermore (*wa*), in sixty-two weeks (*shabuwa'ym sheshym wa shanaym*), she will be restored (*shuwb*) and rebuilt to reestablish and fortify (*wa banah*) the way to grow and expand (*rachob*) by being diligent and decisive (*wa charuwts*) in a troubled time of oppression (*wa ba tsowq ha 'ets*). (Daniel 9:25)

And after (*wa 'achar*) the sixty-two weeks (*ha shabuwa'ym sheshym wa shanaym*), **Mashyach** | the Anointed Messiah (*Mashyach*) will be cut down and uprooted to establish a covenant, removed and exchanged in the new agreement (*karath*), but not for himself and such that he is negated and replaced, his life for naught (*wa 'ayn la huw'*).

Then (*wa*), the people and nation, even the army (*'am*) of the commanding officer and supreme leader who is making copious announcements and prolific declarations (*nagyd*) who is to come (*ha bow'*) will attempt to corrupt and destroy (*shachath*) the city (*ha 'iyr*) and the Set Apart (*wa ha qodesh*).

And (*wa*) its end, and his (*qets huw'*) outrageousness, will be wiped away by an overpowering force (*ha sheteph*). **And yet, to the very last moment (*wa 'ad qets*), it is certain (*charats*) that there will be devastating and desolating (*shamem*) war (*milchamah*).** (*Dany'el* 9:26)

Thereupon (*wa*), he will confirm the prevailing (*gabar*) covenant, this agreement and arrangement (*beryth*) with a great many, including plenty of rabbis, the preponderance of the populous, and with numerous among the elite (*la ha rabym*), for one week and based upon a single promise (*'echad shabuwa'*). But halfway through the week (*wa chatsy shabuwa'*), he will stop the observance of the Shabat (*shabath*), the sacrifice (*zebach*), and the gift of an allocation (*minchah*).

The most extreme aspect (*wa 'al kanaph*) of the repulsive abomination and monstrous religious idolatry (*shiquwtsym*) will astonish and desolate, incapacitate and mortify (*shamem*) such that there is an inability to be perceptive, a great longing, and all-encompassing anxiety, even complete and utter destruction when most will perish (*wa 'ad kalah*).

It will occur quickly and decisively, with determination and decrees (*wa charats*) profusely poured out (*natak*) upon the astonished and stupefied who will perish because they are too stunned to respond (*'al shamem*).'" (*Dany'el* / God is My Means to Judge / Daniel 9:27)

𐤋𐤀𐤅𐤋

When it comes to the next coopted and misappropriated term, a modicum of investigation leads to the inescapable conclusion that the title "Bible" was derived from the name of an Egyptian goddess. Especially incriminating in this regard, *biblos* was not used to describe the Word of God until the 4th century CE, coterminous with the formation of Constantine's Roman Catholic Church. Prior to that time, *biblion*, or in the plural, *biblia*, was a pseudonym for the papyrus upon which the words of the spurious CNT had been written. Other than the fact, one text was inspired and the other not, this is not unlike calling the Torah "parchment."

The papyrus reeds which grew along the Nile in Egypt were imported into the Phoenician port known as Byblos by the Greeks. Priests taught that the city had been founded by the Phoenician sun deity, Ba'al Chronos, "the Lord of Time" (a blending of the Hebrew word for Lord, *ba'al*, and the Greek word for time, *chronos*), according to the scholarly tome *Mythology of All Races*. As such, it was the seat of Adonis (also meaning "my Lord," albeit this time from the Hebrew *'adonay*).

More incriminating still, according to *Ausfuhrliches Lexicon of Grecian and Roman Mythology*, "the ancient city of Byblos in Phoenicia was named after Byblis in Egypt." This town "was named after the sun goddess, Byblis, also known as Byble." Byblis was the granddaughter of Ra. She was eventually inducted into Roman mythology as a descendant of Apollo. According to *Bell's New Pantheon*, "Byblia was also the name of Venus," and thus, "she must be equated with Ishtar," the Babylonian Queen of Heaven and Mother of God for whom "Easter" was named. This connection was affirmed in *An Illustrated Dictionary of Classical Mythology* and also in *Crowell's Handbook of Classical Mythology*. Therefore, considering the title's heritage, "Bible" is a horrible designation for God's Word.

It only gets worse from there. When we turn our attention to Hebrew, the language of Divine revelation, there are three catastrophic problems associated with calling anything associated with Yahowah a "Bible." First, the Hebrew root of Bible is *babel* – which is arguably the lexicon's single most derogatory term. *Babel* is Babylon, the Mother of the Harlots, the civilization that gave birth to the beasts which would plague God's people.

Second, the word *babel* means "to confuse by commingling and to confound by intermixing." This is the antithesis of Yahowah's intent.

Third, *babel* is a compound of *ba*, meaning "with," and *bel*, the "Lord." And now that we know that *Ba'al* | Lord is Satan's title, this is the worst of all possible associations.

As a result, I will only use "Bible" in a derogatory fashion and never in connection with the Word of God. Yahowah's testimony is found in the Towrah, Prophets, and Psalms. End of conversation.

Compounding this mistake, God did not reveal anything even remotely akin to an "Old Testament" or "New Testament." The perpetrator of this fraud was Paul, and his promoter was Marcion, a raging anti-Semite, who rejected Yahowah and the entirety of His Torah testimony to promote Paul's Gnostic-inspired interpretation. In the early 2nd century CE, Marcion became the first, after Paul, to refer to the Torah, Prophets, and Psalms as the "Old Testament."

The reference was intended to demean it as a document such that it was seen as the will of a now-deceased deity. In its place, Marcion promoted his "New Testament," a canon comprised of Paul's fourteen epistles along with Luke and Acts (written by Paul's assistant) – in which almost everything prescribed in the Torah was removed or demeaned. Thereafter, using what Paul and Luke had opined, Marcion entrenched a division which had not previously existed, one that promoted the notion that the Torah was now obsolete, having been replaced by the Pauline concept of the "Gospel of Grace." Anything which did not support this view was either excluded, censored, or discredited. It was a transition in perspective from which

Christianity would never recover. And while Marcion was ultimately labeled a heretic by the Roman Catholic Church for his Gnostic preoccupation, nearly everything he endorsed remains indelibly woven into the fabric of the Christian religion.

In support of this anti-Towrah perspective, Paul, in his letters to the Galatians and Romans, wrote of "two covenants," characterizing the one formalized in the Torah on Mount Sinai as being of the flesh and thus evil, a cruel taskmaster that had not, could not, and would not save anyone. We will allow God to prove otherwise through His many statements which abolish the notion of a "second, new and different" Covenant. Such a claim can only be drawn by mistranslating one statement from *Yirmayahuw* | Jeremiah and taking it out of context.

Yahowah did speak of eventually "repairing and restoring the Covenant," and of this "Renewed Covenant" "not being exactly the same as" the existing one. But the stated beneficiaries are exclusively Yisra'el and Yahuwdah, not a Gentile "church." The reestablishment and renewal is not only in our future, it will be with the Chosen People.

Further, those who actually consider Yahowah's explanation of how His Renewed and Restored Covenant will differ from the Covenant described in His Towrah discover that "Yahowah will give them a copy of His Towrah, placing His Guidance in their [Yisra'el's and Yahuwdah's] midst, writing it upon their hearts" – stating, "I shall be their God, and they shall be My family." Therefore, this is not about Gentiles or Christianity, nor does it endorse replacing the Towrah with Grace. Indeed, it is just the opposite. Therefore, Replacement Theology lacks any validity and completely undermines Christianity's credibility.

Therefore, predicated upon this announcement from God, it would be wrong to refer to the Greek eyewitness accounts as the "Renewed Covenant," much less the CNT. The Covenant has not yet been "renewed." There will never be a "new" one. And since it is His Word, I think it is reasonable to use His terms.

While I am beating a dead beast, there are two additional Christian concepts I feel compelled to expose from the outset so that we can proceed using terminology acceptable to God. The next is the Gospel of Grace. It is based upon the name of the Roman goddesses, the Gratia. They are better known, however, by their Greek name, the Charities, which is how the concept of grace is rendered in the Greek New Testament.

There is no credible source which disputes the fact that "*charis* – grace" is a transliteration of the name of the three Greek Graces known as the *Charites*. The English word "charity" is a direct transliteration. These pagan goddesses of charm, splendor, good fortune, procreation, merriment, and beauty were often depicted ecstatically celebrating the natural world and rejoicing over fertility and sensuality. Collectively, they make four appearances in Homer's *Iliad* and three in the *Odyssey*.

In the capricious mist of Greek mythology, the *Charis* were either the daughters of Dionysus and Aphrodite, Zeus and Eurynome, or Helios and Aegle. And what is particularly troubling is that Paul puts one of Dionysus' most famous quotes in the Messiah's mouth during his conversion experience on the road to Damascus. As it would transpire, Paul's faith came to mirror the Dionysus cult (Bacchus in Roman mythology) which is one of the reasons why so many aspects of Pauline Christianity are pagan. (These troubling associations are detailed for your consideration in the "*Kataginosko* – Convicted" chapter of *The Great Galatians Debate* in *Twistianity*.)

The "Graces" were associated with the Greek underworld, known as Hades, from which the Christian name and concept of "Hell" was derived. Equally troubling, Charis stars in the Eleusinian Mysteries. This exceptionally popular Greek and Roman agrarian cult was based upon the abduction of Persephone from her mother by Hades. The myth plays out like Christianity, with the loss to the underworld, the search, and the ascent, and where the resurrection from hell features a reunion with her mother. Likewise, Persephone's rebirth became the elixir of eternal life, whereby believers were rewarded for their faith.

The cult's popularity, like that of early Christianity, was largely the result of psychedelic drugs. They were used by the faithful to enhance the religious experience and commune with the divine. While noted for their use within the Eleusinian Mysteries and the emergence of the cult of Christianity, drugs were prevalent throughout Greek and Roman religious practices. However, in recognition that *chriso*, upon which Christ and Christian are based, means "to be drugged," if you count yourself among those suffering from this addiction, it is time to detox.

Should you be interested in verifying the early Christian propensity to imbibe psychedelic drugs, you should consider: *The Sacred Mushroom and the Cross – A Study of the Nature and Origins of Christianity within the Fertility Cults of the Ancient Near East,* by John Allegro (an English archaeologist and Dead Sea Scrolls scholar who also wrote *The Dead Sea Scrolls and the Christian Myth* in 1979), *The Mushroom in Christian Art,* by John Rush, *The Psychedelic Gospels – the Secret History of Hallucinogens in Christianity,* by Jerry and Julie Brown, *The Immortality Key,* by Brian Muraresku, *The Road to Eleusis,* by Gordon Wasson, and *Apples of Apollo,* by Carl Ruck. However, be forewarned: while Allegro's claims have been validated regarding the use of hallucinogens by early Christians and the pagan origins of their religion, his desire to connect the Essene's fascination with the 'Teacher of Righteousness' with "Jesus" is universally repudiated. Therefore, since scholarship typically intermixes interesting evidence with absurd deceptions, should you wish to view the prolific influence of psychedelics in the formative years of Christianity for yourself, google "mushrooms in early Christian murals and art" and feast your eyes on the 'shrooms. Turns out, the greatest miracle of Christianity is that so many believed their hallucinations.

The naked form of the Charis stands at the entrance of the Acropolis in Athens. Naked frescoes of the *Charites* adorn homes throughout Pompeii, Italy, which means that they transcended the Greek religion and influenced Rome where they became known as the *Gratia*. Their appeal, beyond their beauty, gaiety, and sensual form, was the alleged mysteries they held known only to religious initiates. Sir Francis Bacon, a Rosicrucian and likely stylist of the *King James Bible*, would have loved them.

And yet, the name of the Greek goddesses, *Charis* | Charity, memorialized today under their Roman moniker, *Gratia* | Grace, is the operative term of Galatians – one which puts Paul in opposition to the very Towrah and God which condemns the use of such names. Simply stated: the "Gospel of Grace" is pagan. It is literally "*Gott*'s spell of *Gratia*."

Most commonly associated with Aphrodite, the goddess of love, the Charis were said to have charmed the gods, Apollo, Dionysus, and Hermes. In Pagan Rome, the three *Gratia*, or Graces, were celebrated for bringing joy, beauty, charm, and happiness to their feasts. As personifications of prosperity and good fortune, and as the messengers for Venus and Cupid (and later for Aphrodite and Eros), the *Gratia* served as clever counterfeits for Yahowah's *chanan* | mercy. Therefore, those who conceived the religion of Christianity simply transliterated *Gratia*, and then based their faith on a new mantra called "the Gospel of Grace," unashamed by the fact that their credo bore the name of pagan deities. This is deeply troubling. It is a scar, indeed a mortal wound, to Paul's epistles, and another deathblow to Christendom.

In ancient languages, it is often difficult to determine if the name of a god or goddess became a word, or if an existing word later became a name. We know, for example, that Greek goddesses, like those in Babylon, Assyria, Egypt, and Rome, bore names which described their mythological natures and ambitions. Such is the case with the *Charites*. The *Charis* came to represent: "joy, favor, mercy, and acceptance, loving kindness and the gift of goodwill." So, while we cannot be certain if the name, *Charis*, was based on the verb, *chairo*, or whether the verb was based upon the name, *Charis*, once *Charis / Gratia* became a name, it doesn't matter, because conveying it in a positive manner is contrary to Yahowah's instructions on this matter.

There are a number of related Hebrew terms which convey the concepts of "mercy, affection, love, acceptance, kindness, and favorable treatment." And they are all devoid of pagan baggage. The first is *chen*. It is used in its collective forms 193 times in the Towrah, Naby', wa Mizmowr. *Chen* is derived from the verb, *chanan*. As a noun, it means "to favor and to accept by providing an unearned gift," which is why it is often mistranslated as "grace" in English Bibles. To be *chanan* is "to be merciful, demonstrating unmerited favor."

Racham, which appears 77 times in the Torah, Prophets, and Psalms, means "merciful, loving, compassionate, and tenderly affectionate." Its shorter form, *raham*, meaning "mercy," makes 44 appearances, and the longer form, *rachuwm*, which also means "merciful," is scribed 13 times.

In the whole of the incredulous narrative of the Christian New Testament, *charis* only appears once in what could be perceived as a credible voice. If we are to believe that a spiritual messenger had reason to speak to "John" circa 70 CE, he would have addressed him in Hebrew, not Greek. Therefore, in the extremely remote possibility such a discussion occurred, the *mal'ak* would have said "*chesed* – mercy," not "*charis* – charity." He certainly would not have spoken of the Latin "*Gratia* – Graces." And since we do not have a copy of this portion of Revelation dating prior to Constantine legitimizing Paul's faith, there is no credible evidence to suggest this revelation occurred.

Further discrediting it, we find another highly problematic placement of this pagan name in the first chapter of the Gospel of John. The oldest extant copy of John's introductory narrative dates to the late 2nd or early 3rd century. And while it was professionally scribed in Alexandria, Egypt, Pauline influences permeated the profession and place by this time. For more on this, I invite you to read *Twistianity*, where this topic is covered in much greater detail.

At best, *charis* / *gratia* / grace is misleading. At worst, it attempts to associate one's salvation with faith in a very popular and seductive trio of pagan goddesses. So, while using the term to convey "mercy" is misleading, promoting salvation under the auspices of "you are saved through faith by Grace" is unquestionably deceitful, deadly, and damning.

Throughout *Yada Yahowah*, and thus also in *An Introduction to God*, *Observations*, and *Coming Home*, the title "Church" is only used in a derogatory sense. It is another of Christianity's ignoble myths. With "church," we not only discover that nothing remotely akin to it appears anywhere in the Towrah, Prophets, and Psalms – the word does not exist in the Greek New Testament.

The notion of a "church" began when Catholic clerics chose to replace the Greek word, *ekklesia*, meaning "called-out assembly," rather than translate it (replicating its meaning (which is required for words)) or transliterate it (replicating its pronunciation (which is permissible with titles)). This counterfeit has served to hide the fact that the meaning of "*ekklesia* – called out" is similar to the Towrah's presentations of the *Miqra'ey*. The title Yahowah uses to describe His seven annual Feasts means: "Invitations to Be Called Out and Meet." One might reasonably assume that Dowd would have shared his intention to fulfill the Miqra'ey which may be the impetus for *ekklesia*.

Christian apologists, however, will protest that their "church" was derived from the Greek *kuriakon*. But that is absurd. Why would someone translate a Greek word *ekklesia* by replacing it with a different Greek word such as *kuriakon*, especially when they have entirely divergent meanings? It is as odd as replacing Torah with Tadpole. Worse, even if the Greek text said *kuriakon* rather than *ekklesia*, the case cannot be made that *kuriakon* sounds like church, further incriminating the religious men who justify this exchange. As such, all of the religious arguments that "church" is a transliteration of *kuriakon*, which is somehow a translation of *ekklesia*, fail the test of reason.

Should you be curious, *kuriakon*, or *kuriakos* as it is sometimes written, is based upon *kurios*, which means "lord and master, the one who rules by usurping freewill." And yet, since the Catholic Church needed a system whereby they could control and fleece the masses, subjecting them to their control, buildings were built and a religious institution was established under the dominion of those who would curtail freedom of choice.

I find it interesting to note that a derivative of the Greek *kuriakon* was used by the false prophet Paul in his first letter to the Corinthians (verse 11:20) to obfuscate the celebration of "*Pesach* – Passover," replacing it with the religious notion of "the Lord's Supper" – which has subsequently evolved to become the Eucharist and Communion.

Turning to Webster's International Dictionary, in the 1909 edition, their explanation begins: "Church, noun. [of Medieval origin. Chirche from the Anglo-Saxon circe...]." They then describe church as "1. a building; 2. a place of worship for any religion." And yet, there is no connection between "*ekklesia* – called out" and any of these things.

Worse, while "church" is not a translation of *ekklesia,* or even a transliteration of *kuriakon,* there is an unmistakable phonetic link to the Druid, and thus Anglo-Saxon and Germanic, words *chirche* and *circe* – consistent with what we just discovered in Webster's Dictionary. The Oldest Druid temples were built as circles, a transliteration of *circe,* to represent their god, the sun. Almost every encyclopedia of mythology reveals that *Circe* was a sun goddess, the daughter of Helios. And if that were not enough, as I have already shared, the "Savior" of the Druid religion (where the "Horned One" is god) was named "Gesus," which was pronounced: "Jesus."

The connection between the Christian Church and Circe is further complicated by the goddess' appearance in Homer's *Odyssey.* We are told that Odysseus' men could hear Circe within her palace. She was singing beautifully as she worked her loom, making a web so fine, and of such dazzling colors, it was one but a goddess could weave. Using her divine ability to lure men to their demise, Circe was said to have turned Odysseus' men into pigs. Transformed back into men, they became Circe's guests, where they found themselves so enthralled by her charms, they were unable to leave.

The best that can be said is that "Church," unlike the word it replaced, *ekklesia,* conveys no relevant message and is wholly unrelated to God. It is yet another Christian deception.

There is also no Godly basis for a cross, the primary symbol of Christendom. The gruesome crucifixes that ghoulishly adorn Catholic cathedrals and the towering crosses set atop Church steeples and worn around the necks of the faithful are a legacy of Babylon's sun-god religion. The Lamb's body was indeed affixed to an upright pole on Passover, but just like Passover, his blood served as a witness on an upright pillar – akin to a lintel forming the doorway to heaven. Worshiping a Dead God on a Stick is as moronic as it is macabre.

Religious deceptions have become so commonplace, our first order of business has been to clear away these societal and religious myths so that the truth can be known and appreciated. *Yada Yahowah,* as you are discovering, was written to confirm what Yahowah had to say regardless of how many lucrative money-making schemes and entrenched religious rituals it skewers.

𐤔𐤅𐤄𐤉

Prophecy

Future History…

Before we leave this introduction to *Yada Yahowah* and move into the creation account, I would like to share a prophecy with Yahowah's target audience – *Yahuwdym*. It is something every Jew should know, even though it will be uncomfortable to hear. The following profession may be the most revealing ever written regarding the Last Days.

Through the prophet *Yasha'yah* / Freedom and Salvation are from Yahowah / Isaiah, Yahowah spoke to His wayward children…

"Woe, this is a warning (*howy* – a cautionary notice of impending trouble) **to *'Ary'el* | the Lion of God and to *'Aruw'el* | Those Gathered by God** (*'Ary'el* / *'Aruw'el* – the Lion of God is a pseudonym for *Yahuwdym* | Jews, Those Gathered by God is a metaphor for *Yisra'el* | Those who Engage and Endure with God, and the Ark and Hearth of God addresses the warmth and light of Yahowah's *Beyth* | Family Home in Yaruwshalaim; a compound of either the Masoretic *'ary* – lion of *'el* – God (the lion is representative of the tribe of Yahuwdah) or the Dead Sea Scroll (1QIsa) *'aruw* – to behold and *'arown* – chest and ark of *'el* – God [note: *'ary*, *'aruw*, and *'arown* are based upon *'arah* – those gathered by *'el* – God (which is indicative of the Chosen People, especially as they were taken home out of the crucibles of human oppression in Egypt)]).

'Ary'el | the Lion of God and _'Aruw'el_ | Those Gathered by God (*'Ary'el* / *'Aruw'el* – a pseudonym for *Yahuwdym* | Jews, a metaphor for *Yisra'el* | Those who Engage and Endure with God, and symbolic of the warmth and light of Yahowah's *Beyth* | Family Home in

Yaruwshalaim): **Dowd** (*Dowd* – the Beloved, David) **was loved and favored when he camped out for a while** (*chanah* – he encamped and was shown mercy and kindness; from *chanan* – to be considered favorably, to be loved, and to receive mercy (qal perfect)) **because of continually** (*yasaph* – repeatedly, doing it again) **being immersed in the annual cycle of the feasts** (*chag naqaph* – encompassing the festivals to be celebrated (singular feminine imperative [from 1QIsa and thus addressing the role Dowd's soul would play in their fulfillment])) **year to year** (*shanah 'al shanah*)." (*Yasha'yah* / Freedom is from Yah / Isaiah 29:1)

Dowd | David, Yahowah's Chosen One, the declared Son of God and the anointed Messiah, the Passover Lamb and King, is the most important *Yahuwd* | Jew who ever lived. He is also the most articulate and brilliant prophet. He resided on Mount *Mowryah* | Moriah just down the ridgeline from Yahowah's Home in Yaruwshalaim. As the Lion of Judah, as the embodiment of the Covenant, and as the one who gathered God's people into a single nation, he is the living manifestation of the Covenant.

The more we learn from the Towrah and Prophets, the more we will come to appreciate the Beloved's role in guiding God's people, enlightening them, protecting them, saving them, and calling them home. Within ten years of this writing in the summer of 2023, *Dowd* | David is returning with Yahowah to transform the Earth such that it reflects the conditions enjoyed in 'Eden six thousand years ago.

Therefore, the reference to Dowd being "immersed in the annual cycle of the feasts" is prophetic of the fact that he has fulfilled the first three Miqra'ey and will return with Yahowah to honor the final two on *Yowm Kipurym* | the Day of Reconciliations, such that we can camp out with Father and Son during *Sukah* | Shelters. By working together over the years, Yahowah and Dowd will have brought us to this place, not only by fulfilling the *Mow'ed Miqra'ey* | Invitations to be Called Out and Meet with God of Pesach, Matsah, and Bikuwrym, his sacrifice nearly two thousand years made the Shabuw'ah and Taruw'ah Harvests possible. And by fulfilling the Kipurym Homecoming he will be King of Sukah ten years from now. And in between these dates, we find Shabuw'ah, which we are cultivating by bringing this all to your attention.

By acknowledging Dowd's role in fulfilling the annual Miqra'ey, we find Yasha'yah contributing to our understanding of Dowd's prophecy to Daniel. Also relevant, Dowd is one of only four individuals whose names are mentioned in this revelation, placing him among 'Abraham, Ya'aqob, and Yahowah, which is good company.

"Therefore (*wa*), **I will incessantly and emphatically nag** (*tsuwq* – even when oppressed, I will seek to influence, speaking clearly so as to plead with and encourage (hifil perfect)) *'Ary'el* | **the Lion of God and** *'Aruw'el* | **Those Gathered by God** (*'Ary'el* / *'Aruw'el* – the Lion of God is a pseudonym for *Yahuwdym* | Jews, Those Gathered by God is a metaphor for *Yisra'el* | Those who Engage and Endure with God, and the Ark and Hearth of God addresses the warmth and light of Yahowah's *Beyth* | Family Home in Yaruwshalaim; a compound of either the Masoretic *'ary* – lion of *'el* – God (the lion is representative of the tribe of Yahuwdah) or the Dead Sea Scroll (1QIsa) *'aruw* – to behold and *'arown* – chest and ark of *'el* – God [note: *'ary*, *'aruw*, and *'arown* are based upon *'arah* – those gathered by *'el* – God (which is indicative of the Chosen People, especially as they were taken home out of the crucibles of human oppression in Egypt)]).**"

Yes, this actually says "nag." God is pleading with His people to return, to come home, to stop being religious, and to start embracing the Covenant relationship. He also wants them to acknowledge Dowd as His Son and their Savior, as

Messiah and returning King. His testimony is clear and compelling. The failure to connect is ours alone.

If you are not yet part of the Covenant, please understand that between now and 2033...

"**There shall be a limited time** (*wa hayah* – while it will not last forever, there will be a period (qal perfect)) **to approach and meet Yah** (*ta'nyah wa 'anyah* – an opportunity for something favorable to occur in the midst of emotional distress; both compounds of *'anah* – to opportunistically approach and encounter Yahowah).

Then, *'Ary'el* will exist for Me, and will approach Me, as if she were the Lion Gathered by God (*wa hayah la 'any ka 'Ary'el / 'Aruw'el* – and so it will come to pass that she will be Mine)." (*Yasha'yah* / Salvation is from Yah / Isaiah 29:2)

You have a reprieve, but not for long. Not only is it risky to press one's luck and hope that you are among the few who survive until the end, there is nothing to be gained by postponing your acceptance of Yahowah and His Covenant. Every aspect of life is better with God.

The following is a depiction of *Yowm Kipurym* | the Day of Reconciliations, when Yisra'el and Yahuwdym will be once again reunited with God. It is followed by *Sukah*, during which this will occur...

"**And** (*wa*) **I will camp out** (*chanah* – I will show favor and be merciful (qal perfect)) **as if I were your home, wrapped all around you** (*ka ha dowr 'al 'atah* – as a dwelling place for you and others living at the same time).

I will be your rock (*wa tsuwr 'al 'atah* – I will be your enclosure such that you are secure (qal perfect)), **a stone pillar and watchtower** (*mutstsab* – a memorial of the Covenant; from *natsab* – to take a stand and be upright). **And I will establish** (*quwm* – I will stand up and confirm, raising up (hifil perfect)) **defensive fortifications for you**

(*'al 'atah matsuwrah* – a means to protect you from attack)." (*Yasha'yah* / Deliverance is from Yah / Isaiah 29:3)

From the time 'Adam and Chawah were expelled from the Garden of Great Joy for having chosen to act defiantly upon an errant rendition of the Word of God, Yahowah has been looking forward to our return. And in this case, Yahowah is offering to protect His family during the Time of Ya'aqob's Troubles – particularly within the borders of Yisra'el. Jews outside of the Covenant and living elsewhere will still be in jeopardy.

"However (*wa*), **outside of the Land** (*min 'erets* – away from the country) **you will be humbled** (*wa shaphel* – then you will be defeated and humiliated). **There** (*wa*), **you shall speak** (*dabar* – your oral and written expressions (piel imperfect)) **from the gutter and out of the rubble** (*min 'aphar* – from the dirt and debris).

Your teachings and commandments, your prayers and promises (*'imrah 'atah* – your words and platitudes, your speeches and statements) **will cause your demise** (*shachach* – your downfall and collapse, reduced in status, becoming downcast in grief, having been brought down (nifal imperfect)).

The sound of your voice (*qowl 'atah*) **shall come to exist as if it were** (*hayah ka* – will be comparable to (qal perfect)) **a ghost** (*'owb* – the communications of the dead, a necromancer) **from the Land** (*min 'erets*).

Then, from the rubble (*wa min 'aphar* – so out of the sewer, from the dirt and debris), **your commandments and prayers, your instructions and promises** (*'imrah 'atah* – your words and sayings, your speeches and utterances), **will resonate in guttural undertones and doleful whispers** (*tsaphaph* – will sound like mournful mutterings, the peeps and chirps of dying birds)." (*Yasha'yah* / Freedom is from Yah / Isaiah 29:4)

This occurred time and time again during the Diaspora. It was foretold and should not have come as a surprise. Nonetheless, it is haunting.

Never in the annals of human history have a people been so mistreated. Jews have had their homeland ransacked by invaders and then infected by the political and religious – defeated and then humiliated. Carted off as slaves to the Middle East and Europe by the Assyrians, Babylonians, and Romans, for centuries they endured sewers, rubble, and other debris in their ghettoes. While Roman Catholics and Muslims will be held accountable for this ordeal, God's people were complicit because the "commandments, prayers, instructions, and promises" made by Jews were as doleful to God as were their imposed surroundings.

If you are a Gentile, please move on to the next verse. This was not written to you or of you. More importantly, gowym are responsible for the deadliest and most damning genocidal conspiracies in human history, most of which blame Jews – not for the horrors they would impose on God's people, but for how they have imagined that Jews have influenced the world to the detriment of Gentiles.

They have always been wrong. But that is not what this is about. Yahowah is telling *Yahuwdym* | Jews that their religious prayers and political platitudes are the reason that they have fallen in stature. It is the reason Yisra'el endures a common fate. Those Gathered by God have endured the worst man can impose because they continue to proclaim the destructive decrees of the dead, murmuring the doleful teachings, edicts, and promises of the rabbis.

I beg your indulgence for one example: Rabbi Akiba. He is the Father of Rabbinic Judaism, which has become the lone surviving form of the religion. And yet, no one throughout the long history of God's People has done more to bring the world crashing down upon Jews. He did so with his teachings and edicts, his prayers and platitudes. Akiba foisted a false Messiah upon Yahuwdym and in so doing caused Rome to suppress the uprising with her legions. As a result, Yahuwdah was ransacked, Jews were starved and crucified, the land was renamed, and all who survived were hauled off as slaves, initiating the Diaspora which concluded in the Holocaust. Trusting Rabbi Akiba with your soul is less rational than believing the mercurial wannabe Apostle Paul or even maniacal Muhammad, the self-proclaimed Messenger of Allah.

If you are Jewish, you know how hard it is to break away from the traditions of your people, especially to disavow Judaism. The mentality is that Jews must stick together if they are to survive. And yet, according to Yahowah, it is the political, cultural, and especially religious glue holding the people together, that is corrosive and toxic, eating away and destroying the Chosen People.

I am a gowy, chosen and enlightened by Yah, whose mission is to awaken the Chosen People such that they disavow the lies of man and return to God in accord with His teachings and promises. And yet, as I ponder what we have just read, my head aches and my heart throbs for Yahowah and Yahuwdym. Please do not remain blind and deaf to His warning. It is time for reconciliation.

Toward this new beginning, you may have noticed that I have been translating Yasha'yah progressively after each citation from the prophet. And that is because Yasha'yah is comprised of *yasha'* and *Yah*, meaning: deliverance and freedom, and thus salvation, are from Yah. If you want to be delivered from the cruel bonds of religion and freed from the political snares of man, then saved, you know to whom you should turn and trust.

As we approach this next statement, we are confronted with a number of interesting options. The Masoretic Text speaks of "*zar 'atah* – your illegitimate foreign invaders, those among you who are unauthorized, loathsome, and nauseating in their alien presence." The *Septuagint* reads "impious and ungodly." The Great Isaiah Scroll (1QIsa) reveals "*zed 'atah* – of your arrogant and presumptuous rebels who are boiling over with religious fervor and seething with anger."

The difference between the two Hebrew texts is Zayn Rosh | ࠆࠇ versus Zayn Dalet | ࠄࠇ – *zar* or *zed*. Therefore, are these foes "foreigners" or are they "insolent and rebellious individuals who are audacious, disrespectful, and impudent, brazen and bold in their audacity?" According to the *Dead Sea Scrolls Bible*, the audacious and disrespectful are "enemies" and thus adversarial.

In this context, and aware of what led us to this place, I suspect that the Great Isaiah Scroll (copied 200 BCE outside *Yaruwshalaim* | Jerusalem) is correct and would trust it over the Masoretic Text (with the oldest credible manuscript copied in Europe around 1100 CE by rabbis). Yahowah likely said…

"Then (*wa*)**, the accumulation of possessions and wealth of the multitudes emboldened by the perception of power and the confusing clamor** (*hamown* – the commotion caused by the disorderly uproar of the agitating protesters) **of your arrogant and presumptuous rebels who are boiling over with religious fervor and seething with resentment** (*zed 'atah* – your insolent and rebellious, your audacious, disrespectful, and impudent, your brazen and emboldened in their audacity; from *zuwd* – to boil, those who are proud of their rebellious nature and boil with religious fervor, who seethe with resentment and act proudly, rebelliously, and arrogantly [from 1QIsa]) **shall come to be like** (*hayah ka* – will be as (qal perfect)) **the soot from a furnace** (*'abaq daq* – thin clouds of unhealthy and emaciated ash) **even like chaff** (*wa ka mots* – akin to that which is useless and easily blown away)**, with the confusing clamor of the cruel agitators, their**

possessions, wealth, and claims of authority (*hamown 'aryts* – the accumulation of power of the oppressive and dreadful people) **angrily and arrogantly passing through en route to being banished** (*'abar* – traveling by while intoxicated and fuming mad as they are expelled, these immoral failures who are unjustified in their arrogance).

This shall come to pass (*wa hayah* – it will exist (qal perfect)) **suddenly and unexpectedly, in an instant** (*peta'* – surprisingly in an extremely short period of time)." (*Yasha'yah* / Deliverance is from Yah / Isaiah 29:5)

Recognizing that the *zar* | foreign invaders and the *zed* | the rebelliously arrogant and presumptuous rebels have a lot in common, in that they are both taunting Yahowah and warring against His people, had it not been for what was stated previously, the difference between *zar* and *zed* might have been somewhat inconsequential. Should the 1,300-year-older witness found in the Great Isaiah Scroll be correct with regard to the *zed* | the arrogant and presumptuous, then Yisra'el's greatest foes can be counted among them.

Nevertheless, we should know that as a masculine noun *zed* and *zadown* (*Strong's* H2086-7) were written thirteen and eleven times, respectively, with an additional ten occurrences of the verbal root, *zuwd* (*Strong's* H2102). *Zuwd*, the actionable basis of *zed*, means: "to boil," and addresses those who are "proud of their rebellious nature, who seethe with religious fervor, who are fervent in their resentment, and who rebelliously and arrogantly act as if they are important to God." The term fits many political leaders and most religious rabbis, even some academic scholars.

As a noun, *zed* is used twice in *Mal'aky* / My Message / Malachi to address those who are "*zed* – presumptuous, with an inflated view of themselves," whose actions tempt Yahowah by denigrating and violating His Towrah. The audience, however, throughout the prophecy is comprised of *Yahuwdym* and *Yisra'el* | Jews and Israelis – notably rabbis – as they are exposed and condemned by Yahowah's witnesses in advance of His return.

The most infamous Torah-debasing Jew in human history was Sha'uwl, a Benjamite known as the "Apostle Paul" to Christians. And while there are far more Gentiles than Jews beguiling believers with his false testimony, in this context, *zed* | conceit is more likely targeting Talmud-touting rabbis (from *rab*, meaning exalted) who have led the Chosen People away from Yahowah. The good news, should you be genetically Jewish, is that *Mal'aky* / Malachi was written for you. Yahowah remains devoted to His people and is calling you home: to His and your *Towrah* | Source of Guidance and Teaching, to His and your *Beryth* | Covenant Family, by way of His and your *Miqra'ey* | Invitations to be Called Out and Meet.

Fortunately, those who are fervently religious will be extinguished. Their only trace is the soot from the furnace in which they will be incinerated. It is an ode to the Holocaust – something Jews would never have endured had it not been for the edicts and platitudes of Rabbinic Judaism pushing the people away from Yahowah and into the clutches of the Gentiles who abused them.

This does not exonerate the Greeks or Romans, the Roman Catholics or Muslims, the Fascists or Socialists, for the abhorrent crimes they have perpetrated against God's People. It only means that had rabbis not intervened between Yahowah and Yahuwdym, and blocked access to God, it would have turned out differently.

I would like to share another example or two. Had rabbis accepted the obvious and proclaimed that Dowd served as the *Pesach 'Ayil* | Passover Lamb in 33 CE, and had they celebrated *Dowd* | David as the Son of God, their Shepherd, Messiah, Redeemer, and King, there would have been no Jesus Christ and no Christianity. Had rabbis in Yathrib circa 622 CE not sold the Talmud tales to a floundering barbarian, Islam would have been stillborn. Two of the most menacing religions to Jews would not have existed if it were not for Jews.

As is the case in the parallel prophecy – *Mal'aky* / Malachi 4 and 5 – through *Yasha'yah* / Isaiah, God affirms that He is fair. Those who have misconstrued and maligned His *Towrah* | Teachings will be found responsible for committing this heinous crime which precipitated the people's fall.

"You will be held accountable by (*paqad min 'im* – there will be a time of reckoning for you with and on account of (nifal imperfect – a period of being held accountable which you have earned and will receive your just due and it will have ongoing implications over time because of)) **Yahowah** (𐤉𐤄𐤅𐤄 – the pronunciation of *YaHoWaH* as guided by His *towrah* – teaching regarding His *hayah* – existence) **of the vast array of spiritual implements** (*tsaba'* – of the command and control company of heavenly envoys) **through thunderous proclamations** (*ba ra'am* – loud spoken declarations, lightning and thunder), **with earthquakes and discordant sounds** (*wa ba ra'ash* – with the rumbling movement of the earth), **with a great voice** (*wa gadowl qowl* – a surprising degree of clamor and commotion following an important verbal declaration), **and with a strong and raging wind** (*wa ba suwphah wa sa'arah* – with hurricane-force gusts and tornadoes; from *suwph* – devastating and life-ending), **in addition to the flames of a devouring fire** (*wa lahab 'esh 'akal* – flashes of fiery light which consume and destroy)." (*Yasha'yah* / Salvation is from Yah / Isaiah 29:6)

Accountability is good. It is fair. It is just. For a crime of this magnitude, there must be a consequence, a judicial sentence and penalty. In these words, we have witnessed all of these, even before they occur. It is the purpose of prophecy. We are not only enlightened, forewarned, and prepared, we have been appropriately instructed. We know what Yahowah detests and how He will respond. If you do not want to be among those excoriated, incinerated, and then buried, you know what to avoid.

Just prior to His return, following the best efforts of His witnesses, Yahowah will be taking out the trash – removing all of the world's religious, political, patriotic, conspiratorial, and militaristic rubbish – starting right at home with Judaism. His words will destroy as surely as they once created. The Earth that He formed billions of years ago will violently reject the edifices and institutions mankind has venerated. They, and everything associated with them, including the individuals who promoted them, will be vehemently condemned, blown away, and incinerated, and then entombed, ashes to ashes, dust to dust. Without doing so, without removing these toxins, the ensuing 'Eden would be hopelessly polluted.

For most of those who remain estranged from God, especially those who are averse to His name, Torah, Covenant, people, and land, this will be horrifying. And while rabbis will be cowering beneath their Talmudic edifice, those most astonished will be Christians, Muslims, and Socialist Secular Humanists – all of whom expected that their animosity toward Jews would lead to an entirely different result…

"And it shall be akin to (*wa hayah ka*) **a nightmare** (*chalowm* – a dream)**, with the darkness being exposed** (*chazown laylah* – a vision of the night)**, this confusing clamor and commotion caused by the agitating protests of those whose wealth has made them powerful and oppressive** (*hamown kol* – the accumulation of possessions of the oppressive multitudes of confounded activists) **from all the Gentiles and their nations** (*kol ha gowym* – of all the people acting as animals, the walking dead as if zombies, those who are not Jewish and who believe religions based upon pagan theology) **that have come to fight** (*ha tsaba'* – that are conscripted into armies and mustered into militias to battle, fighting a war (qal participle active – actually and actively confront and demonstrably and vigorously combat)) **over and against** (*'al* – upon) *'Ary'el* | **the Lion of God and** *'Aruw'el* | **those Gathered by God** (*'Ary'el* / *'Aruw'el* – a pseudonym for *Yahuwdym* | Jews and a metaphor for *Yisra'el* | Those who Engage and Endure with God).

This includes all who battle against her (*wa kol tsaba' hy'* – and all those who fight to harm, dispossess, or oppose her) **construction of walls and barricades** (*matsodah* – defensive fortifications [from 1QIsa as the MT has 'mountain stronghold']) **and who deliberately distress and harass her, seeking to constrain and narrow her** (*wa ha matsyqym la hy'* – and who insist on trying to control her, inflicting hardships on her, troubling her leadership and people; from *tsuwq* – to oppress and constrain)." (*Yasha'yah* / Deliverance is from Yah / Isaiah 29:7)

This is breathtaking in its implications. God just said that after eradicating Judaism, He will annihilate Christians, Muslims, and Socialists, the dominant strains of discontent plaguing Gentiles. This is to say that He will clean His own house first. It is gut-wrenchingly sad, not only for Jews but for the walking dead.

As I categorically stated, Yahowah will absolutely and unequivocally, responsibly and justifiably, hold *gowym* and their nations accountable for the appalling atrocities they have instigated against His people. The only Gentiles who will survive the gauntlet will be Covenant.

The darkness of the Babylonian-inspired religions will be exposed to the light, eliminating them. Neither their loud clamoring nor their abundant wealth, neither their protests nor power, will insulate them from judgment. All who have come to fight against *Yisra'el* and *Yahuwdym* | Israel and Jews will be extinguished.

That last line would include the vast preponderance of people on Earth. Foolishly, politically, academically, or religiously, they have been led to believe that there is such a thing as a Palestinian people whose rightful homeland is a place called Palestine. Having bought into this deception, they not only claim that Jews have wrongfully expelled these supposedly indigenous people, but that Jews are now depriving the 'Fakestinians' of their homeland through an illegal occupation. These lies are then extrapolated into an advocacy of a "Two-State Solution" which confines Israel, depriving the Chosen People of the Promised Land, but which also necessitates the demolition of the walls Israelis have erected to keep the terrorists at bay.

Neville Chamberlain's attempt to appease the Nazis and avoid war by capitulating to a bogus claim and giving the socialists, who would call themselves fascists, much of Czechoslovakia was a dream with an unsatisfactory conclusion – a.k.a., a nightmare. The world awoke to war. History is about to repeat itself.

Although this time, even though right has might, Yahowah's response will follow the rabbinical abuse and Gentile attacks. Darkness will precede the Light…

"And it will be like when (*wa hayah ka 'asher*) **someone who is hungry** (*ha ra'eb*) **dreams of growing physically stronger** (*chalam* – imagines becoming healthy again (qal imperfect)), **and then he envisions himself eating** (*wa hineh 'akal* – he pictures himself being nourished (qal participle active)) **but is aroused from his sleep** (*wa qyts* – is awakened from his stupor and becomes alert (hifil perfect)) **and his soul** (*wa nepesh huw'* – his inner nature, character, and consciousness) **is not satisfied**

by the fantasy (*ryq* – is without benefit, empty and longing).

It can be compared to when (*wa ka 'asher*) a thirsty individual (*ha tsame'*) dreams of recovering (*chalam* – has thoughts and imagines becoming healthy again (qal imperfect)), and then he envisions himself drinking (*wa hineh shatah* – he pictures himself having his thirst quenched (qal participle active)), but awakened (*wa qyts* – is roused from his stupor and becomes alert (hifil perfect)), notices (*wa hineh huw'* – becomes aware) he is weakened and needs to recuperate ('*ayeph* – is weary and weak, requiring food and water to recover) and his soul (*wa nepesh huw'* – his inner nature, character, and consciousness) is unsettled and suddenly anxious, longing (*shaqaq* – is crazed for a quick solution).

So shall it be (*ken hayah*) the accumulation of power and wealth of the multitudes emboldened by the confusing clamor (*hamown kol* – the agitation and turmoil caused by those seeking to impose their influence, these very large crowds of loud and disarrayed activists), of all the Gentiles and their nations (*kol ha gowym* – of all the people acting as animals, the walking dead as if zombies, those who are not Jewish and who believe religions based upon pagan theology) that have come to wage war (*ha tsaba'* – that are conscripted into militaries and mustered into militias to battle, fighting (qal participle active – actually and actively confront and demonstrably and vigorously combat)) over ('*al* – against) Mount (*har*) Tsyown (*Tsyown* – the Signs Posted Along the Way, commonly transliterated Zion (the ridgeline of Mount *Mowryah* | Moriah between the City of *Dowd* | David and the Temple Mount))." (*Yasha'yah* / Freedom is from Yah / Isaiah 29:8)

They call this cognitive dissonance. No matter the prophetic warnings or obvious indications otherwise, people are preconditioned to believe that tomorrow will be like today because there have been so many similar yesterdays. But regional and world events can and do change one day to the next – often catastrophically. Never, in the history of human events, has this been as evident as today, in the Summer of 2023, following the world's collective and universally asinine response, not only to Covid-19 but also to the deaths of several nefarious black criminals with lockdowns and riots. Worldwide the consequence has been the deprivation of liberty and livelihoods, the obliteration of economies and currencies, along with widespread death and destruction. And the greatest casualty of all has been the truth, with all manner of lies proliferated by politicians and reverberating throughout the media. Far more people will lose their way, suffer, and die as a result of the misguided lockdowns and protests than would have succumbed to a virus no more deadly than the flu or to police brutality.

If you are a Jew, you may not yet see the graffiti painted on the walls, nor have heard what is being said about you. But Yahowah has, which is why He is calling you home.

When it comes to responding to Yahowah's Invitations to meet with Him, when your very life depends upon accepting the terms of His Covenant, when we realize the importance of His Towrah Teaching, and as we come to see the merits of distancing ourselves from the growing anti-Semitism erupting around the world, we ought not hesitate.

The world has grown to hate Zionists and Zionism, which is why Yahowah referenced Tsyown as the focus of "Gentillian" wrath. Moreover, Yahowah is a Tsyownist, having personally inscribed the signs posted along the way.

This is such great advice. It is one of the many reasons I wanted you to consider Yasha'yah 29 prior to our exploration of the creation account.

"Consider the consequence, and of your own volition avoid allowing any societal influence to persuade you to linger** (*mahah* – reflect upon the meaning but do not be swayed by any individual or institution to delay considering the consequences (hitpalpel, hitpael, imperative – of your own volition and initiative)) **because otherwise, you will have chosen to be astonished and bewildered** (*wa tamah* – you will be astounded and may be stunned by the situation (qal imperative)).

Of your own initiative, choose to close your eyes (*sha'a'* – shut your eyelids such that you are protected (imperative hitpalpel hitpael – you should of your own volition choose to protect yourself from what you would otherwise see, even though doing so will require that you act independently, undeterred by societal influences)) **and shield your vision** (*wa sha'a'* – making the conscious decision to close your eyes (qal imperative)).

Drink it in, and you will become intoxicated (*shakar* – opt to become incapacitated for the moment, inebriated (participle [from 1QIsa] imperative – it will be your choice to act demonstrably in this manner)), **but not from wine** (*wa min lo' yayn* – and yet not with something which has been fermented and causes drunkenness [1QIsa actually includes *min* – from whereas "from" is only implied in the MT]).

You may be shaken and stumble (*nua'* – you might stagger and sway, wandering away (qal perfect imperative – it will be at your option)), **but not with beer** (*wa lo' shekar* – not as a result of alcoholic beverages fermented with yeast)." (*Yasha'yah* / Salvation is from Yah / Isaiah 29:9)

Yahowah wanted His people to know that they would become irreparably and negatively affected by the jaundiced reporting and anti-Semitism brewing beneath issues like Black Lives Matter, Covid fear-porn, and the notion of land for peace. He does not want His people capitulating to the terrorist tactics of Muslims either, no matter how horrific. Jews are news junkies at a time when most of what is presented is inaccurate and misleading. And then there is the horrific proxy war America is waging in the birthplace of pogroms and Hasidic Judaism – murdering the people of the nation with the most nuclear weapons rather than seeking peace by not promoting NATO.

I am unaware of another occasion in which Yahowah says that the world is going to deteriorate to the point that our eyes, minds, and consciences may be scarred by what we witness – so much so that it may be irrecoverable. I suspect, based upon what we are seeing today, that He is addressing the problem of gang mentality, whereby individuals, who would otherwise refrain from horrific behavior, join in, their consciences conceding to the will of those around them. When it comes to the ways advocated by men, abstinence is the best policy.

There is also a tendency to believe that the majority is right and that it is reasonable to assume that most people are not misled. But this conclusion has never been valid in the entirety of the human experience. A lie circles the planet before the truth is even considered.

In this light, what Yahowah reveals next may seem surprising in that God's primary purpose is for us to know Him. But nonetheless, in His infinite wisdom, the Almighty had for a time closed His book on His people. I suspect that this occurred for a number of reasons. Had He not done so, the rabbis would have made a bad situation much worse. If their religion had been based upon the Towrah rather than the Talmud, had it incorporated Yahowah's name rather than hidden behind *ha Shem ha 'Adonai* | the name of the Lord, they may have made it impossible for anyone to pierce the lies and find the truth.

The text of Yasha'yah makes it abundantly clear that, for the longest time, no one was willing to work with Yahowah, making it impossible for Him to do as He had done in the past. Without an acceptable prophet, there would be no prophecy. Without a willing witness, there would be no additional testimony.

It is also likely with Jewish leadership remaining so overwhelmingly religious and rebellious, with Jews equating being Jewish with Judaism and vehemently attacking those who would dare differ, that the worst possible outcome would have been to give rabbis the capacity to make their religion appear somewhat credible or actually beneficial. It was better for everyone involved, especially those who were religious, to remain defiantly unaware of Yahowah's plans, than for Jews, after conceiving Judaism, Christianity, and Islam, and arguably, Socialist Secular Humanism, to create a belief system capable of intoxicating rational individuals and plaguing the world.

Think about it for a moment. Jews have managed to convolute Passover to the point that, at a Seder, they no longer serve an edible portion of lamb. They have convinced their brethren that the best way to observe *Kipurym* | Reconciliations is through deprivation. They have made the Shabat the most difficult day of the week with so many rules it has become a tedious trial. And that is not to mention all they have done to deny the essential nature of Yahowah's name. They have gone so far as to ascribe a star to David rather than a shepherd's staff. Their Menorah has nine candles rather than Yahowah's prescribed seven. They continue to search for a nameless Messiah even though God has clearly announced his name and has even let us know that he will be returning. They deny that Dowd served as the Pesach *'Ayil,* and as a result, have forfeited the benefits of his sacrifice. Worst of all, they have replaced Yahowah's Towrah with their Talmud.

Fortunately, however, at least for the rational, and as a result of Yahowah's intervention, their resulting religion is no more credible than Christianity or Islam. For secular Jews, the truth is accessible and not hidden under the tomes of religious chicanery and buffoonery that they naturally discard.

There is another reason that God may have incapacitated the descendants of Ya'aqob – especially their leadership. The *zed* | hubris of these people likely played a role. The malignant residue of rabbinical arrogance and their sense of superiority, their audacity to misrepresent Yahowah's testimony and malign His name must be exposed and repudiated for there to be reconciliation. For that to occur, someone from outside the fold would have to correct, discredit, and humble the rabbis. Considering the abuse they would endure, such a task is one few Jews would dare to undertake. Moreover, those with the courage and conviction to do so would likely be sectarian antagonists. And they would have disavowed interest in Yahowah and His Towrah for having wrongly associated both with their religious foes.

Therefore, after millennia of using Yisra'elites, and mostly Yahuwdym, exclusively as His prophets, His messengers to the world, God realized that the most appropriate way to get His people's attention would be to repudiate and bypass those who have errantly and presumptuously claimed to represent Him. God would therefore serve His words up to secular Jews on a gowym platter. Sure, it would be humiliating, but that has become the only effective prescription.

Speaking to Jews…

"Therefore (*ky* – emphasizing this point)**, Yahowah** (*YaHoWaH* – an accurate presentation of the name of *'elowah* – God as guided by His *towrah* – instructions regarding His *hayah* – existence) **will pour out for a time**

(*nasak* – has or will cause an overshadowing (qal perfect)) **upon you** (*'al 'atah*) **a spirit** (*ruwach*) **of diminished consciousness** (*tardemah* – a supernaturally induced state of incapacitation).

He will close your eyes (*wa 'atsam 'eth 'ayn 'atah* – He either has or will impair your vision, shutting your eyes (piel imperfect – those God is addressing suffer the effect of this visual impairment for a very long time such that they are precluded from properly observing)) **with regard to the prophets** (*'eth ha nabym* – concerning those who speak for God about the past, present, and future).

And concerning your leadership (*wa 'eth ro'sh 'atem* – regarding those at the top, your heads of state and chief priests, your government and religious leaders), **He has withdrawn** (*kasah* – He has removed and made unresponsive, kept hidden the knowledge and understanding (piel perfect – the leadership Yah is addressing will not be able to find or process this information for a period of time)) **the ability to receive or communicate messages from God as prophets** (*chozeh* – any association with the agreement or ability to be inspired or perceptive)." (*Yasha'yah* / Deliverance is from Yah / Isaiah 29:10)

The last of the prophets, *Mal'aky* / Malachi, revealed an equally riveting rendition of these same events, but that was 2,400 years ago. It has been a long time since God has been able to speak through His people. Fortunately, He provided us with a sufficient and satisfying written legacy of prophetic declarations, so we are not deprived of a lack of words.

Should you be curious, the reason that I did not include "John" in the line of prophets is because there is no mention of Yahowah's name in the revelations attributed to him, and there is no fulfilled prophecy to validate his testimony. Moreover, there are some 40 citations from Ezekiel that are overtly Satanic. Therefore, when we apply the Towrah's test Yahowah provided to ascertain the inspiration behind the statements attributed to them, his do not meet that standard. The same would hold true with Paul and every rabbi who contributed to the Talmud.

If you are Jewish and reading these pages and have been wondering why they differ so significantly from the religious rhetoric you have become accustomed to hearing, it should be apparent why this is so. Rabbis tout what they have written, and thus the Talmud is oblivious to the implications of the prophecies we are considering. You are hearing it here first because no one else was willing to present Yahowah's testimony accurately.

To retain the possibility of reaching you, God had to incapacitate the ability of the Jewish religious and political leadership to comprehend His revelations. But, since you are reading this, you were not among them, and for you, that time is now over.

And now for your benefit, this introduction to Yahowah, to His *Towrah, Beryth, wa Miqra'ey* | Guidance, Covenant, and Invitations has been provided by a *gowy*, Yahowah's *Choter* | Stem from the main Branch, His *Nakry* | Observant Foreigner, and Dowd's *Basar* | Herald. Yahuwdym were bypassed in this regard because they were unwilling to listen and would have continued to lead you astray.

This is the last thing Yahowah wanted. And yet, He knew that not countering such deception would have been catastrophic.

"Therefore (*wa***), the prophecy regarding the consequences of this entire revelation (***chasuwth ha kol*** – the prominence and appearance of this in its entirety, the totality of the distinguishing presence and manifestation of it) shall exist concerning you (***hayah la 'atem*** – it will be applicable to you (qal imperfect)) in the manner (***ka*** –

like) **of the words** (*dabar* – of the statements and message) **of a written document** (*ha sepher* – of an inscribed communication in a book or scroll) **which is sealed** (*ha chatam* – which is genuinely shut and actually locked up and closed (qal passive participle – a verbal adjective or a descriptive action which should be interpreted literally)).

When, to reveal the way (*'asher* – to provide the path to walk), **the book** (*ha sepher* – the scroll inscribed with written information) **is placed before someone** (*nathan 'eth huw 'el* – it is put in front of a person or given to an individual) **in an effort to help them become aware and understand** (*yada'* – to find out, process the information, and come to know what was revealed by Yada' (qal participle)), **they will say** (*la 'amar*), **'Please** (*na'* – we implore you with a sense of urgency), **read this** (*qara' zeh* – recite and proclaim what it says, welcoming it by inviting and summoning the name by which it is known)**!' But he will answer** (*wa 'amar*), **'I am unable to comprehend it** (*lo' yakol* – I cannot grasp its meaning and I fail to understand (hofal imperfect – I am not going to invest the effort to succeed)) **because** (*ky*) **it is sealed** (*chatam huw'* – it is closed, blocked, and shut with an impenetrable personal signature stamp sealing the document (qal passive participle)).'"** (*Yasha'yah* / Isaiah 29:11)

It is interesting to note that rabbis combat translations and insights such as the ones you are reading by claiming that they, alone, are qualified to provide them. They will go so far as to suggest that you, as a literate and rational individual, could not possibly understand the words 'G-d' wrote on your own. But having just read Yahowah's prophetic announcement, we know that God *begs* to differ. It is they who have been rendered blind, deaf, and truly incompetent. They lack humility, too.

The very people who claim to know the most about God know the least. Those who would claim to be spiritual guides are hopelessly lost. There is no saving a rabbi. God is not going to contaminate 'Eden with the likes of them.

"**And should they give** (*wa nathan* – should they offer (nifal passive perfect)) **the book** (*ha sepher* – the scroll inscribed in writing) **to someone who is ignorant and illiterate and who cannot understand what was written** (*'al 'asher lo' yada' sepher* – to someone who does not know the language or appreciate the inscribed message (qal perfect)), **asking** (*la 'amar* – to say), **'Please** (*na'* – we implore you with a sense of urgency), **read this** (*qara' zeh* – recite and proclaim what it says, welcoming it by inviting and summoning the name by which it is known)!' **He will reply** (*wa 'amar*), **'I am clueless and cannot read the written words** (*lo' yada'* – I am illiterate and thus ignorant, I neither know nor understand how to read or write, and I am clueless about Yada (qal perfect))." (*Yasha'yah* / Isaiah 29:12)

Methinks God is less than impressed with rabbinical lore. I do not suspect that you will find a Talmud on His list of recommended reading. In fact, I am sure of it.

There is a reason God chose to repeat this sobering prophecy. There is a reason it was written at a level even a child would understand. And there is a reason that the Great Isaiah Scroll is protected by a moat surrounding an inverted windowless mushroom comprising the Shrine of the Book and why it is backlit. It has become a monument to ignorance.

"**Then** (*wa*), **Yahowah** (*YaHoWaH* – an accurate presentation of the name of *'elowah* – God as guided by His *towrah* – instructions regarding His *hayah* – existence [from 1QIsa because the Masoretic reads 'Adonai]) **said** (*'amar* – stated and declared (qal imperfect)), **'Indeed** (*ky* – emphasizing this point), **forasmuch as** (*ya'an* – since with intent, and on account of this reason, because) **these people** (*ha 'am ha zeh* – the nation and clans) **approach**

Me (*nagash 'any* – present themselves before Me and confront Me) **with their mouths, and with their lip service** (*ba peh huw' wa ba sapah huw'* – language that is ironic, statements which depict a false sense of light in deep shadows and utter gloom, words which vainly seek approval), **putting on airs** (*kabad* – pretending to be somebody special, acting in a pretentious way), **they avoid exercising good judgment and distance themselves** (*wa rachaq leb huw'* – they have wandered away spiritually, emotionally, and intellectually, allowing their feelings, thoughts, and ambitions to become distant) **from Me** (*min 'any*).

As a result, the fear (*wa yira'th* – therefore, a sense of dread and distress (qal infinitive active) [1QIsa does not include '*hem* – their' as is the case with the MT]) **of Me** (*'eth 'any* – regarding Me) **exists** (*hayah* – is and occurs (qal imperfect)) **as** (*ka* – is akin or similar to [from 1QIsa]) **a condition** (*mitswah* – an authoritative directive or prescription) **of men** (*'iyshym* – of individuals and mankind) **which is taught** (*lamad* – is part of their instruction and training, even indoctrination (pual passive participle – these individuals suffer the effect passively and yet demonstrably as a verbal adjective)).'" (*Yasha'yah* / Freedom and Salvation are from Yah / Isaiah 29:13)

We would have to look hard and long to find a more relevant statement. Lords want to be feared, Fathers do not. Approaching God on this basis, respecting Him rather than fearing Him, is a necessary step in the right direction.

Fearing God is purely religious in origin – part of the manipulation. It is born of ignorance.

There is an abundance of good news here for God's people. He has not forgotten them or abandoned them. In spite of their propensity to reject Him, He is committed to serving them.

"**Therefore** (*la ken* – as a result), **behold** (*hineh* – please pay attention), **as for Me** (*la 'any* – to approach Me and concerning Me [from 1QIsa]), **I will once again at yet another time** (*'any yasaph* – I will increasingly, additionally, and repeatedly) **approach to do wonderful things** (*la pala'* – do astounding things, awesome and amazing, inspiring things, fulfilling something special (hifil infinitive)) **with the people who are closely related** (*'eth ha 'am ha zeh* – with those who are family and associated through the agreement), **with surprising fulfillments and inspiring signs, along with that which is marvelous and miraculous** (*pala' wa pala'* – wonderful and astounding things, difficult and special things).

And then (*wa*), **the wisdom and technical acumen** (*chakmah* – the capacity to understand and the skill to live in accord with the guidance which has been provided) **of their scholars, theologians, and sages** (*chakam huw'* – of their shrewd and technically trained as well as those who claim to be learned and wise), **as well as** (*wa*) **the discernment and understanding** (*bynah* – the insights derived from making connections between things leading to comprehending how to properly respond) **of their most educated teachers** (*byn huw'* – of those instructing them who are perceived to be knowledgeable and educated), **shall vanish, ceasing to exist** (*sathar* – will be tossed aside and away, becoming undiscoverable and unknowable, hidden and concealed from them)." (*Yasha'yah* / Freedom and Salvation are from Yah / Isaiah 29:14)

While there would be an intermission, there is no indication that the people, for whom these inspiring deeds would be fulfilled, have changed. *'Am* | people is most commonly used in reference to Yisra'el and is often translated as "family." The Chosen People were temporarily sidelined, not replaced.

It would be 700 years from the time this prophecy was revealed until Father and Son worked together to fulfill the first three Miqra'ey: Pesach, Matsah, and Bikuwrym. By doing so in Yaruwshalaim, Yahuwdah, our Heavenly Father honored His promise to provide the Covenant's benefits. Then it would be another twenty centuries, many of them exceedingly painful for His *'am* | family, before God's appointed would return on Kipurym to celebrate Sukah.

Along the way, one of the promises He will fulfill is to provide His *Nes* | Banner written by the *Nakry* | Observant Foreigner which will be lifted up to call His people home. Considering the dearth of Gentiles willing to confront the world's most popular religions through the insights derived by translating the Towrah, Prophets, and Psalms, the very thought of it seems miraculous.

But one thing is for sure. It would be foolish to follow the rabbis and religious scholars to their demise. That is God's advice, anyway. And arguing with Him is a poor life choice.

By the time we reach *Yowm Kipurym* | the Day of Reconciliations in year 6000 Yah, the wisdom and technical acumen of the scholars, theologians, and sages will be nothing more than a blight on the past. The alleged wisdom of the most celebrated and educated teachers will vanish, ceasing to exist.

However, since Yahowah will tell us that understanding His Towrah would be easy for those who are open-minded, we can reasonably conclude that this advice is for those who are anything but receptive…

"So this is a warning (*howy* – woe and alas) **to those who lack understanding and have become profoundly difficult** (*'amaq* – to those who are different deep down than they are on the surface, who are intensely hypocritical and who have dug a deep hole for themselves) **with regard to** (*min*) **Yahowah** (𐤉𐤄𐤅𐤄 – a transliteration of *YaHoWaH* as instructed in His *towrah* – teaching regarding His *hayah* – existence).

Your counsel and schemes (*'etsah 'atah* – your advice, your plans and purpose, and of you telling others what they should or should not do) **will no longer be known** (*sathar* – will be absent, concealed and hidden, vanish and perish in shame).

Those whose undertakings (*ma'aseh hem* – those whose pursuits and deeds, whose labor and works, whose business and endeavors; from *'asah* – that which they have engaged in and acted upon) **they have tried** (*wa hayah*) **to conceal in the dark** (*ba machshak* – are unenlightened and secretive and thus dimwitted, obscure, and confusing) **will say** (*wa 'amar* – will inquire and protest)**, 'Who will see us, and why will we be exposed** (*my ra'ah 'anachnuw* – how will our views be revealed and perceived)**? Who** (*wa my*) **actually knows and genuinely understands the nature of our actions** (*yada' 'anachnuw* – has discovered what we are all about and is aware of our thinking (qal participle – a literal interpretation of a verbal adjective))**?'"** (*Yasha'yah* / Freedom and Salvation are from Yah / Isaiah 29:15)

As a result of Yahowah's guidance, I have seen what they have done, and I am committed to exposing them. The first religion I impugned was Islam. I invite you to read *Prophet of Doom – Islam's Terrorist Dogma in Muhammad's Own Words* (now replicated in *God Damn Religion*) for that stinging indictment. I would also like you to read it so that you understand my methodology and realize that I am consistent – going where the evidence leads.

I was also able to prove beyond any doubt that the religion of Christianity – every aspect of it – was false in *Twistianity*. From its assumptions to its terminology, from its accusations to its doctrines, from its incorporation of pagan lore to its internal contradictions, it is all invalidated by comparing its claims to Yahowah's testimony.

Rabbinic Judaism has become my current target, one that was highlighted throughout *Babel* and is being fleshed out during the final edits of the many volumes of *Yada Yahowah*. God hates religion, and so do I. Nothing has been as beguiling, as corrupting, as destructive, or as deadly.

Just as *Moseh* | Moses was chosen because he understood and despised the religion and politics, the economics and militarism, and even the conspiracies he was exposed to in Egypt, I am here largely because of my willingness to excoriate these same menacing malignancies.

In this regard, the Covenant's lone prerequisite is to walk away from the *babel* | confusion of man. Doing so will not occur to the degree Yahowah desires until someone speaks against them all in His name. I do not think this has been done previously on God's behalf.

It has been my experience that the most famous religious clerics know that they are deceiving the faithful. I have addressed this issue with them and can assure you that they are knowingly perpetrating fraud. But, as God is indicating here, it is hell to get them to publicly admit that they are wrong, especially since it means that those they are fleecing will stop donating. It is not good for business.

Religious deceptions have become exceedingly obvious and odious to me. And I am not alone…

"Your perversions have inverted reality, having turned things upside down by claiming the opposite of what is actually true (*hephek 'atah* – your beliefs are the antithesis of that which is credible, your allegations are averse to reason and contrary to evidence such that they are perversions, twisting the facts and convoluting rational thought).

They are comparable to (*'im ka* – they are like) **the potter's clay** (*chomer ha yowtser* – the malleable substance out of which the craftsman and creator fabricates using mud, mortar, and mire which are otherwise worthless, becoming hardened and fragile when baked in the sun) **continually reckoning and regarding itself** (*chashab* – considering and determining itself, valuing itself (nifal imperfect – is consistently influenced by its own determinations of itself)) **such that it should claim** (*ky 'amar*) **of the one who designed and fabricated it** (*ma'aseh la 'asah huw'* – of the one who worked on it, who engaged and acted to make it)**, 'He did not make me** (*lo' 'asah 'any* – He did not engage nor act regarding me. He did not bring me into existence, He did not conceive nor create me (qal perfect))**.'**

Or (*wa*) **should the thing conceived and created** (*yetser* – that which was fashioned and formed as the result of rational thinking, imagination, and reasonable motives, expressing the wants and desires of another) **say of the one who formed him** (*'amar la yowtser huw'* – who, like a potter and craftsman, shaped and fabricated him out of malleable clay)**, 'He is the one without knowledge or understanding** (*huw' lo' byn* – he is ignorant and irrational, uninformed and imperceptive, lacking the ability to comprehend by making reasoned connections (hifil perfect))**?'"** (*Yasha'yah* / Freedom and Salvation are from Yah / Isaiah 29:16)

When we came to realize that the universe had a beginning and was, therefore, created, when we recognized that all living organisms are programmed using the language of DNA, when we noticed that our cosmic assessments were 95% inaccurate, and once it became obvious that macroevolution from the simplest to the most complex being was unrealistic and rationally impossible, we should have accepted the fact that we are clay on a brilliant potter's wheel. It should have been the perfect opportunity to appreciate our Maker. And yet, those claiming to be the smartest among us, the scientists and philosophers, screamed otherwise.

Obviously, it is not God who lacks understanding, but instead men. Without the proper perspective, we have become lost in a cosmic ocean of extraneous details. We were told that this would occur, but we did not listen. Most never will.

When the choice is between reason and faith, reason prevails. When choosing between science and the church, it is an easy choice, which is why science prevailed. But when the debate is between science and God, academia does not fare well. Worse, scholars tend to become presumptuous and arrogant.

Fortunately, Yahowah is fond of the inquisitive and unpretentious, those who seek knowledge and strive for understanding, and those who will follow the evidence even when it leads to some very unpopular realizations. It is for such people that this was written…

"**Whether or not it will take a while** (*ha lo' 'owd* – perhaps now, if not then not much longer, but expectedly and simultaneously) **before, in a relatively short and subsequent period of time, a few individuals** (*ma'at miza'r* – a number so small they can be easily counted as a remnant who will be collected) **will return and they will be restored** (*shuwb* – are changed and brought back).

It will be determined that they are (*chashab* – credited as being and considered (nifal imperfect)) **white** (*labanown* – purified and radiant; from *laban* – to be white and purified, with the *own* suffix indicating that this is a celebration of all things white in the fullness of light) **when approaching a fruitful garden** (*la ha karmel* – a productive orchard and especially fertile and cultivated land) **filled with trees** (*la ha ya'ar* – which is heavily wooded as a healthy forest)." (*Yasha'yah* / Freedom and

Salvation are from Yah / Isaiah 29:17) If only this would dash the hopes of the "Black Hebrew Israelites" and their ludicrous claims and anti-Semitic rhetoric.

Regarding the timing, Yahowah is not being equivocal. He knows the moment when this will transpire. But He also recognizes that time is relative, and therefore, it is not the same for all who will read these words. For a precious few, this awakening has begun. More will join them along the way, but not so many that they cannot be readily counted. The Covenant Family will not be large. It has never been a popular choice.

At the conclusion of the Second Statement etched on the First Tablet, the one that warns us against being religious, Yahowah reveals that the recipients of His mercy will be thousands among billions. Those who will enter Heaven's door will, therefore, be one in a million overall. Although, through the prophet Amos, the odds appear better for Yisra'el, where one in ten of the remnant who survive the upcoming Time of Ya'aqob's Troubles will return to the Covenant.

There should be no doubt regarding the fulfillment of this prophecy. The souls who return and are restored to fellowship with Yah will be deemed sparkling white as they enter God's beautiful garden. This will occur in year 6000 Yah – celebrating the transition from *Kipurym* | Reconciliations to *Sukah* | Camping Out on October 7th, 2033.

So that you are aware, within this prophecy, *labanown* could have been transliterated as "Lebanon," and address the country infected with Muslims north of Israel. But it seemed more reasonable to translate *labanown* – "all things purifying, white, and radiant." In that God is addressing the individuals who return to Him and who are restored in the process, He is addressing His people, not foreigners, making this option superior to the other.

Beyond this insight, God is affirming something profoundly important. He will be reestablishing the conditions experienced in 'Eden. He is, therefore, not only restoring souls, but also the planet on which we live. It will return to its prior state and resemble the Garden.

What occurred in 'Eden is God's view of perfection. It is why *Kipurym* | Reconciliations occurs prior to *Sukah* | Camping Out. We are restored so that we can return.

Just as the timing is firmly established, Yahowah will be unyielding when it comes to the filter He will apply to determine who should be allowed inside. Restored souls will be transformed because they will have chosen to return to God. They listened to what Yahowah conveyed and acted accordingly. You, therefore, by reading these words, are doing as Yahowah prescribed.

There is no quarter for Replacement Theology in these words. Yahowah is restoring the sight of those He blinded long ago – His People – such that they will be able to comprehend His love for them. The audience remains *'Ary'el* | the Lion of God and *'Aruw'el* | those Gathered by God.

"So, in that day (*wa ba ha yowm ha huw'* – at this specific time of His)**, those deaf to what has been inscribed who have now been cut into the agreement** (*cheresh* – those who are now in accord with the relationship based upon what has been written; from *charash*) **shall hear, and they will listen** (*shama'* – they will pay attention, receiving this information (qal perfect)) **to the words** (*dabar* – to the statements, speeches, and message conveyed using language which has been declared) **of this book** (*sepher* – inscribed within a written document; from *saphar* – to recount and relate).

So, it will be out of (*wa min* – removed from) **the shadows, the dysfunctional nature and spiritual nonreceptivity** (*'opel* – the depression, terror, and gloom)

clx

of the darkness and ignorance (*choshek* – of a confusing place and time where there is no light) **that the eyes of the blind** (*'ayn 'iwer* – the sightless unobservant) **will choose to see now and forevermore** (*ra'ah* – will want to become observant, perceptive, and to be shown (qal imperfect jussive – literally see by choice aware of the ongoing consequences))**."** (*Yasha'yah* / Freedom and Salvation are from Yah / Isaiah 29:18)

Considering how universally ignorant and irrational people have become as a result of academic, political, religious, and cultural conditioning, I long for a day of true enlightenment when everyone will be observant and receptive. Yahowah's words, His Teaching and Guidance, will no longer be obscured.

It is interesting to ponder which "book" God was addressing. We know that it leads His once deaf and blind children into the light, from the dysfunctional nature of the spiritually unreceptive to understanding. In this regard, we have a number of options to consider. It would be reasonable to ascribe it to any prophetic account, and specifically to the prophecy we are reading from Yasha'yah. It was, after all, from prophecy that His people were blinded.

However, while relevant and revealing, even the entirety of Yasha'yah has never been sufficient. Not a single soul responded to the prophet's message during his lifetime – nor for thousands of years thereafter.

If it is the entirety of Yasha'yah that Yahowah is inferring, there is yet another challenge. Most Jews speak and read English, so translating it accurately to read it correctly would require as much time as we have left. And still, without the Towrah and Mizmowr, it would remain inadequate.

While the Towrah would be sufficient in and of itself to lead Yahowah's people home, existing translations are grossly inaccurate. And without the addition of the insights provided by the Prophets, what would motivate secular Jews to turn to it at this time?

It is the Psalms, the Songs Dowd wrote to Yahuwdym, which resonate most profoundly at this time. The insights and teachings of the Son of God, the Chosen One, Yisra'el's Shepherd, Messiah, and returning King convey Yahowah's longing for His people in unmistakable terms. Dowd is the centerpiece of creation, the Cornerstone of the Covenant, the Passover *'Ayil*, which is why this prophecy was presented in his name. To appreciate the relationship Yahowah cultivated with *Dowd* | David, His Beloved, is to understand the purpose of Yah's *Towrah* | Teaching, His *Beryth* | Covenant, His *Miqra'ey* | Invitations to Meet, *Yahuwdym* | Yah's Beloved, and the inspiration behind His *naby'* | prophets.

With this in mind, this is the first in a series of books appropriately entitled *Yada Yahowah* – To Know Yahowah, where the Towrah, Prophets, and Psalms are accurately translated. Exceeding fifteen thousand pages, it is not only comprehensive, but these volumes are also replete with insights seldom if ever considered. And throughout, this series relies upon the Prophets and Psalms to explain the Towrah.

If this is the first of the 35 volumes of the *Yada Yahowah* series that you have begun to read, you may not fully appreciate that God has equipped and provided an observant foreigner (a *nakry* in Solomon's parlance) who is a stem from the main Branch (a *choter* according to the terminology found in Yasha'yah 11) to compose a *Nes* | Banner comprised of the words of the Towrah, Prophets, and Psalms, which God will promote prior to His return to call His people home and restore His relationship with them. Since there does not currently appear to be another viable candidate, this comprehensive translation and commentary on Yahowah's testimony serve this purpose…

"So, in that day (*wa ba ha yowm ha huw'*), those deaf to what had been inscribed and who have now been cut into the agreement (*cheresh*) shall hear, and they will listen (*shama'*) to the words (*dabar*) of this book (*sepher*).

So, it will be out of (*wa min*) the shadows, the dysfunctional nature and spiritual nonreceptivity (*'opel*) of the darkness, confusion, and ignorance (*choshek*) that the eyes of the blind, those who had been the sightless unobservant (*'ayn 'iwer*), will choose to see, now and forevermore (*ra'ah*)." (*Yasha'yah* 29:18)

Inferring that *Yada Yahowah* may serve Yisra'el and Yahuwdym in this way may seem presumptuous based upon such a tenuous reference. And should you question this conclusion you may benefit from reading the *Why You, Why Me* presentation in the 1st volume of *An Introduction to God*.

As we consider the prophet's next line, be aware that reentering the *Gan 'Eden* | Garden of Joy will be a three-step process. First, we must come to know and understand Yahowah's path and conditions. Then we must, of our own freewill, accept His terms as valid. And finally, to enter, we must act upon what God has asked.

This process exists because eternity is a very long time and Yah does not want the pretenders to fake their way in and ruin the experience for the rest of us. Therefore, it will be...

"Those who answer and respond, the straightforward and unpretentious (*wa 'anaw* – those who reply and are sincere, without hubris; from *'anah* – to reply and answer) will be enriched exponentially (*yasaph* – shall be enhanced and enlightened, increased in every way) by (*ba* – with) Yahowah (*Yahowah* – a transliteration of 𐤉𐤄𐤅𐤄, our *'elowah* – God as directed in His *towrah* – teaching regarding His *hayah* – existence), becoming

jubilant (*simchah* – joyful and happy with a cheerful disposition).

Those who have willingly eschewed political power and religious influences, making themselves subject to criticism (*'ebyown* – those who live apart from the religious establishment and have limited societal status, those who are opposed and disparaged based upon their choices; from *'abah* – to be willing to accept) **among men** (*'adam* – descendants of the first man with a conscience), **who are in association with** (*ba*) **the Set-Apart One** (*qodesh* – who are separated unto the one who is the most unique) **of Yisra'el** (*Yisra'el* – Individuals who Engage and Endure with God), **shall rejoice over their favorable outcome** (*gyl* – will be happy with the advantageous circumstances (qal imperfect))." (*Yasha'yah* / Freedom and Salvation are from Yah / Isaiah 29:19)

The Set-Apart One of Yisra'el is Dowd. By referring to him in this way, Yahowah is not only affirming the conclusions we have shared, but He is also confirming that the audience has not changed.

The most direct way to establish a relationship with *Dowd* | David is to read what he wrote and then capitalize upon what he has done for our benefit. For this reason, *Observations* focuses on his *Mashal* | Proverbs and *Coming Home*, his *Mizmowr* | Psalms. If you stay the course, you will come to know and love this man and will be inspired by his prose.

Yahowah has issued His invitations. Our job is to accept them. They are His parties, and we participate on His terms.

The benefits of doing so are out of this world. By attending the first three Miqra'ey, we are adopted into Yah's Covenant Family, becoming perfected and immortal. We are enriched exponentially by Yahowah, enlightened and empowered by Him.

Just as the first celebration of Passover and UnYeasted Bread freed Yisra'el from bondage and death in Egypt such that God's Children could enjoy life and liberty in the Promised Land, to be part of the Covenant, we too must walk away from oppressive and deadly human schemes – especially religion and politics. The Set-Apart One of Yisra'el is here to help those who willingly forego these human entanglements.

The opposite is true, of course, for religious and political terrorists. Fortunately, the bloodstains they have left on our world will vanish. Their slogans will be heard no more. But it is not just those who ridicule Yahowah with taunts of *"Allahu Akbar* – Allah is Greater" who will be gone, it will also be those who sought to accommodate this virus.

"Then, indeed (*ky* – truthfully, making this contrast)**, the ruthless terrorists** (*'aryts* – the cruel, violent, and fierce, the physically imposing and aggressive, those who terrorize and elicit fear) **will fail, they will be stopped and then vanish** (*'aphes* – will cease and no longer exist (qal perfect))**. Those who ridicule and mock** (*lets* – the babblers who are condescending and derisive, the conceited who speak arrogantly) **will all be gone** (*kalah* – will be finished, they will be destroyed and wiped out, perishing and eliminated (qal perfect))**.

Then** (*wa*)**, all who do not hesitate when it comes to participating in that which is corrupt and damaging to the relationship** (*kol shaqad 'awen* – everyone who seeks to control others through perversions of the truth, all who are notorious for the hardships they have imposed, and all who are intent on promoting troubling ideas, who desire the misfortune of others) **shall be cut off and separated** (*karat* – will be cut down and estranged, uprooted and die)**."** (*Yasha'yah* / Freedom and Salvation are from Yah / Isaiah 29:20)

God is intolerant of evil and will not accommodate those who support hypocritical and conspiratorial myths, whether they be religious or political, cultural or conspiratorial. Today this would also include the fearmongering tactics promoted by the advocates of Black Lives Matter, the claims of the 'Palestinians,' and the constraints on liberty and livelihood imposed by those using a virus to force their will on others. Be careful whom you support lest you lose the support of Yah.

"Those who have caused a man to be excluded from the relationship by missing the way (*karath 'adam* – those who wrongly inspire the killing of men, separating humankind from life in the Covenant, who are destructive and encourage cutting off arms and legs, even decapitating men) **through their words** (*ba dabar* – with their statements, speeches, and declarations), **and for those who argue, trying to prove their case** (*wa la ha yakah* – those who establish laws and who seek to resolve disputes, offering vindication or punishment, administering justice (hifil participle)) **within the doorways of public meeting places** (*ba sha'ar* – inside the courtyards or marketplaces where people assemble within cities and towns, within temples, palaces, or civic buildings) **so as to mischaracterize or falsify and wrongly convict** (*quwsh* – to misconstrue, improperly condemn, wrongly exonerate, or ensnare, luring astray (qal imperfect paragogic nun – consistently choosing to actually misappropriate justice)), **they promote and disseminate that which misleads and thrusts aside** (*natah* – they publish and circulate, broadcast and spread that which causes many to wander away (hifil imperfect)), **devaluing and negating, even confusing and convoluting** (*tohuw* – making useless and worthless, invalidating), **that which is right** (*tsadyq* – that which is correct and vindicating, trustworthy and valid, just and fair, appropriate and in accord with the proper standard).**"** (*Yasha'yah* / Freedom and Salvation are from Yah / Isaiah 29:21)

This would include every religious cleric, many teachers, most politicians, journalists, judges, philosophers, and all those who promote conspiracies. It is one thing to be mistaken, and another altogether to cause others to miss the way.

What we say matters. The truth matters.

For those who may have thought that I was overreaching by suggesting that the religious and political are offensive to God, this statement should have resolved those concerns. Yahowah rightfully detests the falsifications which mislead and confuse because they preclude souls from engaging in a relationship with Him. These are not work-related problems. They are not disagreements in personal relationships. This has nothing to do with our disparate tastes in music, movies, clothing, or climate. The only declarations that rise to this level are religious, political, and conspiratorial.

The family of Ya'aqob and 'Abraham has one thing in common: the Covenant. Therefore, Yahowah is announcing the restoration of His Family.

"**For this reason, therefore** (*laken* – as a result)**, thus says** (*koh 'amar* – here is what is being said now by) **Yahowah** (*Yahowah* – the proper pronunciation of YaHoWaH, our *'elowah* – God as directed in His *ToWRaH* – teaching regarding His *HaYaH* – existence and our *ShaLoWM* – restoration) **concerning the House and Family** (*beyth* – the household and family line) **of Ya'aqob** (*Ya'aqob* – Yisra'el and the Covenant, to acknowledge the consequence and reward of grasping hold of the Covenant's blessings)**, who, to show the way to the benefits of the relationship** (*'asher* – to reveal the correct path to walk to get the most out of life)**, redeemed and liberated them** (*padah* – ransomed and freed) **through 'Abraham** (*'eth 'Abraham* – with the Merciful Father, the Father of Many, and the Enriching Father),

'**Ya'aqob** (*Ya'aqob* – Yisra'el and the Covenant Family, the one who acknowledges the consequence and reward of grasping hold of the familial blessings) **shall no longer be confounded nor shamed** (*lo' 'atah bowsh* – you will not be humiliated or bewildered, ashamed, distressed, or disapproved of anymore). **No longer** (*wa lo' 'atah*) **will his face appear** (*paneh huw'* – will his presence be) **pale from being perplexed and humiliated** (*chawar* – anemic and sick).'" (*Yasha'yah* / Freedom and Salvation are from Yah / Isaiah 29:22)

Yisra'el was liberated and redeemed because of the promises Yahowah made to 'Abraham during the formation of the Covenant. Unfortunately for the House of Ya'aqob, God's people violated its terms and were excluded from the family for a considerable period of time – one that is now over. Estranged from Yahowah, life has been rough for men and women in general, but far more so for Jews. Once reunited, blessings will ensue.

The way *beyth* | home for the descendants of Ya'aqob, who is the forefather of Yisra'el, is through the Covenant God established with 'Abraham. Its five terms and conditions, and its five benefits, are found in only one place: the Towrah. There is no other means to salvation.

This means that being "Jewish" is not enough for anything other than an engraved invitation. The only way anyone approaches Yahowah or enters His home is through the Covenant. It is in this way that *gowym* also become part of Yah's Family. The next volume of *Yada Yahowah*, an entire volume of *An Introduction to God*, and the second volume of *Observations* were all written to share what Yahowah asked of 'Abraham and explain what God offered him in return.

The children referenced in this next statement are Ya'aqob's. They are Yisra'el. And they have become Covenant once again. This promise was made and affirmed in *Bare'syth* / Genesis, *Howsha'* / Hosea, *Yirma'yah* / Jeremiah, and here in *Yasha'yah* / Isaiah, as well as in the parallel prophecy in *Mal'aky* / Malachi. You can be assured that it is a priority to God and that it will occur as stated.

"**Because when** (*ky ba* – indeed, in that) **he sees** (*ra'ah huw'* – he observes and witnesses) **his descendants** (*yeled huw'* – his offspring), **the accomplishments of My hands** (*ma'aseh yad 'any* – the work of My influence), **in his midst** (*ba qereb*), **they will treat My name as special and set apart** (*qadash shem 'any* – they will be devoted to the unique attributes of My personal and proper designation).

And they will also treat Ya'aqob as being set apart, acknowledging and appreciating his unique attributes (*wa qadash Ya'aqob* – they will be devoted to the special nature of Yisra'el and the Covenant Family). **They will be in awe** (*'arats* – they will be respectful) **of the God of Yisra'el** (*'elohym Yisra'el* – of the Almighty and the Individuals who Engage and Endure with God)." (*Yasha'yah* / Freedom and Salvation are from Yah / Isaiah 29:23)

The first thing the Covenant Family will acknowledge is Yahowah's name, affirming that it is uniquely and vitally important to them. As such, this should be a wake-up call for those who would claim that God does not care what we call Him.

Reflect on that thought for a moment. You have never heard Yahowah's name mentioned in association with Judaism, Christianity, Islam, Hinduism, Buddhism, or Socialist Secular Humanism. There is no political party which promotes it either. And therefore, we can exclude all of these when it comes to the restoration of *Yisra'el* | Israel in addition to serving as a means for anyone to approach the God of Israel. And that would be a problem for those who do not know and use Yahowah's name because there is no other God.

Before we move on, it is worth mentioning that Yahowah's name is not the only one being acknowledged as being set apart and thus special. Ya'aqob, who is synonymous with Yisra'el, will go from an object of scorn to being celebrated for what he uniquely represents.

Also, please note that Yahowah is taking credit for the assemblage of people Ya'aqob will witness as his descendants. It is Yahowah, not Ya'aqob, who has made this possible. Said another way, being a descendant of Ya'aqob, a Yisra'elite, remains insufficient. To appear before Yahowah we must avail ourselves of what God has done on our behalf.

The difference between the following extremes is bridged through knowing. Understanding is the means to restoration. Everything we are going to translate and discuss over the next thirty-five volumes will be to advance this process.

"**Then** (*wa*)**, they will come to know** (*yada'* – they will come to realize, recognize, and acknowledge as revealed by Yada' (qal perfect – literally at that moment in time will become aware)) **that they have erred spiritually** (*ta'ah ruwach* – that they have gone astray and were wrong about the Spirit (qal participle construct / absolute – had actually and demonstrably been mistaken but, while now connected to the Spirit, are no longer bound by those errors)) **and will make the proper connections to understand** (*binah* – will comprehend by being discerning regarding the insights being revealed and respond appropriately).

Even those who have grumbled and complained, having expressed their discontent (*ragan* – those who were at fault and said disparaging things under their breath (qal participle absolute – were actually disparaging but are no longer bound by their discontent)) **will continue to actually learn from this instruction** (*lamad leqah* – they will be consistently taught, demonstrating that they are genuinely capable of literally accepting the directions, benefit from the education, and respond to the guidance (qal imperfect active – with continuous teaching and active learning throughout time))." (*Yasha'yah* / Freedom and Salvation are from Yah / Isaiah 29:24)

It is Yahowah's intent for us to learn from His instruction. It is why Towrah means to teach. So long as we are receptive, so long as we are willing to accept His directions, God will guide us to the Promised Land.

It is by knowledge, not faith, that we approach Yahowah. And part of this process is acknowledging that we have erred spiritually.

This concluding statement contains two of my favorite words: *yada'* | to know and *binah* | to understand. One can lead to the other so long as we are discerning and discriminating and recognize what we should consider and then make the proper connections to comprehend. To *yada'* Yahowah requires *binah*. It is the key which opens Heaven's Door. It is the password into the Covenant. It is how we answer Yahowah's Invitations to Meet. It is the byproduct of the Towrah.

Books are repositories of instruction. They are the most effective teaching aids the world has ever known.

If we write it, they will read it…

"Now at this time (*'atah*)**, choose to approach** (*bow'* – come here and elect to be included in the return (qal imperative active – genuinely and actively by choice come back))**, writing this** (*kathab hy'* – inscribing this, communicating a written record (qal imperative active infinitive – actively, actually, demonstrably, by choice writing it)) **on an illuminated tablet** (*luwach* – on a panel, screen, or surface which radiates light; from *luwach* – to glisten brightly) **for them** (*'eth hem* – with them and alongside them).

Inscribe it (*wa chaqaq hy'* – engrave it and portray it; from *choq* – to inscribe the prescriptions and conditions (qal imperative active)) **in a book** (*'al sepher* – in written form within a written manuscript or document) **so that it may actually be chosen as a means to perpetuate one's existence** (*wa hayah* – such that it is literally and continually an option subject to the reader's freewill to continually exist (qal imperfect jussive active – expressing a genuine relationship actually established under the auspices of freewill on behalf of the reader with ongoing implications over time)) **during the last days** (*la acharown yowm* – for the end of time) **and serve as a witness regarding eternity** (*la 'ad 'ad 'owlam* – as testimony which shall always endure throughout time)." (*Yasha'yah* / Freedom and Salvation are from Yah / Isaiah 30:8)

Yahowah has been speaking to us in first person through Yasha'yah and so it is reasonable to assume that He is still doing so. Moreover, He previously asked His prophet to write all of this down for future generations, so telling him to do so once again would be redundant. And after telling Yasha'yah that his people will not be able to comprehend his prophecies, what's the point? Further, Yasha'yah is already there, in Yah's presence, so there would be no reason to ask him to "*bow'* – come."

Therefore, while the beneficiaries of this book are the descendants of Ya'aqob, and thus Jews, the individual writing it down for the last days as a witness could be anyone willing to devote the time to do so. That is, however, with a couple of caveats. First, this individual would be explicitly called by Yahowah based on this text. He would have to cover this particular prophecy in a salient way – as well as most of Yasha'yah.

Since Dowd's name was one of only four mentioned in this address, the referenced writer would have to be someone who cherished Dowd's Psalms and Proverbs, too. He would also have to understand why 'Abraham's and Ya'aqob's names were introduced and thus detail all that can be known about how we can participate in the Covenant.

Unlike 99.9999% of humankind, this witness would have celebrated Yahowah's name as opposed to changing or ignoring it. With the mention of the Feasts, he would explain the purpose of the seven Miqra'ey. And let's not forget the mandate to detail why Yisra'el was estranged and then why they will be reunited with Yahuwdah and Yahowah. Ahh, and he would have to be a Gentile, too, because by writing this " *'eth hem* – for them," he could not be a descendant of Ya'aqob.

That is a lot of salient material to cover for one writer, and yet, all of it is required based upon this directive if it is to achieve its purpose. Further, for his calling and his book to have been mentioned prophetically, he would likely have to meet the criterion presented earlier in Yasha'yah 11 regarding the *Choter*. And if not this same individual, who is the *Nakry* of whom Solomon spoke during the dedication of the Temple? Their identity and purpose coincide.

There are four other clues we ought not overlook. This author has likely used Yada as a pseudonym. He, unlike Yasha'yah, will "*kathab hy'* – write this" on "*luwach* – an illuminated screen or tablet." And this scribe's book, unlike Yasha'yah's, which chronicles Yisra'el's and Yahuwdah's religious rebellion circa 700 BCE, will serve as something God's People can choose to read to extend their existence during the last days. Yahowah's latter-day scribe will be an "*'ad 'ad 'owlam* – witness to eternity" and thus not a "*naby'* – prophet" as was the case with Yasha'yah. It is a lesser calling – one which is reliant on the inspiration of Yahowah's prophets.

Now that Yahowah is mentioning it, our writer would have to fall in love with the purpose of the Towrah, learning from it and teaching based upon it. He would be unique because God's Chosen People have chosen poorly in this regard.

Those unwilling to listen for so long, those who are rebellious and contentious, and those who prefer their Talmud over Yahowah's Towrah, will need a delicious slice of humble pie. And who better to serve it up than a Gentile…

"Because (*ky***) they are a rebellious and contentious people** (*'am mary huw'* – they are an embittered and revolting group, a disobedient and antagonistic nation), **mendacious and deceitful children** (*kachash beny* – stubborn and rebellious, untruthful sons)**, unwilling to listen** (*lo' 'abah shama'*) **to the *Towrah* | Teaching and Guidance** (*Towrah* – Instruction and Direction) **of Yahowah** (*YaHoWaH* – an accurate presentation of the name of *'elowah* – God as guided by His *towrah* – instructions regarding His *hayah* – existence)**."** (*Yasha'yah* / Freedom and Salvation are from Yah / Isaiah 30:9)

The Towrah has been and remains the only viable answer to what plagues humankind. It is the means to return to God and to be restored into fellowship. It guides and teaches, enriches and enlightens, empowers and liberates.

Let's reflect on where we have been…

"Woe, this is a warning, a cautionary notice of impending trouble (*howy*) **to the Lion of God and those Gathered by God** (*'Ary'el* / *'Aruw'el*)**.**

The Lion of God and those Gathered by God (*'Ary'el* / *'Aruw'el*)**: Dowd** (*Dowd*) **was loved and**

favored when he camped out for a while, receiving mercy (*chanah*) because of repetitively (*yasaph*) choosing to allow and celebrate the feasts running through their annual cycles (*chag naqaph*) year to year (*shanah 'al shanah*). (*Yasha'yah* 29:1)

Therefore (*wa*), I will incessantly and emphatically nag, seeking to plead with and influence (*tsuwq*) *'Ary'el* | the Lion of God and *'Aruw'el* | those Gathered by God (*'Ary'el* / *'Aruw'el*).

There shall be a limited time which will not last forever (*wa hayah*) to approach and meet Yah (*ta'nyah wa 'anyah*).

Then, *'Ary'el* will exist for Me, and will approach Me, as if she were the Lion Gathered by God (*wa hayah la 'any ka 'Ary'el* / *'Aruw'el*)." (*Yasha'yah* 29:2)

And (*wa*) I will camp out, showing favor and mercy (*chanah*), as if I were your home, wrapped all around you (*ka ha dowr 'al 'atah*).

I will be your rock (*wa tsuwr 'al 'atah*), a stone pillar and watchtower, a memorial of the Covenant (*mutstsab*). And I will establish (*quwm*) defensive fortifications for you, protecting you from attack (*'al 'atah matsuwrah*). (*Yasha'yah* 29:3)

However (*wa*), outside of the Land, and away from your country (*min 'erets*), you will be humbled and humiliated (*wa shaphel*). There (*wa*), you shall speak (*dabar*) from the gutter and out of the rubble (*min 'aphar*).

Your teachings and commandments, your prayers and platitudes (*'imrah 'atah*), will cause your demise, reducing your status. They have brought you down (*shachach*).

The sound of your voice (*qowl 'atah*) shall come to exist as if it were (*hayah ka*) a ghost, echoing the thoughts of the dead (*'owb*) from the Land (*min 'erets*).

Then, from the rubble (*wa min 'aphar*), your platitudes and prayers, your instructions and teaching (*'imrah 'atah*), will resonate in guttural undertones and doleful whispers, akin to the peeps and chirps of dying birds (*tsaphaph*). (*Yasha'yah* 29:4)

Then (*wa*), the accumulation of possessions and wealth of the multitudes emboldened by the perception of power and the confusing clamor (*hamown*) of your arrogant and presumptuous rebels who are boiling over with religious fervor and seething with resentment (*zed 'atah*) shall come to be like (*hayah ka*) the soot from a furnace (*'abaq daq*) even like chaff (*wa ka mots*), with the confusing clamor of the cruel agitators, their possessions, wealth, and claims of authority (*hamown 'aryts*) angrily and arrogantly passing through en route to being banished (*'abar*).

This shall come to pass (*wa hayah*) suddenly and unexpectedly, in an instant (*peta'*). (*Yasha'yah* 29:5)

There will be a time of reckoning for you and you will be held accountable (*paqad*) by (*min 'im*) Yahowah (𐤉𐤄𐤅𐤄) of the vast array of spiritual implements (*tsaba'*) through thunderous proclamations (*ba ra'am*), with earthquakes and discordant sounds (*wa ba ra'ash*), with a great voice and verbal declaration (*wa gadowl qowl*), and with a strong and raging wind (*wa ba suwphah wa sa'arah*), in addition to the flames of a devouring fire (*wa lahab 'esh 'akal*). (*Yasha'yah* 29:6)

And it shall be akin to (*wa hayah ka*) a nightmare (*chalowm*), with the darkness being exposed (*chazown laylah*), this confusing clamor and commotion caused by the agitating protests of those whose wealth has made them powerful and oppressive (*hamown kol*) from all the

Gentiles and their nations, the walking dead as if zombies, those who are not Jewish and who believe religions based upon pagan theology (*kol ha gowym*) that have come to fight (*ha tsaba'*) over and against (*'al*) *'Ary'el* | the Lion of God and *'Aruw'el* | those Gathered by God (*'Ary'el / 'Aruw'el*).

This includes all who battle against her (*wa kol tsaba' hy'*) construction of walls and barricades (*matsodah*) and who deliberately distress and harass her, seeking to constrain and narrow her (*wa ha matsyqym la hy'*). (*Yasha'yah* 29:7)

And it will be like when (*wa hayah ka 'asher*) someone who is hungry (*ha ra'eb*) dreams of growing physically stronger (*chalam*), and then he envisions himself eating (*wa hineh 'akal*) but is aroused from his sleep (*wa qyts*) and his soul (*wa nepesh huw'*) is not satisfied by the fantasy (*ryq*).

It can be compared to when (*wa ka 'asher*) a thirsty individual (*ha tsame'*) dreams of recovering (*chalam*), and then he envisions himself drinking (*wa hineh shatah*), but awakened (*wa qyts*), notices (*wa hineh huw'*) he is weakened and needs to recuperate (*'ayeph*) and his soul (*wa nepesh huw'*) is unsettled and suddenly anxious, longing (*shaqaq*).

So shall it be (*ken hayah*) the accumulation of power and wealth of the multitudes emboldened by the confusing clamor (*hamown kol*), of all the Gentiles and their nations, of all the people acting as animals, the walking dead as if zombies, those who are not Jewish and who believe religions based upon pagan theology (*kol ha gowym*) that have come to wage war (*ha tsaba'*) over (*'al*) Mount (*har*) Tsyown, the Signs Posted Along the Way and thus Zionists (*Tsyown*). (*Yasha'yah* 29:8)

Consider the consequence, and of your own volition avoid allowing any societal influence to persuade you to linger, reflect upon the meaning but do not be swayed by any individual or institution to delay (*mahah*), because otherwise, you will have chosen to be astonished and bewildered by the reality of this situation (*wa tamah*).

Of your own initiative, choose to close your eyes, protecting yourself, from what you would otherwise see, even though doing so will require that you act independently, undeterred by societal influences (*sha'a'*), making the conscious decision to shield yourself (*wa sha'a'*).

Drink it in, and you will become intoxicated and incapacitated (*shakar*), but not from wine (*wa min lo' yayn*). You may be shaken and stumble, even be swayed (*nua'*), but not with beer (*wa lo' shekar*). (*Yasha'yah* 29:9)

Therefore (*ky*), Yahowah (*YaHoWaH*) will pour out for a time (*nasak*) upon you (*'al 'atah*) a spirit (*ruwach*) of diminished consciousness (*tardemah*).

He will close your eyes, impairing your vision (*wa 'atsam 'eth 'ayn 'atah*) with regard to the prophets and concerning those who speak for God about the past, present, and future (*'eth ha nabym*).

And concerning your leadership, regarding those at the top, your heads of state and chief priests, your government and religious leaders (*wa 'eth ro'sh 'atem*), He has withdrawn (*kasah*) the ability to receive or communicate messages from God as prophets, to be inspired or perceptive (*chozeh*). (*Yasha'yah* 29:10)

Therefore (*wa*), the prophecy regarding the consequences of this entire revelation (*chasuwth ha kol*) shall exist concerning you and be applicable to you (*hayah la 'atem*) in the manner (*ka*) of the words (*dabar*) of a written document (*ha sepher*) which is sealed (*ha chatam*).

When to reveal the way (*'asher*), the book (*ha sepher*) is placed before someone (*nathan 'eth huw 'el*) in an effort to help them become aware and understand, perhaps even to process the information, and come to know what was revealed by Yada' (*yada'*), they will say (*la 'amar*), 'Please (*na'*), read this (*qara' zeh*)!' But he will answer (*wa 'amar*), 'I am unable to comprehend it (*lo' yakol*) because (*ky*) it is sealed (*chatam huw'*).' (*Yasha'yah* 29:11)

And should they give (*wa nathan*) the book (*ha sepher* – the scroll inscribed in writing) to someone who is ignorant and illiterate and who cannot understand what was written (*'al 'asher lo' yada' sepher*), asking (*la 'amar*), 'Please (*na'*), read this (*qara' zeh*)!' He will reply (*wa 'amar*), 'I am clueless and cannot read the written words (*lo' yada'*).' (*Yasha'yah* 29:12)

Then (*wa*), Yahowah (*YaHoWaH*) said (*'amar*), 'Indeed (*ky*), forasmuch as (*ya'an*) these people (*ha 'am ha zeh*) approach Me (*nagash 'any*) with their mouths, and with their lip service (*ba peh huw' wa ba sapah huw'*), putting on airs (*kabad*), they avoid exercising good judgment and distance themselves (*wa rachaq leb huw'*) from Me (*min 'any*).

As a result, the fear (*wa yira'th*) of Me (*'eth 'any*) exists (*hayah*) as (*ka*) a condition (*mitswah*) of men (*'iyshym*) which is taught (*lamad*).' (*Yasha'yah* 29:13)

Therefore (*la ken*), behold (*hineh*), as for Me (*la 'any*), I will once again at yet another time (*'any yasaph*) approach to do wonderful things by fulfilling something special (*la pala'*) for and along with the people who are closely related (*'eth ha 'am ha zeh*), with surprising fulfillments and inspiring signs, along with that which is marvelous and miraculous, indeed, very special (*pala' wa pala'*).

And then (*wa*), the wisdom and technical acumen (*chakmah*) of their scholars, theologians, and sages (*chakam huw'*), as well as (*wa*) the discernment and understanding (*bynah*) of their most educated teachers (*byn huw'*), shall vanish, ceasing to exist (*sathar*). (*Yasha'yah* 29:14)

So, this is a warning (*howy*) to those who lack understanding and have become profoundly difficult, to those who are different deep down than they are on the surface, who are intensely hypocritical and who have dug a deep hole for themselves (*'amaq*) with regard to (*min*) Yahowah (𐤉𐤄𐤅𐤄).

Your counsel and schemes, your advice and your plans (*'etsah 'atah*) will no longer be known or considered, as they will vanish (*sathar*).

Those whose undertakings (*ma'aseh hem*) they have tried (*wa hayah*) to conceal in the dark (*ba machshak*) will say (*wa 'amar*), 'Who will see us, and why will we be exposed (*my ra'ah 'anachnuw*)? Who (*wa my*) actually knows and genuinely understands the nature of our actions (*yada' 'anachnuw*)?' (*Yasha'yah* 29:15)

Your perversions have inverted reality, having turned things upside down by claiming the opposite of what is actually true (*hephek 'atah*).

They are comparable to (*'im ka*) the potter's clay (*chomer ha yowtser*) continually reckoning and regarding itself (*chashab*) such that it should claim (*ky 'amar*) of the one who designed and fabricated it (*ma'aseh la 'asah huw'*), 'He did not make me (*lo' 'asah 'any*).'

Or (*wa*) should the thing conceived and created (*yetser*) say of the one who formed him (*'amar la yowtser huw'*), 'He is the one without knowledge or understanding (*huw' lo' byn*)?' (*Yasha'yah* 29:16)

Whether or not it will take a while (*ha lo' 'owd*) before, in a relatively short and subsequent period of time, a few individuals (*ma'at miza'r*) will return, and they will be restored (*shuwb*).

It will be determined that they are (*chashab*) white, purified and radiant (*labanown*) when approaching the fruitful garden (*la ha karmel*) filled with trees (*la ha ya'ar*). (*Yasha'yah* 29:17)

So, in that day (*wa ba ha yowm ha huw'*), those deaf to what had been inscribed and who have now been cut into the agreement (*cheresh*) shall hear, and they will listen (*shama'*) to the words (*dabar*) of this book (*sepher*).

So, it will be out of (*wa min*) the shadows, the dysfunctional nature and spiritual nonreceptivity (*'opel*) of the darkness, confusion, and ignorance (*choshek*) that the eyes of the blind, those who had been the sightless unobservant (*'ayn 'iwer*), will choose to see, now and forevermore (*ra'ah*). (*Yasha'yah* 29:18)

Those who answer and respond, the straightforward and unpretentious (*wa 'anaw*) will be enriched exponentially, enlightened and increased in every way (*yasaph*) by (*ba*) Yahowah (*Yahowah*), becoming jubilant (*simchah*).

Those who have willingly eschewed political power and religious influences, making themselves subject to criticism (*'ebyown*) among men (*'adam*), who are in association with (*ba*) the Set-Apart One (*qodesh*) of Yisra'el (*Yisra'el*), shall rejoice over their favorable outcome (*gyl*). (*Yasha'yah* 29:19)

Then, indeed, making this contrast (*ky*), the ruthless terrorists and those who elicit fear (*'aryts*) will fail, they will be stopped and then vanish (*'aphes*). Those who ridicule and mock, including the condescending who are divisive and derisive (*lets*) will all be gone (*kalah*).

Then (*wa*), all who do not hesitate when it comes to participating in that which is corrupt and damaging to the relationship, everyone who seeks to control others through perversions of the truth, all who are notorious for the hardships they have imposed, and those who are intent on promoting troubling ideas (*kol shaqad 'awen*) shall be cut off and separated (*karat*). (*Yasha'yah* 29:20)

Those who have caused a man to be excluded from the relationship by missing the way (*karath 'adam*) through their words (*ba dabar*), and for those who argue, trying to prove their case, those who establish laws and who seek to resolve disputes their way, those offering vindication or punishment, administering their take on justice (*wa la ha yakah*) within the doorways of public meeting places (*ba sha'ar*) so as to mischaracterize or falsify and wrongly convict (*quwsh*), they promote and disseminate that which misleads and thrusts aside (*natah*), devaluing and negating, even confusing and convoluting (*tohuw*), that which is right (*tsadyq*). (*Yasha'yah* 29:21)

For this reason, therefore (*laken*), thus says (*koh 'amar*) Yahowah (*Yahowah*) concerning the House and Family (*beyth*) of Ya'aqob [a synonym for Yisra'el and metaphor for the Covenant] (*Ya'aqob*), who, to show the way to the benefits of the relationship (*'asher*), redeemed and liberated them (*padah*) through 'Abraham (*'eth 'Abraham*),

'Ya'aqob (*Ya'aqob*) shall no longer be confounded nor shamed, neither bewildered nor humiliated (*lo' 'atah bowsh*). No longer (*wa lo' 'atah*) will his face appear (*paneh huw'*) pale from being perplexed and weakened (*chawar*).' (*Yasha'yah* 29:22)

Because when (*ky ba*) he witnesses (*ra'ah huw'*) his descendants (*yeled huw'*), the accomplishments of My hands (*ma'aseh yad 'any*), in his midst (*ba qereb*), they will treat My name as special and set apart (*qadash shem 'any*).

And they will also treat Ya'aqob as being set apart, acknowledging and appreciating his unique attributes (*wa qadash Ya'aqob*). They will be in awe (*'arats*) of the God of Yisra'el (*'elohym Yisra'el*). (*Yasha'yah* 29:23)

Then (*wa*), they will come to know, to realize, recognize, and acknowledge (*yada'*) that they have erred spiritually (*ta'ah ruwach*) and will make the proper connections to understand (*binah*).

Even those who have grumbled and complained, having expressed their discontent (*ragan*) will continue to actually learn from this instruction (*lamad leqah*)." (*Yasha'yah* 29:24)

"Now at this time (*'atah*), choose to approach (*bow'*), writing this (*kathab hy'*) on an illuminated tablet (*luwach*) for them (*'eth hem*).

Inscribe it (*wa chaqaq hy'*) in a book (*'al sepher*) so that it may literally and always be (*wa hayah*) for the last days (*la acharown yowm*) and serve as a witness regarding eternity (*la 'ad 'ad 'owlam*). (*Yasha'yah* 30:8)

Because (*ky*) they are a rebellious and contentious people (*'am mary huw'*), mendacious and deceitful children (*kachash beny*), unwilling to listen (*lo' 'abah shama'*) to the *Towrah* | Teaching and Guidance (*Towrah*) of Yahowah (*YaHoWaH*)." (*Yasha'yah* / Freedom and Salvation are from Yah / Isaiah 30:9)

We found what we sought, and we have what we need. We are better prepared to deal with the choices before us and with what the world will bring. It was kind of our Father to provide these insights – especially since we have not been the most attentive children.

ᛌᛦᛨᛦᛚ

The words we are about to read were spoken by *Shalomoh* | Solomon. He was *Dowd's* | David's son. Standing atop Mount *Mowryah* | Moriah, with the recently completed Temple gleaming in the background, the man noted for his wisdom was dedicating the Home Yahowah had designed to showcase the Ark of the Covenant, the Tablets of Stone, and the original autograph of the Towrah Moseh had scribed.

With Ya'aqob's descendants gathered before him, Solomon spoke of the promises Yahowah had made to his father. Then turning to the future, and desirous of guiding his people's footsteps, Solomon used *nakry* to speak of a "discerning foreigner from a distant place and time, someone who would speak a different language, and who, as a result of being observant, would come to understand." Projecting well into the future, he told the Children of Yisra'el how they should respond to the words this individual would write on their behalf.

Solomon reiterated many of the wonderful things which would benefit Yisra'el if the people continued to observe the Towrah. But knowing they would not, he said the following…

"Therefore (*wa gam*), regarding someone else, the observant and discerning foreigner from a different ethnicity and geographic location who will come to understand (*ha nakry* – this person from a different place and culture, speaking a different language, who, having paid attention will comprehend; from *nakar* – by being attentive and astute will become acquainted, recognize, and acknowledge something which deserves our attention and consideration), **who, to show the way to the benefits of the relationship (*'asher*), is not of your people (*lo' min 'am 'atah*), this Yisra'el (*Yisra'el huw'*).**

He will come (*wa bow'*) from a distant country in a distant time (*min 'erets rachowq*) for the express purpose of being a witness and providing answers regarding (*lama'an*) Your (*'atah*) tremendously important (*ha gadowl*) name (*shem*), the influence of Your Hand (*wa yad 'atah*), the powerful and passionate ruler who is prepared to lead (*ha chazaq*), and (*wa*) the protective ram who shepherds His flock as well as His Sacrificial Lamb (*zarowa' huw'*) whom You have extended (*'atah ha natah*).

When (*wa*) he arrives on the scene and chooses to pursue this (*bow'*), then (*wa*) he will help interested parties reconcile their relationship by providing those who exercise good judgment with the information and justifications needed to make a correct and reasoned decision (*palal*) regarding this familial relationship (*'el ha beyth ha zeh*). (*Dabarym ha Yowmym* / 2ⁿᵈ Chronicles 6:32)

When you hear it out of the heavens, coming from the atmosphere (*wa 'atah shama' min ha shamaym*) within the location where you live (*min makown yashab 'atah*), then (*wa*) engage and act accordingly, doing everything (*'asah ka kol*) which, to show the way (*'asher*), the observant foreigner from a different ethnicity and geographic location who understands (*ha nakry*) has invited you to read (*qara' 'el 'atah*), for the express purpose of being a witness who provides answers such that (*lama'an*) all peoples of the Earth (*kol 'am ha 'erets*) will have a genuine and ongoing opportunity to become familiar with, to know,

acknowledge, accept, and understand (*yada'*) **Your name** (*'eth shem 'atah*).

He will come to respect and revere You (*wa la yare' 'eth 'atah*) **along with** (*ka*) **Your people** (*'am 'atah*), **Yisra'el** (*Yisra'el*). **This is so** (*wa la*) **they may know** (*yada'*) **that, truthfully** (*ky*), **I have built** (*banah*) **for Your family this house** (*'al ha beyth ha zeh*) **which, to reveal the correct path to give life meaning** (*'asher*), **is designated and called** (*qara'*) **by Your name** (*shem 'atah*)." (*Dabarym ha Yowmym* / Words for the Days / 2nd Chronicles 6:33)

Other than Yahowah speaking directly to all humanity in His own voice, which isn't possible in this context because He's not a *Nakry* | Observant Foreigner, imagine the wonderment in the minds of those listening to Solomon three thousand years ago trying to ascertain how this would occur. How would everyone on Earth listen and benefit concurrently? And why, they may have wondered, would God want to speak through a foreigner to Yisra'el and Gowym concurrently, from outside of Yisra'el, and in a language other than Hebrew?

And yet, here we are. The ability for everyone the world over to listen to someone whose words and voice come out of the sky is now possible. Advancing technology, communication satellites, broadband internet, and seven billion smartphones have made it possible for almost everyone to listen simultaneously along with Yisra'el.

The preamble to this prophecy is amazing, and yet now, since this capability is so integrated into our lives, with the average individual spending seven hours a day listening, looking, and reading content selected from the cloud, the fulfillment appears almost mundane. But still, consider the unlikely intersection of someone thousands of years and thousands of miles from Yisra'el, a complete stranger in a distant place and time, becoming so enthralled with Yahowah's words that he would compose fifteen thousand pages of insights on the Towrah, Miqra'ey, and Beryth, all gleaned by translating Yahowah's Word into the lingua franca of the world – the language spoken by more Yahuwdym than Hebrew – somehow stumbling upon the realization that Dowd is the Son of God, the Mashyach and Melek, Yahowah's Right Hand, Protective Shepherd, and His Sacrificial Lamb – all of which was conveyed in this prophetic message.

Three thousand years ago Yahowah revealed that He would use a Gentile to reach His people and call them home. He would even endorse what he would write and say, telling His people to do as he said, recognizing that this *nakry* would "*nakar* – come to know Him by being observant, that he would come to understand Him by being discerning," then base everything he would write upon what he "observed by closely examining and carefully considering" the *Towrah* and *Naby'* | the Guidance and Prophets. He would even Yada' Yah! – focus on the importance of knowing and understanding Yahowah's name.

This may be the one and only time that Yahowah asked His people to engage based upon something a foreigner had to say. Yet it was said of this *nakry* that he would serve as a *Lama'an* | Witness, as someone "who would provide answers," which can be "*qara'* – read and recited" on behalf of people the world over, beginning with Yisra'el.

Beyond the written translations and insights found in *Yada' Yahowah*, *An Introduction to God*, *Observations*, *Coming Home*, *Babel*, *Twistianity*, and *God Damn Religion*, beyond the reach of Yah's Word being recited throughout *Yada' Yah Radio* and *Shattering Myths*, might this also be inferring that Yada' will be invited to serve alongside 'Elyah as the unnamed Witness during the Time of Ya'aqob's Troubles (*Malaky* / Malachi 4:5 and *Zakaryah* / Zechariah 4:14)?

Beyond all of this, there is but one reason that *ha Nakry* | the Observant and Discerning Foreigner in a faraway place and time would have been introduced and authenticated by Yahowah during the dedication of His Home. Yahowah wants Yisra'el, and the world at large, to consider what he has translated and shared because the information, insights, and perspective he is providing are relevant and credible, valid and reconciling, and indeed trustworthy because it is all based upon the words of Moseh and Dowd, Yasha'yah and Yirma'yah. By engaging in something others were unwilling to do, the *Nakry* became so uniquely relevant to knowing Yahowah, to appreciate what He is offering, and to recognize what He is asking in return, that God saw fit to validate his Witness – one based entirely upon the *Towrah, Naby', wa Mizmowr*.

ᵚᎽ᎒Ꮍᎏ

1

Bara' | Creation

In the Beginning...

One of the most revealing, intellectually stimulating, and least appreciated prophetic passages peers fourteen billion years into our past. It is found in Genesis One – known in Hebrew as *Bare'syth* – In the Beginning.

In it, Yahowah introduces Himself, explains the creation process, and presents His plan to reconcile our relationship with Him well in advance of humankind collectively walking away. Through brilliant allusions and captivating symbolism, God also chronicles the seminal events of human history – past, present, and future – providing the framework to understand His seven-thousand-year timeline: from life in the Garden of Joy to our scheduled, and impending, return.

In addition to these three essential stories, Yahowah answers mankind's most important questions: is there a God, and why do we exist? He even provides a precisely accurate portrayal of universal creation and the conception of life, both within the correct epochs of time. In so doing, God proves His existence, demonstrates His role as our Creator, and validates His inspiration of the resulting witness.

It is not uncommon for God to paint several pictures with the same brush. For example, when one reads the story of 'Abraham and *Yitschaq* | Isaac on Mount *Mowryah* | Moriah (meaning: Revere Yah) with a knowledge of archeology and history, it's apparent that their story, which chronicles an actual event in year 2000 Yah (1968 BCE), foreshadows another. And, indeed, their journey culminates with the prophetic announcement that the Passover Lamb would be provided at the opportune time and in this same place. And that is precisely what occurred forty Yowbel / 2,000 years thereafter.

Each word spoken between father and son points to what our Heavenly Father and His Son, Yahowah and *Dowd* | David, experienced fulfilling the *Miqra'* | Invitation to be Called Out and Meet of *Pesach* | Passover in year 4000 Yah / 33 CE. With this recognition, we come to appreciate that these dates serve as the preeminent meeting times on God's calendar, such that the parameters of His timeline emerge, enabling us to date the formative events pertaining to our relationship. And it is these same lessons which can be discerned from a thoughtful analysis of *Bare'syth* / Genesis one.

Another example of a timeline embedded in an inspired account and of three stories existing in one narrative is *Howsha'* | Hosea's marriage to the temple prostitute, Gomer. The betrothal served to acquaint the prophet and Yisra'el, circa 700 BCE, with a tangible means to anticipate the consequence of their infidelity with God. Howsha's marriage to Gomer, therefore, served as a metaphor, illustrating how the *Yahuwdym* | Jews (meaning: Related to Yah and Yah's Beloved) had broken their Covenant relationship with Him. The story also provided Yahowah with an opportunity to explain why He had to divorce His people to remain moral. In addition, this account reveals relevant lessons for us today – particularly for Orthodox Jews whose belief system and culture are very similar to those assailed in Howsha's open letter to the Northern Kingdom. Finally, Howsha's troubled marriage presents the framework on which to ascertain the time of Dowd's arrival as the Pesach 'Ayil in *Yaruwshalaim* | Jerusalem (meaning: Source from which Guidance on

2

Reconciliation Flows) in 33 CE (Year 4000 Yah) as well as his return with Yahowah in 2033 CE (Year 6000 Yah) for redemption and reconciliation respectively.

There are multiple timelines and simultaneous narratives embedded in *Bare'syth* / In the Beginning / Genesis One, but the brush strokes are much broader, bolder, and more complex. As is His custom, Yahowah chooses His colors for a reason and shades each word with great precision. Therefore, we will honor this great communicator by examining His selections under the etymological microscope of Hebrew lexicons, allowing us to amplify His message.

Along with what we discover in the expansive examination of these words, I will share the insights which can be derived from them, associating this painting with other illustrations the ultimate Artist has drawn. If nothing else, my commentary will slow us down so that we can reflect on the majesty of our Maker's message.

However, be forewarned: this chapter on "Existence" requires an additional layer of complexity in the midst of what is already an extremely challenging interwoven tapestry. To comprehend the creative side of Yahowah's testimony, we will have to understand aspects of the theory of relativity, some physics, astronomy, biology, and evolution, as well as have some familiarity with the fossil record, statistical analysis, the concept of spacetime, and the nature of light. I will do my best to provide the necessary insights for the uninitiated while not boring scientists or overwhelming those who have a limited interest in these discoveries. But no matter where you reside on the spectrum of contemporary scientific awareness, what lies before us is challenging by design.

Before we begin, there is some reassuring news. Yahowah is correct. From His perspective, it took precisely six twenty-four-hour days to create the universe and our

3

planet, conceive plant and animal life, and then design 'Adam to His specifications. And scientists are mostly right. Looking back from our perspective, the inception of the universe occurred between 14 and 15 billion years ago as energy coalesced into matter and time began to flow.

Yahowah is correct in that plants and animals reproduce after their kind, and evolutionists are accurate in saying that species have evolved. Yahowah not only agrees with the concept of the Big Bang, He was the first to use the term. God even uses scientific jargon in His presentation of dinosaurs. His testimony is in complete harmony with the fossil record, especially as it is presented in the Cambrian Explosion 500 million years ago.

Therefore, this scientific review of *Bare'syth* isn't going to pit Creationism against the Big Bang and Evolutionary Theory but, instead, demonstrate that they are in accord, right down to the details. The controversy that we have become accustomed to hearing only rages between the advocates of religion and secular humanists. God's accounting and the evidence are not in conflict, nor is *Bare'syth* / Genesis contrary to reason.

ﭏﬓﬞ

Yahowah begins His open letter to man with a seven-word instruction. *"Ba-re'shyth 'elohym bara' 'eth ha-shamaym wa-'eth ha-'erets."* Beyond their meaning, the realization that there are seven words in God's opening statement is not a coincidence. Every important aspect of Yahowah's plan, from the duration of the human experience to the creative timeline, from the *Shabat* | Sabbath to the *Miqra'ey* | Invitations to be Called Out and Meet, is based upon the formula: one (representing God) in addition to six (representing humankind) equals seven (a perfect relationship and result). Man, a carbon-based

4

lifeform (with an atomic number of six), was created on the sixth day. And while there is only one God, with one name and one purpose, without developing a relationship with us, God cannot grow and thus ceases to be infinite. Wanting to experience the joys of raising a family, Yahowah initiated this creative process, emphasizing the one special word among these seven: "*bare'syth* – in the beginning."

Translated into English, *Bare'syth* / In the Beginning / Genesis 1:1 reads…

"**In** (*ba* – near, within certain limits of, and in proximity to, regarding the account of) **the beginning** (*re'shyth* – at the start of time and the initiation of the process of existence, concerning the first fruits of the labors of the head of the family, while addressing the thing which is of first and foremost importance; from *ro'sh* – the head, the top and uppermost, the sum and total, first and beginning), **the Almighty** (*'elohym* – God), **for accompaniment and association** (*'eth* – accordingly and therefore, near and in proximity), **created** (*bara'* – conceived and caused a new existence, choosing perfect transformation and birth, planning, preparing, shaping, producing, and fashioning something out of the elements and making it happen) **the** (*ha*) **spiritual world** (*shamaym* – heavens and abode of God) **and** (*wa*) **alongside** (*'eth* – to accompany it as part of a relationship) **the** (*ha*) **material realm** (*'erets* – matter, the physical and natural world)."

Sometimes, even within the scale of universal creation, it is the smallest things that are the most revealing. The shortest word, *'eth*, is the only one which is repeated. And yet, it is the only one every religiously and politically inspired translation ignored.

While I did not have to translate either occurrence of *'eth* in God's opening statement, as ignoring its presence has become scholastically acceptable when rendering ancient Hebrew into English, *'eth* indicates that God was "in proximity to" His creation and that He initiated the process for the purpose of "accompaniment and relationship," and was, therefore, seeking a "close association." These concepts are germane to our understanding.

By using *'eth*, God makes us aware of His proximity to this creative event. That is exceedingly important because in the presence of great energy, mass, or velocity the rate that time flows slows appreciably. This realization will allow us to correlate a clock on Earth to one at creation and thereby sync the creative timeline using the now-proven Theory of Relativity.

God is also providing us with the reason for creation. He is seeking a relationship and wants to remain in close association with us. This in turn serves to underscore the purpose of the Towrah which is to present the Familial Covenant Relationship.

Speaking of that association, the letters which comprise the Towrah's first word are telling. In Ancient Hebrew, the alphabet Moseh used to scribe the original autograph of the Towrah, and reading right to left, *ba-are'syth* reads: 𐤁𐤓𐤀𐤔𐤉𐤕. The first letter, Beyth, when used as a preposition means "in" or "with." Its name is derived from *beyth*, meaning "home and family."

Beyth serves as the root of *beryth* – the Hebrew word translated as "Covenant." thereby explaining the nature of the intended relationship. That is why the character 𐤁 was originally drawn to depict the floor plan of a home – one with a singular entrance or doorway. Brought together, these concepts convey God opening the door and inviting us into His Home to be with Him and to become part of His Family.

The second letter, a Rosh, originally written 𐤓, explains how we can avail ourselves of this opportunity. Drawn to depict a human head, the letter indicates that we should use our eyes to observe and our ears to listen to what God has to say about His Covenant Home and Family. After we process this information, we can then use our mouths to respond appropriately. Beyond this, Rosh, which is derived from *re'sh*, reveals that this quest should be our "primary objective and foremost priority" because this is the "first" Family.

The third alphabetic character in Yahowah's first word to mankind is an Aleph. Initially drawn in the form of a ram's head 𐤀, it conveys strength and power in addition to the ability to lead and protect the flock. As such, the Aleph is the first letter in the title God: *'el* – which means "Almighty" and in *'ab* | father.

This brings us to the fourth letter, a Shin. It was scribed to symbolically represent teeth ᗏ. This was done to depict words and convey language, specifically the nourishment His words provide.

The next letter is a Yowd. It was based upon, and drawn to depict, a *yad*, the Hebrew word for "hand." It conveys the idea of reaching out to accomplish something. Especially relevant in this regard, a ᨪ reveals that God is reaching down and out to us with an open hand because He wants to lift us up and raise us as His children. In particular, the Yowd was not communicated with a closed fist engendering fear but, instead, as an open hand extended in friendship and support.

Lastly, we are greeted by a Theth, presented by a ⊗ in Ancient Hebrew. This letter was drawn to depict an enclosure, symbolic of God's protection. Then, the internal marking denotes a signature, affirming that Yahowah signed His name on the Torah's first word and upon those who have sought His protection.

Re'shyth conveys many pertinent thoughts, including "first and best." It speaks of "the beginning or initiation of a process." Its "first fruits" connotation is very significant

7

spiritually because it identifies "something of value which is set aside and dedicated to God."

Re'shyth describes the idea of being the "head of the family." Also, with regard to Yisra'el and Yahuwdym, who serve as the control group in Yahowah's revelation, *re'shyth* means "to make a division and distinction."

I use the term "control group" because that is the role Yahuwdym perform in God's unfolding story. By choice and covenant, by word and deed, by land and spirit, they were and remain separate from all others. The Chosen People serve as a living, quantifiable, and documented example of the benefits of choosing to form a Covenant relationship with Yahowah, as well as the consequences of separating from Him. Through these people, we also witness the consequence of foregoing the relationship God prescribed through an ill-fated affinity for the religions and politics of man.

The most significant aspect of *re'shyth,* and its second most frequent translational rendering, is: "first fruits" – symbolic of reaping the harvest of purified grain [a metaphor for saved souls] and waving a sheaf before Yahowah so that it will be accepted. This Called-Out Assembly known as Bikuwrym (*Qara'* / Leviticus 23:9-11) is indicative of men and women being born as children into Yahowah's Covenant Family – something we will learn a great deal about in subsequent volumes.

Suffice it to say for now, as Yahowah's third of seven *Miqra'ey,* the Festival Feast of FirstFruits, which is accurately translated as "Firstborn Children," follows Passover and UnYeasted Bread. It is the first of three harvests of saved souls included in God's seven-step plan of redemption and reconciliation. It signifies our acceptance before God and our reunification with Him after we accept the gifts of life and perfection represented by the *Miqra'ey* of *Pesach* and *Matsah.* On *Bikuwrym* |

Firstborn Children, we are adopted into our Heavenly Father's Family. Therefore, the first word provides a foreshadowing of Yahowah's ultimate intent.

Since this is important, let's linger here a moment longer. The three spring Feasts commemorate actual historical events experienced by the Children of Yisra'el during their rescue from political, religious, economic, and military oppression in *Mitsraym* | Egypt.

These days are also prophetic, predicting when Yahowah will honor His promise to provide the Covenant's benefits. They are instructive, too, explaining precisely how God will ransom us from our misguided propensity to be religious.

During the *Yatsa'* | Exodus, and during the ultimate fulfillment of the Miqra'ey, the blood of the Passover Lamb was smeared on an upright pole forming the doorway to eternal life. The following day, and as a result of the Feast of UnYeasted Bread, the invasive fungus of yeast was removed from the grain. This is synonymous with the removal of religious and political guilt from our souls. This confers an immortal and perfected status, enabling the beneficiaries to be adopted by God, redeemed and reconciled on the third day in commemoration of FirstFruits.

God used a term that suggests He has a plan to redeem that which He had yet to create, bringing mankind back into eternal fellowship. In many ways, the first word's diverse meanings summarize all the words which follow.

Continuing to focus on *re'shyth*, we discover that it is based upon *ro'sh*, which means "head, top, summit, chief, sum, and beginning." And in this vein, the "summit" of Mount *Mowryah* | Moriah (meaning revere Yah) is where God's beloved Son, *Dowd* | David, fulfilled Passover and UnYeasted Bread, leading to Firstborn Children so that

9

those who accept his sacrifice become perfected and immortal children of God.

In this regard, Yahowah could well be revealing an aspect of creation I've long suspected, that the experience for Him and the benefit for us is entirely cerebral and, therefore, something for us to contemplate in our heads. The most fascinating aspect of creation is the thought process which made it possible, both the purpose and expectations. It required precise planning and exacting calculations for the result to serve this purpose. Trying to glimpse into Yahowah's head, if we may be so bold, is the most interesting aspect of the account of the inception of the universe and conception of life. Why did God do it?

Even for a seven-dimensional being, creating the perfect six-dimensional environment for life and exploration, revelation, interaction, and choice was not easy. It required a multi-variable equation which had to be the most complex ever contemplated. It was not so much the enormous amount of energy needed to accomplish this ambitious goal but, instead, the nature of that energy and how it was applied, in addition to establishing the parameters by which it would interact to form matter.

Then there was the challenge of creating DNA, the three-dimensional language of life. Using it, an endless array of distinct lifeforms was possible. But how would the living interact, evolve, and grow? Especially intriguing, all of this had to be the product of intelligent planning such that the end result would be somewhat predictable and the desired result achieved. And yet, there also had to be an infusion of sufficient chaos to make the process interesting and freewill possible.

At least one iteration of a resulting lifeform would have the capacity to reflect Yahowah's nature, showing a desire to form a family. Individually, this creature would have the capacity to be upright and observant, thoughtful and industrious, and be able to understand spoken and written language while being capable of loving and raising children. And collectively, the focus of God's intent would possess the capacity for evil.

Then there is the issue of time. As we shall discover, the universe and the life within it were conceived to play out from beginning to end over seven days or some fourteen billion years, depending upon the relative point from which time is experienced. The most relevant lifeform would exist in the ordinary flow of time and yet have a lifespan long enough to come to know his Maker and make a choice regarding Him. It would necessitate creating an aspect of his being capable of experiencing emancipation from the bounds of time should he choose to be elevated beyond 3D and join His Creator in the seventh dimension.

While the result may have been calculable, even foreseeable, Yahowah would refrain from witnessing most of it play out, otherwise; nothing would be gained by it. For the desired relationship to be genuine and meaningful, the future children of the Covenant would have to be capable of making good and bad decisions, accepting or rejecting God, and thus becoming a source of amusement or aggravation.

There would be a beloved child in the midst of it – someone to love and to return his Creator's devotion – similar to a Father and Son. Indeed, there was. The man in the center of it all, the individual who embodies creation's purpose, the ultimate recipient of Yahowah's compassion, is *Dowd* | David. The more we come to appreciate their relationship, and what they achieved together, the better we will understand the reason we were created.

To this end, Yahowah conceived language and then He used it creatively. Since Hebrew is His chosen dialect, every linguistic nuance of this lexicon is worthy of our consideration. In that light, we discover that *re'shyth* has a scientific connotation in addition to its spiritual meaning. *Re'shyth* "denotes the point when and where space and time began." This is something we only came to understand quite recently.

Despite what you may have heard suggesting that scientists dismiss God's *Bare'syth* account, the truth is just the opposite. With each new discovery, the position of science is changing. The scientific community has migrated from being in conflict with Yahowah's 3,500-year-old testimony to being in harmony with it.

Old science has been refuted, not God. For example, throughout the first half of the 19th century, prior to the discovery and acceptance of the redshift found in light was formed by retreating galaxies and the observation of CMB radiation, the overwhelming majority of scientists, some 99% of them, believed the universe was a constant without beginning or end. They claimed that it always existed and was not created. They were obviously wrong.

While Alexander Friedmann was the first to publish a set of equations showing that the universe might be expanding in 1922. Then in 1929, Edwin Hubble proved that the recessional velocity of a galaxy increases with its distance from Earth. He did so based on the idea of a redshift, where the wavelengths of light are stretched when emerging from retreating objects. Then, in 1978, the co-discoverer of CMB emanating from the Big Bang, Arno Penzias, a Jewish physicist, won the Nobel Prize for his affirmation of a creational event.

To capture the moment, England's most acclaimed astronomer, Arthur Eddington, said, "Philosophically, the notion of a beginning of the present order of Nature is repugnant to me." The truth is often repulsive to those who focus on the creation rather than the Creator. Yet if they were to change their perspective and observe Yahowah's

Torah, they would come to better understand our universe and life in it.

They would have understood long ago that the cosmos had a starting point, a place where space and time began. After all, the truth was revealed nearly three thousand five hundred years before man stumbled upon it. They would know that life was the result of an intelligent design – one commissioned for a particular purpose.

While Yahowah's creation account isn't merely a scientific explanation of our genesis, it has proven scientific implications that humankind would not be able to fully appreciate before Einstein's Theories of Special and General Relativity. They demonstrate that before matter was created through the transformation of energy into mass, there was no time or space. Time began when matter and space were formed. That is precisely what *re'shyth* reveals: "the initiation of the process of the state of being, the first point in spacetime."

Consistent with Einstein's Theory, where light is the universal constant, *'owr* | light was the first thing God made manifest. Like Yahowah, Himself, it exists outside of and beyond the constraints of time. According to Relativity, at the velocity of light, the past, present, and future exist simultaneously. That is why the verb, *hayah*, "I was, I am, and I will be," lies at the heart of Yahowah's name.

God exists beyond the confines of the four dimensions of time and space we understand. When He so chooses, He can see yesterday, today, and tomorrow as if they are all here and now. However, to relate to us and to enter our more finite realm, Yahowah can either use emissaries such as *mal'ak* or He can convert some of His light energy into matter.

Science has recently come to recognize that all matter is stabilized light. This transformation through the shedding of dimensions and energy from light to matter is what enabled a diminished aspect of Yahowah to tread alongside 'Adam in the Garden of 'Eden, to meet with 'Abraham in the Promised Land, and to converse with Moseh while providing His Towrah.

Today, we have an even clearer view of our Creator. We not only have the perspective that history, science, and time provide, but we have unfettered access to the words He shared with these men and with all of His prophets.

Light, like Yahowah, is the universal constant. Light is the purest form of energy. And energy is the source and substance of the physical world. At creation, when energy became matter consistent with Einstein's $E=mc^2$ (energy is equivalent to mass when matter is multiplied by the speed of light squared), the four-dimensional construct we call "spacetime" began. This is important because everlasting life – the nature of light, the definition of Yahowah's name, the substance of FirstFruits, and the essence of prophetic revelation – requires a transition from our mortal three-dimensional existence and beyond, to the fourth dimension where time eternally exists in the past, present, and future.

That is not to say that Yahowah and the universe He created are limited to four dimensions. The empirical evidence confirms that there are more. For example, scientists are completely baffled when it comes to explaining the nature of the strongest macro-influence on the universe – gravity – the tendency of matter to attract. And even if we were to stumble on an explanation of gravity's nature, we would then only understand four percent of the forces influencing our observable reality.

Ninety-six percent of the energy and matter at work in the universe is invisible to our observations. This unknown influence, labeled "dark energy" and "dark matter" provides either a counterforce to gravity, demonstrating a repulsive nature, or just the opposite, keeping things bound together. String Theory suggests this could be the result of

14

several more dimensions, albeit within a point and thus acting at the micro-atomic level.

While I could neither fully understand it nor prove it directly, I would not be surprised if there are seven dimensions – Yahowah's favorite number – with three dimensions intersecting at right angles at the micro level. If that is so, the fifth dimension might explain "dark energy," the repulsive nature of the unknown force influencing our universe. God might call this dimension *bachar* | choice, as it provides the ability for us to separate from God if we make light of His gravity. Under this premise, the sixth dimension would be "dark matter" – the unknown source of universal attraction, the tendency of things to draw closer together. He might call it *'asher* | relationship.

The seventh could provide the basis of consciousness and communication, the language of perfect communion, the essence of thought and creativity which binds us together and causes all things to occur. Many aspects of our universe, especially at the subatomic and galactic levels, demonstrate cognitive awareness. Examples of this phenomenon include the fact that light responds differently when it is observed, the half-lives of radioactive decay whereby individual particles demonstrate coordinated behavior, and the ability of living cells to communicate with and influence the behavior of wave particles. Yahowah might call the seventh dimension "the Word" because it brings us to the Spiritual Realm in Heaven.

Before we leave our study of *re'shyth*, I would be remiss if I did not share that there are many appropriate ways to transliterate the sound of this Hebrew noun in English. Comprised of the letters Rosh, Aleph, Shin, Yowd, and Theth, you will find this word which is pronounced ray·**sheeth,** conveyed as: *resit, re'sit, resith, re'sith, resyth, re'syth, resiyth,* and *re'siyth* in Hebrew dictionaries and lexicons. These are all acceptable

15

variations, each transliterating the sounds of the Hebrew letters in an appropriate manner. Some represent the vowels Aleph and Ayin with apostrophes and others do not. Some lexicons transliterate the Hebrew Yowd with an "i," some with a "y," while others use both to designate the source of the sound.

Further, while the Hebrew letter Shin is most similar to the English "s," it usually conveys a "sh" sound. Similarly, the Hebrew Theth is akin to the English "t," but most often is spoken with a "th" pronunciation. Accordingly, you will find many variations of the same word in this book. Also, so that you know, the use of *italics* is the customary way to convey foreign words in a translated text. It helps distinguish them from the primary language in which the document is written.

While we are on this subject, I would like to dispel a myth. Scholars will tell you that Hebrew is a consonant-only language, but that is not true. The purpose of this deception is to artificially elevate the status of the Masoretic Text, which is vocalized through diacritical markings, and to underscore the invalid impression that Yahowah's name is unpronounceable. But in fact, there are five vowels among the 22 letters which comprise the Hebrew alphabet. They are: Aleph, Hey, Wah, Yowd, and Ayin. Yahowah's name is pronounced using three of these vowels: Yowd Hey Wah Hey (𐤉𐤄𐤅𐤄 - hwhy- יהוה) – vocalized: Y·aH·oW·aH. Collectively, there are 260 individuals and places in God's Towrah and Naby' which incorporate aspects of Yahowah's name – all of which can be accurately pronounced.

When read from the perspective of the subject-verb-object sentence structure we are accustomed to in English, *'elohym* is the second word in Yahowah's opening salvo. It is the plural of *'el*, meaning "almighty, mighty one, deity, or god." And both *'el* and *'elohym* are based upon *'elowah*. Written right to left in the original Hebrew alphabet it looks like this: 𐤀𐤋𐤅𐤄, or like this in the contracted plural form: 𐤀𐤋𐤄𐤉𐤌.

'Elowah begins with an Aleph: 𐤀 (א), the first letter of the Hebrew alphabet. In its pictographic form, it represents a ram's head which symbolizes strength, power, might, and authority. It conveys the will and ability to lead and protect.

The second letter, a Lamed 𐤋 (ל), was drawn in the shape of a shepherd's staff. It conveys leadership, direction, guidance, nurturing, and protection. Used commonly as a prefix, a Lamed serves as a preposition in Hebrew, communicating movement toward a goal – in this case toward God, Himself.

The Wah 𐤅 (ו), which designates the "o" sound in *'elowah* and is the reason its contracted plural form is pronounced, *'elohym*, resembles a tent peg. This is important because they were used to enlarge and secure the homes of those who first heard Yahowah's title. These sturdy stakes also secured the Tabernacle, which represented God's home among His people. Today, as then, the Wah is used as a conjunction and conveys the ideas of increasing, connecting, adding, and enlarging.

In this regard, it is interesting to note that the oldest extant example of the Wah is from the time of the Exodus 3,500 years ago. In this depiction on a lead tablet, the upper portion of the letter was drawn with an enclosed circle rather than the open v shape. As such, it was able to hold the ropes needed to secure a tent.

The final letter, a Hey 𐤄 (ה), was the most elaborate in its detail. Like the Wah, it is found in both Yahowah's name and His title. The highly distinctive Hey was drawn in the form of a person standing up, pointing and reaching up to the heavens. It screams, pay attention, be observant, and take notice of what God has done and said. Today, *hey* still means "Hey, I'm over here! Look at me! Pay attention!"

To achieve the plural form as it was scribed in the opening line of the Towrah we must add two letters, a Yowd ⊃ and a Mem ᴧᴧ. The Yowd ⊃, which depicts God's arm reaching down and out with an open hand, is the first letter in His name 𐤉𐤄𐤅𐤄 | Yahowah. It reveals that God is not only reaching out to us with an open hand of friendship to lead us to Him and to lift us up but also that He, Himself, will engage personally to do this work on our behalf.

The Mem ᴧᴧ was drawn to show waves on water. The visual image could be of the *ruwach*, wind and spirit, driving them. Water is not only the universal solvent and shown throughout the Towrah as the source of cleansing, it is also depicted as the source from which life emerged.

Bringing this all together, the characters which comprise *'elowah*, and its contracted plural form *'elohym*, meaning "Almighty God," paint a picture of Yahowah being supremely powerful while acting in the role of a shepherd who cares for His flock, leading, nurturing, and protecting His sheep. He is focused on enlarging His Family while defending them.

By using the plural form, Yahowah implies that His parental nature as our *'Ab* | Heavenly Father and *Ruwach* | Spiritual Mother were present at creation. Yahowah will affirm this in His next statement, which focuses on the role of the Spirit during the creative process. It is also something Yahowah's Son, *Dowd* | David, confirms throughout his *Mashal* / Word Pictures / Proverbs. They were written from the perspective of our Heavenly Father and Spiritual Mother to us as God's children.

While there is only one God, *'elohym* serves to affirm that Yahowah perceives Himself as part of the relationship which is being created through the Covenant Family.

Reinforcing the single unity of *'elohym* | God and the *beryth* | Covenant, the verb *"bara'* – create" was written in the third-person singular, not plural (i.e., He created, rather than they created).

Speaking of *"bara',* it is the lone verb in God's initial statement to His creation. Its primary meaning is "to create," both in the sense of "initiating something new which had not been in existence before" and of "renewing and transforming that which already exists." Consistent with its procreant and regenerative connotations, *bara'* conveys: "the choice to transform and to perfect, performing whatever it takes to bring something or someone into a preferred state." It speaks of "initiating" in the sense of "cutting a covenant," and of "life's beginnings," and thus "birth."

A composite of *bara's* overall influence on Yahowah's message might read: the *Creator chose to begin a relationship, initiating the process* by *dispatching* part of Himself to *perform whatever was needed to bring about a preferential state* so that we could *exist creatively*.

By using *re'shyth, 'elohym* and *bara',* or in Ancient Hebrew – ᴧᴧ⋌ᴸᵭᒍᕈᓍ ᕈᓍᡫ ᠗ᐳᒫᒫᒍᕈᓍᡫ – Yahowah is saying that He wants us to join Him in His Family and that He is first and foremost our Father and our Shepherd, the one who leads us, who protects us, who cleanses us, and who restores and nurtures our life, empowering and enriching us. He is not only introducing us to His Covenant Family, but He has also provided us with His Word, the means to know Him, the means to understand what He is offering, and then respond appropriately.

In the world's only credible creation account, the Spirit who inspired *Bare'syth* is putting us on notice: we can accept or reject the claimant and His claims. In the thousands of pages which follow His *Bare'syth* | Genesis testimony, the Author provides what He deems to be

19

sufficient evidence for us to evaluate the veracity of His claims and determine the wisdom of choosing to acknowledge Him as our Creator. What you choose to do with this information is up to you.

The fourth and sixth words in *Bare'syth* share a common base, *'eth*. As we discussed previously, this Hebrew term doesn't require translation into English, but since it enhances the content, *'eth* reveals that Yahowah was "in close proximity to" His creation and that He initiated the process for the purpose of "accompaniment and relationship." He was, therefore, seeking an " *'eth* – close association" with its culminating event – the creation of man. *'Eth* can be rendered as "with, among, through, accordingly, and also." It is derived from *'owth*, meaning "sign or signal," which is something "to be observed and remembered." It is related to *'uwth*, meaning "consent," as in "reaching an agreement."

The most revealing aspect of *'eth*'s presence, not once but twice in the Creation account, is that Yahowah certifies His proximity to the epicenter of what was about to occur. This is significant because time is relative to the observer. In the presence of tremendous energy or velocity, even mass, the rate at which it flows slows dramatically. By sharing and confirming His location relative to these events with *'eth*, we are able to synchronize a clock on Earth with one at the inception of the universe and thereby validate the timeline Yahowah provided.

Nearly as revealing, albeit in a different way, with the second inclusion of *'eth*, God is conveying the reason He was there in the first place. Yahowah was seeking to create something He did not have and yet wanted. It was the one thing that would make His existence interesting, indeed, meaningful and rewarding. He wanted the very thing He designed us to value above all else: our children. God sought to develop a mutually beneficial and familial

20

relationship with humankind. And He wants to remain in close association with us throughout the universe and time.

Pronounced differently, the Hebrew letters in *'eth* (Aleph Taw אֶת) can be rendered as *'ath*, which speaks of a "miraculous sign." According to the *Bare'syth* account in particular, it could be considered the most "extraordinary sign." It is, therefore, indicative of the insights it conveyed in this account – all of which can be corroborated.

Shamaym, Yahowah's fifth word to mankind, is often used to describe the "heavens – the spiritual abode of God." It is also the principal Hebrew word to address the "physical universe – the realm of stars." Both are relevant to the expressed storylines.

Shamaym is based upon a Hebrew root meaning "to be lofty and elevated." As such, it speaks of God's plan to elevate us to His spiritual abode.

But more than this, and in recognition that *shamaym* is the plural of *sham / shem,* several additional insights are possible. *Sham* speaks of a "specific place" or "location" which is identified by the "*shem* – personal and proper name" of its principal occupant and associated with His "reputation and renown." *Sham* also serves as the base for two of Yahowah's most repeated requests: that we "*shama'* – listen" to Him by "*shamar* – observing" His words, "hearing what He has to say by closely examining and carefully considering His testimony." *Shem, shama',* and *shamar* take us to this *sham.*

In this regard, the term "anti-Semite" actually means "against the name and place." The name is Yahowah, and the one He gave His people: *Yahuwdym* | Jews. The place is *Yahuwdah* | Judaea and *Yisra'el* | Israel.

One of the more interesting verifications that *shamaym* can be used to describe Yahowah's Home in the spiritual realm is found in the 78ᵗʰ Psalm. There we learn that heaven

21

has a doorway – at least metaphorically. Speaking of His frustration over His children's total lack of appreciation for what He had done for them during the Exodus, their infidelity, rebellion, and overall irritating attitude, we find:

"Yahowah became frustrated...with Yisra'el because they did not trust (*'aman*) in God (*'elohym*) and did not rely (*batah*) on His deliverance, freedom, and salvation (*yashuw'ah*). And yet He had directed (*tsawah*) the clouds and sky (*sachaq*) from a higher dimension (*ma'al*), and He had opened (*pathach*) the door (*deleth*) to the Heavens in the Spiritual Realm (*shamaym*)." (*Mizmowr* / Song / Psalm 78:21-23)

Consistent with this declaration, Passover is the Doorway to Life in Heaven. It was opened for the Children of Yisra'el the night before the Exodus began and again for all mankind by Dowd when he fulfilled the Miqra' in year 4000 Yah.

As this *Mizmowr* / Psalm suggests, God does not ask a great deal of us. But there are some baseline requirements for the relationship to be mutually beneficial. These include walking away from religion and politics, trusting and relying upon Yahowah, and walking to God along the path He has provided so that He can perfect us. In addition, He asks us to observe the instructive conditions of His Covenant – all of which are presented in *Bare'syth* / Genesis. And it is here that we learn that He wants us to circumcise our sons as a sign to demonstrate that we are set apart unto God and are committed to raising our children within this unique relationship.

The seventh word of God's first sentence is *'erets*. Its primary definitions include: "land, region, territory, earth," or "material realm," which is the preferred rendering in this declaration because it speaks of the physical universe. In this context, *'erets* cannot represent our solar system, the planet, 'Eden, or Yisra'el because these things wouldn't come to exist for another ten billion years – although they are all derivative parts of the physical universe.

'Erets is the fourth most prevalent noun in the Towrah and Prophets. It is found an astonishing 2,500 times to describe related concepts which often differ in location and scale. At the heart of *'erets* is a concept both small and large of the "natural material," especially the "minute physical particles of matter" from which men, the land, earth, and the universe are comprised. Its root means "to be firm," associating it with that which is tangible, physical, and material as opposed to spiritual. Therefore, in this declarative statement, at this time and in this context, the most natural and appropriate way to distinguish between *shamaym* and *'erets*, is to differentiate *shamaym* and *'erets* as the spiritual and material realms.

It is important to acknowledge that the first people who heard this message had no concept of planet Earth, much less any notion of what comprised the other planets, moon, sun, or abundance of stars. It is likely that they would have understood *'erets* as the material world beneath their feet, as the ground itself. And they would have seen the heavens as the opposite of that which they could touch, as the abode of God, and as the place they wanted to be welcomed into at the end of their mortal life.

So long as this distinction was between physical and spiritual, their perceptions would have been accurate and meaningful. And yet today, blessed as we are with a worldview and with a partial understanding of the universe, we can deduce a much bigger and more profound sense of these words. In that way, Yahowah's Word is meaningful to all people throughout time.

Bringing it all together, the first seven words reveal…

"In (*ba* – near, within certain limits of, and in proximity to, regarding the account of) **the beginning** (*re'shyth* – at the start of time and the initiation of the process of existence, concerning the first fruits of the labors of the head of the family, while addressing the thing which is of first and foremost importance; from *ro'sh* – the head, the top and uppermost, the sum and total, first and beginning)**, the Almighty** (*'elohym* – God)**, in proximity to while closely associated with** (*'eth 'eth* – for the purpose of a relationship and close association)**, created** (*bara'* – conceived and caused a new existence, choosing perfect transformation and birth, planning, preparing, shaping, producing, and fashioning something out of the elements and making it happen) **the** (*ha*) **spiritual world** (*shamaym* – heavens and abode of God) **and** (*wa*) **the** (*ha*) **material realm** (*'erets* – matter, the physical and natural world)." (*Bare'syth* / In the Beginning / Genesis 1:1)

In this light, let's take a moment to ponder the massiveness of our earthly spaceship and its intergalactic home. There is a reason for its enormous scale in energy, space, and time. It had to be precisely as it is for us to exist temporally as stardust transformed into life, and for us to have the option to choose greater dimensions, to be reborn in the Spirit of Light.

Should *any* aspect of the universe as it was conceived differ by so much as one part in a million (1 in 10^{120}), the ripple effect on every other aspect would cause the cosmos to implode. We could not and would not exist – nor could any form of life. While this does not prove the role of a creator, it does demonstrate just how marvelously creation is tuned for our existence.

In our present form, trapped in the flow of time, humankind will never visit another planet, much less leave our solar system. Three-dimensional mass cannot be accelerated to the speed of light because the faster something moves, the greater its mass becomes. If an object were to reach the speed of light, its mass would become infinite, filling the entire universe.

Further, to move an infinite mass would take an infinite amount of energy – more energy than there is in the universe. Therefore, no material object can attain the speed of light, leaving the universal distances at 93 billion light-years across, far too great to navigate – even in a billion lifetimes. Complicating the matter, not only is the preponderance of the known universe beyond our reach, but because the most distant stars are moving away from us faster than the speed of light due to the stretching of space, even if we could travel at the speed of light – a physical impossibility – we still wouldn't be able to reach them.

Our only hope of exploring the universe is to become greater than we are and eternal like our Creator. When that happens, when we become akin to light, we will embark on a grand voyage. There are over 100 billion galaxies, each averaging 100 billion stars to explore. Many, if not most, are replete with solar systems, planets, and moons.

Therefore, when we avail ourselves of the Covenant's promises and our souls are empowered such that we become spiritual beings, we will be able to travel through time and thus explore the vastness and brilliance of Yahowah's creative genius. We will become like God and enjoy the photon's perspective where, from its point of reference while traversing enormous distances (186,282 miles per second), it requires no time to do so. Since speed is the rate at which an object covers distance over time, when time does not move, the velocity, which is the degree at which the position changes, becomes infinite. From the human perspective on Earth, a photon of light requires 93 billion years to traverse the cosmos, while from the photon's perspective, it would occur in an instant.

Not only is the vast scale of our universe instructive, demonstrating the need for a designer, but its minute scale is also thought-provoking. The molecular realm diminishes in scale equally rapidly and marvelously. The micro realm is comprised of molecules, atoms, electrons, and quarks retreating infinitely inward beyond our vision. This suggests that our eternal investigations may one day be limitless in all directions and dimensions. This is why even agnostic scientists are anthropocentric – recognizing that man is actually at the center of the universe with regard to its scale, and that the cosmos was tuned precisely for human existence. But why was it tuned for us and by whom, are the questions we are exploring?

‏לֶאֱוֹהַ‎

Before we turn the page and consider Yahowah's second sentence, since our initial chapter was based upon the "creative, renewing, and transforming" aspects of *bara'*, let's ponder its implications relative to God's prime objective: His Covenant. We will be enriched.

Bara' conveys an essential aspect of the Covenant's role in Yahowah's plans. And the best way to understand God's Word is to observe how He uses His words.

Bara' was deployed in conjunction with cutting the Covenant in *Shemowth* / Names / Exodus 34:10. Long after the universe had been created, long after the Covenant had been established with 'Abraham, and in the immediate aftermath of Yahowah's liberation of His children from the crucible of human religious and political oppression in Egypt, we find God reestablishing His relationship with *beny Yisra'el* | the Children of Israel through His prophet and shepherd *Moseh* | Moses.

The path to *bara'* begins…

"Then (*wa* – so and in addition), **Yahowah** (*Yahowah* – the proper pronunciation of YaHoWaH, our *'elowah* – God as directed in His *ToWRaH* – teaching regarding His *HaYaH* – existence and our *ShaLoWM* – restoration) **descended** (*yarad* – He came down, lowered and diminished Himself, and He bowed down, coming from a higher dimension to a lower one) **in** (*ba* – within certain limits positioned in proximity to) **the visible mass of condensed water vapor** (*ha 'anan* – the relatively dense and opaque occlusion within the atmosphere of moisture or smoke sufficient to block most of the light, similar to a cloud) **and stood** (*wa yatsab* – made a commitment to appear, present Himself, and take a stand) **with him** (*'im huw'* – in association with him and in a close relationship with him) **there** (*shem* – here and by name, close by to be properly known).

And he called out to, summoned, and proclaimed (*qara'* – he recited aloud, invited, welcomed, encountered, and announced) **Yahowah** (*YaHoWaH* – an accurate presentation of the name of *'elowah* – God as guided by His *towrah* – instructions regarding His *hayah* – existence) **by name** (*ba shem* – with the personal and proper designation)." (*Shemowth* / Names / Exodus 34:5)

If you are accustomed to viewing God from a religious perspective, there are many surprises here. First, God had to diminish an aspect of Himself to meet with a man. Had He not done so, the power of His presence would have incinerated Moseh. According to the implications of *yarad* and *yatsab*, Yahowah "diminished Himself" to "take a stand" alongside Moseh, concepts which are incompatible with religion.

Yahowah wants us to pronounce His name, to call out to Him by His name, to summon Him as we come to know Him. Those who do not use His name do not know Him. Those who do not invite Yahowah into their lives by name are estranged from Him.

Even more than pronouncing Yahowah's name and calling out to Him, *qara'* serves as the basis of *miqra'* – the title Yahowah chose to represent His seven "Invitations to be Called Out and Meet." They provide the path Home, opening the doorway to Heaven.

Now that Moseh had followed God's instructions, and had summoned God by name:

"**And** (*wa* – so) **Yahowah** (*Yahowah* – written as directed by His *towrah* – teaching regarding His *hayah* – existence) **led him so He could send him** (*'abar* – extended Himself toward him then passed over him to remove his transgressions) **on account of and alongside** (*'al* – along with, before, and by) **His presence** (*paneh huw'* – His appearance)." (*Shemowth* / Names / Exodus 34:6 (in part))

Passover is the first of seven steps Home. It opens the doorway to Heaven and is required for us to exist in Yahowah's presence. It was conceived to make us immortal. Here, the root of Pesach, *'abar*, was used to reveal that Yahowah was going to extend Himself to lead Moseh, thereby sending him to liberate His captive children.

The promise of a forgiving and compassionate God offering undeserved and unbounded mercy, who is longsuffering and loving, is neither recent nor religious. He has always been there for us, waiting in His words and ready to respond. These benefits are inherent in the Covenant and describe Yahowah's primary intent in creation. His desire to share these things is why we exist.

Best of all, the God who conveyed His personality and inner nature to us through Moseh in the Towrah is trustworthy and reliable, dependable and steadfast. He is what He has always been. His offer to provide these benefits remains unchanged and unwavering.

"**And he called out, summoned, and proclaimed** (*wa qara'* – he recited aloud, invited, welcomed, greeted, and announced), **'Yahowah** (*Yahowah* – a transliteration of 𐤉𐤄𐤅𐤄, our *'elowah* – God as directed in His *towrah* – teaching regarding His *hayah* – existence), **Yahowah** (𐤉𐤄𐤅𐤄), **Almighty God** (*'el* – the Mighty One) **of benevolent, favorable, and forgiving, compassionate and affectionate relationships** (*rachuwm* – generous and kind, deeply devoted and caring, tender and passionate, advantageous and dedicated personal interactions; from *racham* – deeply loving and friendly, sympathetic and concerned associations) **and genuine mercy** (*wa chanuwn* – in addition to a heartfelt response to intervene and give an undeserved gift to those He befriends, predisposed to bestowing blessings; from *chanan* – merciful), **longsuffering and slow to anger** (*'arek 'aph* – patient and enduring, not prone to resentment; persevering), **in addition to abounding** (*wa rab* – considerable and abundant, pertaining to the upper end of the scale, tremendously great) **in steadfast love and unfailing devotion** (*chesed* – providing benefits, goodness and kindness, enduring affection, and favorable relationships), **while completely trustworthy and reliable** (*wa 'emeth* – true, dependable, honest, sure, supportive, confirming, unwavering, and unchanging, and thus absolutely certain)." (*Shemowth* / Names / Exodus 34:6)

Moseh knew Yahowah personally. God spoke directly with him. He inspired him to write the Towrah and revealed many prophetic insights through him. Therefore, Moseh's depiction of Yahowah is as wonderful as it is reliable.

Yahowah, the God of the Covenant, the Voice of the Towrah, our Creator, is "compassionate, forgiving, merciful, patient, devoted, honorable, and dependable." With the actual, living God being all of these things, what was the purpose of creating religious gods?

"Loyal love and unfailing devotion (*chesed* – providing benefits, goodness and kindness, enduring affection, and favorable relationships) **spares, protects, and preserves** (*natsar* – watches over, guards, saves, keeps, and maintains within an observant and protective relationship) **so that** (*la* – enabling the approach of) **the thousands who learn and adopt the instruction as their own** (*ha 'eleph* / *'aleph* – the thousand-fold who are discerning, and become familiar, then teach the tribes, imparting wisdom through evidence and reason while urging others to respond promptly so as to be increased a thousand-fold) **will be raised, supported, sustained, and carried away** (*nasa'* – will be lifted up and forgiven) **from widespread religious rebellion** (*pesha'* – from societal revolt against the established standard and defiance against the authority figure, from being liable and invalidated as a result of being contrary), **from that which distorts, corrupts, and perverts** (*wa 'awon* – from that which twists and warps and is therefore wrong, depravity from which guilt and punishment are incurred), **and from missing the Way** (*wa chata'ah* – as well as from having been on a wrong and incorrect path).

They will be pardoned and vindicated (*wa naqah* – they will be considered innocent, released from the consequence of what has been done, and not left destitute, they will not be banished or punished (piel infinitive – the individual acquitted is acted upon by God in a demonstrable way)) **while counting and recording** (*paqad* – taking stock and inventory of while holding accountable), **and not pardoning or forgiving** (*lo' naqah* – not leaving alone or exempting from punishment), **that which corrupts, distorts, and perverts** (*'awon* – guilt from twisting and warping as a consequence of being wrong) **of fathers** (*'ab* – of parents) **on sons** (*'al beny* – over children), **and on their son's sons** (*wa 'al beny beny*– with regard to their children's children) **to the third and fourth generation** (*'al shileshym wa 'al ribea'* –

addressing sons, grandsons, and great-grandsons)." (*Shemowth* / Names / Exodus 34:7)

One of the benefits of amplification, which is the process of using as many words as are appropriate to convey the full extent of the intended thought, is that when we come upon a word which can be vocalized in different ways, like "*'eleph* – thousands" and "*'aleph* – learn," both connotations can be conveyed. And while God may have intended one over the other, preferring learning and teaching over thousands, both fit the context and both renderings are consistent with Yahowah's previous and subsequent instructions.

What's particularly interesting here is that God just provided considerable specificity regarding the three types of crimes which we would otherwise be held accountable: "widespread religious rebellion which leads societies astray," "distorting, corrupting, and twisting" His testimony, and "missing the way." If we are among the thousands who adopt His teaching and embrace it, we will be among those He will lift up and raise as His children. What is surprising is how relatively few individuals will capitalize upon His instructions and benefit from the "love" and "mercy" which "spares, protects, and preserves those who are observant in a protective relationship."

Yahowah etched this same realization in stone as part of His Second Statement. He said that thousands, which among billions is just one in a million, would benefit from His mercy by closely examining and carefully considering the terms and conditions of His relationship agreement. Numbering those who will be saved from man's oppressive religious schemes in the thousands, as opposed to millions or billions, should send shivers down the spines of religious Jews, Christians, and Muslims. There are millions and billions of them.

31

The conclusion of this message is one that mankind doesn't want to hear. People don't want to accept responsibility for corrupting and perverting Yahowah's message with religious schemes or acknowledge the consequence on children into future generations. But Orthodox Jews breed Orthodox sons and daughters. And Christian parents raise Christian children. The same is true with children born into socialist secular Humanist societies.

Yahowah provided and enabled the path from mankind's oppressive religious and political world to His Home where we can live forever. But the path is narrow, specific, restrictive, and very unpopular. Few find it. Fortunately for you, and for those you love, you are now looking in the right place.

As we move ahead to the next statement, we find that Moseh was pleading with God. He knew that his people deserved to be abandoned for their infidelity. They had acted like today's Christians, Muslims, and Jews, and had mocked the Creator, and His willingness to save them, by worshiping something they, themselves, had created. He was asking God for forgiveness, for a second chance. And that would require two things: God responding based upon His nature, not man's nature, and a different attitude toward Him. So...

"**Moseh** (*Mosheh* – One who Draws Out) **impulsively and anxiously** (*mahar* – hurriedly and emotionally, demonstrating considerable distress regarding the future, while clearly disturbed) **inclined himself toward** (*qadad* – may have knelt down as he was motivated by thoughts of) **the earth** (*'erets* – the territory, region, and land) **and of his own accord tried to explain** (*chawah* – verbally explained, communicated, and declared with words, independently informing while making known (hitpael imperfect – speaking of his own accord without being

32

influenced by anyone, neither being predisposed or assisted in this regard)), (34:8) **saying** (*'amar* – expressing),

'Please, I am pleading with You (*na'* – I am requesting of You because it is my desire), **if** (*'im* – as a concession) **I have found** (*matsa'* – if I have attained) **favor** (*chen* – mercy, and considered fondly, deserving compassion) **in your eyes** (*ba 'ayn 'atah* – in Your sight and from Your perspective), **my Upright One** (*'edon 'any* – my Upright Pillar and my Foundation, my firm and established base), **would You reconsider and travel** (*na halak 'edon 'any* – it is my desire and request that You, Sir, walk) **in our midst** (*ba qereb 'anachnuw* – among us)?

Indeed, it is true (*ky* – because surely), **the people** (*'am* – the members of this family) **are stiff-necked, stubborn, and difficult** (*qasheh 'oreph huw'* – hard-headed, and harsh, trying and perplexing, obstinate and vehement), **but You can forgive** (*wa salach* – You can pardon and remove) **our propensity to be wrong** (*la 'awon 'anachnuw* – our tendency to pervert the message and engage in depravity, becoming incorrect by twisting, corrupting, and distorting things) **and miss the Way** (*wa la chata'ah 'anachnuw* – regarding our offenses against the standard), **and provide us with an inheritance** (*wa nahal 'anachnuw* – and then You can accept us as Your heirs)." (*Shemowth* / Names / Exodus 34:8-9)

Moseh was naturally embarrassed for his people, which is why he was so anxious, something Yahowah neither desired nor acknowledged. However, he did not "worship" God as most every English Bible proclaims. This false notion is derived by inappropriately translating *chawah* as such when its primary meaning is "to tell, to explain, to verbally communicate, announce, inform, and declare," all of which fit the context.

Moseh was quite literally imploring Yahowah, asking Him to forgive one of the most inappropriate and revolting acts in human history. After being miraculously freed from the most powerful and oppressive nation on Earth, the Children of Yisra'el showed their true nature by creating and worshiping a false god.

Speaking of fraudulent representations, our ears are more accustomed to hearing "my Lord," a translation of *'adony*, than they are to hearing "Upright One" or "Upright Pillar," which are from *'edon*. *'Adon* and *ba'al* mean "lord" in Hebrew, and because they serve to define Satan's ambition, Yahowah uses them as the Adversary's name and title. *'Edown* speaks of the "Upright Pillar" of cloud and then of fire which traveled with the Children of Yisra'el from this day forward, honoring Moseh's request.

More telling still, *'edown* is descriptive of the upright pillar placed in the center of the Tabernacle of the Witness. Therefore, in this case, the more familiar " *'adony* – my Lord" depiction is " *'awon* – an errant corruption" which causes people to "*chata'ah* – miss the Way." And the " *'edon* – Upright One" designation is the only one who can "*naqah* – forgive and pardon" us.

Before we move on, let's consider Moseh's evaluation of the Yisra'elites in his company circa 1450 BCE. He said, "Indeed, it is true that the people are stiff-necked, hard-headed, and stubborn, both perplexing and obstinate." It would be fair to say, at least considering how few *Yahuwdym* | Jews acknowledge Yahowah and follow His guidance, that not much has changed in the past three and a half millennia other than that the relationship has degraded politically and religiously.

Yet even then, as now, Moseh recognized that Yahowah "can forgive our propensity to be wrong and miss the Way." Should we do our part, Yahowah remains willing and able to "provide us with an inheritance" – one we find by engaging in the Covenant.

This enlightening excursion brings us to the passage in which Yahowah used "*bara'* – create" in conjunction with trying to reestablish His Covenant with children who had already turned their backs on Him. So, long after the universe had been created, long after the Covenant had been established with 'Abraham, and in the immediate aftermath of His children's rebellion, we find God renewing His relationship with His wayward family. And in this declaration, we find Yahowah doing far more than Moseh had asked...

"**And He said** (*wa 'amar* – then God replied)**, 'Behold, here and now** (*hineh* – look up and pay attention)**, I am cutting** (*'any karat* – I am establishing by confirming through separation) **a Familial Covenant Relationship** (*beryth* – a family agreement based upon a binding oath and promise; from *beyth* – family and home) **and conspicuously announcing it before** (*neged* – in the presence of) **all of your people** (*kol 'am 'atah* – your entire family)**.

I will act and engage, doing** (*'asah* – I will perform, bringing about) **wonderful and marvelous things** (*pala'* – amazing and extraordinary acts which are awe-inspiring to fulfill that which is exceedingly special) **which relationally** (*'asher* – to show the way to the benefits of the relationship and provide guidance to get the greatest joy out of life) **have not been conceived nor created** (*lo' bara'* – have not been begotten or fashioned, nor have they previously existed) **throughout the earth** (*ba kol 'erets* – in all the material realm) **nor among any of the people from different races and places** (*ba kol gowym* – in any other nation or ethnicity)**.

And the entire family** (*wa kol ha 'am* – so all of the people) **will see** (*ra'ah* – will be shown, consider, and perceive (qal perfect – literally at this moment in time)) **who** (*'asher* – is leading the way to the blessings and benefits of the relationship) **is in your midst** (*'atah ba* *qereb* – is among you): **Yahowah** (𐤉𐤄𐤅𐤄 – a transliteration of *YaHoWaH* as instructed in His *towrah* – teaching regarding His *hayah* – existence), **He is doing this work** (*huw' 'eth ma'aseh* – He is engaged, expending the energy to accomplish what must be done).

Indeed (*ky* – truthfully and by contrast) **it will be awe-inspiring** (*yare' huw'* – it will be awesome, engendering respect and reverence) **what I will do when engaged and acting with you to lead you along the proper path** (*'asher 'asah 'im 'atah* – what, to show the correct way to receive life's most rewarding benefits I will bring about and accomplish in conjunction with and together with you (qal participle masculine singular absolute – Yahowah acting alone will literally accomplish such that He is described and known by His actions)).'" (*Shemowth* / Names / Exodus 34:10)

Yahowah was not kidding. This is the most extraordinary response a beggar has ever received. Moseh had pleaded with God, imploring Him to overlook the fact that the Children of Yisra'el had left Egypt, but not their gods. He somehow knew that, in spite of the people's obstinance, Yahowah had a plan to resolve their propensity to miss the way. Sure, they were dead wrong, but God could make them right such that they could still be His heirs. He had implored God to continue with them, and God said that He would do far better than that. He would reconcile the relationship such that they would remain His children.

Yahowah conceived the work He was going to do on behalf of the Covenant and His Family long before this announcement, so the only thing "new" was that His means and methods were previously unknown within the human experience. No pagan god had ever bowed down to or suffered for man, but the only real God would do these wonderful and amazing things.

Yahowah's most "marvelous and astounding" deed was His willingness to support the decision His Son had made to save his people. Dowd would offer to burden his soul with our guilt, taking it to She'owl to personally pay the price required to enable our reconciliation. It is the most amazing episode in the Greatest Story Ever Told.

𐤋𐤅𐤅𐤃

2

Hayah | Existence

The Big Bang...

The second sentence of the Towrah is even more enlightening than the first – especially scientifically. After introducing the concept of *"bara'* – creation," Yahowah said...

"And (*wa* – then) **the material realm** (*ha 'erets* – the physical world and the natural substance of which the universe is comprised, that which is perceived to be solid) **existed** (*hayah* – came to be and was (qal perfect – actually for a finite period of time existed)) **formless, without shape** (*tohuw* – lacking organization, in a state of lifeless confusion, as something which would dissipate into nothingness without additional energy), **an orderless, chaotic, and empty space** (*wa bohuw* – a randomized void, a deserted and unoccupied place, desolate of life), **dark, hidden, obscure, and unknowable** (*wa choshek* – a dark matter, incomprehensible and indecipherable, appearing confusing and black, incapable of being perceived or seen) **in proximity to** (*'al* – along with, upon, and near the spatial position of) **the presence** (*paneh* – the face and appearance of the visible aspects) **of the vast, inexhaustible power and inaccessible, mysterious energy of the big bang** (*tahowm* – of the great commotion from the agitated and loud, enormous and yet controlled explosion, with wave following wave without intermission)." (*Bare'syth* / In the Beginning / Genesis 1:2 (in part))

38

Dissecting God's message, we learn that without light, without Yahowah who is Light, *the* universe, as well as *our* existence, is *"tohuw, bohuw* and *choshek* – lifeless, orderless, and dark." *Tohuw* is "formless confusion, lifelessness and nothingness." It is "chaos which would dissipate into nothingness without energy and intervention." Symbolically, it represents the "idolatry of worthless worship that emanates from false testimony."

Bohuw depicts "a lack of order," of something that appears "random and chaotic." It is descriptive of "an unoccupied place, desolate of life within an empty void."

To be *choshek* is to be "obscured in darkness." It, therefore, speaks of "dark matter," of that which is "hidden and obscure," even "unknowable and incomprehensible." It is so "obscure, it appears indecipherable, absolutely incapable of being seen or perceived."

This was all " *'al paneh* – in proximity to the presence" of "*tahowm* – the vast, inexhaustible power and inaccessible, mysterious energy of the big bang." *Tahowm* speaks of the "great commotion of the agitated and loud, enormous and yet controlled explosion, with wave following wave of light and radiant energy without intermission." *Tahowm* is also the "deep, dark, inaccessible, and inexhaustible place of separation" created for the eternal sorrow of Satan, his fellow demons, and those who league with them. This is a rather profound Spiritual insight.

There are clearly several scientific revelations here. The first comes from the realization that matter is actually nothing more than organized energy. Therefore, the first of four words describing the creative process depicts an energetic state where matter has not yet formed. It is "*tohuw* – lacking organization, formless, and without shape." The transition to matter occurred when the energy emitted to cause the Big Bang cooled sufficiently for quarks to be confined. It was only then that time began to flow. *Tohuw* is, therefore, the perfect word to initiate the process.

By following "*ha 'erets* – the physical and material realm composed of the natural substance of which the universe is comprised, and that which is perceived to be solid," the juxtaposition of "*tohuw* – lacking organization" serves to affirm both their definitions and the science behind them. It leads us to the conclusion that matter does not exist until energy is properly organized. Further, since the text transitions from formless matter to the existence of enormous energy, we begin to see the connection and relationship between them. Matter is a diminished form of energy.

The temperature at which quarks can be confined, changing energy into matter, which is the starting point of time, is the subject of considerable speculation with significant implications regarding the age of the universe. Physicists modeling creation in reverse have calculated that quarks and their particle pals, gluons, can break free from their confinement inside protons and neutrons at 2,000,000,000,000 Kelvin. And while physicists extrapolated from this data that the Big Bang's initial temperature had to be in the range of two trillion Kelvin, scientists have shown through experimentation that free quarks can exist in gluon plasma at seven to ten trillion degrees Fahrenheit (4 to 6 trillion Celsius / Kelvin) which is 300,000 times hotter than the center of the sun – and two to three times hotter than the original estimate of the Big Bang.

That is interesting for several reasons. First, "quark soup" is the transitional state between energy and matter in which, at extremely high temperatures and/or density, the nuclei and electrons, confined within atoms by electrostatic forces at ambient conditions, can move freely. That is to say, they are "*tohuw* – formless and unorganized."

Second, once confined, a quark can never actually be liberated and isolated. Their elastic bands break, destroying the quark and replacing it with a new quark-antiquark pair created out of the energy in the field.

And third, if quark confinement occurs at 4 to 6 trillion Kelvin, then the initial temperature of creation was likely two to three times hotter than originally thought, which would make its post-quark confinement age older than the current assessment of 13.8 billion years. This will become especially relevant when we use these findings to prove that six twenty-four-hour days at creation are equivalent to fifteen billion years looking back in time from the Earth.

The Creation account's second descriptive term is equally insightful scientifically. Before energy in the form of light could be introduced, an area had to be created for it to exist. And that space would have to be enormous and expansive. For life to exist, it would have to be three-dimensional. For time to manifest itself as Albert Einstein demonstrated, the "*bohuw* – empty space" would have to be at least four-dimensional. (It is likely six, but more on that in a moment.)

The space needed is really big. The universe, by our best estimates, is ninety-three billion light-years across, and it is expanding into this "*bohuw* – void" faster than the speed of light, traveling at three hundred million meters per second (precisely 299,792,458 m/s).

When I first wrote this chapter, I noted but did not discuss a fascinating aspect of *bohuw*: chaos. I sidestepped it because its implications seemed contrary to my perception of the multivariable equation God had to solve to know just how much energy He had to introduce to derive the desired result. There was nothing in my mind "*bohuw* – random" about this calculation. With math, no matter how complex, there is an answer.

41

But not this time. There could not be. Without chaos, the entire experiment would have been a colossal waste of time and energy (literally). Had Yahowah known the outcome, had God calculated the result He desired, everything would have been predictable and freewill would have been for naught.

Enter *Bohuw* | Chaos Theory, an interdisciplinary postulate stating: within the apparent randomness of chaotic complex systems, there are underlying patterns, interconnectedness, constant feedback loops, repetition, similarities, connections, and commonality manifesting self-organization. With the apparent randomness of chaos, there could be freewill and individual determination. With the underlying patterns and interconnectedness, it would allow billions of approaches to the same path, thereby making our lives unique, individual, and interesting.

God could be consistent without being boring. We could come together in the desired fashion but as a result of our choices. It would be entertaining, amusing, and exciting, sometimes wonderful, and at other times horrible to watch. With randomness buffered by the underlying patterns, interconnectedness, and feedback loops, we would be able to observe the similarities, note the organizational structure, and deduce the connections which facilitate understanding and thus think our way to God.

Rather than toss out the notion that Yahowah calculated the right amount of energy to introduce into the proper dimensions of space, the multi-variable equation preceding creation presented sufficient complexity to make the process more interesting. And what is especially fascinating, the postulates which comprise chaos theory actually define the process which leads to understanding. The transition from knowing to comprehending is predicated upon making connections between things and recognizing patterns. Our minds seek similarities to file information in the proper place such that it can be retrieved and used appropriately to guide future responses. And it is by repetition that we learn.

Supporting this view, *Bohuw* | Chaos Theory is a branch of mathematics that studies probable outcomes. This statistical analysis of probabilities underpins logical thinking, thus allowing us to use reason to transition from observations to comprehension. We have discovered that apparent disorder is actually governed by deterministic and universal laws of nature and physics which were designed into the initial conditions. And yet, there is still the possibility of the "Butterfly Effect," whereby a small change in one place and time can result in large differences elsewhere, even in a different period or place. As a result, Chaos Theory is used to predict and understand weather and climate change, the stock market, transportation and logistics, the recurrence of patterns of behavior on a national and global scale, artificial intelligence, engineering, economics, anthropology, and pandemic crisis management.

Turning our attention to the third scientific revelation, *choshek* is as descriptive of "dark matter" as is possible within the Hebrew lexicon. Back in 1933, astronomer Fritz Zwicky was the first to discover what scientists now call dark matter. We don't actually know anything about this phenomenon other than its existence and effect. *Choshek* is "obscure and hidden." It is "unknowable and incomprehensible," which is why it is called "dark." Its nature exceeds our capacity to understand, just as a being in two-dimensional flatland would be unable to perceive the infinite expansion and opportunity a third dimension would provide.

Choshek | Dark Matter is attractive in nature, which is why it is described as "matter." Its influence is so prevalent, it represents 27% of the substance of the universe Yahowah created, which is six times greater than the total value of everything we can currently perceive. So, if you have been led to believe that science holds the answers and that God requires faith to believe, you may want to table that thought for a moment.

Yahowah said that "*choshek* – dark matter, that which is hidden and obscure, unknowable and incomprehensible, indeed, indecipherable, appearing confusing and black and incapable of being perceived or seen" was " *'al paneh* – in proximity to the spatial position of the presence and appearance of aspects" of "*tahowm* – the vast, inexhaustible power and inaccessible, mysterious energy of the big bang." Thereupon, we are introduced to dark energy as well as to Yahowah's sense of humor.

Tahowm | Dark Energy is repulsive in nature, exceedingly powerful and prevalent. Representing a staggering 68 to 70% of the universe, it counters the effect of gravity and not only keeps the cosmos from collapsing upon itself, it is the reason behind its expansion. Without it, for example, the furthest any form of energy, not matter, could have traveled from the epicenter of the Big Bang some 15 billion years ago would be 15 billion light-years. Assuming that it was random, as astronomers suggest, we would expect to find a spherical universe 30 billion light-years across. And yet, within the four dimensions of spacetime that we comprehend, the cosmos is flat and over three times that size.

Tahowm is derived from *huwm*, meaning "great movement and noise." Its most fitting definition would be "an enormous explosion, the great commotion from the agitated and loud, massive and yet controlled outburst, with wave following wave of light and radiant energy without intermission," also known as "the big bang." This means that Yahowah coined the term *Tahowm* | Big Bang a few thousand years before the sponsors of mankind's most acclaimed alternative to *Bare'syth* / In the Beginning / Genesis One plagiarized Him. Methinks God is demonstrating a sense of humor.

44

And yet, this is no laughing matter. If you are being reasonable, Yahowah has already garnered your undivided attention. You have surmised that Moseh, the aforementioned stuttering sheepherder, didn't pull the concepts of *tohuw* | formless, *bohuw* | chaos theory, *choshek* | dark matter, and *tahowm* | dark energy and big bang out of the thin desert air atop Mount Choreb. How you respond to this newfound knowledge and understanding is between you and your Maker.

Most people are aware of the Big Bang Theory – or at least the popular sitcom based upon the lives of four Caltech nerds which capitalizes upon its nomenclature. It is a proposition in which the universe is said to have started out a hundred billion times smaller than a photon of light. How one would get that much energy into that small a space is worth pondering, but so is how it got there and who created the space in which it would expand.

It should be noted that according to MIT's *2002 Physics Annual:* "the theory doesn't explain the big bang but instead its aftermath – that period of time in which the universe expanded and cooled. The theory says nothing about the underlying physics of the primordial explosion and provides no clues about when the bang occurred, what caused it to bang, or what happened before it banged.... The explosion theory gives no explanation for the razor-sharp fine-tuning of the universe...and thus does not describe a universe that resembles the one in which we live."

Now that is the kind of honesty they don't typically teach in schools or reveal in the media. That which is purported to be science, and thus is assumed to be testable, even taught as fact, isn't either. And by comparison, Yahowah's testimony is both factual and testable.

The simple truth is, scientists still have more questions than answers and even their conclusions are constantly changing. But do not accept my testimony on this, consider P.J.E. Peebles' conclusion. He is an acknowledged leader in the field of universal beginnings, a professor of Cosmology at Princeton University:

"Cosmology – the study of the beginnings, formation, and evolution of our Universe – is currently in a badly confused state. At the moment, scientists don't know what makes up 99% [more accurately, 96.5%] of the Universe. This, needless to say, is a rather embarrassing situation. Although much of what is visible in the Universe is becoming comprehensible, with great recent strides in understanding star formation, galactic structure, and spectacular events such as supernovae, it would appear that there is another component of the universe – possibly making up most of its mass – which we cannot see, and we do not understand."

If I may beg your indulgence for a moment. Regarding the previous mention of Fritz Zwicky and Caltech, there is something you ought to know – something of which Yahowah is surely aware. Fritz Zwicky was likely Jewish on his father's side. In 1925, when the controversial Nobel Laureate, Robert Millikan, recruited Fritz Zwicky from Switzerland, it was out of character because Millikan and the institution were anti-Semitic. Caltech had their token Jew, German physicist, Paul Epstein. He did not think that the scientific institution would tolerate another Jewish faculty member because they were dependent upon the Christian, Anglo-Saxon population of Southern California for financial support. Although, there was that other Jew, where fame trumped racism because Albert Einstein was invited to serve as a visiting professor from 1930 to 1932.

Speaking of Robert Millikan, while he was the first Caltech professor to win a Nobel Prize, certainly his judgment and character played no role in the committee's selection. Millikan led an organization that advocated the forced sterilization of people with disabilities and actively

46

supported Nazi Germany's 1933 forced sterilization laws. Millikan served on the Board of the Human Betterment Foundation and also worked at the Pasadena, California campus of Caltech. They promoted compulsory sterilization as "the greatest advancement in modern civilization" through "race betterment by eugenic sterilization."

Millikan has recently been charged with "crimes against humanity." A petition to have his name removed from the Caltech campus reads: "It is unconscionable and un-American to place anyone in a position of reverence who was in any way involved in the forced sterilization of African American servicemen and women. The Human Betterment Foundation, housed at Pasadena's California Institute of Technology, played a role in developing the Nuremberg Laws and provided the intellectual underpinning for the extermination of Jews." The Neighborhood Unitarian Universalist Church in Pasadena, which Millikan founded and was a lifelong member, removed his name from the plaques honoring him in 2019.

As for Fritz Zwicky, he was brilliant but not particularly moral. In 1971 he self-published a 23-page rant designed to settle scores with his colleagues. He would brand them: "scatterbrains, sycophants and plain thieves" who "have no love for any of the lone wolves who are not fawners and apple polishers," who "doctor their observational data to hide their shortcomings and to make the majority of the astronomers accept and believe in some of their most prejudicial and erroneous presentations and interpretations of facts," and who therefore publish "useless trash in the bulging astronomical journals." They were charmed, I am sure. Or perhaps not. His colleagues regarded him as "an irritating buffoon" who "promoted goofy notions." And speaking of such, one of his daughters, a born-again Christian, said of dark matter: "I think it's the Lord."

Returning to Someone who does understand, whose judgment and character are impeccable, here is a summation of my translation of Bare'syth 1:2. It reveals that Yahowah was the first to address the scientific concepts of "chaos theory," "dark matter," "dark energy," and the "big bang."

"The natural and material realm existed formless, without shape or organization, random and chaotic in empty space, dark, hidden, obscure, and unknowable as dark matter, incomprehensible and indecipherable, in proximity to the presence of the vast, inexhaustible power and inaccessible, mysterious dark energy of the big bang." (*Bare'syth* / In the Beginning / Genesis 1:2)

If the scientific community only knew where to look, long ago they would have come to recognize that God was explaining what happened, defining the very concepts which frame our study of the universe: "Matter Not Yet Organized," "Chaos Theory," "Dark Matter," "Dark Energy, and "Big Bang." These are things that astronomers and physicists are just beginning to ponder.

In these statements, Yahowah is also introducing the concept of relationship and separation. We must choose which side of the divide we want to be on – darkness, confusion, and lifelessness *or* light, instruction, and life – the family or the void. It should therefore be no surprise then that light, instruction, and life occupy Yahowah's thoughts over the first three days of creation, and that on the fourth day, He presents the ultimate guide to them.

While we are on the subject of God knowing that which man does not know, of God being light, and of man stumbling in the darkness, the most recent tests conducted by the Wilkinson Microwave Anisotropy Probe satellite experiment have affirmed that indeed, dark energy, a repulsive force completely unknown to man, occupies 68 to as much as 73% of the universe, and dark matter, the attractive effect which is equally mysterious and inaccessible to man, represents 23 to 27% of universal content. Thus, our known and testable theories can only account for 4 to 5% of the structure of the cosmos. All we know is that they work together harmoniously such that the universe exists in a manner which is hospitable to life – evidence that suggests intelligent design behind such fine-tuning.

It isn't pertinent to our discussion, but should you be interested, the reason scientists know that a substance they call "Dark Matter" exists is because spiral galaxies are spinning ten times faster than the laws of physics specify, based upon the gravitational effect of their observed mass. And the reason we know that something scientists refer to as "Dark Energy" exists is because the universe's expansion is accelerating. If it were not for an unknown source of enormous energy, the cumulative effect of gravity would slow and then contract the universe – the opposite of what we are observing. Further, "dark" is not a pejorative adjective. It simply means that we are unable to see it, much less understand what it is. These things remain a "mystery, unknowable and inaccessible." Also, as we move forward, keep in mind that "matter" is a form of diminished energy. The ability to transition from one to the other will help us understand much of what Yahowah is sharing with us.

𐤋𐤉𐤄𐤅𐤄𐤉

Before we advance further into Yahowah's testimony, let's establish a more complete foundation so that we can better appreciate what God has to say. In that regard, it is important to recognize that *how* God created the universe was well beyond the comprehension of His initial audience. The languages of astronomy, physics, and

49

calculus, the matrix of spacetime and relativity, the equivalency of energy and matter, and the language of life, DNA, would not be understood for another 3,400 years. Without them, the Towrah's purpose for most of its existence could not explain *how* the universe and life were conceived. Even with these advances, mankind's quest to comprehend our existence remains clouded and unfulfilled. Therefore, for the Creation account to be relevant for all people in all ages, for there to be something all generations could understand and apply regardless of their time or circumstance, there would be equally revealing storylines regarding the who and why of our genesis.

Sadly, these themes are not commonly known. And what is even more egregious is that educational institutions teach incorrect propositions. Fortunately, today we are in a position to appreciate the significance of each message.

For example, in the last thirty years, scientists have discovered that Yahowah was right regarding every important aspect of the beginnings of the universe and of life. The cosmos had a genesis, contrary to what most astronomers believed in the middle part of the 20th century. The universe began with an enormous, practically infinite, concentration of energy in a singular place and time, a big bang, consistent with Yahowah's declaration and terminology. Light was in fact the first thing to exist. This energy would eventually coalesce to form matter. We even find that the universe is stretched out and consists of spacetime, again harmonious with Yahowah's accounting.

Plants preceded animals, and simple forms of life emerged from the sea the moment liquid water existed on the Earth, consistent with Yahowah's assertions but not with Darwin's. Plants and animals are comprised of the elements of the earth, and they literally exploded onto the scene in separate eras, in absolute accordance with the Bare'syth testimony.

The fossil evidence confirms that there was no gradual mutation from simple to complex lifeforms nor was there an evolutionary tree between phyla, the basic categories of life. As we shall discover, Yahowah's witness is accurate. Representatives of each of the thirty-four animal phylum alive today were present among the fossils of the Cambrian Period. They all came to exist, reproduced after their kind, and flourished in their complex forms within a cosmic nanosecond of less than five million years. Insects and fish, vertebrates and invertebrates, complex bone structures and most sophisticated internal organs, even male and female forms all appeared simultaneously in one enormous explosion of life – precisely as Yahowah described it, and in complete discord with macroevolutionary theory.

In fact, it is the macroevolutionary theory which is errant. Not only do harmful mutations (which destroy information) outnumber beneficial ones by a million to one in the genome (genetic structure including chromosomes, genes, and nucleotides), natural selection, acting on the phenome (entire body) rather than the genome, is unable to keep pace, meaning that every animal species is irrevocably degenerating over time – not evolving to become more complex organisms. Further, no scientist has been able to demonstrate that any animal gene mutation has actually added a meaningful amount of new information. While some random mutations have been beneficial, they are insignificant in quantity compared to destructive changes, and they are irrelevant in comparison to the vast differences between species. We will return to this subject (which forms the foundation of the scientific mindset and secular humanism) and discuss it in great detail in the "Chay – Life" chapter.

Yahowah's creation account, barring three potential exceptions, is completely consistent with the evidence mankind has most recently discovered. And yet, high school and college textbooks still cling to the notions scientists have since disproved. Proper science would be advanced in schools if *Bare'syth* / Genesis were understood and taught.

Now do not get me wrong. This will not be a religion versus science debate. I despise the former because clerics are misguided. And I enjoy the latter because the evidence scientists discover almost always points to God, confirming His witness. Such is the case regarding our existence. Yahowah's testimony has not changed in 3,450 years. He was right all along, which is not surprising since He was an eyewitness. It is the late 20th-century scientists who have come full circle. Based on the evidence, they now agree with God, although it remains too painful for most of them to admit it. Moreover, their predecessors, the fathers of modern science – Copernicus, Kepler, Galileo, Newton, and even Darwin and Einstein – were theists, not atheists.

In this light, let's review some scientific highlights that are pertinent to our discussion. We begin by recognizing that without the existence and active engagement of God, or an inconceivably enormous energy system completely unknown to us, the universe could not be expanding at an accelerating pace. Its expansion would slow due to the effect of gravity if there was not an active and enormous source of energy currently at work.

Next, we must consider DNA, the double helix computer code of life. This blueprint is a language, and languages require a creator, a beneficiary, and a purpose. No designer, no language – especially one with billions of character combinations providing instructions to trillions of human cells.

Further, the odds of elements unintentionally, inadvertently, and fortuitously engaging in a manner capable of forming life, and doing so with nutrients available, a means to acquire and process a food source, and a means to reproduce itself, all within the ten-to-fifteen-million-year timeframe this actually occurred, astronomically exceeds the odds beyond reason, beyond belief. Statistically, it is less than one chance in ten to the billionth, billionth power. This probability is so ludicrously extreme, the number exceeds the quantity of fundamental molecular particles in the entire universe by a million billionfold.

Furthermore, since life existed on Earth immediately after liquid water was available, there was no time for random chance in either inception or mutation. Mathematically, biologically, and physically speaking, macroevolution from inorganic matter to complex lifeforms through natural selection rather than intelligent design is so improbable that belief in such a theory ironically requires a blind leap of faith, one that requires ignorance of the evidence and a complete suspension of reason.

Moreover, the universe is clearly built around man in scale, substance, and tuning. It retreats inwardly just as significantly as it expands outwardly. Life requires the specific elements, parameters, and behaviors which resulted from the Big Bang. According to current scientific models, if any one of a thousand physical aspects differed by as little as one part in 10^{120th} power, life could not exist in any form. Therefore, our reality is both consistent with God having created the universe for man and inconsistent with random chance.

There are three places where some may envision *Bare'syth* / Genesis to be in conflict with the still touted, yet irrational and unverifiable theory of non-causal creation and random chance macroevolution. They are as follows:

First, the Towrah speaks of microevolution, of all phyla replicating after their kind. It does not advocate macroevolution, which is the progression of chemicals to amoebas to humans by chance. In support of God's position, there is but one transitional body form in the fossil record (archaeopteryx – which is the one that the prophets anticipated us finding, which is a blend between bird and reptile), though there would have to be millions of transitional fossils for macroevolution to be accurate.

Further, the second law of thermodynamics, the notion of entropy, that disorder and randomness evolve in closed systems, or that systems mutate from ordered complexity to confused disarray without outside influence, has always served as macroevolution's death certificate. This law states that information is lost, not gained, in transmitted messages and that there is a universal tendency for all matter and energy to evolve toward an inert and deteriorated state. Animals evolve downward, losing genetic information with time, consistent with the laws of thermodynamics.

The second perceived difference between creation and science is the early timing of water on day one and its emphasis on the second day of *Bare'syth*. But even here, God's testimony is accurate. He is not talking about liquid water on Earth but instead interstellar molecular clouds. When we apply the lessons of relativity to creation, day one covers seven to eight billion years from our perspective, and the second day, three-and-a-half to four billion years.

Calibrated to the perspective of the witness, the focus on water during these stages is essential. Water is the second most abundant molecule in the universe, ranking only behind molecular hydrogen, H_2. Interstellar clouds are especially loaded with it, and they serve as the maternity wards of the universe where new stars, planets, and comets are born. Moreover, water is the central ingredient in all organic systems, which is why scientists look for it first when searching for extraterrestrial life. Therefore, in *Bare'syth* / Genesis, water takes its rightful and scientifically accurate position in its contribution to the birth of stars on day one, in our solar system on the second day, and in the emergence of plant life on the third day.

But there is more to it: water plays a crucial role during this period of our spiritual development as well as in man's history. So its inclusion makes perfect sense when the creation account is seen depicting the *why* of creation and the *when* of our salvation, replete with Yahowah's plan of redemption. Water is the Towrah's primary metaphor for the purification of human souls. Moreover, in the second millennium of human history, the waters of the flood were used to purge corruption from the region surrounding the Garden. We will detail how these events relate to the Bare'syth account as the days unfold.

The third perceived conflict between science and the Towrah is the most glaring. If the fourth day were about the creation of the sun and the moon, it is out of place. Vegetation, which is said to have blossomed on the third day, could not have existed without the sun.

However, if as God shall demonstrate, the fourth day is the fourth millennium in the story of man's reconciliation after expulsion from 'Eden, then its "signs, signals, and remembrances" are precisely where they must be – tied directly to the arrival of the Passover Lamb and the fulfillment of the first three Mow'ed Miqra'ey in year 4000 Yah (33 CE).

Additionally, God does not say that He *created* the sun, moon, and stars during the fourth day. He said that they would be "signs" and thus would be *visible* at this time.

Scientifically speaking, the Bare'syth testimony is an accurate chronological depiction of what actually occurred. The sun had existed for billions of years before the atmospheric debris from the onslaught of volcanic activity and the aftermath of countless asteroid impacts settled sufficiently for the sun to be seen. The dust cleared and plants gradually filtered out the carbon dioxide that had been spewed into the air, creating and transforming the atmosphere into the oxygen-rich and nearly transparent condition which exists today. The sun and moon could finally be *seen* in the fourth era of universal creation.

Also pertinent, we find in the fossil record that there is a billion-year gap between the "earth bringing forth simple plant life" and the emergence of complex "sea animals which exploded onto the scene," using the parlance of Bare'syth. This gap is acknowledged in God's accounting. Further, having the creation of plant and animal life separated by a cosmological epoch enables Yahowah to devote the fourth day to a different form of life – eternal and spiritual life.

The biggest barrier for most people, however, between science and the Towrah, is it's obvious that all of this could not have occurred in six Earth days. Unfortunately, most everyone deals with the conundrum by either accepting the impossible as fact or by discrediting the *Bare'syth* / Genesis account, and therefore all of the prophets along with it. Not only are both choices errant, but they also lead away from God.

On the subject of a cosmological day, over the course of the first three chapters, we'll reveal how the universe can be both six days and approximately 14 billion years old – depending upon the perspective of the witness. But for now, appreciate the fact that the best current estimation of cosmological age is 13.8 billion years. (Although, HD140283, known as the Methuselah star, has been measured by the European Space Agency's Hipparcos satellite at 16 billion years old. Curiously, not only is it our cosmic neighbor in the constellation Libra and just 190 light-years from Earth, but it also travels across the sky at a staggering 800,000 mph.)

There are two primary astronomical methods of measure for universal age, pulsars and redshift, but they both employ a substantial array of unproven and even untestable assumptions. For example, we know that the universe has not been constant, as it is always changing, and consistency is required for either method to render a reasonable result. In addition, both astronomical calculations are forced to speculate regarding the composition of 96% of the universe, rendering our conclusions based upon the observable 4 to 5%.

This known and assumptions aside, man's most enlightened guesstimate, inclusive of studies of carbon dating, star evolution, and nuclear fuel consumption is that the universe was created in a "Big Bang" close to 13.8 billion years ago when energy was first transformed into matter.

The lower end of that range is all too often touted as being factually accurate and confirmed. However, there are three problems with that assessment. First, there is no telling how much time passed for the initial explosion to cool sufficiently for quarks to confine and time to commence. Second, the temperature conducive to the formation of matter, marking the beginning of time, could be as cool as 2 trillion Kelvin or as hot as 6 trillion degrees. Third, the universe is 93 billion light-years in diameter, not 27.6 light-years, and there are stars with apparent ages exceeding 15 billion years.

The initial galactic formation stage lasted just shy of eight billion years. Our planet, orbiting around a second-generation star, was formed 4.5 billion years ago. The first signs of plant life on Earth manifested themselves shortly thereafter as liquid water formed on the surface. These plants produced oxygen, helping to clear the atmosphere two billion years ago. This provided the catalyst needed for the emergence of more complex and energy-dependent animals one billion years later.

As you may have noticed, these events not only parallel the Bare'syth testimony, but they also occurred in the same order God specified. Equally important, the duration of each cosmological epoch became successively shortened at the rate of what is known as nature's spiral. Each successive epoch is approximately half the duration of the one which preceded it.

While it would be too premature at this point to get into a discussion on the longevity of man's time on Earth, the evidence indicates that *Homo sapiens* have existed a hundred thousand years or more. In the "*'Eden* – Joy*"* chapter, we will discuss why this too is completely harmonious with God's testimony.

Since we have broached the subject of "testability," there are two popular and contemporary myths I would like to bust. First, despite secular humanist claims to the contrary, many of the scientific theories taught in schools as "science," which by their definition comprise those things which can be empirically tested, cannot, in fact, be validated. Even worse, many, if not most of man's cosmological, molecular, and biological evolutionary theories are in conflict with the empirical evidence and reason. While we know many things, most of the fundamentals currently escape our grasp.

For example, we don't know how many dimensions actually exist. Some scientists claim two within a holographic construct, the mundane say three, relativists claim four inclusive of time, but the more adventurous string theorists promote seven to ten. Based upon what I've learned over the past twenty-two years of translation and thought, I think the universe is six-dimensional and was created by Yahowah in the seventh dimension.

Mankind does not actually know how many forces are operating within these unknown dimensions. Electricity and magnetism are both forces, but they not only change from one form to another in moving fields, but they also coexist in light, which is not a force. Gluons are thought to generate the strong nuclear force, holding quarks together, but explanations of how that occurs require untestable String Theory in which the math itself is too complex to formulate or calculate. According to the theory, as many as 10^{60th} colors, or variations, of these invisible rascals are needed to rationalize our reality.

Gravity remains a complete mystery to scientists, with Quantum Theory and Relativity mired in irresolvable conflict as to what generates its attraction. The first calls it a force but cannot qualify the mechanism and the second says it's an effect. Within this macro realm, ninety percent of the universe's energy cannot be accounted for within the matrix of spacetime or within the assumed construct of three to five fundamental forces. And that means that our calculations regarding the Big Bang theory, apart from an intelligent designer and instigator, are errant by 96%. Only arrogant fools would postulate a theory as being "true" when it is in fact 96% invalid.

Turning to molecular constructs, there is no assurance that quarks and gluons represent the minutest atomic particles, but only that something smaller in scale eludes our ability to detect it or them. More befuddling still, there is no assurance these or any particles actually exist. The material world could be, and probably is, nothing more than organized manifestations of energy with everything in motion.

On the biological front, every attempt to mathematically demonstrate that life, given enough time, could have emerged by random chance from inorganic matter has failed. The fossil record of the Cambrian period confirms that the two billion years needed for the improbable to become probable has evaporated by at least 99%, thereby rendering man's conclusions errant once again. Further, in the transition from plant to animal life, macroevolutionary theory predicts the opposite of what we have observed. Rather than a single and simple animal body type gradually coming to exist from which all others eventually evolved, every animal phylum known today burst onto the scene at the same time.

Without a Creator there is no way to explain the development of life's extraordinarily complex blueprint, the quaternary language of cell communication, DNA. And the simultaneous existence of male and female forms occurring in one species, much less every species, by random chance and evolutionary mutation is absurd. Moreover, even if these things could be miraculously resolved, science still has no concept of what consciousness is or how it came to exist. Nothing is more fundamental to life.

Therefore, the core building blocks of cosmological, molecular, and biological science remain mysterious and untestable. Scientific assumptions not only have not been proven, but they also cannot be tested, and those which can be demonstrated have been found to be wrong. And that would explain why secular humanists do not want intelligent design taught in schools. They know that their theories will not stand up to scrutiny. But it begs the question: why are the promoters of the West's liberal and communal religion so arrogant as to say that they are right and that God is wrong when the opposite is actually true?

That leads us to the second myth. All of these things, and especially the existence of the male and female forms, are explained in *Bare'syth* / Genesis, with God providing His rationale for everything He did. Moreover, the notion that is advanced in popular culture, that the Towrah and Prophets cannot be tested and therefore cannot be taught as science, is not accurate.

Yahowah's Word can be validated. God even told us how to do so in *Dabarym* / Deuteronomy 18: rely on the accuracy of His prophetic predictions. Yahowah inspired men to document His account of future history centuries and millennia before the events they foretold occurred. He provided us with tangible evidence of their existence – proof in the form of a paper trail of His prophetic proclamations. We can therefore test His witness against the ledger of history and archeology.

By checking to see if each prediction was fulfilled exactly when, where, and how the prophets predicted it would occur, as evidenced by archeology and recorded history, we create a testable environment consistent with scientific theory. Then using statistical analysis, we can compute the probability of these events unfolding as they were foretold by random chance versus the actual foreknowledge of the Author. In the "Playing the Odds" chapter of *Tea with Terrorists,* we calculated the probability that twenty very specific prophecies could have been fulfilled randomly. I chose these because, with the Dead Sea Scrolls, we possess actual written copies of God's predictions that predate the forecast enactment as well as eyewitness records of the fulfillment. The odds against Yahowah being this "lucky" were at least 10, 000, 000, 000, 000, 000, 000, 000, 000, 000, 000, 000, 000, 000, 000, 000, 000, 000, 000, 000, 000, 000 to one – more commonly known as impossible. Mathematicians call odds worse than one in 10 to 50th a "mathematical absurdity."

Testing aside, there is another measure of proof. Consider the fact that God's testimony regarding the creation of life and the universe was revealed over 3,450 years ago, and yet it is accurate. The scientific assumptions over that period have been reassessed a thousand times, with each new theory repudiating the prior one. The moral of this story is that it is wise to trust someone who has consistently told us the truth.

That said, the universe is not 6,000 years old as the Creationists advocate. When they postulate such nonsense, they embarrass themselves and prevent many from trusting the lone Source that can explain the existence of life but can also provide the means to sustain it. Moreover, they affirm that their god is a deceiver, someone who would make that which is relatively recent appear ancient just to toy with us.

ᛈᛇᛈᛄ

The word for "day" used in Bare'syth is *yowm*. It is based upon an unused root meaning "to be hot." *Yowm* can mean "daytime, an undisclosed period of time, and even a year," or simply "warm." As a day, *yowm* can last from sunrise to sunset, from sunrise to sunrise, or from sunset-to-sunset, as is Yah's custom. A *yowm* is "a lifetime, an indefinite period in time, a generic temporal reference, today, yesterday, or tomorrow." It is only a twenty-four-hour period of time when *yowm* is modified by the definite article or by a cardinal number. In the Towrah, Prophets, and Psalms, *yowm* is translated: "afternoon, age, always, chronicles, continually, daily, day, days, first, forever, life, long, period, time, today, when, year, and years," on multiple occasions.

This known, I have a confession to make. Not long ago I viewed the creation account through this lens. I considered *yowm* to designate a general period of time or an unspecified era. But live and learn: time is not a constant, and like matter, it did not always exist. Time is relative, differing considerably in relation to the velocity, energy, and/or mass of one observer or in the proximity of one observer relative to another. At the velocity of light, for example, time seems to stand still as all time exists simultaneously.

As we progress in this study, with the help of physicists, we shall prove scientifically that from Yahowah's vantage point at creation, not only is the universe six twenty-four-hour days old, but that each day uses a natural spiral to lay out a timeline from light to life over the course of nearly 15 billion years looking back in time from our perspective. If proving Yahowah's existence, validating His testimony, coming to know what He is offering and expects in return are of value to you, then you will come to prize this realization due to the implications it will have on your life.

But there is more because, as I have shared, the Bare'syth revelation is three stories in one. In addition to creation, Yahowah is providing us with an accounting of our reconciliation and of human history. Therefore, to appreciate how and when the events unfolded, and to understand Yahowah's timeline past and present, we will search the prophets for further elucidation. And for that, there is no better place than the 90th Psalm.

In the 90th Mizmowr, Moseh (commonly known as Moses, meaning: to draw out) provides us with the quantification of the unit of measure Yahowah is using to depict time. But before he gets to it, the great liberator and prophet shares some valuable insights for living that are worth exploring.

If you are checking, the 90th Psalm (actually Mizmowr, meaning "Lyrics to be Sung") would appear to commence with "Lord," regardless of which English Bible you are reading. Lord was rendered from the Masoretic substitution of *'adonay* for YHWH, pronounced, **Y·ah·ow·ah.**

Fortunately, based upon the *Septuagint*, we know Moseh wrote "𐤉𐤄𐤅𐤄 – Yahowah." This is one of 132 times that the Masoretes were guilty of making this specific copyedit, purposely changing the Towrah to suit their

63

agenda—which was to keep God's name unknown. On 6,868 other occasions, the rabbinical Masoretes (meaning: those who vocalize) left 𐤉𐤄𐤅𐤄 – Yahowah's name in the text but wrote " *'adonay*" above it so that whoever read the passage wouldn't commit the religious crime of actually revealing God's personal and proper name.

Then, rather than transliterate (replicating the sound of) the name which actually appears in the text 7,000 times, consistent with scholarly convention, English translators ignored 𐤉𐤄𐤅𐤄 – יהוה –YHWH and translated the rabbinical substitution instead. The combination of these errors has robbed billions of people of a personal relationship with God and has served as a catalyst in the growth of religions. The systematic removal of Yahowah's name from His Towrah and Prophets may be the greatest crime ever perpetrated against humanity.

The 90th Mizmowr / Song provides additional clues to suggest that Yahowah's creation account is a spiritual guide to the Covenant, a scientific explanation of our existence, and a prophetic history of time all melded together. As such, it is among the most brilliant and inspired treatises ever committed to paper.

"A request and petition, expressing a desire to be set apart and distinct (*taphilah* – a psalm, an earnest plea for favor, a sincere request for intervention and intercession, an assessment that calls for a decision which is morally and justly discerned; from *palah* – be special and unique, *palal* – to assess and estimate leading to a favorable reassessment through intervention and *pilel* – to decide and then settle an affair, reconciling a relationship) **of** (*la* – by, concerning, and on behalf of) **Moseh** (*Mosheh* – the one who draws out (errantly transliterated from the Greek as Moses)), **a man** (*'iysh* – male individual) **of the Almighty** (*ha 'elohym* – of God):

Yahowah (𐤉𐤄𐤅𐤄 – the pronunciation of *YaHoWaH* as guided by His *towrah* – teaching regarding His *hayah* – existence), **You** (*'atah*) **have been** (*hayah* – have existed as (qal perfect – genuinely for this finite period of time)) **concerned about being our** (*la 'anachnuw* – near us, approaching us regarding our) **helper, provision, and support** (*ma'own* – refuge and dwelling, habitation and home; from *'ownah* – to cohabitate as if married) **throughout** (*ba* – in, among, and with) **time and generations** (*dowr wa dowr* – for the entire household and family, including everyone surrounding the encampment and dwelling place for all those who are related by birth, including every successive lifetime and place of habitation)." (*Mizmowr* / Song / Psalm 90:1)

Hayah, translated as "have been," is the second most prevalent word in Bare'syth one. In *Shemowth* / Names / Exodus 3:14-15, we were told that *hayah* serves as the basis of Yahowah's name – affirming that God exists. Here in the 90th Mizmowr, *hayah* is linked to our existence in God's dwelling place. It is speaking of our ultimate provision, with Yahowah helping and supporting us along the way.

As we have discovered, *hayah* plays a significant role in the account of our creation. The Hebrew verb is all about God enabling us to exist throughout time with Him. It also serves as another way of Yahowah telling us that He and His accounting of time combine past, present, and future together as if they were one and eternal.

Noting Yahowah's proclivity for symbolism, it is instructive to note that *hayah* reads the same from right to left as it does from left to right. It is the same, no matter the perspective – as is time from Yahowah's perspective. It signifies that God does not change, nor does His Word, no matter the time, place, or occasion.

The verb which serves as the basis of Yahowah's name helps define the nature of time, where the past, present, and future are the same, no matter the perspective, because they exist simultaneously. This in turn explains prophecy. God is not "predicting" the future, because He has already witnessed it. He reported what He had seen of our future in our past so that we might recognize that He inspired His prophets.

There are few words more basic to the Hebrew language than *hayah*. No one disputes its pronunciation. And yet, two of the three vowels which comprise Yahowah's name are presented within it. The missing letter is Wah – which is hardly a mystery since it is the most often repeated letter within the text.

In the first two sentences of Bare'syth, the Wah has already been used to convey the "oo" and "o" sound in *tohuw, bohuw,* and *tahowm*. And in the next two verses, a Wah will convey the same vowel sound in "*ruwach* – spirit," "*'owr* – light," and "*towb* – good." The Hebrew letter Wah even helped us properly transliterate *ma'own*, the Hebrew word for "help." A Wah was also found in the midst of "*dowr* – generations" in the Psalm. It is also the source of the "o" sound in "*Towrah*." Therefore, scholars and theologians deceive when they claim that "no one knows the proper pronunciation of 𐤅𐤄𐤅𐤄𐤉 – YaHoWaH."

In this passage, *ma'own's* triple meanings coalesce within the nature and purpose of Yahowah. God's principal ambition is to "help" His children. If we will let Him, He will "provide" for us and "support" us. As is the case with any devoted and loving parent, Yahowah wants us to "live with Him in His Home." We are afforded the opportunity "to cohabitate as if we were married."

Similarly, *dowr's* dual connotations coalesce into one when they are considered in this context, which is one of the reasons the word was repeated in the text. Yahowah didn't want us to miss the fact that He is there for "every generation throughout all periods of time, no matter the place." The Covenant is His Family. His "encampment" is for those who are "related by birth (racial descendants or spiritual adoptees)."

The etymology of *dowr* is particularly interesting in light of God's symbolism. It was first used to describe an orderly arrangement of harvested grain, which is symbolic of saved souls. And then it was used to depict a protective courtyard surrounded by homes – and thus a secure dwelling place. *Dowr* evolved to convey the circle of life from the womb and then back to the earth, symbolic of time as generations mark its onward march.

As a general rule when a word is repeated in Hebrew, it not only underscores the importance of whatever it is conveying, it calls us to consider every implication of the word. You could consider the repetition of words like "*dowr dowr*" to denote the fullest and most extreme aspects of their meaning. It is exponential in its connotations, making it *dowr*^{2}.

So by emphasizing "*dowr* – to live, to surround, to enclose, to harvest, to bring into a home and a dwelling place, to be part of a family for generations over time," in the context of *ma'own*, and of Yahowah helping His children, providing for them and supporting them so that they live and camp out together, in conjunction with "*taphilah* – an earnest plea for favor following an honest assessment," Moseh is introducing the underlying purpose of the *Miqra'ey* of *Pesach* | Passover, *Matsah* | UnYeasted Bread, *Bikuwrym* | Firstborn Children, *Shabuw'ah* | the Promise of Seven, *Taruw'ah* | Trumpets, *Kipurym* | Reconciliations, and *Sukah* | Shelters.

Passover is the Doorway into God's "*dowr* – home." UnYeasted Bread depicts His "*taphilah* – favor and intervention on behalf of the set apart." Firstborn Children represent the initial *"dowr* – generation born into Yahowah's Family. Seven Sevens is an all-encompassing harvest that alludes to the concept of *dowr dowr* or of the enormous growth in God's Spiritual household.

The purpose of the *Taruw'ah* Harvest, which is "to signal an alarm," "to shout for joy," and "to announce the gateway to healing," is encapsulated in the twin connotations of *taphilah*: "an earnest plea for favor and to be set apart," as well as "a sincere request for intervention and judgment, for a decision which is morally discerned." *Kipurym*, meaning "reconciliations," is based upon *ma'own*. Because of God's "great care and concern for us" during *Yowm Kipurym,* He "summons us, calls and pleads with us, to come into the presence" of His "provision, help, and support" which is provided by the Set-Apart Spirit. By way of our Spiritual Mother, Yisra'el and Yahuwdym are reconciled and thus prepared to "camp out" with God.

This in turn leads us to *Sukah*, meaning God's "encampment for life and protective shelter," His "tabernacle and home." *Sukah* is thus synonymous with the entirety of the passage.

Before we continue, I would like to pause here for a moment and reflect. What we have done thus far with Mizmowr 90, verse 1, is to meticulously examine the complete meaning and shading of each Hebrew word using the best etymological lexicons and dictionaries, and then consider the full implication of these words within the context of the passage and the Towrah, Prophets, and Psalms as a whole. This is not unlike viewing blood under a microscope as opposed to the naked eye. The microscope doesn't change or alter the blood in any way; it simply reveals what was always there, enabling us to better understand its nature, design, and function.

This does not make my translations inerrant nor my commentary inspired. I'm currently completing my eighth edit of this material, and each time the translations and insights improve. Besides, the only inspired commentary is when Yahowah or one of His prophets explains the meaning behind the text. Moseh did this throughout *Dabarym* / Words / Deuteronomy and *Dowd* | David did the same in His *Mashal* / Word Pictures / Proverbs and *Mizmowr* / Lyrics / Psalms.

Admittedly, all translations are inadequate and imprecise – especially recognizing that they are a human undertaking. Therefore, my advice to you is the same as God's: trust Yahowah and not men – and that includes me. Purchase some of the tools listed in the *Composition and Methodology* prologue and with the aid of the Spirit, examine Yah's Word yourself. Do what Moseh did: "*taphilah* – make a sincere request for good judgment and for decisions which are morally discerned regarding being set apart and uncommon." Test the evidence and be judgmental, discerning, and discriminating.

As mentioned before, the 90th Song provides some of the keys needed to decipher and quantify the *Bare'syth* / Genesis revelation. That is why I believe it references the formation of the Earth. But you will also notice here that God accurately depicts the Earth's violent beginnings.

"Even before (*ba terem* – previous to the time) **the mountains** (*har* – hills, ridges, ranges, and elevated land formations) **were born** (*yalad* – were conceived through labor and begotten) **and** (*wa*) **You brought forth through trembling and twisting** (*chuwl* – You patiently formed through violent shaking and agitation) **the earth** (*'erets* – ground comprised of natural material) **and** (*wa*) **the world** (*tabel* – the planet and its habitable places), **even from** (*wa min*) **before time** (*'ad 'owlam* – from perpetuity, from as far back as eternity, and continuously existing, forever), **You** (*'atah*) **always existed as God** (*'owlam 'el* – were infinite and unlimited, eternal in time, as the Almighty)." (*Mizmowr* / Song / Psalm 90:2)

This, too, is scientifically accurate, depicting the violent upheaval of massive volcanoes, trembling earthquakes, twisting plate tectonics, and the battering of asteroid and comet impacts which served to form the uneven surface of our planet. Yahowah used *'erets*, meaning "land, region, realm, area, ground, or earth in the sense of natural matter which is firm," and *tebel*, meaning "world or planet," to help distinguish between these concepts. Keep this in mind as we cover the subject of *Noach* | Noah and the scope of the flood.

By announcing that "God has always existed," *Mizmowr* / Psalm 90:2 reinforces the meaning of *hayah*, and it explains why Yahowah selected it as the basis of His name. While He is "*'ad 'owlam* – infinite" in relation to time, the religious are wont to make God infinite in all areas, suggesting that He is omnipresent, omnipotent, and omniscient.

In actuality, for God to be omnipresent, and thus be unlimited in scale or size, He would cease to be unique. He would become indistinguishable from the universe itself and thus would be in all things from rocks to slugs.

For God to be omniscient, and thus know all things, there would be no merit to creation or to Him forming a relationship with us. God grows by experiencing us grow, by enjoying our company, just as parents grow from the experience of raising their children.

Moreover, if God were omniscient, there would be no salvation, because He would be continuously aware of our mistakes in judgment, as opposed to having them vanish in the presence of the Spirit's Garment of Light. And since this is the purpose of Dowd's fulfillment of the Miqra'ey in concert with the Set-Apart Spirit, recognize that by depositing our guilt in She'owl, it is now unknown to God.

Continuing deeper into the Mizmowr, we discover that just like the Earth, our mortal birth is fraught with pain, so to exist with God, we must be transformed.

"**You can return or restore** (*shuwb* – You can change and renew, thereby transforming) **mortal humankind** (*'enowsh* – mankind; from *'anash* – to be weak and wicked) **forever from** (*'ad* – eternally as a witness until) **being crushed, diminished, and destroyed, becoming dust** (*daka'* – being reduced to nothingness by grinding and pressing minute natural and material particles into annihilation, becoming destroyed; from a state of despondency pertaining to emotional grieving).

So You say (*wa 'amar* – therefore, You instruct, declare, and encourage)**: 'Return, be changed, and restored** (*shuwb* – turn around, be renewed and transformed, reestablish relations, be repaired, and be refreshed, come back) **children** (*ben* – sons and offspring, descendants; from *banah*, meaning those who build a home and family, who are restored and established) **of *'Adam* | man** (*'adam* – human beings and people, the name of the first man with a *neshamah* | conscience).'" (*Mizmowr* / Song / Psalm 90:3)

Mortal men and women must change, returning to God to be restored by Him in order to avoid returning to the dust from which we came. God has put us on notice that our souls are mortal, and that unless we are willing to leave the world of men and return to Him, the consequence will be the destruction of our consciousness.

While we turned to this passage for the unit of measure needed to unlock the prophetic implications of the *Bare'syth* / Genesis One timeline, the journey into this Song has been priceless. God has revealed that His plan is to "restore and renew" the souls of the mortal men and women who answer His request to return. God wants us to change our ways and thus to be transformed so that we can

71

live forever in His presence. This is the embodiment of *Yowm Kipurym*, of the Day of Reconciliations leading to *Sukah* | Camping Out, where God seeks to reconcile our relationship so that we can spend an eternity together.

Over the course of three statements, there have been three words for "man." The first was " *'iysh* – individual," which was used in reference to Moseh representing a "man of God."

The second was " *'enowsh* – mortal humankind" on the precipice of destruction. God, Himself, defines this term as it is based upon *'anowsh*, which means: "terminally ill as a result of an incurable disease." He is speaking of the consequence of religious poison.

Third, we found *'adam* representing the descendants of the first man with a "*neshamah* – conscience," the unique ability to distinguish between right and wrong. Without transformation, " *'enowsh* – mortals" return from whence we came: dust to dust. The sons of 'Adam, however, who respond to God's call, choosing to change and to be restored, are able to establish eternal spiritual relations with Yahowah.

Now, from the perspective of *Bare'syth*, here is the payoff line:

"**Indeed because** (*ky* – for truly and surely) **a thousand** (*'eleph* – a thousand-fold for those who learn such that they adopt the teaching and instruction, incorporating it into their lives) **years** (*shanah* – a repetitive division of time marked by the cycle of every season and equating to alteration and change, making a difference and being different) **in Your sight and from Your perspective** (*ba 'atah 'ayn* – in Your eyes and in Your presence, by way of Your thinking and perceptions) **are like** (*ka* – exist the same as and equate to) **a day** (*yowm* – from sundown to sunset)**, the same as yesterday** (*'ethmowl* – the day before today) **when** (*ky*) **it passes by** (*'abar* – it passes through) **a perceptive observer** (*wa 'ashmuwrah* – one who takes notice and pays attention, the focused and watchful; from *shamar*: to closely observe and carefully examine) **during the time of minimal light** (*ba ha laylah* – in time of darkness when there is limited visibility during the night)." (*Mizmowr* / Song / Psalm 90:4)

According to the Mizmowr, "perspective" and "presence" are essential elements in the calibration of time. This is the same claim Albert Einstein made in support of Special and General Relativity. Time moves differently relative to the observer, and slows appreciably in the presence of great energy, mass, or velocity.

But more than that, from our "perspective" and from our "presence" here on Earth as mortal men, one of our "days" is "like a thousand years" from God's perspective. Therefore, if we extrapolate to the portrayal of the unfolding story of our salvation in the Creation account, each of the seven days depicted in Bare'syth represents a one-thousand-year period. This aspect of time is not random but instead has been quantified.

Therefore, as it relates to cosmological time, *Bare'syth* / Genesis readers have a number of options – albeit some are considerably less informed than others. They can believe that the universe, our solar system, life, and man were created in six solar days, one of which occurred before our sun was created, two before the Earth existed, and three before sunrises and sunsets were even visible, all in complete disregard for the scientific evidence to the contrary. And yet, according to recent surveys, most Americans believe the unbelievable. If you are one of them, visit the Creation Institute on the web. You will find many like-minded fools.

The second option, at least before Yahowah introduced us to the concept of relativity, is to render the word *yowm* as an imprecise "period of time" and not fret about the details. But if you were of that inclination, you probably wouldn't be reading this book. *Yada Yahowah* celebrates the details and is fully committed to taking Yahowah at His word.

Third, Bare'syth can be scrapped as a scientific explanation and be read exclusively for its spiritual insights. This is the Vatican's most current view. The Church, which has a knack for being wrong, recently issued a statement saying that the creation account was not accurate and that, at best, God played a distant, fatherly role in our genesis.

I am partial to the fourth option, viewing *yowm* as a precise quantitative measurement, as an accurate accounting, but relative to the "presence and perspective" of the eyewitness providing this testimony. That is the course we shall chart throughout *Yada Yahowah* because it provides the best fit between God's revelation, evidence, and reason.

However, within the framework of six plus one and of a day being equivalent to one thousand years, the readers of *Bare'syth* / Genesis cannot be faithful to the text and ignore the fact that the "days" of creation are prophetic. They reveal key aspects of our salvation history – past, present, and future – from the expulsion of 'Adam to the fall of man, and then to the final Millennial Sabbath. For this accounting, Mizmowr 90 was essential because it provided the scale we must deploy: one day represents one thousand years. Nearly six millennia of human history have passed since man, as we know him, began to record his existence. In that, God's word and history all agree.

In this regard, 'Abraham and Yitschaq affirmed the *Beryth* | Covenant with Yahowah on Day 2, year 2000 Yah, which was 1968 BCE. Forty Yowbel, which is 2,000 years, later Dowd served as the *Pesach 'Ayl* | Passover Lamb on the same mountain on Day 14 in year 4000 Yah, as he fulfilled the first three *Mow'ed Miqra'ey* | Invitations to Meet at the Appointed Time in 33 CE. Working together, Father and Son enabled the promised benefits of the Covenant with *Pesach* | Passover providing eternal life, with *Matsah* | UnYeasted Bread perfecting our souls, and *Bikuwrym* | Firstborn Children certifying adoption into His Covenant Family so that we can be enriched and empowered by God.

The next two events are Ingatherings, the Shabuw'ah Harvest and Taruw'ah Gleaning, both of which we are cultivating. The first will transpire in May of 2026 and the second in September of 2033.

Then, forty *Yowbel* | Redemptive Years where debts are forgiven, captives are freed, and the land is returned, Dowd will return for the Family Reunion, so that in year 6000 Yah, Father and Son will fulfill the final two Miqra'ey, starting with *Yowm Kipurym* | the Day of Reconciliations on October 2, 2033, when they return at sunset in Yaruwshalaim. Five days later, on *Sukah* | Shelters, those who have answered His invitation will Camp Out with their Heavenly Father for all time.

ᛚᛘᛂᛉᛘᛈ

3

Ruwach | Spirit

God's Feminine Side...

Now that we have our bearings, let's move on to the second half of Bare'syth's second statement, picking up the relative cosmological timeline at the end of day one. We are told that the Creator is Spirit (a radical concept at the time idols were ubiquitous) and that God set apart an aspect of Himself for a purpose.

The *Ruwach* | Spirit is introduced as "purifying, cleansing, and protecting by hovering over" creation. This is the same role the *Ruwach* | Spirit plays in the lives of those who are adopted into the Covenant Family. And while that should not come as a surprise, it may be shocking to many, while comforting to others, that God has a feminine side. The Ruwach is unabashedly maternal.

In context, Yahowah began: **"In the beginning, the Almighty, for accompaniment and association, created while being alongside and closely associated with the spiritual world and the material realm.** (*Bare'syth* / Genesis 1:1)

And the natural physical material realm existed formless, without shape, lacking organization, a chaotic place of empty space, dark, hidden, obscured and unknowable, like dark matter, in proximity to the vast, inexhaustible power and inaccessible, mysterious energy of the big bang." (*Bare'syth* / Genesis 1:2)

To which Yahowah added:

"**Then** (*wa*)**, the *Ruwach* | Spirit** (*ruwach* – the maternal manifestation of Divine power, courage, attitude, and acceptance, the heart and mind of God; from *ruwm* – to lift up and raise to a higher elevation and dimension, to help by keeping safe and secure, *ruwah* – to experience the full effect and extent of complete satisfaction, to be drenched in a healthy abundance of water to be revived, refreshed, and renewed, and *ruwayah* – the abundant and overflowing acceptance and vast amounts of freedom with Yah providing more than enough for alleviation of troubles and relief from burdens; a feminine noun) **of the Almighty** (*'elohym* – God) **hovered over and quickly administered to, cherishing** (*rachaph 'al* – She moved back and forth, supervising everything, brooding over Her infant creation as a loving Mother, instigating an exceedingly fast quivering motion, flying rapidly over while suspended above to increase the pace of accomplishments, acting expeditiously while managing the process and advancing the action; She served by energizing and promoting growth and development through superintendence; the derivative meaning of cleansing and purifying is from *rachats*) **the appearance** (*paneh* – the surface and presence) **of a fluid state** (*maym* – waters as a symbol of the source of life and means to cleanse; plasma scientifically)." (*Bare'syth* / In the Beginning / Genesis 1:2)

In the previous chapter, I offered my conclusion, which is that Yahowah, as a seven-dimensional entity, created a six-dimensional universe. Whether or not that is correct, as a statement of fact, larger-dimensional beings cannot enter lesser-dimensional space. They can interact with implements, communicate with words, or set apart an aspect of themselves to engage in lower realms. That is why Yahowah dispatched the *Ruwach* | Spirit.

While Mickey and Minnie Mouse are not living beings, and while Walt Disney didn't actually fabricate two-dimensional space, when we consider his options

77

regarding interactions with his cartoon creations, we are better able to appreciate God's limitations. Not only would it have been impossible for Mickey or Minnie to envision 3D in Flatland, but Mr. Disney was also limited to using words and implements. He would not fit in 2D.

The reason that mankind cannot perceive how Yahowah constructed the universe or appreciate how something this large and energetic would have left God undiminished is that we cannot actually envision dimensional space beyond our own. And the reason mankind has consistently conceived gods in our image is that we do not understand the infinite possibilities of greater dimensions.

Contemplating the opportunities inherent in dimensions beyond our own 3D existence challenges our imagination and potentially elevates our understanding of the universe and our place in it. It enhances our appreciation of who Yahowah is and what He is offering. It also aids our ability to comprehend why God uses words and implements to communicate and interact, in addition to His *ruwach* | spirit and *nepesh* | soul. Over the course of the next fifteen thousand pages of translations, commentary, and insights, we will constantly build upon these ideas.

Before we examine *rachaph* | hovered, the operative term in this passage, a word regarding transliteration is once again in order. While there are several acceptable ways to alphabetically convey the proper pronunciation of *ruwach* or *'elohym*, there is only one correct way to present them. Titles such as these should be transliterated (conveying their pronunciation) and translated (accurately rendering their meaning).

So that you know, the reason I include the "w" in *ruwach*, beyond the realization that this is how the word was written, is so that you might come to appreciate the source of the "u" sound. It is why I provide the "y" in *'elohym* as opposed to using an "i." And as I have shared before, the "w" in God's name is a vowel. It conveys the "u," "o," or "oo" sound in English.

While on the subject of *'elohym*, there are many who prefer to see the Hebrew word transliterated rather than translated. While I prefer both because it is more instructive, let's not lose sight of the fact that it means: "God, Gods, god, gods, the Almighty, or Mighty One."

The principal argument rendered against translating *'elohym* as "God" is that the English word has a pagan origin, based as it is on Gott and Gad. But not only does this condition permeate our language, and thus eliminate thousands of words like those which designate days and months on our calendars, Yahowah uses *'elohym* to identify Himself and also to describe false gods. In this regard, *'elohym* carries the same baggage as does "god" with the exception that "God" can be capitalized in English to distinguish the real one from the frauds.

And as for the religious predilection among Orthodox Jews to write "G-d," there is no justification for doing so. God is a title, not a name, so it does not fall under Yahowah's admonition against promoting the names of false gods.

Now that you know how the Hebrew words, titles, and names are rendered, let's shift our focus back to the meaning of Yah's message. Not only are we introduced to Yahowah's *ruwach* | Spirit before we meet God by name, but we are also confronted by two amazing realizations. Yahowah is shaping His new creation by dispatching the *ruwach* | Spirit, and She is feminine. It took a woman's touch to shape the universe and conceive life. Considering its beauty, it should be obvious.

While we have already noted the practical reason behind the Spirit's involvement, Her introduction to us is far more important. The *ruwach* | Spirit is the projection of Yahowah's nature which is available to us here and now. She is here to hover over and administer to the needs of the Covenant's children. Her purpose is to serve us while promoting our growth and development.

This understanding is advanced by a most curious verb, *rachaph*, which suggests that the *Ruwach* "brooded over Her infant creation as a loving Mother." It presents the imagery of a mother bird fluttering her wings, hovering over her newborn chicks.

As this story unfolds, we will discover that the "*ruwach* – Spirit" highlights by contrast the mortal nature of our "*nepesh* – souls." Most are unaware that "consciousness" is something which both men and animals received on the sixth creative day. Shortly thereafter we will learn that the *ruwach* of '*elohym* is distinguished from the "*neshamah chay* – conscience of life" which is "*napah* – breathed" into 'Adam, making him more like God and less like all other animals. Our "*neshamah* – conscience" enables us to exercise good judgment and discern the things which are of God and those which are of man.

From a scientific perspective, God's Spirit is shown "*rachaph* – rapidly moving and hovering over, while administering to and protecting" creation in its infancy. There is a sense of advancing the pace of what is being accomplished and of managing the process as it rapidly expands and unfolds. The Spirit is engaged to promote growth.

Therefore, the Big Bang was not a set-and-forget explosion. There was a time in which physical laws were stretched and guidance was required to achieve the desired result. This occurred early on, during what is called "the inflationary period" of the cosmos' formation.

Physicists claim that almost all physical laws were suspended, enabling a great, instantaneous expansion (10^{26}

increase in three dimensions in 10^{-32} seconds) to take place instantly after the Big Bang commenced. This period of "*rachaph* – quickly moving and hovering over" was so extreme that two objects an inch apart prior to the inflationary period would be 2.5 septillion meters separated after it. Not only did the inflationary period commence on creation's first day, but its influence on our reality also remains at the heart of all universal explanations.

This understanding is also consistent with the primary purpose of Yahowah's testimony, to convey *why* He created the universe and us, illuminating His plan of redemption therein. It would get rough out there, so Yahowah put a plan in place whereby His Spirit is shown protecting while encouraging growth, providing responsible oversight while using water to conceive life and cleanse.

Spirit and purification are well-developed aspects of salvation and eternal life, but so is water. For example, *Howsha'* | Hosea equates water with life: "'**The Spirit (*ruwach*) of Yahowah will ascend out of the desolation. Her source of life, Her basis for purification, and Her fountain of joy'**" are equivalent to "'**His cistern of mercy, His source of blessings, well of sustenance, and fountain of life....'**" (*Howsha'* / Salvation / Hosea 13:15)

If I am right about what seems to be the natural implication, "*rachaph* – swiftly moving to conceive and cleanse, and hovering over to protect in a maternal fashion," used in the third statement of Bare'syth in conjunction with Yahowah's Spirit, will convey as much about the Spirit's role in our lives as it does the formation of the universe. And fortunately, such theories are not hard to verify because Yahowah almost always defines His terms. (More on this in a moment.)

Consistent with this review of the nature and purpose of the *Ruwach* | Spirit, it is instructive to learn that the root of *rachaph* is *rachats,* which means: "to cleanse and to make pure by washing." It is analogous to the Towrah instructions related to being immersed in water to become pure prior to entering the House of Yahowah. In conjunction with the *Ruwach* | Spirit's role in our lives, *rachats* describes a "trusted female servant at a bath who washes and cleanses." In this light, *rachsah* means: "to purify, removing all contaminants and filth."

Formed from the same Hebrew base, we find *racham*, meaning "tender love and mercy," whereas *rachuwm* is "compassion." *Racham* also conveys "familial and affectionate nurturing derived from motherly love." *Racham*, therefore, explains the reason for and the means to the gift of renewed life.

Another variant of the same root, *rachamah*, is a "mother's womb," reinforcing the fact that the *Ruwach* | Spirit is our "Spiritual Mother." Along these same lines, *rechem* is "a matrix, the source from which life originates, develops, and takes form." And *rachmany* is a "compassionate woman."

The insights gleaned from *rachaph* are particularly telling in the context of God's *ruwach* being credited with the "formation," and thus "birth," of the universe, as well as its development and expansion. Further, She (remembering that *ruwach* is a feminine noun) filled the "void," just as the Set-Apart Spirit does in our lives, enabling us to live eternally in Yahowah's presence.

As a result of Her work and Her enlightenment, we are able to avoid mankind's "ignorant confusion" of lifeless deceptions and thus preclude our souls from "dissipating into nothingness" or descending into "darkness and death." By "hovering over" the source of Divine energy and protecting the young universe from potential adversarial influences, She perfected creation, just as Her Garment of Light makes us look perfect in God's eyes.

And that makes the Set-Apart Spirit the implement of Yahowah's *rachem*, "mercy." And just as *rachaph* speaks of "enlarging," *rachab* is "expansive," addressing that which is "enormous in scope and breadth," even "growing and liberating." *Rachash* is "to move and stir, to awaken, invigorate, and motivate." A *rachath*, also a feminine noun, depicts a "winnowing implement which separates the wheat from the chaff."

Rachal helps identify the intended benefits of Passover because it signifies "a young lamb." And *rachats* means "to trust and to rely upon" which, in this case, is the source of Yahowah's means to eternal life, purification, and continual protection.

By focusing on this verb, we discover that the *Ruwach* is the manifestation of God's power which we can personally experience "*rachaph* – hovering over us, purifying and protecting us, engaged in our lives and playing an active role influencing us, empowering and increasing us so that we can grow." If we accept Her, She makes us acceptable.

The *Ruwach* renews and restores us, reconciling us with God, enabling us to understand and flourish. She is not only the breath of eternal life, She enlightens the path to life. So as a result, it is safe to say that this portion of *Bare'syth* contains an essential ingredient relative to the benefits of the *Miqra'ey* | Invitations to be Called Out and Meet with God. And of course, in this context, *rachaph* explains proven aspects of our creation, especially regarding the inflationary period in the growth of the universe and the presence of molecular water – but more on that later.

In this form, *rachaph* was only used three times in the Torah, Prophets, and Psalms. With a little digging, we will be able to determine its associated meanings and thereby ascertain precisely why Yahowah used it in His early creation reference. However, because the second and third use of *rachaph* are so amazingly revealing, I am going to ask for your patience and present both at the conclusion of this chapter. Learning is always relevant, but so is focus, so let's do both by keeping our attention directed at creation before we explore the long tributaries to where *rachaph* leads.

It was not until a couple of years ago, coinciding with the launch of the Herschel Space Observatory by the European Space Agency, that an abundance of water was equated to star and planet formation – as is suggested here in Genesis. Some 50 signatories published a peer-reviewed article in Astronomy & Astrophysics in April 2021 using data from Herschel demonstrating that water continues to be a key molecule in the physics and chemistry of stellar nurseries. It was entitled: Water in Star-Forming Regions: Physics and Chemistry from Clouds to Disks as Probed by Herschel Spectroscopy. Providing the first confirmation of the Genesis account in 3,500 years, the opening line of the Abstract reads: "Water is a key molecule in the physics and chemistry of star and planet formation, but it is difficult to observe from Earth." The Herschel Space Observatory provided unprecedented sensitivity as well as spatial and spectral resolution to study water.

The first news of this was reported in October 2011 after oceans of cold-water vapor were discovered in the accretion discs of young stars. It is an amazing corroboration of God's testimony.

𐤉𐤅𐤄𐤅

In the next statement, the Creator revealed the root of His name and His nature. Here Yahowah links four extraordinary words together, connecting God, instruction, light, and eternal existence. It reads:

"**Then** (*wa* – in addition), **God** (*'elohym* – the Almighty [depicted in the original alphabet as ⴎⵘ – the protective ram shepherding His flock]) **said** (*'amar* – He declared by intending (qal imperfect – actually and literally spoke with ongoing ramifications)), '**Let there continuously be** (*hayah* – it is the ongoing will and desire of the light for it to always and genuinely exist (with the qal stem – there is an actual and literal relationship between God and the light, in the imperfect conjugation – we see a continued emphasis on this process, including its unfolding implications over time, such that in the jussive mood – there is the indication that this is occurring under the auspices of freewill)) **light** (*'owr* – illumination, enlightenment, the ability to see, and brilliant guidance) **and** (*wa*) **light** (*'owr* – illumination, enlightenment, the ability to see, and brilliant guidance) **exists** (*hayah* – actually was and will literally always be (qal imperfect)).'" (*Bare'syth* / In the Beginning / Genesis 1:3)

The universe was spoken into existence. This would make words, and thus communication, the ultimate source of causation. It would also make the Word of God more powerful than, and even superior to, the universe.

That being so, it makes every word we read, from Bare'syth to Malaky, from the Towrah through the Prophets, more empowering, indeed enlightening, than all of the stars in the sky. We ought to respect God's terminology and contemplate its full intent. And if we do, we will inherit, as Yahowah promised 'Abraham, a universe with 70 billion trillion (7×10^{22}) stars and two trillion galaxies, each festooned with an average of 100 billion stellar inhabitants.

Analyzing one word at a time, *wa*, which was translated as "then," is a conjunction which ties things together and adds one thing to another. It is used in the Hebrew text in lieu of punctuation, revealing that one sentence is complete and the next follows. Originally drawn to depict a tent post Y, *wa* symbolically addresses the function of the peg deployed to erect, enlarge, and secure a home – which in the context of this revelation were tents, including the Tabernacle of the Witness, Yahowah's Home on Earth and shelter for the Ark of the Covenant. The word and letter, *wa* and Wah, expound on the concepts of adding to, continuing with, making connections, increasing and enhancing, strengthening and enlarging, protecting and securing.

'Elohym is the plural of *'el* and means "god, God, gods, Almighty, or Mighty One." It was written in the original alphabet as ᴊᵧ – which presents a strong, protective ram engaged in shepherding his flock. This is consistent with *Dowd* | David description of Yahowah as his "Shepherd" in the 23rd *Mizmowr* | Psalm, especially when he describes God walking with him when they fulfilled Pesach, Matsah, and Bikuwrym in year 4000 Yah / 33 CE.

'El is a title, not a name. It is used to reveal that Yahowah is "God" but also that there are many false "gods." While the plural form is intriguing and subject to much speculation, every verb we have encountered thus far was scribed and spoken in third-person singular, either as "He" or "She." Therefore, there is only one actual God whose one and only name is Yahowah.

I have thought, and the creation account seems to confirm, that the plural form of *'el* was used to convey that Yahowah has paternal and maternal characteristics and serves as our Heavenly Father and Spiritual Mother. Creation was for the benefit of the Covenant Family, after all.

Hayah, translated as "let there continuously be" and then "exists," may be the lexicon's most relevant verb – especially in this context. In addition to serving as the basis of Yahowah's name, *hayah* defines the unique nature of the Hebrew language where verbs are liberated in time. Therefore, Hebrew is like the subject of this revelation – light. On a photon of light, time does not move. Its existence is akin to a dimension, such that it can be experienced as it has and will exist.

This enables an energy-based being to see the future before it occurs and report what they have witnessed in the past. When things transpire exactly as reported, those who read these "prophecies" will know that they can trust the source. This means that God exists outside the constraints of time, just as is the case with light, as well as with Hebrew verbs. As a dimension which can be navigated, the past and future can be experienced as we currently engage in the present. If we were like light, we would be able to move in time as easily as we can step back and forth, right or left, up and down in three dimensions.

In this direct and simple statement, we are presented with evidence of God's existence, an explanation of our existence, the nature of time, and the basis of prophecy. We are introduced to light and find the interconnectedness of light and the language used to create it.

In this case, on both occasions, *hayah* was scribed with the qal stem and imperfect conjugation. The qal stem depicts a literal and genuine relationship between God and light. The imperfect conjugation means that light's existence will be continuous.

From a scientific perspective, light is as Yahowah describes it – continuously existing. Energy cannot be destroyed; it can only change forms, such as going from light to heat. Light epitomizes the imperfect conjugation.

In Hebrew, there are three ways to express volition, in the first, second, and, like this occurrence, in the third person. This indicates that Yahowah is equating Himself with light by projecting His will upon it. Literally, the statement reads: it is the ongoing will and desire of the light for it to always exist.

This perception is advanced even further by the grammar, where the pronouns ascribed to both verbs convey: "And He, God, said, He is light and He exists as light."

Also interesting, the Hebrew text renders the first *hayah* as *yhy*, which is the qal imperfect singular, masculine, third person, jussive active tense of the verb *hayah*. The second time the verb appears, it is written as *whyh*, which includes the conjunction "*wa* – and" along with the qal stem, imperfect conjugation, and third-person singular masculine. Collectively, these letters convey the full basis of Yahowah's name. So, in this way, we find God identifying His name and associating Himself with our existence.

Light is one of the metaphors Yahowah uses to describe Himself in tangible terms. The others include: the Word, the Upright Pillar, the Bread of Life, the Rock of our Salvation, and Living Waters.

'Owr, the word rendered as "light," can convey "the light of instruction and guidance, the light of judgment, the light which removes someone from darkness, trouble and danger, the light of life, the light of a lamp, or the light of God." *'Owr* can also convey the "light of the sun and stars" which is significant because, while universally present on day one, it was not visible on Earth until the fourth day. *'Owr* can be translated as: light or illumination, providing the ability to see along with brilliant directions.

In a related statement in Yasha'yah (meaning: Freedom and Salvation are from Yahowah, errantly known as Isaiah), God introduces Himself as Light. But first He sets the scene. The discussion begins by predicting that the Chosen People would disavow their relationship with God to such an extent that there would be no witnesses among the Chosen People as they stumbled in the darkness. Therefore, Yahowah would deploy a third Zarowa', enlightening him to garner Yisra'el's attention prior to His return. Significantly, all of the pronouns in the relevant portion of this prophecy continue to address the *Zarowa'* | Arm Sowing the Seeds which will take root and grow. For the arriving Light to be of benefit, He must be anticipated and recognizable...

"**Truth is lacking, and no one is honest** (*wa hayah ha 'emeth 'adar* – the truth has gone missing because there is a lack of integrity, and no one is dependable). **Furthermore** (*wa*), **anyone who turns away from what is wrong** (*suwr min ra'* – who departs from that which is perverted and objectionable, harmful and disagreeable) **is victimized, attacked, and discredited** (*shalal* –abused then plundered). (*Yasha'yah* / Isaiah 59:15)

When (*wa*) **Yahowah** (*YaHoWaH*) **witnesses this** (*ra'ah*), **it is disturbing** (*ra'a* – it is displeasing) **in His sight** (*ba 'ayn huw'*) **that, indeed** (*ky*), **no one exercises good judgment** (*'ayn mishpat* – no one is just, fair, or moral). (*Yasha'yah* 59:16)

He has looked and seen (*wa ra'ah*) **that there was not a single individual** (*ky 'ayn 'ysh*). **So** (*wa*), **He was devastated** (*wa shamem* – He was appalled) **that there was no one to intercede and plead His case** (*ky 'ayn paga'* – that there was no one to intervene).

It was then (*wa*) **His *zarowa'* | the one who sows His seeds to shepherd the flock** (*zarowa' huw'* – His capable arm, the prevailing and effective nature, resolve, and ability of His guide, His productive and protective ram, the defender and caretaker engaged as a shepherd among His sheep who is fruitful in His ways, accomplishing His mission, especially when sowing the seeds which take root and grow while denoting and advancing the purpose of the arm of God and that of His shepherds and sacrificial lamb) **will come to the rescue on His behalf** (*yasha' la huw'* – delivered for Him, liberating those approaching Him).

'**Therefore** (*wa*), **the realization that he will be right for you and will engage correctly** (*tsadaqah huw' 'asah* – the fact he is correct regarding you, will decide fairly and act in accord with the standard, working on behalf of your vindicatation [*'asah* is from 1QIsa]) **will be upheld and sustained** (*huw' samak huw'* – will be supported and established, embraced, even relied and capitalized upon). (*Yasha'yah* 59:17)

He will be adorned (*wa labash*) **correctly in righteousness** (*tsadaqah* – in what is considered right, acquitting and vindicating, just and fair, honest and reliable) **as a breastplate and coat of armor** (*ka ha shiryown* – as a form of protection, thwarting any attack) **and a helmet** (*wa kowba'* – a protective head covering worn by someone engaged in battle) **of deliverance** (*yashuwa'ah* – of liberation, freedom, and salvation) **will be on his head** (*ba ro'sh huw'*).

He will be clothed (*labash*) **in garments** (*beged*) **of retribution** (*naqam* – designed to inflict vengeance and repay harm with hostility, to punish and avenge) **as a raiment** (*talbosheth*), **and he will be covered** (*wa 'atah*) **as if cloaked in** (*ka ha ma'yl*) **passion and desire** (*qin'ah* – the devotion and zeal of knowing that he has a perceived advantage in advocating exclusivity in the relationship). (*Yasha'yah* 59:18)

Seeking recompense in accordance with their deeds (*ka 'al gamuwlah* – requiring a penalty and reprimand as a form of repayment commensurate and consistent with what they have done), **he will achieve a sense of closure** (*ka 'al* *shalem* – he will compensate the victims, restoring a sense of fairness, repaying the guilty for what they have done, fulfilling the will of God in the process**), showing righteous indignation** (*chemah* – displaying antagonism, a strong sense of displeasure) **toward his opponents and adversaries** (*la tsar huw'* – toward those who are opposed to him and who seek to restrict and confine him, narrowing his outreach) **by doing what is necessary and deserved** (*gemuwl* – for achieving what is right, advantageous, and beneficial, dealing out repayment) **against those showing animosity and rancor toward him** (*la 'oyeb huw'*).

Against a land of woe surrounded by water with greedy people living along the coasts (*la 'iy* – toward a covetous nation situated between large bodies of water**), he will complete the requirement to obtain restitution** (*shalem* – he will fulfill the need to find closure) **based upon what was done and is deserved** (*gemuwl* – in accordance with their deeds, requiring an appropriate penalty and reprimand commensurate with the crimes committed). (*Yasha'yah* 59:19)

Therefore (*wa*)**, there will be one suited to deliver recompense who requires restitution** (*ga'al* – one who redeems the deprived by eliciting retribution, demanding a repayment to provide relief on behalf of those who were wronged).

Then, those who are part of Ya'aqob (*wa ba Ya'aqob* – those in Yisra'el) **will turn away** (*la shuwb* – will change and be restored) **from their political revolt and religious rebellion** (*pesha'* – their overt and public defiance and offensive nature),' **prophetically declares** (*na'um*) **Yahowah** (*YaHoWaH*). (*Yasha'yah* 59:20)

'As for Me (*wa 'any*)**, this is My Covenant** (*zo'th beryth 'any* – this is My Family and Relationship Agreement) **with them** (*'eth hem* – masculine plural),' **announces** (*'amar*) **Yahowah** (*Yahowah*). **'For the**

benefit of the relationship (*'asher* – to show the way to get the greatest enjoyment out of life), ***Ruwach 'Any* | My Spirit** (*ruwach 'any*) **is upon you** (*'al 'atah* – over, before, and beside you (singular masculine)).

And to show the way to the relationship (*wa 'asher*), **I have placed** (*sym*) **My words** (*dabar 'any*) **in your mouth** (*ba peh 'atah* – masculine singular).

Therefore, what comes from your mouth (*wa min peh 'atah*) **shall not fail nor cease** (*lo' muwsh*), **nor out of the mouths of your offspring** (*wa min peh zera' 'atah* – from what is sown by you), **nor from the declarations sown through your seeds** (*wa min peh zera' zara' atah*),**'** **says** (*'amar*) **Yahowah** (*YaHoWaH*), **'from this moment** (*min 'atah*) **and forevermore** (*wa 'ad 'owlam*).'"** (*Yasha'yah* / Yahowah Liberates / Isaiah 59:21)

The one speaking the words and sowing the seeds regarding the Covenant, and the one who receives the Spirit for the benefit of God's people is the Zarowa'. Throughout this prophecy, the pronouns have remained singular as they have addressed the role of the Zarowa', while attributing a feminine title to this Witness. The recipients of his message, however, remain masculine plural, especially when addressing the returning remnant of Yisra'el. This is relevant because as we address the prophecies pursuant to the arrival of the Light, the pronouns are decidedly feminine.

"'Choose to rise and be illuminating (*quwm wa 'owr* – of your own volition, stand up and enlighten, choosing to take a stand by shining a luminary which establishes the source of the Light (both verbs are qal imperative second-person singular feminine active thus addressing the Zarowa')) **because** (*ky*), **he will come, arriving with and pursuing your light** (*bow' 'owr 'ath* – he will return your source of enlightenment at this moment in time he has arrived (qal perfect third-person masculine singular while the light is associated with the Zarowa' in the feminine singular)).

And the presence and overall significance, the manifestation of power, and the resulting reward (*wa kabowd* – the splendor and ensuing status, the personal abundance, the distinction and magnificence) **of Yahowah** (*YaHoWaH*) **will shine forth, becoming more apparent** (*zarach* – will become visible, arising and appearing (qal perfect third-person masculine singular active)) **upon you** (*'al 'ath* – you is feminine singular and thus addressing the *zarowa'*). (*Yasha'yah* 60:1)

By contrast (*ky*), **behold** (*hineh* – take note), **ignorance, confusion, and terror** (*choshek* – the lack of enlightenment and the dearth of illumination when so much is obscured and unknown) **will have enveloped and overwhelmed the Earth** (*kasah 'erets* – will cover the land and conceal the material realm) **such that an archaic and misled world** (*wa la'om*) **will be shrouded in darkness** (*'araphel* – clouded in gloom, hardship, and trouble, appearing hopeless).

But then, Yahowah will appear with you, shining upon you (*wa 'al 'ath zarach Yahowah* – will appear, becoming visible to you ('ath is feminine singular while the verb is qal imperfect third-person masculine singular)) **and His glorious presence, His power and reward** (*wa kabowd huw'* – His splendor and status, His person and abundance, as well as the significance and distinction of His magnificence), **will be seen** (*ra'ah* – will be witnessed around you (nifal imperfect)) **upon you** (*'al 'ath* – you remains singular feminine and thus is addressing the *zarowa'*). (*Yasha'yah* 60:2)

Then, even (*wa*) **the gentiles** (*gowym* – those who are from different ethnicities and cultures other than Yisra'el (a masculine plural noun)) **will be drawn** (*halak* – will travel, walk, and move) **to your light and enlightenment**

(*la 'owr 'ath* – toward your illuminated and brilliant guidance (with your conveyed in the feminine singular)).

Those who are thoughtful (*wa melak* – leaders who carefully consider and wisely respond to counsel and advice) **will be drawn to your knowledge and brilliance** (*la nogah* – your enlightenment and radiance) **which has dawned upon you** (*zarach 'ath* – which shines forth from your presence and is apparent (in the feminine singular, you remains the *zarowa'*))." (*Yasha'yah* / Isaiah 60:3)

"And so (*wa*), **the offspring** (*beny*) **of the *Nakar* | Observant and Responsive Foreigner** (*nakar* – the little appreciated and often misunderstood non-Yisra'elite from a distant land who closely examines and carefully considers, then recognizes and acknowledges the truth, making it known through declarative statements, the discerning friend who highly regards what can be perceived) **will reestablish** (*banah* – will restore and rebuild) **the means of separation and protection** (*chowmah 'ath*) **while those who are thoughtful and responsive among them** (*malak hem*) **will render assistance and serve you** (*sharath 'ath*).

This is because (*ky*), **in My frustration** (*ba qetseph 'any*), **I lashed out against you** (*nakah 'ath*), **and now, with My acceptance and approval** (*ba ratsown 'any*), **I will be merciful toward you** (*racham 'ath*)." (*Yasha'yah* 60:10)

"Whereas rather than succeeding (*tachath*), **you have been** (*hayah 'ath*) **forsaken, separated, and abandoned** (*'azab*) **and** (*wa*) **you have been abhorred and shunned** (*sane'*).

And yet, without anyone passing through (*wa 'ayn 'abar*), **I shall appoint and establish you** (*sym 'atah*) **to be preeminent with the highest possible status forever** (*la ga'own 'owlam*), **a delight** (*masows*) **for many generations to come** (*dowr wa dowr*)." (*Yasha'yah* 60:15)

The choices are simple, the answers easy, the process straightforward, and yet for nearly one hundred generations, Jews, rather than succeeding, have stumbled in the darkness. More than any other ethnicity, they have been disliked and detested. Collectively, religiously, and culturally, they have been oblivious to the orderly arrangement of events that Yahowah laid out for us to explore. They have failed to appreciate the connections between cause and consequence.

Without the benefits of the Covenant, without the result of Passover, UnYeasted Bread, and Firstborn Children, there is only "*azab* – separation and abandonment." Those who do not walk through this doorway from man's oppressive religious realm to God's Home and across the cleansing threshold where we are perfected are "*azab* – forsaken, disassociated, and neglected."

Unfortunately, the Chosen People have opted out of the Covenant. The restoration of the relationship is now up to God. For the fortunate few who return to Him in the end, He will reestablish them such that they return to the preeminence Yahowah intended. A litany of travesties will be vanquished in a moment's time, such that Yahuwdym will once again become a cause for celebration.

And there is nothing more empowering or joyous than *yada' Yahowah*...

"Then, you will know (*wa yada'* – you will be aware and understand) **that I, Yahowah** (*ky 'any Yahowah*), **am your Savior** (*mowshya' 'ath* – the One who rescued and delivered you) **and your Redeemer** (*wa ga'al 'ath*), **the Mighty One** (*'abyr* – the strength) **of Ya'aqob** (*Ya'aqob* – a synonym for Yisra'el)."** (*Yasha'yah* 60:16)

"No longer (*lo' 'owd*) **will terrorism resulting in destructive and deadly violence** (*hamas*) **be heard** (*shama'*) **in your Land** (*ba 'erets 'ath*), **neither willful**

destruction and demonic carnage (*sed* / *sod* – the presence of an evil spirit who finds it acceptable to be worshiped as a god and inspires looting by compulsion, force, and oppressive subjugation) **nor** (*wa*) **crippling injuries and resulting disfiguration** (*seber*) **within your borders** (*gabuwl*).

Then (*wa*), **you shall call** (*qara'* – you shall designate and name) **your walls and barriers** (*chowmah 'atah*) *'Yashuw'ah* | **Salvation & Deliverance** (*yashuw'ah*) **and** (*wa*) **your doors and gates** (*sha'ar 'atah*) *Tahilah* | **Brilliant & Praiseworthy** (*tahilah*)." (*Yasha'yah* 60:18)

"*Yada' Yahowah* – knowing Yahowah" is the first step toward becoming part of the Covenant, to benefiting from the Miqra'ey, and to coming Home. A day will come when those who avoided His name as if it were a plague will acknowledge it, appreciate, respect and even understand it. Then they will know that Yahowah saves, not HaShem or the Lord, not Jesus Christ, and especially not rabbis.

Yahowah is light – or at least light is the most similar analog to His nature, a concept He knew we should be able to understand. As the Creator of 400 billion galaxies, each with as many as 400 billion stars like our sun, it would not take much of Him to brighten our world and replace the brilliant orb at the center of our solar system.

As we consider God's next statement, we find that *tiph'arah* is from *pa'ar*, which means "to adorn in a garment which glorifies and beautifies." In the context of "Yahowah existing for us as our everlasting and eternal light, as our God, and as our glorifying and beautifying adornment," this is speaking of the *Tiph'arah* | Garment of Light which makes us appear perfect in God's eyes and thus enables us to live in His presence as His children. Provided by the *Ruwach Qodesh* | Set-Apart Spirit, the Garment of Light empowers and enlightens us, immortalizes and enriches us, beautifying us to the point of perfection. As light, we become ever more like our God – which is the point.

That is the nature of light. It is immortal. What we perceive as beautiful is a result of light. And as Albert Einstein's famous equation reveals – $E=mc^2$ – light, as energy, is enormously more powerful than matter. Most relevant of all, light eliminates darkness, such that we appear magnificent, dazzling and radiant in Yahowah's eyes. And in this regard, while darkness cannot eliminate light, nor even faze it, light obliterates darkness.

Within the testimony of Yahowah being Light and saving us by purifying and protecting us with His Garment of Light, the next statement could be literal in the sense of illumination, or symbolic in the sense of curtailing the Adversary's influence – given that the sun and moon have long served as the most common guise for false gods.

"The sun's (*ha shemesh*) **light** (*'owr* – illumination) **will no longer be a means of persistent renewal** (*lo' hayah 'owd* – will not exist as a restoring witness) **for you** (*la 'ath 'owd*) **by day** (*la yomam*)**, nor the moon** (*ha yareach*) **a source of information on when to respond** (*wa la nogah* – make known or enlighten) **by night** (*layl*) **to provide light** (*lo' 'owr*) **for you** (*la 'ath*)**.**

Instead (*wa*)**, Yahowah** (*Yahowah*) **will be for you** (*hayah la 'ath*) **an everlasting light** (*'owr 'owlam*)**. And your God** (*wa 'elohym 'ath*) **your glorious adornment** (*la tiphe'reth 'ath*)**.** (*Yasha'yah* / Isaiah 60:19)

Therefore (*wa*)**, your time of sorrowful rituals and mourning over death** (*yowmym 'ebel 'atah*) **shall be ended by way of restitution and restoration** (*shalem*)**.** (*Yasha'yah* 60:20)

Then, your family (*wa 'am 'ath*) **will be entirely right** (*kol tsadyq* – they will all be correct, validated, and vindicated). **They will be heirs to the land** (*hem yarash 'erets*) **forevermore** (*la 'owlam*).

This observant sprout and shoot, indeed this sucker from the original rootstock preserving the life of the tree (*netser* – this new growth emerging from an old stump which rises to the next generation, this extension grafted into the main branch which can be used as an implement to spare lives by revealing that which was not readily known; from *natsar* – to be observant, watchful, and trustworthy, to guard, protect, and preserve), **is the one whom Yahowah planted** (*ha mata' Yahowah* – the one whose base and roots Yahowah established), **the work and accomplishment of His hands** (*ma'aseh yad huw'* – the labors, acts, and products of His influence), **to endow a higher status through clarifying explanations** (*la pa'ar*). (*Yasha'yah* / Isaiah 60:21)

That which is determined and readily known (*ha qaton*) **will be** (*hayah*) **magnified a thousandfold** (*la ha 'alaph* – will become abundantly productive) **and the child with older siblings** (*wa ha tsa'yr*) **will be an accomplished and effective gentile** (*gowy 'atsuwm*). **I** (*'any*)**, Yahowah** (*YaHoWaH*)**, am prepared to accomplish this quickly** (*chuwsh hy'*) **at the proper time** (*ba 'eth hy'*).'" (*Yasha'yah* / Isaiah 60:22)

In a way, this is an unveiling of eternity. The God who created the universe for us to enjoy, beginning with light, is replacing an aspect of what He conceived with Himself. The realization that we will come full circle in the physical sphere helps reinforce something much more profound, something which will become essential to our understanding of where we have been and where we are going. Yahowah's plan is to take us back to 'Eden where our relationship began and flourished. Upon His return, after removing all traces of religion and politics, God is going to restore the planet so that we can camp out together – enjoying one another's company. Without the sorrowful religious rituals men have conceived, life will be joyous. It is the promise of "*shalem* – restitution and restoration."

The point of our excursion through this portion of Yasha'yah has been to affirm the correlation between our Creator and the first thing He conceived. In the process we found that Yahowah is not only equating an aspect of His nature with *'owr* | light, but He is also saying that He eternally exists as our light.

The same individual who spoke the universe into existence inspired these words, affirming the profound correlation between Himself and His Word, between Himself and light, and between enlightenment and our path to eternity.

In the end as it was in the beginning, it is all about light. Its energy is the essence of our *hayah* | existence. From the perspective of science, this is precisely what light accomplishes. Einstein discovered, and others have confirmed, that light defines time, illuminating what it means to be eternal – existing in the past, present, and future simultaneously. Light is the purest form of energy, its speed is considered the universal constant, the source and measure of time, the means to enlightenment, and to life itself.

So whether **"God (*'elohym*) said (*'amar*), 'Let there continuously be (*hayah*) light (*'owr*) and light (*wa 'owr*) exists (*hayah*),'"** or said…**"I was, am, and will be Light, always existing as light,"** He was speaking about how light, the first thing He created, could be equated to His nature so that we would better understand Him and what He is offering. His essential nature would lead directly to our enlightenment and immortality. Yahowah through creation shed light upon the path to Him, so that we might become like Him.

Yahowah completed His opening *Bare'syth* declaration with…

"**And so** (*wa*), **the Almighty** (*'elohym* – God) **saw** (*ra'ah* – viewed, perceived, and regarded, appeared and presented Himself, becoming visible to delight in and distinguish, revealing (qal imperfect)) **that the association with** (*'eth* – the accompaniment of) **the light** (*ha 'owr* – enlightenment and illumination) **was truly** (*ky* – was indeed and truthfully) **good** (*towb* – beneficial and productive, having desirable and positive qualities, especially valuable and beautiful, pleasant and prosperous, enjoyable and festive, agreeable and pleasing, useful and enriching, of a higher nature and empowering, best and right).

God (*wa 'elohym* – the Almighty) **caused the ongoing separation** (*badal* – divided and set apart, choosing then creating an exclusion based upon His ongoing preference (hifil imperfect – influencing the light such that it would act in consort with God with ongoing implications throughout time)) **between** (*bayn* – such that we could look closely and process this information, ponder the implications, and then respond appropriately by being discerning regarding) **the light** (*ha 'owr* – the source of energy, illumination, empowerment, and enlightenment) **and** (*wa* – in addition to being) **concerned about the understanding made possible through this connection with** (*bayn* – for association during an interval of time between things, isolating them for the purpose of enhancing comprehension; from *byn* – to be discerning so as to realize and comprehend, developing understanding by being observant and recognizing the connections between what is related and distinct regarding) **the darkness** (*ha choshek* – obscurity, that which shrouds in blackness, veils by withholding knowledge, perplexes and clouds revelation with sinister suggestions, concealing and mystifying by way of ignorance and confusion, the absence of light)." (*Bare'syth* / In the Beginning / Genesis 1:4)

According to God, light is good – simple and accurate. Light is truly as Yahowah expressed: "*towb* – beneficial and productive, having desirable and positive qualities, especially valuable and beautiful, pleasant and prosperous, enjoyable and festive, agreeable and pleasing, useful and enriching, of a higher nature and empowering."

But that is where it gets interesting because light is separated from darkness, just as we must distance ourselves from religious and political schemes if we wish to be with God. The Covenant's prerequisite is to be "*badal* – set apart and excluded" from the confusion of religion, the politics of our nation, the customs of our people, and the family of man.

The root of *bayn*, *byn*, is among my favorites. It describes the process by which we make connections regarding the things we come to know by being observant and contemplating the relationship between them such that we come to understand. To be *byn* is to ponder the implications of what we perceive in order to respond appropriately. It is to view and consider everything in context.

Doing so is what I enjoy most of all. *Byn* is how I came to understand what most have missed. Everything you will read in these pages is ultimately the product of *byn* – of connecting the dots, or in this case – letters, words, statements, and thoughts – to better understand.

It is a lack of *byn* that I abhor because it leads to truncated thinking, worthless opinions, irrational religions, inane politics, hypocritical pronouncements, absurd causes, counterproductive missions, and senseless protests and policies. A lack of *byn* is why politicians curtailed liberty and livelihoods to confront a virus and made everything worse. A lack of *byn* is why America made a bad situation horrific following its ill-fated invasions of Afghanistan and Iraq. A lack of *byn* is why the Roman

Catholic Church still exists. A lack of *byn* is responsible for the counterproductive hypocrisy and societal upheaval wrought by the emergence of the Black Lives Matter movement. (While all lives matter, should one decide to only advocate for one ethnicity, then one should be careful about blaming other races for their plight, especially when Blacks are responsible for 93% of all Black murders.)

In this case, Yahowah contrasts light with darkness. He wants us to closely examine these two extremes and consider the implications of being surrounded by one rather than the other. This is the contrast between enlightenment and ignorance, the words of God and beliefs of man, of right and wrong, of life or death, of *Shamaym* | the Spiritual Realm of Heaven or *She'owl* | the Place of Separation akin to a black hole.

All who avail themselves of the Light are called out of the darkness and separated unto Yahowah. This is one of a dozen times that separation and division are discussed in Yahowah's opening statement.

The other two aspects of this revelation worth considering are that darkness is not the opposite of light; it is the absence of light. And Satan is not the opposite of God; the Devil is the absence of God. Death is not the opposite of life; it is the absence of life.

Second, the dark spirit's deceptive arsenal is itemized in *choshek*. He conceals his true nature as the adversary. He lurks in the shadows, behind the scenes, obscuring his purpose. His religious and political schemes are seldom considered satanic, for if they were, they would not be seductive. Satan is clandestine, wrapping himself and his beguiling institutions in mystery and secrecy. The Devil preys on ignorance. A confused and distracted society is his sandbox. He has been so successful that he is actually worshiped as God in most religions.

The reason darkness and separation are making a second appearance on day one is to highlight the choice we must all make – to choose God or the Adversary. Choice remains paramount to Yahowah because it is the prerequisite of all loving relationships.

Bringing it all together, Yahowah's salutation to humankind reads:

"**In** (*ba* – near, within certain limits of, and in proximity to, regarding the account of) **the beginning** (*re'shyth* – at the start of time and the initiation of the process of existence, concerning the first fruits of the labors of the head of the family, while addressing the thing which is of first and foremost importance), **the Almighty** (*'elohym* – God), **for accompaniment and association** (*'eth* – accordingly and therefore, near and in proximity to), **created** (*bara'* – conceived and caused a new existence, choosing perfect transformation and birth, planning, preparing, shaping, producing, and fashioning something out of the elements and making it happen) **the spiritual world** (*ha shamaym* – heavens and abode of God) **and** (*wa*) **alongside** (*'eth* – to accompany it as part of a relationship) **the material realm** (*ha 'erets* – matter, the physical and natural world). (1:1)

And (*wa*) **the material realm** (*ha 'erets* – the physical world and the natural substance of which the universe is comprised, that which is perceived to be solid) **existed** (*hayah* – came to be and was for a finite period of time) **formless, without shape** (*tohuw* – lacking organization, in a state of lifeless confusion, as something which would dissipate into nothingness without additional energy), **an orderless, chaotic, and empty space** (*wa bohuw* – a randomized void, a deserted and unoccupied place, desolate of life), **dark, hidden, obscure, and unknowable** (*wa choshek* – a dark matter, incomprehensible and indecipherable, appearing confusing and black, incapable of being perceived or seen) **in proximity to** (*'al* – along with, upon, and near the spatial position of) **the presence** (*paneh* – the face and appearance of the visible aspects) **of the vast, inexhaustible power and inaccessible, mysterious energy of the big bang** (*tahowm* – of the great commotion from the agitated and loud, enormous and yet controlled explosion, with wave following wave without intermission).

Then (*wa*), **the** *Ruwach* **| Spirit** (*ruwach* – the Maternal manifestation of Divine power, courage, attitude, and acceptance, the heart and mind of God) **of the Almighty** (*'elohym*) **hovered over and quickly administered to, cherishing** (*rachaph 'al* – She moved back and forth, supervising everything, brooding over Her infant creation as a loving Mother, instigating an exceedingly fast quivering motion, flying rapidly over while suspended above to increase the pace of accomplishments, acting expeditiously while managing the process and advancing the action, She served by energizing and promoting growth and development through superintendence) **the appearance** (*paneh* – the surface and presence) **of the fluid state** (*maym* – of the source of life and means to cleanse symbolically or plasma scientifically). (*Bare'syth* 1:2)

In addition (*wa*), **God** (*'elohym* – the Almighty [depicted in the original alphabet as ⅃𝄪 – the protective ram shepherding His flock]) **said** (*'amar* – He declared by intending with ongoing ramifications), **'Let there continuously be** (*hayah* – it is the ongoing will and desire of the light for it to always and genuinely exist) **light** (*'owr* – illumination, enlightenment, the ability to see, and brilliant guidance) **and** (*wa*) **light** (*'owr*) **exists** (*hayah* – actually was and will literally always be).' (*Bare'syth* 1:3)

And so (*wa*), **the Almighty** (*'elohym* – God) **saw** (*ra'ah* – viewed, perceived, and regarded, appeared and presented Himself, becoming visible to delight in and distinguish, revealing) **that the association with** (*'eth* –

the accompaniment of) **the light** (*ha 'owr* enlightenment and illumination) **was truly** (*ky* – was indeed and truthfully) **good** (*towb* – beneficial and productive, having desirable and positive qualities, especially valuable and beautiful, pleasant and prosperous, enjoyable and festive, agreeable and pleasing, useful and enriching, of a higher nature and empowering, best and right).

God (*wa 'elohym* – the Almighty) **caused the ongoing separation** (*badal* – divided and set apart, choosing then creating an exclusion based upon His ongoing preference) **between** (*bayn* – such that we could look closely and process this information, ponder the implications, and then respond appropriately by being discerning regarding) **the light** (*ha 'owr* – the source of energy, illumination, empowerment, and enlightenment) **and** (*wa* – in addition to being) **concerned about the understanding made possible through this connection with** (*bayn* – for association during an interval of time between things, isolating them for the purpose of enhancing comprehension; from *byn* – to be discerning so as to realize and comprehend, developing understanding by being observant and recognizing the connections between what is related and distinct regarding) **the darkness** (*ha choshek* – obscurity, that which shrouds in blackness, veils by withholding knowledge, and clouds revelation with sinister suggestions, concealing and mystifying by way of ignorance and confusion, the absence of light)." (*Bare'syth* / In the Beginning / Genesis 1:4)

ﭞ�﬩ﭞ�﬩

Since *Bare'syth* / In the Beginning / Genesis 1:2 introduces the first use of *rachaph*, the uniquely challenging verb deployed in conjunction with the Spirit of God, it is time now to consider the second occurrence so that we might better appreciate its implications. *Rachaph* is found again in the 32nd chapter of *Dabarym* / Words / Deuteronomy.

The context begins similarly to the opening lines of *Bare'syth* / Genesis, speaking of "heaven and earth," and of "Yahowah's spoken words." This passage, like Yahowah's initial Towrah testimony, even mentions "water" in the forms of "droplets, dew, and rain" in Moseh's poetic couplet. Then Dabarym turns its focus to God's influence in our lives, perhaps in similar fashion to *Bare'syth*. We are told that "Yahowah is God's name," that "He is the Rock of our salvation," and that "His work is perfect, just, dependable, and upright." By contrast, we are also told that Yisra'el would "act corruptly toward Him" and that a time would come when they "would not be His children" but instead be considered "a perverse and crooked generation" of "foolish and unwise people."

Yahowah provided this contrast to make the benefits associated with *rachaph* readily apparent. In addition to introducing Himself as our "Savior" in Dabarym, Yahowah, consistent with His Bare'syth implications, says that He is "our Father," the "Rock who begot us," and "the God who gave us birth"—in this case, Spiritual birth from above.

In the midst of this treatise on salvation, Yahowah introduces *rachaph* in a metaphor:

"Of your own freewill, pay attention, come to understand, and respond (*'azan* – choose to hear, be perceptive, and comprehend, then reply (hifil imperative – the subject (who is *Moseh* | Moses) is encouraging the objects (those listening) to choose of their own freewill to hear what he has to say such that their response will be similar to his own)) **to the Spiritual Realm** (*ha shamaym* – to the Heavens and abode of God) **because** (*wa*) **I want to speak** (*dabar* – I would like to communicate using

106

words, expressing this in speech (piel cohortative – an expression of first-person volition whereby the individual listening is directly affected and put into action by what is message)) **and** (*wa*) **may the material realm** (*ha 'erets*) **decide to listen** (*shama'* – opt to hear (qal imperfect jussive – expressing a genuine relationship between the parties with ongoing implications throughout time as a result of choices made by those on Earth who decide to listen)) **to the words of my mouth** (*'emer peh 'any* – to what I say and share verbally, especially the promises; from *'amar* – to say, answer, question, and promise)." (*Dabarym* / Words / Deuteronomy 32:1)

I chose to introduce Moseh's statement regarding *rachaph* in advance of his actual use of the word because it presents an opportunity to explore some of the wonderful nuances of the Hebrew language. Here we find volition expressed in first, second, and third person. This was demonstrated in the imperative (conveying that the individual being addressed has freewill, and thus choice in the second person), cohortative (a first-person expression of desire used to share the speaker's will), and jussive (third-person volition). These moods convey the options and opportunities, choices and decisions, will and desire of the parties participating in the conversation. Freewill is so vital to establishing mutually beneficial and loving relationships, volition underscores much of what Yahowah has to say. He has it and so do we.

The stems all establish a relationship between the subject and the object of the verb's action. Here, the qal stem reveals that we should interpret this relationship literally because the action is actual and genuine. With the piel stem, the relationship is voiced a little differently in that it is used to reveal that the object of the verb receives the effect and is put into action by the subject of the sentence. In that the entire reason Yahowah created the universe and conceived life was to establish the Covenant

107

Family, these relationships are paramount, especially as we interact with each other. Hebrew stems range from simple to exceedingly complex, adding nuance and depth to each conversation.

In Hebrew, the verbs of Yah's testimony are all liberated in time such that there is no past, present, or future tenses. Everything that is said is forever. However, not every action is eternal. As a result, there are two conjugations. The imperfect describes ongoing action throughout time, often with unfolding implications. The perfect is a completed act, whether that occurred in the past or will transpire in the future, and thus is finite in time. Our actions are often habitual, in that we do the same things over and over again – sometimes with undesirable results. Yahowah's response is to completely resolve the problem at a moment in time, thereby making the imperfect perfect.

To correctly convey the intended implications of each stem, mood, and conjugation in Hebrew requires additional wording in English since the language does not have a counterpart. Therefore, translators have the option of ignoring their influence, making the result shorter and simpler, or conveying it, resulting in a longer and more accurate rendering.

Moseh may have been old. He may have had imperfect diction. But that did not keep him from waxing poetic. He wanted to build upon some of the metaphors implied by water.

"May the persuasive words of my teaching (*leqach 'any* – my instruction based upon what I know to be true, including the insights and information which can be grasped hold of and incorporated into one's life) **continually trickle down** (*'araph* – drip and fall (qal imperfect – literally and genuinely, continually and consistently)) **like the rain** (*ka matar* – as a natural and widespread shower)**, distilled** (*nazal* – enveloping) **as the**

dew with abundant benefits (*ka tal* – like a mist bringing prosperity), **my instructive promises** (*'imrah 'any* – my communication and speech; from *'emer* – to share promises and convey intent) **are similar to** (*ka* – like) **showers** (*sa'yr*) **upon new growth** (*deshe'* – verdant growth, tender grass, herbs and vegetation, all of which sprout, bringing forth new life), **like** (*wa ka*) **a substantial soaking rain** (*rabybym* – the ideal amount of water to stimulate and sustain growth; from *rabab* – great, plentiful, and abundant) **on vegetation** (*'eseb* – plants, herbs, and vegetables for human consumption)." (*Dabarym* / Words / Deuteronomy 32:2)

From Moseh's perspective, words are like water. They are life-giving and sustaining when the teaching and instructions are valid. And for that to be so, it all begins with...

"Indeed, therefore (*ky* – as a result), **I will continually call out and summon** (*qara'* – I will read and recite, proclaim and invite, invoke and encounter (qal imperfect)) **the name** (*shem* – the personal and proper designation) **of Yahowah** (*YaHoWaH* – an accurate presentation of the name of *'elowah* – God as guided by His *towrah* – instructions regarding His *hayah* – existence), **choosing to draw your attention to it while encouraging you to take action regarding** (*yahab* – wanting to extol its virtues, asking you to make a decision regarding it and actually respond to it while there is still time, to give it your undivided attention and come to embrace it literally of your own volition, ascribing and disclosing (qal imperative – literally and genuinely of your own freewill)) **its unrivaled importance and enormous power** (*godel* – its extraordinary significance and majesty, its magnitude and magnificence; from *gadal* – ability to empower, enhance, magnify, and promote growth, enabling great things to be accomplished) **to approach our God** (*la 'elohym* *'anachnuw* – to draw near the Almighty).**" (*Dabarym* / Words / Deuteronomy 32:3)

If you are influenced by religion or societal customs into believing that God has many names, that He does not care what we call Him, that there is no value in knowing or using His name, or that the four vowels which comprise it are unpronounceable (but nowhere else), then perhaps after reading *Moseh's* | Moses' declaration you'll reconsider. And should you do so, are you also going to disassociate from and disparage the religious institutions and individuals deliberately misleading you and so many others about the single most important realization in the universe?

Other than to preclude you from knowing His name and forming a relationship with Him, what is the purpose of writing "the Lord" all 7,000 times Yahowah appears in the Towrah, Prophets, and Psalms? Why do the religious react angrily to Yahowah's name being spoken and write "G-d" when doing so is in absolute conflict with the Towrah? Why claim to be "Torah-observant" when opposed to its guidance?

Nothing is more important than *Yada Yahowah* | Knowing Yahowah. God's one and only name is "*godel* – unrivaled in importance." It is "enormously powerful and empowering." Yahowah "promotes growth, magnifying us in knowledge, riches, and days, especially dimensions and thus capability, enabling us to do great things."

"The Rock (*ha tsuwr* – the massive, impregnable, strength of the foundation of stone, the sure edifice and stronghold), **His work** (*po'al huw'* – His labor, actions, and expenditure of energy; from *pa'al* – to do, performing to carry out and prepare, fashion, and forge, making ready) **is entirely perfect** (*tamym* – totally right, completely correct, and absolutely genuine and sincere, is in universal accord with reality and the truth, sound and complete, without defect).

110

Indeed (*ky* – it is truthful and reliable), **all of** (*kol* – every one of) **His ways** (*derek huw'* – His path and the subsequent journey of discovery, His actions pertaining to the conduct of one's life) **are directed by exercising good judgment, especially regarding the means to justly resolve disputes** (*mishpat* – are just and justifiable, evidentially and logically valid, found through rational decision-making; a compound of *my* – to question, ponder, and contemplate *shaphat* – the process of judging and deciding, of being just and right, discerning and discriminating, separating right from wrong, truth from fiction, and beneficial from counterproductive):

God (*'el*) **is trustworthy, steadfast, and reliable** (*'emuwnah* – is honest, dependable, truthful, firm, and unchanging; from *'emuwn* – trusting and trustworthy which is from *'aman* – to be established and readily verified, confirmed, and validated, to be supportive and dependable).

In addition (*wa*), **He is devoid of anything which is wrong, dishonest, invalid, or unjust** (*'ayn 'awel* – He is never incorrect, hypocritical, or contradictory and He never deviates from the proper way).

He (*huw'*) **is right** (*tsadyq* – is correct, upright, and in accord with His standard, is honest, fair, and consistent, having integrity and character because He is ethical and moral, accurate and just, even justified when vindicating and acquitting) **while also straightforward and unwavering** (*wa yashar* – on the level, frank and blunt, never beating around the bush, open and honest, preferring full disclosure, consistent without ever being contradictory, and as such is the Upright One)." (*Dabarym* / Words / Deuteronomy 32:4)

What are we to make of the idea of God working, doing whatever is required to plan, implement, and then pursue His ambitions? Since His enterprise is called "perfect," it is obviously good, beneficial, and appropriate. But why labor? Couldn't God have willed the desired result into fruition without lifting a finger?

Perhaps, but then what is the purpose? If we could enjoy an ideal relationship without engaging, achieve the perfect family without effort, or acquire everything we want without doing anything to merit it, where is the sense of achievement or value? What would anything be worth? How would we otherwise grow? What is the purpose of life? Why have freewill?

Yahowah is setting an example for us, showing us the benefit and importance of work. It is a good thing, a wonderful thing, to work. It creates a sense of appreciation, develops confidence, and forges our character, making us stronger and more capable. Our investment in time and energy makes everything, from learning to relationships, from grand adventures to businesses, even homes, families, friendships, and hobbies, more rewarding and enjoyable. Simply stated: work is good.

One of the many things differentiating Yahowah from the men He created and the institutions they conceived is that God is always right, in full accord with reality, logical and rational. God never contradicts Himself. The flaws that we see in every human endeavor do not exist with Yahowah.

The path to God is found by exercising good judgment, which is to say, being judgmental and embracing the truth while discarding that which is invalid. We think our way to God, making faith irrelevant. To know Yahowah is infinitely superior to believing.

To capitalize upon the way Yahowah has provided to leave the corrupt and unreliable world of mortal men and enter into His company, we must be knowledgeable and logical, exercising rational decision-making. We know this because, like so many Hebrew terms, *mishpat* is a compound word. It is comprised of *my*, which asks us to question, to ponder, and to contemplate that which is required to *shaphat*: make quality decisions. To know the truth, we must be discerning and discriminating, separating right from wrong, fact from fiction, and that which is beneficial from things which are counterproductive. This is the opposite of the moral relativism and conformity imposed through political correctness.

Judaism, Christianity, and Islam all require Yahowah to be vastly different than He presents Himself. For the Talmud, New Testament, or Quran to be valid, everything God stated in His Towrah and through His prophets must be subject to change, be flexible and invalid – indeed untrustworthy. But since the Towrah and Prophets are readily verified, and Yahowah is truthful, consistent, and reliable, anything that changes His approach or contradicts Him is invalid. The moment a religion claims that the Towrah and Prophets were inspired by their god, as do Judaism, Christianity, and Islam, and then contradict what God said, changing His approach to suit their own, they are wrong.

The religious position is preposterous. Why would anyone put their faith in a god who isn't trustworthy or dependable, who is dishonest and unjust, who is like them, both contradictory and hypocritical? If His original plan were invalid when He claimed it was right, nothing attributed to Him would be reliable. Faith in that which is incorrect is stupid.

While it requires a considerable amount of work to find and know God, because He is straightforward and unwavering, an open and honest search through evidence and reason will consistently lead to Him. Yahowah favors full disclosure, with all of His words placed face up on the table for our inspection.

And yet, men have long sought to hide them, to write other things all over them, and to shuffle them around and remove them from their context – as if playing a game with the souls of humankind.

And perhaps now you know why this commentary follows much of what Yahowah inspired. I am doing what Yahowah asked of us: contemplating the meaning and consequence of each statement. I am working at it, engaged in the process and going where the words lead. And I want to take you there with me.

Should you be able to process all of this on your own, should you have garnered these insights and developed these conclusions while reading the translations, then rather than finding my commentary repetitive, please see it as reinforcing what you have discovered, recognizing that we were led to the same place. Should you disagree, that is fine too, so long as you are thoughtful and consistent, because then we are both engaged in contemplating the word of God. The more we collectively strive to extract the insights Yahowah sought to convey, the better.

If you are devoted to learning the truth, then you are one in a million. Most…

"They will corrupt everything regarding Him and be devastated as a result (*shachath la huw'* – they will suffer the effect of perverting, distorting, twisting, falsifying, and misrepresenting that which is near and dear to Him, injuring themselves in the process (piel perfect – they will endure the consequence of their corruptions at a point in time)).

No longer His children (*lo' beny huw'*)**, they are shameful and disgusting, verbally abusive, slanderers** (*muwm hem* – they are blemished and sullied to the point of being defective, painful to be around and injurious to others) – **a perverse and dishonest** (*'iqesh* – a convoluted and corrupted, evasive and immoral) **as well as** (*wa*)

deviant and warped (*pataltol* – crooked, wily and shrewd, obstinate and twisted) **generation** (*dowr* – lineage, group of ethnically related individuals at another period of time)." (*Dabarym* / Words / Deuteronomy 32:5)

The Children of Yisra'el were called to be the family of God. But over time, they all left home. God has called out to them, pleading with them to come home, but they do not listen. What was intended to be a showcase for how wonderful life with God could become has soured such that Jews are viewed with contempt and seen as abusive and dishonest deviants. Fortunately, this was scribed in the perfect conjugation, affirming that it will not always be this way.

There is yet another insight here that I do not want you to miss. The Children of Yisra'el were able to slander Yahowah by twisting His testimony. They have convoluted and corrupted the word of God, as have Christians and Muslims following in their footsteps. This means that God allowed it even though He despises it. At times, children can be their own worst enemy, as almost every parent can attest.

Knowing that Jews like Rabbi Akiba (Judaism through the Talmud), the Apostle Paul (Christianity through its New Testament), and the Prophet Muhammad (by way of the Quran) deliberately and dishonestly convoluted Yahowah's message should help the informed steer clear of their disgusting influence.

In the book that presents Yahowah as our Creator, Moseh asks his people...

"Is this how you approach (*ha la*) **and repay** (*gamal* – deal with and treat) **Yahowah** (*Yahowah* – the proper pronunciation of YaHoWaH, our *'elowah* – God as directed in His *ToWRaH* – teaching regarding His *HaYaH* – existence and our *ShaLoWM* – restoration)?

115

As a people (*zo'th 'am* – as part of this family), **you are becoming willfully ignorant** (*nabal* – you are foolish and surprisingly stupid, oblivious and inconsiderate, insolent and impudent, disrespectful and rude, senseless and contemptible). **You simply do not understand** (*lo' chakam* – you are not discerning or discriminating and do not exercise good judgment, having squandered the capacity to understand).

Is He not (*ha 'lo huw'* – have you not negated His role as) **your Father** (*'ab 'atah* – your originator and caregiver, the one whose name you bear and should respect for conceiving and raising you, protecting and nourishing you) **– the One who created you and then ransomed you** (*qanah 'atah* – who brought you forth such that you exist and subsequently acquired and obtained you (from Egypt and Babylon))?

He acted and engaged on your behalf (*huw' 'asah 'atah* – He has and will again perform for you, having worked for your benefit, accomplishing what needed to be done for you (qal perfect)) **and then** (*wa* – in addition) **established you such that you might endure** (*kuwn 'atah* – authenticated and sustained you such that you have survived (piel polel imperfect – reinforcing that Yisra'elites have benefited from what Yah has done such that they, unlike other ancient ethnicities, still exist as a discernable people in their God-given homeland))." (*Dabarym* / Words / Deuteronomy 32:6)

Moseh is letting Yisra'el know as bluntly as words allow that Yahowah was critical of His people's approach toward Him. Today, this is largely the result of Judaism, a religion which is neither valid nor beneficial. With all Yahowah has done for *Yahuwdym* | Jews then and now, this is how they have chosen to repay Him – by corrupting and perverting His testimony.

But please do not gloat, much less entertain anti-Semitic thoughts, if you are a *gowy* | gentile. Christianity, Islam, and Socialist Secular Humanism were conceived by Jews, making them part and parcel of this condemnation.

While I am sure that it sounds harsh to modern ears, there is no denying that religion is as stupid as it is stupefying. A person has to be ignorant or irrational to believe any of them. Even worse, every religion is disrespectful because they all discount and deny the one true God in favor of a substantial collection of bumbling and imbecilic imposters.

Humanity was conceived to be bright and to exercise the capacity to understand. It is religions which have deliberately thwarted people's ability to think. As a result, the masses are more easily manipulated and controlled. Most people fail to appreciate even the basics about God, who He actually is, why He created us, or what He is offering or expects in return.

And it is worse today than ever because those not dumbed down into submission by traditional religious and political schemes are now degraded by the imposition of political correctness – where exercising good judgment is rebuked. The desires of leftists (both communists and socialists) are considered sacrosanct, such that those who dare point out their hypocrisy are ruthlessly condemned and shunned.

In a world of nearly eight billion people, less than one in a million, not even eight thousand people, know, much less understand God. We have been cajoled into believing that we are entitled to our opinions and that faith is of value – when both are worthless. Without the will or capacity to think rationally, freedom and freewill are for naught. Without being judgmental, there is no morality, civility, or justice.

The most basic of all perspectives is the one we humans don't seem to understand. Yahowah wants nothing more or less than to be our Father. As such, He should not be feared or worshiped. We ought never bow down to Him. These are behavioral responses completely incompatible with a parent / child relationship. Families are conceived and grow based on loving relationships, not religious edicts.

As our Father, it is Yahowah who is in a position to get down on His knees and lift us up. He is capable and desirous of doing so. But this is not something we can reciprocate, so it is long past time we get off of our knees such that we are ready to walk with His assistance.

Truth be known, God conceived us and then He rescued His people from the most oppressive and ruthless of nations – and He is offering to do so again. Our Heavenly Father has acted and engaged on our behalf, not only to free us from human abuse but also to enable the benefits of the Covenant.

"Remember the days of long ago (*zakar yowmym 'owlam* – call to mind and consider a time long past (qal imperative – of your own freewill, genuinely reflect)), **choosing to make the connections needed to understand** (*byn* – opt to observe and consider what can be known, coming to comprehend by establishing rational relationships between what you learn, then choose to impart that knowledge by teaching (qal imperative)) **the years** (*shanah* – the sequence of the seasons and of life and light as well as the period of renewal, even the repetitive nature of things), **the lifetimes and succession of generation after generation** (*dowr wa dowr* – the lineage, related births, and dwelling places of the many generations), **asking your Father of your own interest** (*sha'al 'ab 'atah* – genuinely inquiring of and questioning of your own volition your Father (qal imperative)) **and He will convey this information to you** (*wa nagad 'atah* – He will be forthright and open with you, making it conspicuous) **of those of old** (*zaqen 'atah* – regarding your elders) **and they will provide answers for you** (*wa 'amar la 'atah* – they will respond, speaking to you)." (*Dabarym* / Words / Deuteronomy 32:7)

God wants us to question Him. As the best of Fathers, He would love nothing more than to teach His children, sharing what He has come to know – which, might I add, is considerable and inspiring. But many of these answers and most of the insights are already laid out conspicuously before us in the Towrah and Prophets. God's story, His explanation, and even His guidance, begins with 'Adam and then Chawah in the Garden, followed by the venerable captain of the Ark, Noach.

We can learn almost all we need to know from 'Abraham and Sarah, their son, Yitschaq, and his second-born, Ya'aqob, who became Yisra'el. Then there is the man speaking to us through these words, the great liberator, Moseh – who revealed the Towrah. Thereafter, *Yahowsha'* | Joshua would lead Yahowah's people back into their Land, but then considerable time would pass before we would meet the most remarkable of the Judges, Shamuw'el – from whom there is so much we will learn.

In the midst of the generations, in *dowr wa dowr*, we find the Chosen One, the most beloved, the Son of God, the Messiah, Shepherd, and King – *Dowd* | David. He is not only the living embodiment of the Covenant, the man Yahowah consistently called "right," he is the author of the most inspiring and enlightening Psalms and Proverbs.

Exceptional men would follow: the irascible and entertaining 'Elyah, Howsha', Yasha'yah, Yirma'yah, and Zakaryah, then Yahowsha', to name a few. There would also be villains in the midst – none greater than the two Sha'uwls, the wannabe king and, a millennium thereafter, the wannabe apostle.

One of the many things we are going to find during our voyage of discovery through the words Yahowah revealed for us is that we are not all equal in the sight of God. He has absolutely and unequivocally prioritized His relationship with the descendants of 'Abraham and Sarah through His Covenant with Yitschaq and Ya'aqob who became Yisra'el. And even among the Children of Yisra'el, Yahowah favors Yahuwdym over the other descendants of Ya'aqob. Beyond this, our Heavenly Father has one son He loves more than anyone else, *Dowd* | David.

As *gowym* | gentiles, we are invited and welcome. We can become part of Yahowah's Covenant Family too, doing so in exactly the same way God described for His people in His *Towrah* | Instructions. But if Yahowah's enduring devotion to Yisra'el, if His affinity for Yahuwdym, if His love for one man beyond all others, troubles you, that is your choice. But your decision in this regard will not cause God to change His mind and pick a different ethnicity, nation, creed, place, or faith. The attention and promises God afforded Yisra'el endure forever, which is why Gentiles were separated and the boundaries were set and remain.

Gentiles can cross the border and enter the Promised Land, becoming part of Yisra'el, if they come by way of the Towrah's Guidance, answer the *Miqra'ey* | Invitations and join the *Beryth* | Covenant Family. That is to say that Christians, Muslims, and Socialist Secular Humanists are wrong. The path to the Promised Land is in accord with Yisra'el, not in hostility against them or by seeking to replace or control them.

There is one Towrah, one Covenant, and one inheritance for all of God's children...

"When offering an inheritance (*ba nachal* – through the process of bestowing a bequest, birthright, and legacy, an endowment for those who become heirs (hifil infinitive

– the subject, who is God, is engaging the objects, His Covenant children such that they become more like Him in a highly demonstrable way using a verbal adjective to intensify the action)) **to people from different races and places** (*gowym* – ethnicities other than Yisra'el, and the confluence of nations)**, the Almighty** (*'elyown* – the Most High) **thereby** (*ba* – therein and with this) **separated and divided** (*parad huw'* – He created a distinct allocation such that there would be different groups, spreading out the divergent ethnicities (hifil infinitive)) **the descendants of 'Adam** (*beny 'adam* – the children of mankind and the sons of the first man created in God's image).

He took a stand and established (*natsab* – He attended to and was upright in appointing, standing on solid ground with regard to (hifil imperfect)) **the borders** (*gabuwlah* – the boundaries and geographical space and limits) **of the families** (*'amym* – of the peoples (typically used in the singular for the family of Yisra'el and in the plural for the twelve descendants of Ya'aqob but can also be people and nations generally)) **according to the number** (*la misphar* – calculated mathematically based upon the amount of people approaching and quantity of souls over time who draw near; from *saphar* – to count and to relate, to take into account, to calculate the number, enumerate the result, and communicate the result in a census) **of the children of Yisra'el** (*beny Yisra'el* – sons of those who engage and endure with God and the family members who are empowered and set free by God)." (*Dabarym* / Words / Deuteronomy 32:8)

The world at large remains separate and distinct from Yisra'el. And yet, a *gowy* | person of a different ethnicity can choose to become part of Yahowah's Family in accordance with the *Towrah* | Teaching, *Miqra'ey* | Invitations to be Called Out and Meet, and *Beryth* | Covenant Family. This necessitates disassociating from the politics and religions of the Gentiles, coming to know

Yahowah, acknowledging that His revelation is truthful, reliable, and unchanging, accepting the terms and conditions of His Covenant, and answering His Invitations to Meet. We do not change God; God changes us.

In the end as it was in the beginning, the Children of Yisra'el are Yahowah's priority...

"Indeed, this is (*ky* – surely and reliably this is actually) **Yahowah's** (*Yahowah* – the proper pronunciation of YaHoWaH, our *'elowah* – God as directed in His *ToWRaH* – teaching regarding His *HaYaH* – existence and our *ShaLoWM* – restoration) **allotment** (*cheleq* – share and portion, even reward) **to His family** (*'am huw'* – His people, the individuals who are related by ethnicity). **For Ya'aqob** (*Ya'aqob* – One who Succeeds with His Footsteps, son of Yitschaq and grandson of 'Abraham whom God renamed Yisra'el, commonly known as Jacob; from *'aqab* – to succeed and embed, *'eqeb* – with a consequence and reward, and *'aqeb* – heel and footsteps) **this is his share and destiny** (*chebel* – this becomes the pledge he offered expecting a commitment in return, this is for a relatively large amount of property and possessions, a significant portion to an heir whom God has chosen to favor for a joyful existence) **through his inheritance** (*nachalah huw'* – that which is given to successive generations from father to son based upon the relationship and their association serving as his hereditary share of the whole that is apportioned and assigned; from *nachal* – to receive as a possession, acquiring through an inheritance)." (*Dabarym* / Words / Deuteronomy 32:9)

Ya'aqob, the One who Succeeds with His Footsteps, is the forefather of Yisra'el. The twelve tribes are his direct descendants. In the earliest iteration of the Hebrew alphabet, the Semitic font reads right to left as: ⊔•⊙⊶. The ⊶ (*Yowd* | hand) depicts God reaching down and out to His children with an open hand to lift us up. The ⊙ (*'ayin* | eye) is an eye and is indicative of being observant.

The ◦ (*qoph* | horizon) was drawn to reveal the proper perspective. And the ◻ (*beyth* | family home) conveys a home with a single entrance. Therefore, Ya'aqob, in the language of revelation, describes someone with direct access to the hand of God, who, because he is observant and has gained the proper perspective, is included in His Family and lives within His Home.

While Ya'aqob, and thus Yisra'el, are favored, that does not leave *gowym* | gentiles shortchanged. God has more to offer than we can imagine. The universe is large, and its dimensions are expansive. There is much to learn, explore, share, and indeed inherit. It is certain that we will all be pleased with what we receive, and that begins with living forever, being perfected and adopted, then enriched, empowered, and enlightened.

Considering where we are, and where He is willing to take us, given what we are contributing in return, it's an exceedingly favorable arrangement.

"He found (*matsa'* – He discovered and met with, developing a relationship with (qal imperfect)) **him in a desolate land** (*huw' ba 'erets midbar* – him in a realm where the word is not considered, a desert wilderness)**, in** (*wa ba*) **a state of lifeless confusion** (*tohuw* – a place without much to offer, lacking organization, formless, as something which would dissipate into nothingness, a wasteland) **among howling animals** (*yalal* – wailing and shrill shouting) **of an inhospitable and unproductive desert** (*yashymown* – of a place of death, desolation, and destruction).

He enveloped and encompassed him (*sabab huw'* – He surrounded him and protected him, shielding him, while changing his direction). **He gave him the capacity to understand** (*byn huw'* – He made him more perceptive so that he might be more discerning and comprehend) **keeping him safe and watching over him** (*natsar huw'* –

protecting him, delivering him from harm's way, closely observing him, and saving him) **as the most cherished individual** (*ka 'ishown* – as the focus and center of, making him the most precious person; from *'iysh* – man) **in His sight** (*'ayn huw'* – in His view and from His perspective)." (*Dabarym* / Words / Deuteronomy 32:10)

Yahowah created 'Adam but He chose Noach, largely because he chose to disassociate from neighboring cultures and communities and was willing to listen. Yahowah chose 'Abram, whom He renamed 'Abraham, after he, on his own accord, decided to walk away from Babylon. He, too, was willing to listen to God and then act on His instructions. In the process, Yahowah facilitated Yitschaq's miraculous birth but then chose Ya'aqob, his second-born, who, as a shepherd, lived alone without political or religious entanglements.

Yahowah initiated contact with all of His prophets, most notably Moseh and Dowd – selecting these men, men who did not yet know Him, out of a world of others. From this, we can deduce that God chooses to work through people. He introduces Himself to individuals in lowly places who manifest the attributes, aptitudes, and attitudes He desires. The only common denominators among those with whom He initiates contact are that they are all unimpressive individuals who are disengaged from society, they are willing to listen and then act decisively. They are all imperfect people, with flaws of one sort or another, giving Yahowah the opportunity to empower, enlighten, enrich, and embolden them. Such was the case with Ya'aqob, whom Yahowah gave the capacity to understand – the most valuable thing in the universe.

From that moment, Yahowah looked upon Ya'aqob as a Father and Mother would their own child. Even when he behaved badly, God loved him, protected him, educated him, and watched over him. Of the millions of souls on the planet at the time, Yahowah chose to work with Ya'aqob and, through him, offered to engage with humankind.

Here at long last is the reference to *rachaph* we have been seeking. This time the Actor is paternal, not maternal, but the action and result are the same...

"**In the manner of** (*ka* – like and as) **an eagle** (*nesher* – a powerful bird of prey with a large wingspan) **who is alert and ready for action** (*'uwr* – who stirs up and raises up; from *'uwr* – exposes (hifil imperfect)) **regarding his nest** (*qen huw'* – on behalf of his elevated place to conceive, protect, nurture, and raise offspring), **he hovers over it, expeditiously administering to it while supervising everything** (*rachaph* – he moves back and forth, cherishing and brooding over his infant creation, instigating an exceedingly fast quivering motion, flying rapidly over it while suspended above to increase the pace of what is being accomplished, acting expeditiously while managing the process and advancing the action, he energizes the young and promotes growth, developing everything through superintendence (piel imperfect)).

He spreads out his wings (*paras kanaphy huw'* – he extends himself and stretches out his capacity for movement (qal imperfect)) **over** (*'al* – near, before, and in close proximity to) **his young** (*gowzal huw'* – his adolescent chicks as they mature and grow; from *gazal* – to apply significant effort and force), **grasping hold of them, accepting them, and keeping them** (*laqach huw'* – receiving and acquiring them, instructing and carrying them, even suffering for them if needed), **lifting them up and carrying them away** (*nasa' huw'* – supporting and respecting them, raising them, taking them to a higher elevation (qal imperfect)) **upon his pinions so as to empower and liberate them** (*'al 'ebrah huw'* – upon his body and feathers to induce soaring flight in an elevating and protective manner designed to strengthen and free them (note: *'ebrah* shares the first four of five letters in

125

'Abraham's name))." (*Dabarym* / Words / Deuteronomy 32:11)

The eagle is depicted as a male bird with chicks, reinforcing Yahowah's role as our Father. This, in conjunction with the earlier statement where the *Ruwach* | Spirit of God was deployed in conjunction with *rachaph*, completes the picture of Yahowah serving to conceive, guide, and raise the Covenant's children as our Heavenly Father and Spiritual Mother.

By pursuing this, the second of three times *rachaph* appears in the Towrah, Prophets, and Psalms, we are given other clues which help define the nature of the action being described. And that is because *rachaph* was used this time in conjunction with "*nesher* – a soaring and powerful eagle," which is " *'uwr* – ready to engage" with regard to "*qen* – an elevated place where offspring are protected, nurtured, and raised." We once again find that *rachaph* speaks about "*paras* – spreading out and extending something, expanding it," and of "*kanaphy* – wings," and thus of "more rapid movement in three dimensions."

The focus of *rachaph* is once again "*gowzal* – a new and adolescent creation ready to mature and grow with the application of the appropriate effort and force." And this time, young life is "*laqach* – embraced and accepted to the degree the one reaching out is willing to suffer if needed to guide" their children. Reinforcing the parental benefits of *rachaph*, we find "*nasa'* – to lift up those being raised and carrying them to a higher elevation." And if that were not enough to affirm that we were correct when applying parental shadings to *rachaph* when deployed in conjunction with the *Ruwach* | Spirit of God during creation, here it is used in conjunction with " *'ebrah* – to empower and liberate."

Our understanding of *rachaph*'s implications grows even richer with what follows because the action of the

126

verb is directly associated with Yahowah, casting God into the role of Spiritual Mother during creation and as Heavenly Father now hovering over His young family as the papa bird. Better still, Yahowah is "*nachah* – guiding and leading" His fledgling family "*nachah* – along the correct path, creating the opportunity for them to be loved, providing directions which can be trusted."

"**Yahowah** (𐤄𐤅𐤄𐤉 – a transliteration of *YaHoWaH* as instructed in His *towrah* – teaching regarding His *hayah* – existence), **alone** (*badad* – uniquely and by Himself as the only one in the space, separate and distinct from others), **guided him** (*nachah huw'* – lovingly led him along the correct path, shepherding him so as to provide the direction necessary to create this opportunity for him, doing so reliably and dependably such that he could trust Him (hifil – Yah positively influenced Ya'aqob with His guidance, thereby enabling Ya'aqob to lead others, imperfect – doing so consistently and continually with ongoing implications over time, energic nun – emphasizing the benefits of this relationship, jussive – conveyed as an expression of God's will))).

And (*wa*) **there was no foreign** (*'ayn nekar* – none with a familial connection and kinship from a distant place or time, and therefore, unfamiliar: from the negation of *nakar* – to recognize, acknowledge, know, respect, and regard by being observant, paying close attention, being perceptive and discerning) **god** (*'el* – power, influence, or concern) **associated with Him** (*'im huw'* – along with, or in relation to, Him)." (*Dabarym* / Words / Deuteronomy 32:12)

Back in 2005, when I first encountered *nekar* in this statement, and in all subsequent edits prior to 2020, I was unaware of how a derivation of its root, *nakar*, and thus *nakry*, when presented elsewhere would elevate the perceptions of these translations and commentary. Therefore, although I have translated *'ayn nekar* as "no

127

foreign," that rendering, while accurate in this statement due to its negation, benefits from the amplified explanation provided within the parentheses.

𐤉𐤄𐤅𐤄

The third occurrence of *rachaph* | to hover over in a protective and supportive manner is also insightful. It explains God's preference for a relationship instead of religion. Therefore, as we strive to more fully comprehend *rachaph* – the word that described the Spirit's initial role in universal causation, please consider this salvation prophecy. In *Yirma'yah* / Rise Up and Live in Yah's Shelter (errantly known as Jeremiah) 23, our suspicions regarding *rachaph* are confirmed. The paragraph which leads to *rachaph* begins...

"'**Now pay attention** (*hineh* – behold, look now and see), **the day** (*yowm*) **is coming** (*bow'* – will arrive),' **prophetically declares** (*na'um* – announces and reveals before it occurs) **Yahowah** (*Yahowah* – a transliteration of 𐤉𐤄𐤅𐤄, our *'elowah* – God as directed in His *towrah* – teaching regarding His *hayah* – existence), '**when** (*wa*) **I will take a stand, establish, and raise up** (*quwm* – I will stand upright to accomplish, affirm, fulfill, and restore), **approaching alongside** (*la* – by way of and as a result of) *Dowd* | **Beloved** (*Dowd* – meaning loved, but errantly transliterated "David"), **the rightful and upright** (*tsadyq* – the correct, just, proper, innocent, guiltless, and moral, vindicating and acquitting) **Branch** (*tsemach* – a source of growth). **And** (*wa*) **he shall reign** (*malak*) **as King** (*melek* – implying royal lineage and sovereign authority).

He will understand (*shakal* – He will prudently prosper by teaching that which is proper). **He will act upon and actively engage in** (*'asah* – He will endeavor to respond to, profit from, and celebrate) **the means which**

128

will be used to achieve justice and resolve disputes (*mishpat* – the basis upon which judgment will be exercised and sound and just decisions will be made) **along with** (*wa*) **that which is correct and vindicates** (*tsadaqah* – that which is right, just, proper, moral, and acquitting) **in** (*ba*) **the** (*ha*) **Land** (*'erets* – the material realm).'" (*Yirmayahuw* / Rise Up and Live in Yah's Shelter / Jeremiah 23:5)

The *Tsemach* | Branch is used prophetically of *Dowd* | David throughout the prophets, and most notably in *Yasha'yah* / Isaiah 4:2, *Yirma'yah* / Jeremiah 33:15, and *Zakaryah* / Zechariah 3:8 and 6:12. We will review these passages in the chapters dedicated to Yahowah's *Mashyach* | Messiah and *Melek* | King. But for now, please do not miss the connection between "*bow'* – shall arrive, prompting a return, an association, and a harvest" with "*quwm* – taking a stand, establishing, confirming, fulfilling, ratifying, and restoring" in the context of Yahowah working through, and approaching alongside, *Dowd* | David. This is important because almost every attribute ascribed to the mythical misnomer Christians call "Jesus," actually applies to Dowd, the actual Son of God and Messiah, our Savior, who is returning as King.

Christians have tormented Jews with the anti-Semitic mythology of "Jesus" for nearly 2,000 years. They have condemned God's people for not accepting their counterfeit Messiah and have accused them of killing their god. And yet, "Jesus" is nothing but a fable – as mythological as Osiris, Dionysus, and Odysseus.

That said, the Messiah and Son of God lived and died among his people 2,000 years ago. A King was, indeed, crucified by the Romans during Passover in 33 CE as predicted by the sacrificial victim, himself. But unfortunately, Peter and Paul were so insistent upon robbing Dowd of his accolades and achievements to create the myth of Jesus Christ, the actual Passover Lamb, Messiah, Son of God, and King went unheralded.

All the while, Jews were so preoccupied with being religious, political, and militant, they remained oblivious, even in the face of a thousand prophetic affirmations regarding what occurred. Then inexplicably, rabbinical Judaism was foisted upon *Yahuwdym* | Jews with horrific consequences by the acknowledgment of a false Messiah of their own, *bar Kokhba* | Son of a Star. It was this religious and political miscalculation which led to the Diaspora and Holocaust. And it is the legacy of Rabbi Akiba's grotesque affront to everything *Dowd* | David represents which is now emblazoned upon Israel's flag in the form of a six-pointed star. Oh, what a wicked web men have woven.

For the first time in 2,000 years, the foundational claims of Judaism and Christianity are being invalidated by pointing out what Father and Son foretold. *Dowd* | David is far more than the *Tsemach* | Branch from whom we live and grow. He is Yahowah's Chosen One, His Firstborn, the Most Set Apart, the Son of God and the Sacrificial Lamb, our Messiah and King. And for good measure, he was also the exemplar of the Covenant and the most prolific prophet – the one who explained all of this, one to three millennia before he fulfilled his own pronouncements.

The world's focus has been misdirected for the past two to three thousand years. The living embodiment of the Covenant, the beloved Son of God, the once and returning Messiah and King, and our Savior, is *Dowd* | David. It is his life and lyrics, his *Mizmowr* | Psalms and *Mashal* | Proverbs, that we ought to be "*shamar* – observing," which is to "closely examine and carefully consider," if we want to know Yahowah, appreciate what He is offering and accept what He expects in return.

130

As we move through *Yada Yahowah* and deeper into *Observations*, this realization will become increasingly clear. Then in *Coming Home*, as we commence a systematic review of his Psalms, the obvious will become undeniable. And as a result, to engage in a relationship with Yahowah, everyone, and especially Jews, should forego the myth of "Jesus Christ" and focus on the man God chose to fulfill His Mow'edym.

Addressing Dowd, the prophet revealed...

"**'In** (*ba*) **his day** (*yowm*), **Yahuwdah** (*Yahuwdah* – Beloved of Yah and Related to Yah, commonly known as "Jews") **will be liberated and saved** (*yasha'* – rescued and delivered) **and** (*wa*) **Yisra'el** (*Yisra'el* – a compound of *'ysh* – individuals, who *sarah* – strive and contend with, engage, endure, and persist with, and who are set free and empowered by *'el* – God, commonly known as Israelis) **will live and remain** (*shakan* – will camp out and reside, settling in and inhabiting) **confidently by expressing their trust and reliance** (*la betach* – totally assured and worry-free, safe and secure).

And thus, this is (*wa zeh*) **his name** (*shem* – personal and proper designation and renown) **which** (*'asher* – as a result of this relationship and to lead to its benefits) **he shall be called** (*huw' qara'* – summoned, invited, met, and encountered, proclaimed, read about, and recited): **"Yahowah Is Right** (*Yahowah Tsadaq* – Yahowah Vindicates because Yahowah is upright, just, honest, fair, and correct, Yahowah enables us to stand upright, be acquitted, and appear innocent and restored in His presence by doing what is appropriate).**""** (*Yirma'yah* / Rise Up and Live in Yah's Shelter / Jeremiah 23:6)

Tsadaq's root conveys: "to be right" and thus it identifies *Dowd* | David and his message as "the straight and correct path" to Yahowah. In *tsadaq*, we learn that Dowd fulfilled Pesach as the *'Ayil* | Lamb enabling the

131

benefits of the Covenant. He represents everything and more that was wrongly attributed to Jesus. He, along with Yisra'el, was robbed of what is due him through the Christian myth of Replacement Theology and rabbinical ignorance.

The passage goes on to obliterate the notion that the promises God made to Yisra'el were somehow transferred to a Gentile Church. Yahowah predicted that a day would come in which...

"'Therefore (*la ken* – as a direct result), **behold** (*hineh* – look up and pay attention), **the days are coming** (*yowm bow'* – a time will arrive),' **Yahowah** (𐤉𐤄𐤅𐤄 – a transliteration of *YaHoWaH* as instructed in His *towrah* – teaching regarding His *hayah* – existence) **announces before it occurs** (*na'um* – prophetically declares), **'when they shall no longer say** (*wa lo' 'amar 'owd 'asher*), **"Yahowah** (*YaHoWaH* – an accurate presentation of the name of *'elowah* – God as guided by His *towrah* – instructions regarding His *hayah* – existence) **lives** (*chay* – exists and animates life, honoring His promises to sustain life) **who beneficially** (*'asher* – who to show the way to the relationship and reveal the narrow and restrictive path which leads to life's benefits) **lifted** (*'alah* – brought out and elevated) **the people** (*'eth 'am* – alongside the family) **of Yisra'el** (*Yisra'el* – of Individuals who Engage and Endure with God) **out of** (*min* – away from) **the land** (*'erets* – the country) **of the Crucibles of Oppression in Egypt** (*Mitsraym* – of besiegement and subjugation, of the maximum extent of suppression and manipulation, of being controlled and incarcerated)**,"** (*Yirma'yah* 23:7) **but instead** (*ky 'im* – rather), **"Yahowah lives is who** (*Yahowah chay 'asher*) **lifted up** (*'alah*) **as He returned and led** (*wa 'asher bow'* – such that He could arrive and facilitate the return) **the descendants** (*'eth zera'* – with the seed and offspring) **of the family** (*beyth* – household) **of Yisra'el** (*Yisra'el* – of Individuals who Are Liberated and

Empowered by God) **out of** (*min* – away from) **the lands to the north** ('*erets tsaphown* – the region located toward the north)**, and out of** (*wa min*) **all of the countries** (*kol ha 'erets* – every land and region) **where He had scattered them** ('*asher nadach hem* – in which He had banished and exiled them) **by name** (*shem*)**." Then** (*wa*) **they will live, remaining** (*yashab* – will establish a dwelling place) **upon their own soil** ('*al 'adamah hem* – on their land)**."'** (*Yirma'yah* / Rise Up and Live in Yah's Shelter / Jeremiah 23:8)

The first step in this direction began in 1948 when the European Jews who survived the Holocaust traveled south to the Promised Land. There is great specificity in Yah's predictions. And even now, 90% of the Jews in the Diaspora reside north of Israel.

Having just spoken about the dishonest nature of Replacement Theology, it is nice to see God affirming the importance of exposing and condemning the theory which has been used to justify Christianity. Not only was it inappropriate to transfer the promises God made to Dowd, such that the mythical Jesus Christ was acclaimed as the Messiah, Son of God, and King of Kings, there will be no second coming of the one who was never here in the first place. Moreover, Yahowah's focus remains on Yisra'el. God's people have not been replaced.

Should you be seeking to understand the difference between the two proclamations, the distinction serves to introduce Yahowah's intent, which is to let His people know that there will be a second *Yatsa'* | Exodus. Soon, Jews will be leaving political, religious, and geographic Babylon (the United States, the influence of Roman Catholicism, and the Muslim Middle East) to come home to Yahowah in Yisra'el as promised.

In the 9th verse, which was, of course, prefaced by this affirming pronouncement, we find *rachaph*, the word which led us to the prophecy. This next pronouncement is spoken in the voice of the prophet. He is clearly shaken by the onslaught he is witnessing, as God, working through Dowd as the Messiah, seeks to protect the people. Their freedom will not be easily won. Mankind will fight to the end to impose its hostile narrative on Jews – with the most derisive conspiracies promoted by the religious.

"'**Concerning the approach** (*la* – regarding) **of the prophets** (*naby'* – those who claim to be able to predict the future by speaking on behalf of their god)**, my heart breaks** (*shabar leb 'any* – my sense of what is right and wrong is crushed and intellectually and emotionally I am grieved, my motivation is crippled) **in the core of my being in the midst of this conflict** (*ba qarab 'any* – with all the infighting around Me)**.

My entire essence** (*kol 'etsem 'any* – my essential nature and substance, even my very bones) **is brooding over the scene while suspended above it, seeking to increase the pace of what is being accomplished** (*rachaph* – is acting expeditiously while managing the process and advancing the action, hovering over while quickly administering to it).'"

If we were to stop here and take this statement out of context, there would be the natural inclination to believe that these prophets were speaking for Yahowah, and that His actual prophet, Yirma'yah, was now lamenting how poorly they have been treated in the past. And while God's prophets were maligned, this prophecy pertains to the future, long after the last of the prophets had spoken. These men, therefore, are political prognosticators and religious charlatans erroneously claiming divine sanction. We know this because of Yah's clarification two statements hence, where He says that they are corrupt. This is important because, while the prophet is still hovering over the scene and rapidly moving from place to place to take it all in, there is a more aggressive aspect of *rachaph* at play this time. This is a dangerous time and place, not unlike creation in this regard.

Yirma'yah is staggered by what he is witnessing...

"'I am somewhat like (*hayah ka* – I am similar to) an intoxicated individual (*shikowr 'ysh* – an inebriated person), (*wa*) similar to (*ka* – like) a strong man (*gibowr* – a powerful human) who is overcome ('*abar huw'*) by wine (*yayin*) because of (*min* – as a result of) the appearance and presence (*paneh*) of Yahowah (*Yahowah* – the proper pronunciation of YaHoWaH, our *'elowah* – God as directed in His *ToWRaH* – teaching regarding His *HaYaH* – existence and our *ShaLoWM* – restoration), and (*wa*) as a result of (*min* – from) facing (*paneh* – the proximity of) His set-apart and cleansing (*qodesh huw'* – His uniquely purifying and separating) words (*dabarym* – statements).'" (*Yirma'yah* / Rise Up and Live in Yah's Shelter / Jeremiah 23:9)

The reason Yirma'yah claims that he is a little like the *Gibowr* | Most Capable and Courageous Man of God is that all of Yahowah's coworkers, prophets, and witnesses manifest some of Dowd's attributes and attitudes. It is the reason they were chosen over all others.

It is the juxtaposition of Yahowah's presence and testimony compared to what mankind is saying and doing that has Yirma'yah reeling. Even as God returns, men are still divisive and full of themselves.

"'By comparison (*ky* – indeed by contrast), the Land (*ha 'erets* – the material realm) is full of (*male'* – is overflowing and finished with) those who are unfaithful and idolatrous, therefore, religious (*na'ap* – adulterous, dishonest in their vows while cheating those with whom they claim to have a relationship) as a result of (*min*) the presence (*paneh*) of the curse of Allah ('*alah* – of the mournful wailing and swearing of the doomed and their grievous religious confessions and lamentable devotion to the one who is unfit, harmful, and inappropriate).

The Land (*ha 'erets* – the region and the material realm) **is grieving** (*'abel* – mourning over the lamentable circumstances, with despicable parades of men and women weeping for the dead as part of their repulsive political and religious rituals). **The dwelling places and surrounding pastures** (*nawah* – the community developments and agricultural lands) **are withered and dry** (*yabesh* – are parched and lifeless and the people are paralyzed and unresponsive), **even desolate where the word is not considered** (*midbar* – the wilderness where the word is not pondered through questions; a compound of *my* – to question and consider and *dabar* – word).

Their course of life (*maruwtsah hem* – their conduct and patterns of behavior, especially their walk (thereby denouncing Judaism's *Halakhah* | The Walk (through the Jewish religious laws as conceived by rabbis))) **has been and continues to be** (*wa hayah* – consistently, actually, and habitually exists as (qal imperfect)) **wrong** (*ra'ah* – incorrect and harmful, wicked and evil, troublesome and distressful, misfortunate and miserable, creating unwarranted anxiety and unnecessary suffering).

Their politicians and religious factions (*gabuwrah* – their leadership and military might, those they idolize and elect to the most powerful positions, their collective might) **are not honest or forthright** (*lo' ken* – are not telling the truth, are invalid and incorrect, and what they say is so is not so). (*Yirma'yah* 23:10)

Indeed, both (*ky gam* – truthfully, and in addition) **prophet and priest** (*naby' gam kohen* – those who claim to speak for their god and also those who claim to serve their god) **are unGodly filth and useless hypocrites** (*chaneph* – are corrupt and Godless, common and thus profane, hypocritical and irrational, polluted and poisoned, adulterated without backbone or character, full of sh-t and easily swayed).'

'**Even** (*gam* – denoting two related concepts, besides) **in My House** (*ba beyth 'any* – within My Family and Home) **I have discovered and had to expose** (*matsa'* – I have actually found and uncovered, encountered and experienced during this specific time (qal perfect)) **their evil** (*ra'ah hem* – their adversarial wickedness and wrongdoing, their collective, national, and institutional malignancy, maliciousness, and malevolence),' **prophetically declares** (*na'um* – announces long before it occurs) **Yahowah** (*Yirma'yah* / Rise Up and Live in Yah's Shelter / Jeremiah 23:11)

Yahowah's declarations and affirmations of His antagonistic position against religion are prevalent and irrefutable. As a result, everyone, whose religion is based upon the "Bible," is either ignorant of what God revealed or irrational regarding His instructions.

ﭏﻭﭏﻟ

137

4

'Owr | Light

And There Was Light...

Yahowah's open letter to humankind began...

"In the beginning, at the start of time (*ba re'shyth*)**, the Almighty** (*'elohym*)**, for accompaniment and association** (*'eth*)**, created, conceiving and causing a new existence** (*bara'*) **of the spiritual world of the heavens** (*ha shamaym*) **along with** (*wa 'eth*) **the material realm** (*ha 'erets*)**.** (*Bare'syth* 1:1)

The material realm (*wa ha 'erets*) **existed** (*hayah*) **formless and without shape, lacking organization** (*tohuw*)**, a disorderly and chaotic space** (*wa bohuw*)**, dark and unknowable** (*wa choshek*) **in proximity to** (*'al*) **the presence** (*paneh*) **of the vast power and unapproachable energy of the big bang** (*tahowm*)**. Then** (*wa*)**, the Spirit** (*ruwach*) **of the Almighty** (*'elohym*) **hovered over and administered to** (*rachaph 'al*) **the appearance** (*paneh*) **of the fluid state** (*maym*)**.** (*Bare'syth* 1:2)

In addition (*wa*)**, God** (*'elohym*) **said** (*'amar*)**, 'Let there continuously be** (*hayah*) **light** (*'owr*) **and** (*wa*) **light** (*'owr*) **exist** (*hayah*)**.'** (*Bare'syth* 1:3)

And so (*wa*)**, the Almighty** (*'elohym*) **saw** (*ra'ah*) **that the association with** (*'eth*) **the light** (*ha 'owr*) **was truly** (*ky*) **good, beneficial and productive, having desirable and positive qualities** (*towb*)**.**

138

God (*wa 'elohym*) **caused the ongoing separation** (*badal*) **between** (*bayn*) **the light** (*ha 'owr*) **and** (*wa*) **its association with** (*bayn*) **the darkness** (*ha choshek*)." (*Bare'syth* / Genesis 1:4)

God's creative testimony was accurate when He revealed that, cosmologically, time began the moment energy became matter. Before the conversion of energy to matter, time did not and could not exist. In fact, Yahowah's suggestion that the "material realm was formless and disorderly" initially, syncs with current scientific thought, whereby matter is considered to be nothing more than an organized form of energy.

Also noteworthy, *Bare'syth* indicates that before Yahowah created the light energy which became the cosmos, there was a lifeless, purposeless void. Scientists are in lockstep confirming that, before the Big Bang, there were no physical laws, no matter, or life – only a powerful source of energy. Furthermore, we now know that the inception of the universe was incredibly chaotic, and that chaos actually has redeeming qualities.

In the beginning, light was literally separated from darkness. Photons broke free as electrons were liberated. Even today light remains supreme; there are more photons in the universe than particles of matter. God's testimony, "Let there be light and there was light," is consistent with our observable reality.

According to scientists, the universe began approximately fourteen billion years ago, plus or minus a billion years, at least from our perspective on Earth looking back at the Big Bang. That duration equates to six days from the perspective of the Creator at the time and place of universal genesis according to His testimony. Both suggest that the first cosmic epoch – that of initial star and galactic formation – lasted seven billion years from our vantage point, which is one twenty-four-hour day measured from the relative position of creation looking forward. So how is that possible, you may be wondering?

Light, the subject of day one, is the eternal timekeeper. Its wave aspect allows man to measure time throughout the cosmos, even near the place where time began. But to appreciate this we must first understand something about time itself. And for instruction on this subject, the best place to turn is to Albert Einstein. He brought forth the Theory of General Relativity which establishes the relationship between light, mass, energy, space, and time. He was the first to discover that the rate at which time passes is not uniform in all places.

Differences in mass and velocity radically affect the rate at which time flows. This aspect of the General Theory of Relativity is considered to be an established physical law. The only aspects of relativity in dispute are those related to quantum mechanics – to the lack of cause-and-effect, even certainty, at the subatomic level, and whether gravity is a force or an effect (bending of the fabric of spacetime). However, there is no dispute that time is a dimension, not a constant, and that its rate of flow is relative.

The pace of time flows more slowly in proximity to greater mass, energy, or velocity than in proximity to diminished mass, energy, or velocity. We can confirm this shift by measuring the two parts per million a light wave is stretched emanating in the presence of the greater mass of the sun relative to a light wave generated on Earth. The sun's clock runs 2.12/1,000,000 slower than Earth's, losing 67 seconds a year relative to a terrestrial timepiece. But the sun is only marginally more massive than the Earth, especially compared to creation – to the concentration of energy and mass required to give birth to 7,000,000,000,000,000,000,000,000 suns. And that's just the known universe, representing a scant four percent of the total (96% of the energy and mass in the cosmos is considered "dark" because its nature is unknown to us).

We do not have to guess the rate at which time flowed in these conditions. The measurement is screaming out to us in one form, it is observable in a second medium, it is calculable in a third, and the rate is deducible in a fourth venue. The pace time flowed at creation cries out from the entire universe in photon radiation in the form of cosmic microwave background (CMB) – an elongated part of the electromagnetic spectrum with a wavelength of 1.9 millimeters and a frequency of 160.4 GHz.

The CMB is a measure of the residual heat left over from the time photons were first freed to travel – perhaps 300,000 years after the Big Bang. It was discovered when Robert Wilson and Arno Penzias tried to resolve the universal presence of static in their new systems at the Bell Labs in 1964. What they found is that cosmic microwave background radiation is the residue of the aftermath of creation. It provides us with a cosmic clock calibrated to a time close to day one of Genesis (*Bare'syth* | In the Beginning). The CMB wavelength is stretched approximately one million millionfold, confirming that Genesis time flowed slower by a factor of 10^{12}. More on this in a moment...

A second glimpse of the Creator's clock can be gleaned by observing the redshift, or lengthening of wavelengths emitted from the oldest and most distant sources of light and comparing this expansion to the rate the universe has and is growing. To understand this, we turn to Professor Peebles who was named the Albert Einstein Professor of Science at Princeton University. In his textbook, *The Principles of Physical Cosmology* (Princeton University Press), Dr. Peebles, who has established himself as the world's foremost authority on cosmology, explains that when the universe was small, it was doubling very rapidly. But as the cosmos grew, the time required to double in size got exponentially longer. He, concurring with almost all cosmological texts, quotes 10^{12} as the average rate of expansion. This yields a general relationship between genesis time and time today, indicating that they are different by a factor of one million million.

This concept is fairly simple: when space was stretched, so were the wavelengths within it. The redshift, or stretching due to the expansion of space, is commonly observed in astronomical data, and it now confirms that time originally flowed a trillion times slower than it does today.

The calculable, and third, insight into creation's clock, and how it differs from ours today, is found by dividing the temperature of quark confinement, when light energy could be successfully transformed into matter following the Big Bang, by temperature recorded across the universe today of 2.73 degrees Kelvin (the measure of the CMB). By comparison, the temperature at the instant of the explosion precipitating universal genesis was approximately 1.6 x 10^{12} K. This ratio is relevant because the more massive the presence of energy, the more slowly time flows. The resulting calculation serves to indicate that our clock runs 0.85 x 10^{12} (around 600,000,000,000) times faster than the Creator's clock while initiating the Big Bang.

While the 0.85 x 10^{12} calculation implies precision, in actuality, it is a moving target. While physicists have calculated that quarks can break free from their positions inside protons and neutrons at around 2,000,000,000,000 Kelvin, we do not know if this is the temperature at which the quark-gluon plasma changes into matter at certain pressures and distances. And this is vital to our understanding because prior to the transition from energy to matter, the concept of time did not exist.

Due to the influence of distance and pressure on the strong force pursuant to quark confinement, it would be rational to conclude that quarks, which serve as the building blocks of matter, would have begun to coalesce at a lower temperature than they are liberated. The estimate is 130 MeV (Mega electron-volts).

Based upon the research published in 2019 by Adamu Issifu and Francisco Brito, entitled, The (De)confinement Transition in Tachyonic Matter at Finite Temperature, we now know that confinement is favored at short distances and low temperatures, whereas deconfinement shows up at long distances and higher temperatures in the tachyon matter. That is relevant because the confinement of quarks coincides with tachyon condensation. In the confining phase, there is a spontaneous chiral symmetry breaking, while at the deconfining phase, there is a restoration of the symmetry.

While this may seem overly complex, ascertaining the temperature at which point quarks would have been confined, turning energy into matter after the Big Bang, is essential to calculating the age of the cosmos. This determination is the basis for the currently touted, albeit upwardly migrating, 13.8-billion-year estimate of the age of the universe.

Therefore, it is germane to recognize that the strong force between quarks increases geometrically with distance, which means that these particles need large amounts of energy to remain free. Therefore, a quark-gluon plasma, a.k.a., quark soup, exists at exceedingly high temperatures. When the cosmos cooled through separation, quarks and gluons could combine to form composite particles such as protons and neutrons. Exactly what this temperature is, however, has not been easy to work out.

The current data set on quark liberation was derived from the Large Hadron Collider at CERN, but it relies upon an experiment conducted in a very small, confined space with targeted interactions, which is the antithesis of the conditions following the randomness and enormity of universal conception. I share this with you to say that when scientists state that the universe is 13.8 billion years, they are extrapolating based upon the data observed in the LHC, even though they know it does not represent the conditions of creation and that it is for liberation, not confinement.

What this means to us is that we do not know how much time expired from the Big Bang with the enormous release of energy to the point matter formed as a result of the temperature falling sufficiently for quarks to be confined. And it is only from this moment that time began to flow. And since the laws of physics do not apply to the intervening period, and since time did not yet exist at the point of the controlled explosion of energy, we would be wise to look at 13.8 billion years, plus or minus a billion years.

In that he was the first to "*byn* – make the connections which lead to understanding" the timeline of our genesis, I am going to refer to, and on occasion paraphrase, a work called *The Science of God* by Gerald Schroeder. He earned his doctoral degrees in nuclear physics and earth science from M.I.T. His book serves to present relativity, quantum mechanics, biology, and probability in terms we can more easily comprehend and appreciate.

Schroeder not only deduced a similar exponent for the relative difference in the flow of time, but he was also the first to compare creation's clock to Genesis time. His reasoning can be summarized as follows: the wavelength of what we now observe as cosmic microwave background radiation was stretched during the inflationary period, at the outset of time, in the first seconds of day one.

At creation, energy transitioned into matter consistent with Einstein's $E = mc^2$, with c being the speed of light, which is being multiplied by itself, requiring a tiny amount of energy to form a relatively large accumulation of matter. This initial transition from energy to substance occurred when the universe was a million million times smaller and hotter than it is today. We know that this is the point when time began because time only takes hold when matter forms. Yet, from the relative perspective of photon/wave energy, time literally stands still.

The MIT-trained nuclear physicist went on to say that, according to the measurements taken in the most advanced physics laboratories, the temperature, and thus frequency, of radiation at the instant of creation was 10^{12} times hotter than the 2.73° K we now observe in the black of space. Since the Big Bang temperatures were a trillion times hotter, or more energy-intense than today's observed CMB, it means that the electromagnetic wavelength must have been a trillion times shorter than it is now at its present trillion-times-lower temperature.

The higher the temperature, the higher the frequency of the wave, and the higher the frequency, the shorter the wavelength must be. Girded with this knowledge, we can use recent nuclear laboratory calculations to deduce that the CMB is stretched by a factor of approximately 10^{12}, or 1,000,000,000,000 to one – slowing the cosmic clock at creation relative to Earth by that amount.

Therefore, on average, these four measurements serve to confirm that one day in the Creator's life at creation would seem like 0.85×10^{12} days to us. And none of this should be surprising since Yahowah consistently equates His nature to light, and since we now know that at the velocity of light, time stands still. Eternity only exists in the presence of *the* Light.

Before we conclude the calculations calibrating Genesis time to our own to ascertain how God and man can both be accurate and yet differ, let's take a moment to explore some of the cosmological assumptions which led us to our current state of awareness. To begin, physicists contend that a concentration of energy at the initiation of the universe produced electromagnetic waves, or photons, which were forged as the explosion cooled sufficiently to permit them to form. Persisting to this day, the photons have traveled out in all directions.

The thermal soup of quarks, electrons, and photons decreased in temperature, falling from 10^{13} degrees Kelvin to one billion degrees – a temperature still 67 times hotter than the sun's core. Three hundred thousand years later, as universal energy and density dispersed and dissipated, atoms began to coalesce into gas clouds which later evolved into stars.

Moving forward to our time, we find that the black body temperature of space has fallen to 2.73 Kelvin – hovering ever so slightly above absolute zero. This temperature is the remnant of the primordial fireball, still discernable through the stretching of the electromagnetic wavelength.

Visible light lies in the center of the nearly infinite range of electromagnetic waves, also known as traveling packets of energy. This physical phenomenon occurs when an electric field couples with a perpendicular magnetic field. Lengths and frequencies of photon energy vary, but not speeds, at least in a vacuum. All forms of radiant energy, gamma rays, x-rays, ultraviolet, visible light, infrared, microwave and radio waves, are manifestations of the same thing and they all travel at the same speed—a pace so extreme that, from their perspective, time slows to the point that it no longer moves.

The wavelength of electromagnetic radiation determines whether it falls within our range of vision. We see wavelengths of approximately 0.00007 centimeters (700 nanometers) as red and 0.00004 cm (400 nanometers) as violet at the other extreme of the visible spectrum. By contrast, a microwave produces waves that are 10.0 cm long. X-rays and gamma rays from radioactive materials can be as short as 0.000000001 cm to 0.00000000001 cm. The shorter the wavelength, the higher the wave frequency and energy.

A gamma-ray photon, for example, packs billions of times more energy than an infrared photon. This is important because the energy we measure as CMB was emitted as gamma rays (10^{-11} cm), but are now elongated microwaves (10 cm), indicating that they have stretched a million million fold—confirming our 10^{12} exponent once again.

As an interesting aside, while we can only feel infrared light and see visible light, I believe that our senses will be more receptive in our eternal state. We may be able to see and feel things that currently lie well beyond our current limitations. What I am hinting at here is that I think the universe may be comprised of seven dimensions, not just the four we vaguely perceive today, and that dark matter and energy are essential components of these things.

Once we recognize that the CMB is little more than a uniform sea of photons left over from the hot early phase of the universe immediately after quark confinement, we are confronted with a singular plausible explanation for having this uniform CMB radiation exist throughout the universe with such a precise spectrum. It had to be generated at a time when the cosmos was much hotter and denser than it is now.

Hence the CMB spectrum is essentially incontrovertible evidence that the universe experienced a hot Big Bang stage. That is not to say that we understand the initial instant, just that we know the universe used to be vastly more energy-intense and massively dense, and that it expanded rapidly, becoming less dense. It has cooled ever since.

It is therefore certain that the early universe was very hot. The temperature was approximately 4×10^{72} ergs. An erg is a unit of energy equivalent to 10^{-7} joules, the energy required to exert a force of one newton at a distance of one meter. This means that creation was 10^{12} times hotter than the universe is today on average.

There was so much energy around at the time, scientists speculate that pairs of particles and anti-particles were continually created and annihilated. This annihilation was translated into packets of light, known as photons. But as the universe expanded and the temperature fell, particles and anti-particles (quarks and the like) annihilated each other for the last time, and the energies became low enough that they couldn't be recreated again. For reasons still not understood today, the early cosmos had about one part in a billion more particles than anti-particles. So when all the anti-particles had annihilated their counterparts that left about a billion photons for every particle of matter. And that's the way the universe exists today, with light remaining dominant.

Now that we have some familiarity with the elements which comprise the coefficient of variance between our clock and the Creator's, let's examine how long this timepiece has been running. Here, Hubble's law has great significance because it quantifies the expansion of the universe and thus can be used to calculate its age.

The time elapsed since the Big Bang is a function of the present value of Hubble's constant and its rate of change. Astronomers have determined the approximate rate of expansion, but no one has yet been able to measure the effects on what was once considered a constant. Still, one can estimate the rate of change within the context of the universe's average density. Since gravity exerts a force which opposes expansion, galaxies should be moving apart more slowly now than they did in the past. The rate of change in expansion is therefore related to the gravitational pull of the universe as a result of its average density. If the density is that of the visible material in and around galaxies, the age of the universe is between 12 and 18 billion years – a range which allows for the uncertainty in the rate of expansion.

The Wilkinson Microwave Anisotropy Probe provided an estimate of 13.7 billion years in 2014. In 2020, this figure was adjusted upward to 13.8 billion years. Both are a bit suspicious for two reasons. First, the density of the universe isn't remotely equivalent to "the visible material in and around galaxies." Along these lines, this very same satellite confirmed that 96% of the energy and matter in the cosmos is unknown to us. The gravitational influence of "dark matter," and the repulsive effect of "dark energy" has dramatic consequences for all aspects of fundamental physics, so it should have moved the age estimate to one outside of that anticipated by Hubble (12 to 18 billion years). Further, the universe is filled with a uniform sea of quantum zero-point energy or a condensate of new particles that have a mass which is 10^{-39} times smaller than that of an electron. They should not be ignored.

The second reason for skepticism is that the cosmos cannot be younger than the material from which it is comprised. There is considerable evidence that many stars, even relatively close ones, are considerably older than 13.8 billion years. Some may be up to 15 billion years old, revealing that determining the exact time which has elapsed after quark confinement remains a moving target.

Apart from the Hubble redshift expansion model, and the Wilkinson CMB estimates, there are several other ways to evaluate the universe's age. For example, the rate of cooling of white dwarf stars indicates the oldest stars in the disk of the Milky Way galaxy are about 9 billion years old.

The stars in the halo of the Milky Way are much older, appearing to be somewhere around 14 to 15 billion years old – a value derived from the rate of nuclear fuel consumption in their cores.

Additionally, the age of the oldest known chemical elements in the cosmos is also approximately 15 billion years old according to radioactive dating techniques. Scientists in laboratories derived these age estimates from atomic and nuclear physics. It is noteworthy that their results agree with the age astronomers calculated by measuring cosmic expansion.

Now that we have evaluated some of the pieces to our puzzle – God's big bang testimony, man's Big Bang Theory, the age of the universe, the relative nature of time, and the role of photon energy in our genesis – it's time to put it all together. The first conclusion should now be obvious. This discussion on the initiation of time, concentration of energy, inflationary stretching of space, and the transformation of light into matter serves to corroborate Yahowah's testimony.

The Big Bang Theory requires, and our observations confirm, that all of these things actually occurred during the cosmos' birth. It is why Bare'syth 1:2 says the *ruwach* | Spirit of *'elohym* | Almighty God was *paneh* | present, *rachaph* | hovering over and administering to the *tohuw, bohuw*, and *choshek* | the formless, chaotic, dark, and unfathomable void of *tahowm* | inexhaustible power and mysterious energy of the big bang prior to the existence of visible *'owr* | light. Especially notable in this context is that one of *rachaph*'s most prevalent connotations is "agitation and rapid movement," making everything God has said thus far consistent with the evidence.

The second conclusion should now be intuitive. Based upon our analysis of the cosmic clock, Yahowah's claim that the first universal epoch lasted one day is not in conflict with the scientific assertion that it required seven billion years.

In support of this conclusion, consider the fact that while the various scientific methods for estimating the age of our universe provide differing conclusions, they all fall within the same general magnitude. So, while we cannot be dogmatic or assert that the scientific claims are precise, based upon our ability to measure it, looking back in time from the vantage point of Earth, the universe can be reasonably assumed to be between 14 and 15 billion years old plus or minus a billion years or so.

The creative days of *Bare'syth* | Genesis, however, look forward, not back. Yahowah's testimony was recounted as an eyewitness, from the perspective of the Creator at creation, not from that of us on Earth. The simple truth is that no matter how self-important or self-reliant mankind chooses to be, our planet didn't exist when the universe was formed, so our perspective and clock could not have been used.

With that in mind, let's compare time on Earth to its rate of flow at the point of Creation. To do that we must multiply the 14,000,000,000-year estimated age of the cosmos by 365.25 days per year so that both clocks conform to the same unit of measure – that being "days." 14,000,000,000 years x 365.25 days/year = 5,113,500,000,000 days (plus or minus 5 to 10%).

To coordinate this 5.1-trillion-day period with creation's clock, respecting the relativistic nature of time, we must divide this number of Earth days since creation by the coefficient time was slowed at creation. Earlier, we deduced this number by averaging the results derived from the four methods from which it can be calculated. We discovered that Big Bang time ran 0.85×10^{12} (850,000,000,000) times slower than Earth time does today.

So here is the math: 5,113,500,000,000 days (plus or minus 10%) divided by 850,000,000,000 equals: **6 days**. From the vantage point of a witness to creation, existing at the point of inception, the whole process from start to finish took a length of time that equates to six, twenty-four-hour, Earth days.

"And thus, the heavens and earth were finished...and on the seventh day God concluded His work which He had made..." (*Bare'syth* / In the Beginning / Genesis 2:1-2)

This is not a cosmic coincidence. Yahowah's timeline, His accounting, and God's 3,450-year-old written Towrah testimony correspond precisely with the evidence at our disposal. If that doesn't get your attention and cause you to think that His *Towrah* | Teaching might be inspired, nothing will.

But we have only scratched the surface. With every layer and detail He adds, God proves that He knew how the universe was created, when it was created, and how and when life came to exist – because He was responsible. This then compels a singular informed and rational verdict: **"In the beginning, God created the spiritual world and also the material realm."**

𐤋𐤄𐤅𐤄𐤉

The energy Yahowah put into His creation was perfectly calculated to produce a universe hospitable to intelligent life and thus to meaningful relationships. By design, the resulting system required just six days to conceive from God's perspective, and yet, it established the environment necessary for human history to unfurl over the course of precisely 6,000 years – providing humankind with ample time to get to know Him.

The reason for the common denominator is because the redemptive story is interwoven into the future history of mankind, with both appearing throughout the creation account. Both are correct because they are based on the same formula. Six is the number of man (who was created on the sixth day); one is the number of God (who repeatedly tells us that He is one). Bring them together and you have the ideal result – also known as a reconciled relationship. In six days, God created, and on the seventh, the Sabbath, He observed and celebrated what He had achieved.

So, it shall be with us. As is the case with the Sabbath, mankind shall toil for six thousand years before resting and reflecting during the celebration of the seventh and final *Miqra'*, that of *Sukah* | Shelters (also known as Tabernacles but meaning: "to Camp Out" with God) in 2033 (Year 6000 Yah).

Therefore, we are still living in the sixth day of creation. God and man still have much to accomplish.

Yisra'el and Yahuwdym remain estranged from Yahowah. And they will be reconciled prior to Yahowah's return with His Son on *Yowm Kipurym* | the Day of Reconciliations in 6000 Yah, October 2nd, 2033, at sunset in *Yaruwshalaim* | Jerusalem. When God's people come home at long last, we will all celebrate Sukah as it was intended. So, while time is fleeting, we will not rest until the seventh day dawns with the return of the ultimate Yahuwd, the King of Yisra'el, the Messiah Dowd and his Father, Yahowah, our God.

If the willingness to date the inevitable seems presumptuous at this point, rest assured that God's timeline will be firmly established long before we have completed the first few volumes of *Yada Yahowah*. God's plan is so simple and clear, it has taken the onslaught of nearly six millennia of religious corruption to obscure the obvious.

(As for the often-cited, Christian excuse that "no one knows the hour" of God's return, rest assured we will obliterate this objection, turning a perceived criticism into an astounding confirmation.)

What we have already discovered represents an amazing, yet seldom considered, verification of the veracity of Yahowah's witness, but there is much more. You see, the flow of time did not remain constant during the six days of cosmic conception – at least from our perspective looking back. That is because the amount of matter and the rate of stretching at the center of creation diminished over this period at a logarithmic rate approximating natural spirals. Time sped up in parallel with universal expansion.

The infinite curve underlying this phenomenon is manifest in the graceful swirls evident in spiral galaxies (representing 72% of all galaxies) and in the turn of every nautilus shell or ram's horn. Moving from inside out, each successive spiral of the common galactic arms, or shell rings, telescope outward at a rate approximating twice the previous distance. Based on the way living cells grow, you'll find a similar ratio in everything from flower petals to pineapples and pine cones.

There are three widely accepted formulas used to quantify this natural geometric expansion. The first is known as the Golden Ratio. Calculated as the square root of 5 plus 1 divided by 2, it yields a ratio of 1:6180339887.... In his galactic observations, Johannes Kepler equated this proportion to what has been called the Fibonacci Sequence of 0, 1, 1, 2, 3, 5, 8, 13, 21, 34, 55, 89, 144, 233..., where each additional number is the sum of the two previous values. It serves as the best whole-number approximation of the irrational Golden Ratio. A third logarithmic scale defines the exponential rates of decay of radioactive atoms known as a "half-life."

Based upon Yahowah's testimony and the empirical evidence, we can deduce that the clock at the center of creation became more closely synchronized with an Earth-based timepiece at a rate of approximately fifty percent per cosmic day. As confirmation, this diminishment is evident in the relative scale of subjects covered in the creation account itself, from its focus on the universe on day one, to the solar system and earth, to plants and the atmosphere, then to animals, and eventually to man in successive periods.

This logarithmic spiral is pertinent because when we apply the celestial unit of measure, and that revealed through a ram's horn, to the creative timeline described in the Towrah, we discover that each of the six days of creation coincides perfectly with verifiable developments in the cosmos and here on Earth. Yahowah's insights regarding this telescoping unit of measure are manifest in the opening lines of the 19th *Mizmowr* | Psalm. Its words are as riveting as they are precise.

"**Concerning the approach of** (*la* – for, to, and regarding) **the eternal and glorious Leader** (*ha natsach* – the unending and everlasting splendor and majesty of the ultimate Director, the One who endeavors to continuously guide)**: a Song** (*mizmowr* – these lyrics and melody) **of** (*la*) **Dowd** (*Dowd* – the Beloved, commonly known as David)**:**

The heavens (*ha shamaym* – the realm of stars and universe) **quantify the unit of measure, exactly and accurately** (*saphar* – recount and relate, number and reckon, record and proclaim, providing a census to convey) **of the manifestation of power and the abundant presence** (*kabowd* – the profusion and richness, the energy and massiveness, the elegance and great beauty, as well as the rewarding gift) **of God** (*'el* – the Almighty).

Its spreading out in a flat expanse (*ha raqya'* – its expansion and transformation into matter which is round, yet thin) **makes conspicuous** (*nagad* – makes known, enabling a verdict, reporting this information for a purpose, declaring the message which presents and acknowledges) **His handiwork** (*ma'aseh yaday huw'* – the ability to evaluate and ponder His work, actions, influence, achievements, and power involved in creation; a compound of *ma* – to question and *'asah* – to engage and act with *yad* – hand, power, strength and control). (19:1)

Day unto day (*yowm la yowm*) **pours out** (*naba'* – gushes forth, spewing out) **a proliferation of answers** (*'omer* – words of intent, promises and proclamations, declarations and announcements). **Night unto night** (*laylah la laylah*) **reveals** (*chawah* – makes known and illuminates, displays and explains) **knowledge which leads to understanding** (*da'ath* – information which facilitates comprehension regarding the implications of these relationships)." (*Mizmowr* / Song / Psalm 19:1-2)

This passage is particularly astute. We turned to it to help us properly evaluate the Bare'syth timeline. And it does exactly that with the precision of "*saphar* – to quantify the unit of measure, exactly and accurately." Yahowah is as skilled at creation as He is at communication. In addition to telling us that the enormity of His power is evident in the universe, He told us to use the stars to compute creation's timeline. Galactic formations are most often logarithmic spirals where each successive arm extends approximately twice the distance from the center as the previous one.

Even in the details, this rings true. Recent maps of the universe have revealed that it is a "*ha raqya'* – flat expanse, expanding in a manner which is round, yet thin."

According to the inspiration Yahowah offered *Dowd* | David, God's very presence, indeed the verification of His existence, is manifested day and night before our eyes. The universe was created and thus had a Creator. Its enormity reveals God's power and influence. Its design necessitates a Designer. And it is all magnificent and harmonious, addressing God's nature and intent. The fact that we can observe and ponder these things such that they lead us to the same conclusions, not only speaks to the merit of these words but also suggests that this is all fundamental to our existence.

Since no accounting of universal genesis would be complete without a complement of insights into the mind of God, profound truth is woven into the Song's narrative. So, although we have already found the answer we were searching for – the unit of measure for our cosmological timeline – by considering the rest of the *Mizmowr* | Psalm we will grow wiser still. The lyrics and implications of Dowd's 19th Song are among the most brilliant and insightful ever written by man.

Through His Son, Yahowah reveals...

"Nothing exists without (*'ayn* – there is no existence, and it would all be for naught, empty, negated, and senseless, unsearchable and inscrutable, calling everything into question without) **the Word** (*'omer* – the answers and promises, these declarations and announcements, that which has been spoken and its intent).

Everything is senseless and nothing matters when (*wa 'ayn* – and therefore, our existence is nullified where) **the spoken and written words of** (*dabarym* – the statements, accounts, and message, the record and treatise of what has and will happen, communicated by) **the voice which calls out to them** (*qowl hem* – the audible and intelligent sound of speech) **is considered outdated, is corrupted or denigrated, and is therefore not** (*bely* – is considered old and thus arcane and worn out, muted, becoming unimportant, is diminished in relevance, is gone without or negated so as not) **heard** (*shama'* – received, perceived, or processed)." (*Mizmowr* / Song / Psalm 19:3)

157

When we think about it, it becomes immediately obvious that Yahowah is right. Words are essential. Nothing meaningful exists without them. Emphasizing this, Bare'syth repeats: "And God said" before each creative event, each day all the way to "and God said let us make man in our image."

Without His words we would not exist. And without the written report Yahowah gave us in His *Towrah* | Teaching, these very words we are currently considering, there would be no hope of knowing God or of engaging in the Covenant relationship with Him.

The use of words, particularly written words, distinguishes humankind from other animals. It is how we obtain information from our past and pass it on to future generations. Words are the building blocks of knowledge and understanding.

The last line suggests that ignorance and inspiration are related in a surprising way. If we knew everything, there would be no new insights and no discoveries. So, while ignorance isn't bliss, it is also true that the life of a know-it-all would be tedious and uninspiring, especially over eternity.

In this regard, this statement was prophetic of the diabolical nature of the Christian New Testament, particularly as Paul sought to create the impression it was needed to resolve God's inadequacy. In his view, the Towrah was obsolete. Forewarning us, Dowd, who is the antidote for Paul's poison, wrote: **"everything becomes senseless, and nothing God said matters when the written words of the voice which calls out are considered outdated, then corrupted and denigrated, therefore, no longer considered."** This accurately describes the mythos of Christianity.

There are additional insights here because *dabarym* is plural, meaning "words." Without language, we are

158

rendered senseless and powerless as it is the source of enlightenment and of causality. We think with words and act upon them. Language is God's gift to humankind. In written form, it emerged 6,000 years ago, contemporaneously with the first man created in Yah's image. Words are the source of life and the means to relationships. As such, Yahowah is saying that if we fail to regard His message, if we diminish the importance of His Word, we will cease to exist, returning to the dust from which we came.

Before we consider the next line in the Song, I would like to point out something which is foundational. God's equation for life is sensible and fair. If you prioritize Yahowah and His Word, highly regarding Him and carefully listening to what He has to share, Yahowah will reciprocate. He will respond to you and value your soul, not only to save it but to actually adopt you into His Covenant Family. But if you do not care sufficiently about Him, if you elect to accept a corruption of His message, if you ignore His voice, He will ignore your soul. Having chosen to live your life apart from Him, death will be the end of your existence. There will be nothing more because your soul will be seen as having the same value you placed on the source of life. Such souls are diminished to nothingness, which means they simply cease to exist. And while that may strike you as harsh, it's not only completely fair; it's a far better fate than eternal anguish in *She'owl*.

Moving on, there are three ways to consider what follows – all of which are meritorious. Yahowah's *Towrah* | Instruction is the universal standard; it undergirds the laws of nature and the Gentile of life. The Word of Yahowah is the source of mankind's mortal existence as well as immortality. And the heavens accurately calibrate Yah's power.

"**This standard of measure** (*qaw hem* – this ability to assess the underlying rules and overall size which binds everything together and provides hope as in a confident expectation) **has gone forth** (*yatsa'* – been brought up and produced as an extension of the source) **concerning** (*ba* – in association with) **all the material realm** (*kol ha 'erets* – the entire earth)**, along with** (*wa* – together with) **these words** (*milahym hem* – these reasoned arguments and verbal portraits, these communications and proverbs characterizing the truth of this affair) **to the uttermost outskirts** (*ba qatseh* – to a point marking the completion of an epoch, to expose the end and the finite nature of time and space) **of the Earth** (*tebel* – the world or planet)**."** (*Mizmowr* / Song / Psalm 19:4)

Everything fits together and is consistent, from the creation of the universe to its inevitable conclusion, from the similarity between light and the Hebrew language, it all forms an integrated portrait of who we are and why we were conceived. More than any words ever spoken or written, Yah's Word has been known longer and by more people than any other message – affirming the prophecy. However, on the dark side, this has created the opportunity for it to be misquoted, twisted, and misapplied more than any message ever written.

In this light, there is another interesting possibility since *qaw*'s secondary meaning is "the strange blah, blah, blah of nonsensical statements spoken in a foreign language to mock, especially the meaningless guttural rhythmic chants spoken by marchers." Translated as such, Dowd could be seeking to demean both the supposedly enlightened who claim there is no God along with the dunderheads who march against everything Yahowah stands for while chanting irritating and senseless slogans.

To fully appreciate what follows, we need to know that Bare'syth, using the sun as a sign, and the "*mow'ed* – appointed meetings" as a guide, portends that on the fourth day, or fourth millennia of mankind's history, the *Miqra'ey*

| Invitations to be Called Out and Meet with God will be fulfilled. In this light, please consider:

"Along with these words (*ba hem* – in them (masculine plural) and thus denoting the *dabarym* and *milahym* – words (both masculine plural) [from 11QPs]) **He has set up** (*sym* – He has for a time appointed and established, constituted and fashioned, brought about and placed) **a brilliant dwelling** (*'ohel* – household and home, a sheltered tent and temporary tabernacle; from *'ahal* – to be bright, to be clear, to be brilliant, and to shine (speaking of Dowd)) **such that this would be clear regarding the approach of the sun** (*la ha shemesh* – on behalf of clarity provided by the brilliance of sunlight),**..."** (*Mizmowr* / Song / Psalm 19:4)

Yahowah is not constructing a palatial residence for our nearest star. He is instead saying that His words will live in His Home, shining brightly on behalf of His Family.

Based upon other Psalms written by Dowd, it is likely that *shemesh* is a metaphor for Yahowah's most brilliant orator. God is hereby honoring His promise to build a home for Yisra'el's returning messiah and king. Moreover, Dowd's brilliance is equated to the sun at the conclusion of the 89th *Mizmowr* / Psalm.

As we consider the conclusion to Dowd's statement, realize that he was a bridegroom eight times (Michal, Ahinoam, Abigail, Maacah, Haggith, Abital, Eglah, and Bathsheba). Moreover, Dowd metaphorically became Yah's son-in-law by marrying the prophetess, *'Abygayl* | Abigail, a Yahuwdy, whose name means "My Father is Joyful." It was Dowd, therefore, who traveled from his wedding pavilion, delighted to marry a woman who was similarly inspired by Yah.

Dowd is also the paradigm for *gibowr*: an empowered leader with the strength to prevail. He was and will return as the mighty warrior, valiant soldier, and virtuous hero

161

defending his people. He was, and upon his return as king will once again be, a manly man with prominence in the community he has influenced, a man who was audacious and will continue to be courageous, awe-inspiring, and victorious.

"**...similar to** (*ka* – like, as, or comparable to) **a bridegroom** (*chathan* – and son-in-law, the husband of the Father's daughter) **who goes forth** (*yatsa'* – who leaves, extending himself to serve) **from** (*min*) **the tent he has erected for the wedding ceremony** (*chupah huw'* – his sheltered pavilion and bridal chamber for the upcoming nuptials and to consummate his marriage)**, he confidently and joyously speaks about his love for relationship** (*suws* – he expresses his fond feelings of appreciation for the association and how much he enjoys it)**, consistent with** (*ka* – comparable to) **the power and strength of a virtuous and victorious fighter, a competent and courageous man** (*gibowr* – the character of a leader with the strength to prevail, the nature of a mighty warrior, valiant soldier, and honorable hero defending his people, a manly man with prominence in the community he influences, who is audacious and awe-inspiring) **who swiftly and intensely pursues** (*la ruwts* – who drives off pursuers, aggressively chasing them away while summarily following) **the Way** (*'orach* – the road to life, the route to travel, the path to explore, the example of conduct, and the course to journey in the right company)." (*Mizmowr* / Song / Psalm 19:5)

Thankfully, with these edits of *Yada Yahowah*, one during the summer of 2020 and the next three years later in 2023, I have been afforded the opportunity to give God's Son the credit he is due. As our Savior, Dowd is so much more than Messiah and King.

In that it matters, I am likely the first person in three millennia to realize that *Dowd* | David is the Son of God, the Messiah, and the returning King, as well as our Savior

162

since he fulfilled the Miqra'ey, while also acknowledging that these attributes, accolades, and accomplishments were misappropriated from him to create the myth of "Jesus Christ." I share this with you because, to navigate the path to God, we must shatter myths while exposing truth.

Over time, there will be others who parrot these deductions, but for all the wrong reasons. Charlatans will seek to advance their own agenda by claiming credit for my translations, transliterations, commentary, and conclusions. Some have tried to create their own religion by taking something which is true, such as Yahowah's name, His affinity for Hebrew, or His love of Yisra'el, and then go off on some ridiculous tangent. The Black Israelites, Hebrew Roots, Jews for Jesus, Messianics, and Yahwehists are examples of those who remain far more wrong than right. There are even those who advance absurd conspiracies, who are anti-Semitic and plagiarize my work. Please avoid them.

And third, it is actually important that these translations and transliterations reveal thousands of profound insights, previously unknown, many of which are exceedingly important. The sheer magnitude of verifiable insights offered here and nowhere else strongly suggests Divine involvement and support.

Transitioning from brilliant metaphors back to science, and then returning to Yahowah's timeline once again, the Bridegroom, God's Mighty *Gibowr*, and the man devoted to pursuing the Way revealed the following about himself…

"His going forth at this stage of his journey occurs (*mowtsa' huw'* – his pronouncements during this incremental part of his very long mission will be conducted from a place of departure such that his declarations are; from *yatsa'* – to go forth) **at the completion of a long duration of time and commences from the limits** (*min*

163

qatseh – in association with a period marking the conclusion of a prescribed interval of time at the confluence of dimensions regarding finishing the purpose) **of the heavens** (*ha shamaym* – of the abode of God and spiritual realm).

His return to complete his course of action will continue (*wa taquwphah huw'* – his trajectory and established course for each stage of his journey, his ability to encompass time and space and complete the circuit of events, bringing all things back to where they began, cycle forward; from *naqaph* – continue to occur) **until their fulfillment at the end** (*wa 'al qatsah hem* – are distant in lesser dimensions).

And then, nothing (*wa 'ayn*) **will be hidden** (*sathar* – is concealed) **from** (*min*) **his warmth and light** (*chamah huw'* – his sunlight (often transliterated *chamah*); from *cham* – warmth)." (*Mizmowr* / Song / Psalm 19:6)

When Yahowah returns, He is bringing His beloved Son with Him. At that time, we will bask in their warm and brilliant light. Nothing will be hidden when Yahowah fulfills one of His most beneficial prophecies – placing His *Towrah* | Guidance inside of His children upon His return, integrating His Instruction into the fabric of our lives.

Our review of the 19th *Mizmowr* | Psalm brings us to one of Dowd's most vital lines. It unequivocally establishes the prophet's position on Yahowah's *Towrah* | Teaching. It reveals that the Son of God and Messiah was resolutely Towrah-observant. Therefore, it puts *Dowd* | the Beloved and *Sha'uwl* | Question Him in irresolvable conflict. Being on the wrong side of this conflict is deadly for the religious.

With this one statement, and in just seven words, the Messiah destroyed the religions of Judaism, Christianity, and Islam. Most everything Paul, Akiba, and Muhammad wrote was exposed and contradicted by the testimony of the very God all four of these men claimed to represent. As such, the lone informed and rational conclusion which can be drawn from these irreconcilable differences is that they lied. And that means that the religions they founded are untrustworthy and unreliable.

"**Yahowah's** (*Yahowah* – an accurate transliteration of the name of God guided by His *towrah* – instructions regarding His *hayah* – existence) **Towrah** (*Towrah* – Source of Teaching and Instruction, Direction and Guidance [plural in 11QPs]) **is correct, complete, and perfect** (*tamym* – is entirely right, lacking nothing, without defect, totally sound and genuine, helpful and healing, beneficial and true, manifesting great integrity because it is in accord with reality), **returning and restoring** (*shuwb* – changing and transforming, bringing back and renewing, reconstituting the relationship and repairing) **the soul** (*nepesh* – an individual's consciousness representing the essence of their life and character, personality, proclivities and aptitude, a person's perspective, the ability to observe and respond).

Yahowah's (*Yahowah* – the proper pronunciation of the name of *'elowah* – God as directed in His *towrah* – teaching regarding His *hayah* – existence and our *shalowm* – restoration) **testimony** (*'eduwth* – eternal witness; from *'ed* – everlasting verbal and written memorialization of the perpetual agreement, including evidence and proof; from *'ed* and *'edah* – an eternal witness to an enduring and restoring agreement concerning a glorified community of the highest possible status which gathers together with a shared understanding regarding the evidence, and in a common cause which is being memorialized so that its conditions and precepts are forever remembered) **is trustworthy and reliable** (*'aman* – is instructive and informative, verifiable and readily confirmed, supportive and established, dependable and enduring), **making understanding** (*chakam* – enabling the formation of reasoned conclusions by imparting the teaching, instruction, and education needed to make learning and enlightenment leading to comprehension and wisdom) **easy for those who are receptive** (*pethy* – simple for the open-minded and readily deduced for those with the capacity to change; from *pathah* – open and receptive and *pethach* – unfolding events leading to opening and entering the doorway)." (*Mizmowr* / Song / Psalm 19:7)

Since Yahowah's Towrah is correct, Paul's letters assailing it, and rabbinical tomes augmenting it, must be invalid. Therefore, there can be no justification for the Christian New Testament or Talmud. There can be no Divine sanction for the rabbinic Zohar or Islamic Quran.

It is hard to imagine anything more polarizing or unaccommodating. To believe in any of these religions in light of this declarative statement, the faithful must disavow God's testimony.

According to God, and there is no higher authority on the subject, the means to "*shuwb* – restoration and return" is found in His *Towrah* | Guidance. If you want your soul to transcend your mortality, then you know where to look.

In this passage, *shuwb* was scribed in the hifil stem. This means that we are influenced by and benefit from the relationship established between our "*nepesh* – soul" and Yah's "*Towrah* – Teaching." This is what leads to our restoration and renewal. Further, *shuwb* was written in the participle form, telling us that these benefits modify our souls, changing us so that we can return to God.

'Eduwth is such a simple concept, it is easy to miss its profound implications. It reveals that these words comprise Yahowah's "testimony." They are provided from the perspective of an "eyewitness to the events being depicted." *'Eduwth* even reveals the "inspiration behind the ideas being shared." As an *'Ed* | all-encompassing witness, God "has provided an everlasting verbal and written

166

memorialization of the perpetual agreement, offering the evidence required to prove His veracity."

'Aman, like *'eduwth*, proclaims that faith is for fools. There is no reason to believe when we "can trust and rely upon what we know to be true." The "evidence" God provides is not only "instructive, it is verifiable," which is to say, "easily confirmed." His testimony is "enduring and dependable."

Also noteworthy, *'aman* was written in the niphal participle absolute. This means that "trust and reliance" are actionable and that they are linked to Yah's witness. His testimony facilitates our ability to verify and confirm that what we are reading is true.

There is a prerequisite for trust. It is understanding. Without it, we are back to believing. Therefore, Yahowah is committed to "teaching us, imparting instructions which help us learn." When we observe and consider His *Towrah* | Teaching, we are "equipped to make reasonable decisions and form rational conclusions."

Knowledge is good, but understanding is far better. And while one can lead to the other, most never make the connection between the two. This detrimental result is by human design. Those who rise to positions of power and influence do not take kindly to rivals – and the best way to prevent the ascension of others is to circumvent understanding.

This can be done by restricting access to information, offering inaccurate information, or providing so much of it that society is lost in a sea of data. It can also be accomplished by incapacitating a person's ability to think for themselves and thus to exercise good judgment. Such is the role of Political Correctness and its debilitating consequence.

By contrast, I cannot help but marvel and rejoice at the realization that Yahowah is fair, consistent, forthright, forgiving, and merciful. Everything He says makes sense – as we would expect from God.

"**Yahowah's** (*Yahowah* – an accurate transliteration of the name of *'elowah* – God guided by His *towrah* – instructions regarding His *hayah* – existence and our *shalowm* – reconciliation) **principles, directions, and guidance,** (*piquwdym* – instructions and prescriptions which should be considered and acted upon regarding the assigned appointments, as well as the precepts, procedures, and guidelines, because when they are observed, attended to, and cared about; this oversight enables the individual and their circumstances to undergo considerable change; from *paqad* – oversight and caring guidance which we should pay especially close attention to and carefully examine so that we respond appropriately and benefit as intended) **are on the level and correct** (*yashar* – are straightforward (and thus neither crooked or circuitous), upright (and thus do not include bowing down), and agreeable (and thus neither unsuitable or discordant, neither incongruous nor harsh), they are approved, esteemed, right, proper, honest, fair, likable, and pleasing), **resulting in joyful disposition and elated attitude** (*leb samach* – facilitating an attitude of elation, causing the heart to be delighted, as a result of thoughtfully evaluating the directions while happily incorporating them into one's life (piel construct – the quest to know and understand is satisfied by Yah's oversight when a connection is made between His guidance and our decisions)).

Yahowah's (*Yahowah* – the proper pronunciation of the name of *'elowah* – God as directed in His *towrah* – teaching regarding His *hayah* – existence and our *shalowm* – restoration) **instructions regarding the conditions pursuant to His relationship agreement** (*mitswah* – His authorized stipulations pertaining to the codicils of His mutually binding covenant contract) **create heirs who are brilliant and enlightened** (*bar* – providing light for His offspring which leads to understanding, creating supernatural children who are radiant, fostering favoritism among those choosing to participate in a special relationship as sons and daughters, conceiving descendants who are bright and pure, akin to cleansed and purified grain, paving the way to an inheritance, to enlightenment, and to comprehension)**, illuminating the proper perspective** (*'owr 'ayn* – shining a light for the eyes to see, enabling insightful observation and understanding, shedding a brilliant light on the means to enlightenment and thereby obliterating darkness while making the perceptive person aware and thus able to see the light (hifil construct – the conditions of the relationship cause the observant individual to become light and to be bound to the source of the light))." (*Mizmowr* / Song / Psalm 19:8)

Mitswah is a compound comprised of *my*, meaning "to inquire about the who, what, why, when, where, and how of a matter," and *tsawah*, which is a verb. If we were to rely exclusively on the lexicons, our understanding would be limited to it meaning: "command, order, tell, instruct, or give direction to someone pertaining to how they should respond in the context of the relationship between the speaker and the recipient." It is to "appoint and assign a role or function." To this, other Hebrew / English dictionaries indicated that *tsawah* can be rendered: "urge, guide, enjoin, determine, arrange, constitute, and commission."

Cognizant of the harmonious nature of the Father / Son relationship Dowd enjoyed with Yahowah, in concert with the familial nature of the Covenant, and with an eye to God's affinity for freewill, our only rational option is to interpret *tsawah* as "to tell, to instruct, or to give direction pursuant to a specific set of conditions." In the context of a relationship between the speaker and the recipient of the instructions, *tsawah* addresses that which is "arranged and constituted" as "instructive provisions and stipulations of the relationship."

Then in conjunction with the *my* interrogative prefix, we are being encouraged to "question and ponder the who, what, where, why, when, and how" of these specifications and requirements. As a result, I have consistently chosen to render *mitswah* as "terms and conditions of the agreement," which is, in this context, the stipulations and provisions of the Covenant.

Validating my approach, *tsawah* first appears in *Bare'syth* / In the Beginning / Genesis 2:16. Let's check it out since our lives depend upon getting Yahowah's instructive conditions regarding the relationship agreement right. It does not seem plausible, considering the setting and the nature of their relationship, that Yahowah would have been issuing a "commandment" to 'Adam, but I will let you decide…

"Then, Yahowah Almighty provided instructions regarding the relationship (*tsawah*) on behalf of 'Adam, approaching to say, 'From every tree of the Garden you may eat all you would like. However, from the tree of understanding good and bad, of being able to comprehend the difference between that which is beneficial or wrong, you should not make a habit of eating from it. This is because, in the day you eat from it, the ongoing specter of death will be the inevitable result." (*Bare'syth* / In the Beginning / Genesis 2:16-17)

If *tsawah* were a command, there would have been no reason for the explanation. And yet, as an instruction to thoughtfully consider, it is in perfect harmony with 'Adam being granted freewill in this regard.

While I see this proving my point, consider this affirmation inherent in: Yahowah's second up close and personal relationship was with *Noach* | Noah. Regarding God's volunteer shipbuilder and lifesaver, we read:

"Noach acted, doing everything which was beneficial to the relationship that God had instructed in the process of guiding and commissioning him (*tsawah 'eth huw'*). **And in this manner, he consistently engaged."** (*Bare'syth* / In the Beginning / Genesis 6:22)

If Yahowah were interested in acquiring a cargo ship having no connection with the Covenant, He would have built it Himself. If God were desirous of becoming an admiral with the captain of the ark at His beck and call, why bother with the doves, olive branches, and rainbows? Why talk about Noach at all if he was just thoughtless muscle shouldering lumber and following orders? Why create man at all, since robots reliably perform as programmed?

Since Dowd wrote this Mizmowr, it would be fair to say that his characterization of *tsawah* should be definitive, surpassing the opinions of scholars composing lexicons three thousand years thereafter. The first time he dealt with the implication of *tsawah* was right after his anointing as Mashyach on Yahowah's instructions. At this point, Yahowah's Spirit came upon him to empower, enlighten, and enable him. To those in the know, at this moment, and for years thereafter, Dowd became the most important person on the planet.

In that light, these are among the words a father spoke to his son:

"Dowd arose early in the morning and left the flock with an observant individual. Inspired and free of concerns, he set out, traveling in a way which was consistent with Yshay's instructive conditions and guidance regarding the relationship with him (*tsawah huw'*)." (*Shamuw'el* / Listen to Him / 1 Samuel 17:20)

171

Yshay was Dowd's father, not his superior officer barking out an order. He most assuredly was not a wannabe god issuing a commandment. And it is evident that Dowd capitalized upon this guidance because he would soon confront Goliath.

Since the initial reference to *tsawah*, the actionable aspect of *mitswah*, in conjunction with Dowd precludes "command, order, or commandment," I think we are on solid ground in eliminating these incompatible notions from our translations.

Continuing through the text, we next come upon *bar*, which was translated as "create heirs who are brilliant and enlightened." It is a particularly revealing term with three related connotations. It speaks of a perfected son, of His pure radiant light, and of how His enlightenment leads to understanding. These are all Dowdian concepts.

Bar is also the path to purification leading to an inheritance and thus is indicative of *Matsah* | UnYeasted Bread and *Bikuwrym* | Firstborn Children. It is first used in the 2nd *Mizmowr* | Psalm, where speaking of our Heavenly Father's and Spiritual Mother's beloved Son, *Dowd* | David, we read:

"With reverence and respect, even admiration, work alongside Yahowah with great excitement, rejoicing over the prospect. (*Mizmowr* / Psalm 2:11)

Reach out and touch, contacting as a sign of affection, demonstrating your mutual adoration for the relationship (*nashaq* – passionately brush up against and demonstrate your affinity for) **with the radiant and favorite son, the brilliant and purifying heir** (*bar* – the illuminating and enlightening child with an inheritance who chose to provide moral cleansing and intellectual understanding, selected and dispatched to conceive supernatural children who are radiant, fostering favoritism among those choosing to participate in this special relationship as sons and daughters who are bright, thereby paving the way to an inheritance), **lest** (*pen* – to eliminate any apprehension that) **he becomes indignant and displeased** (*'anaph* – he becomes angry and averse) **and you perish** (*'abad*) **in this way** (*derek*).

For indeed (*ky*), **his righteous indignation** (*'aph huw'*) **can be kindled** (*ba'ar*) **for a few and for very little** (*me'at*) **comparatively** (*ka*).

Joyful with me and blessed by me (*'ashery* – fortunate in the relationship with me, stepping along the straightforward and correct path which gives meaning to life with me providing the proper place to stand and live as a benefit) **are all** (*kol*) **who put their trust in him** (*chasah ba huw'*)." (*Mizmowr* / Psalm 2:12)

The magnificence of Mizmowr 19:8 concludes brilliantly, with "*'owr 'ayn* – illuminating the proper perspective." The radiance of Yahowah's beloved Son "shines a light for our eyes to see, enabling insightful observations leading to understanding, providing enlightenment to obliterate the darkness."

As we explore Yahowah's testimony, it is not uncommon for us to progress through a host of reactions. My first response is usually awe, as I am impressed with Yah's profound insights, His creativity and consistency, as well as His literary skill. As a result, I have grown from questioning faith and belief to absolute trust and reliance. That does not mean that my amplified translations are perfect because they are not. I am admittedly not a Hebrew scholar, but there is more than enough here to demonstrate that the thoughts being shared in **bold** are Divinely inspired and thus completely trustworthy.

My next reaction is usually thankfulness, especially as I contemplate the enormous generosity of His plan for us as well as the great price Father and Son paid to enable it. The Way of the Towrah is so well communicated, so completely fair, so beautifully laid out and timed, so overwhelmingly compassionate and merciful, I am overwhelmingly grateful.

I am also enveloped with a great sense of companionship and familial love as I consider what it really means to be adopted into the eternal Family of our Heavenly Father. I often ponder what it will be like to camp out with Him, exploring and discussing those things which are currently beyond my physical reach and mental grasp. In this relaxed relationship, I am sure that we will laugh at my crude attempts to translate and communicate His Word, and yet smile, knowing that, empowered by the Spirit, our work together changed many lives.

And yet, sometimes I experience frustration, even anger, as I ponder the Word. It is a crying shame that God so clearly laid out the way to Him, and so eloquently and brilliantly verified the veracity of His revelation, only to have it corrupted and demeaned by religious, political, and academic institutions. The truth is evident, and yet so very few find it.

Yahowah deserves our respect. He has earned our trust. Not just for His sake, but for our own...

"Reverence and respect for (*yir'ah* – demonstrating a profound appreciation for what it means to be revitalized and restored while astonished by the awesomeness of the superior nature of) **Yahowah** (*Yahowah* – an accurate transliteration of the name of *'elowah* – God guided by His *towrah* – instructions regarding His *hayah* – existence and our *shalowm* – reconciliation) **is cleansing and restoring** (*tahowr* – is perfecting and renewing, enabling individuals to present themselves for purification so that they can be pronounced clean and flawless, free of all impurities and majestically brilliant), **sustaining and establishing one's presence** (*'amad* – causing one to remain and endure, continuing to abide standing upright and present (qal

174

participle)) **forever** (*la 'ad* – for eternity as a result of the witness, to approach and draw near the source of the testimony for an unlimited duration of time).

Yahowah's (*Yahowah* – an accurate transliteration of the name of *'elowah* – God guided by His *towrah* – instructions regarding His *hayah* – existence and our *shalowm* – reconciliation) **means to exercise good judgment and to justly resolve disputes** (*mishpat* – the means used to achieve justice and to make sound decisions; from *my* – to ponder the who, where, why, when, and how of *shaphat* – rendering rational decisions based upon thoughtful evaluations of accurate and complete information) **are continually trustworthy and reliable** (*'emeth* – are enduring, dependable, honest, consistent, and true forever). **They are right and vindicating** (*tsadaq yahdaw* – they are of one accord working in harmony and in unison to prove one's innocence, all together and united, correct and justifying, causing the recipient to be upright, acceptable, cleared of all wrongdoing, righteous and acquitted (qal perfect))." (*Mizmowr* / Melodious Lyrics / Psalm 19:9)

The path to restoration and vindication, to standing in God's presence for all eternity, is through demonstrating sufficient respect and reverence for Him and His Word – the Towrah. Respect Yah, His Way, and His Word, and Yah will revere you sufficiently to adopt you into His Family.

Designating the nature of this "reverent relationship" Yahowah uses *'amad* to convey that He wants us "to be upright and unbowed, standing in His presence." While it is customary to bow down before those who oppress and in front of those whom we have reason to fear, it is inappropriate to cower before someone you love. Loving fathers want their sons and daughters to stand by their side, to walk with them, not grovel at their feet. After telling 'Abraham to leave the religious and political schemes of

175

Babylon, Yahowah asked the father of the Covenant to stand and walk with Him.

The Towrah was written to liberate and save, not control or condemn. Its purpose is to guide us to a relationship and away from religion. Everything we need to know about Yahowah is presented therein. The Towrah gives life meaning.

When it comes to knowing God and being saved by Him, everything that matters is revealed in the Towrah. As such, God did not authorize and will not accept a "New Testament" or "Quran" to undo what He has done. And yet, these religious texts and others exist to enrich the perpetrators, the covetous mongrels who did not listen to God.

For those who may currently be misled by an out-of-context and errant rendering of "judge not lest you be judged," recognize that the statement actually conveys: "Don't separate, or you'll be separated." God does not want us to lead souls away from Him, but since being judgmental is the essence of justice, of morality, of logic and reason, of understanding, and thus of making wise choices, He values judgment. In spite of this, the moral code of man, Political Correctness, makes being judgmental an unforgivable sin.

To be honest with ourselves and true to our God, we should test everything which claims to be Divinely inspired to determine what is reliable and what is seeking to give a false impression. Ascertaining the veracity of a witness' message, especially someone who claims to have been Divinely inspired, can be a matter of life and death. No matter how many people believe, or the fervor of one's faith, being religious, charitable, and good is not going to save anyone.

As an example, it might be helpful if someone wrote the following passage on a slip of paper and inserted it into the offering plate of their local church instead of money, as the pastor or priest flattered his enriching patrons...

"**Desire and covet them** (*ha chamad* – treasure them and find pleasure in the *mishpat* – means to exercise good judgment and resolve disputes) **more than** (*min* – rather than) **money** (*zahab* – gold), **beyond anything man considers worthy** (*wa min paz rab* – instead of what man has refined and values).

They are sweeter and more pleasing than honey (*wa matowq min dabash* – the *mishpat* – means to exercise good judgment and resolve disputes are more satisfying and pleasant, agreeable and acceptable, even more enjoyable than sugar) **or the overflowing flattery of enticing words** (*wa nopheth tsuwp* – or the uplifting of excessively sweet-sounding speech and verbal gymnastics or the brandishing of honeycombs)." (*Mizmowr* / Song / Psalm 19:10)

Yahowah has conceived and implemented a plan to resolve the issues which divide us. The decisions we make regarding His approach determine the eternal fate of our souls. Dowd is encouraging us to do as he has done, which is to exercise good judgment regarding them and to treasure them. And in the process, as a natural consequence of the proper response to His Towrah, we will naturally become opposed to man's religious and political alternatives – no matter how sweet and enticing they may sound.

Continuing to speak of Yahowah's "*mishpat* – means to exercise good judgment regarding resolving disputes and making rational decisions," Dowd writes...

"**Moreover** (*gam* – also in addition) **Your coworker** (*'ebed 'atah* – he who serves with you) **is educated and enlightened by them** (*zahar ba hem* – he shines brilliantly because of them and is taught by them, thereby helping him achieve a higher status and earn respect, even coming to know the consequences of future events).

By focusing upon and observing them (*ba shamar hem* – by closely examining and carefully considering them) **there are tremendous rewards and abundant benefits** (*'eqeb rab* – there is a profound consequence and great merit along with an abundance of trustworthy compensation).**" (*Mizmowr* / Song / Psalm 19:11)

Eternal life is a nice reward, as is being perfected by God. Considering what we inherit, adoption into His Family is highly recommended. Being empowered and enlightened sounds good, too.

The obvious aside, this is what Dowd got out of observing Yahowah's *Towrah* | Instructions. Suffice it to say, if it was this beneficial for the Son of God and the Messiah, it is suitable for us as well.

And now you know the reason our excursions into related revelations are thorough rather than superficial. The investment of our time is always rewarded when we stay the course and go above and beyond the first stop along the way.

While *Dowd* | David was among the brightest men who ever lived, and unquestionably the best-informed regarding the issues vital to our survival, he knew his limitations. That cannot be said of political and religious aspirants…

"Who has the ability to apprehend (*my byn* – asking the question, who can perceive or comprehend, or how would we form the connections to understand) **a misleading statement or lapse in judgment** (*shagya'ah* – an error or mistake, willful or inadvertent ignorance; from *shagah* – an error which leads astray, which intoxicates and clouds one's judgment, misleading them) **among that which is either unknown or unknowable** (*min sathar* –

from that which is concealed from our purview, or is beyond our capacity to know)? **I am innocent of such charges** (*naqah 'any* – I am not guilty of doing this)." (*Mizmowr* / Song / Psalm 19:12)

Whether it is trying to comprehend the nature of dark energy or the fourth dimension, there is much which eludes us. For example, it is all but impossible for us to wrap our brains around anything beyond the 3D world in which we exist. Complicating matters, a physical being cannot enter the fourth dimension. And even if we could, we do not have the mental prowess to navigate it or the capacity to endure it.

The energy in the fourth dimension would incinerate us. The noise, therein, would overpower us. The dynamic instability would evaporate us. Moreover, even if we could survive, the computations needed to function in 4D would overwhelm us. It would be as caustic to us as trying to slice and dice ourselves to fit into two dimensions.

This realization, this perspective of our place in creation, is one of the many reasons that I think the *towrah* | guidance Yahowah will be integrating into our thought processes upon His return will include instructions necessary to enjoy life in the 4th, 5th, 6th, and 7th dimensions. This subject is one we will explore at great length when we consider the promised reconciliation of the Covenant relationship with Yisra'el and Yahuwdah as it is presented in *Yirma'yah* | Jeremiah 31.

What we will surmise is that Yahowah's existing and external *Towrah* | Teaching will bring those to Him who reach out and grasp hold of it, choosing to incorporate its guidance into their lives. Then Yah will be integrating His internal *towrah* | instructions into the fabric of His children's lives on *Yowm Kipurym* | the Day of

Reconciliations in year 6000 Yah, enabling His Family to enjoy being together with Him.

ⵣⵉⵉⵣⵍ

The creative act of day one is explained with these words...

"**God** (*wa 'elohym* – then the Almighty) **accordingly** (*la*) **called out in a welcoming way and proclaimed** (*qara'* – He saw as inviting, summoned, and met with, issuing an invitation for us to read and recite, designating and announcing (qal imperfect – creating an actual ongoing relationship between God and the illumination)) **the approaching light** (*la ha 'owr* – the extension and intent of the brilliant illumination) **day** (*yowm* – a unit of time, the twenty-four hours from sundown to sunset; from an unused root meaning hot and glowing or radiant heat).

And concerning (*wa la* – therefore, the approach of) **the darkness** (*ha chosek* – the obscurity, that which shrouds in blackness, veils by withholding knowledge, that which clouds revelation with sinister suggestions, concealing and mystifying by way of ignorance and confusion with the absence of light; from *chashak* – to conceal by eliminating the light) **He called it** (*qara'* – He designated it, calling it out as (qal perfect – actually limiting its time, making its existence finite)) **night** (*laylah* – time of darkness and gloom, the absence of light; from an unused root meaning to fold back space and time and enclose)." (*Bare'syth* / In the Beginning / Genesis 1:5)

It is telling to see *qara'* used this early in Yahowah's accounting of creation because *Miqra'*, which means to ponder the implications of *qara'*, serves as the title of God's seven annual Invitations to be Called Out and Meet. Collectively, they comprise the path Home and provide

180

each of the Covenant's benefits. They not only comprise the seven essential days on Yahowah's yearly calendar – Pesach, Matsah, Bikuwrym, Shabuw'ah, Taruw'ah, Kipurym, and Sukah – Dowd's fulfillment of the first three and final two are days we should all celebrate.

The *Miqra'ey* | Invitations to be Called Out and Meet with God are so essential to life in the Covenant, we devote three entire volumes of *Yada Yahowah* to them and discuss them in every book along the way. The Creator of the universe, the Author of life, announced on day one that He would be inviting us to meet with Him, welcoming us into His presence.

To *qara'* is to "read and recite" the Word of God. To be *qara'* is "to be called out" of the realm of man and come Home to God. *Qara'* is "to be invited into God's presence and welcomed by Him." *Qara'* is Hebrew's most inviting and welcoming term.

The distinction in this declaration is between light and darkness. It is the difference between enlightenment or ignorance and thus between life or death. To be with Yah in *Shamaym* | Heaven is to become like Him, which is to be light. Separation from Him in *She'owl* | Hell would be in eternal darkness and is, therefore, best described as a black hole.

Yowm is an effective and important means to express the concept of time. The Hebrew day always begins at sundown and continues up to sunset the following evening. Seven *yowmym* | days, of course, constitute a week.

Light is associated with time, not only because light defines time, but also because Yahowah's Light is the source of enlightenment and life eternal. The absence of light renders us confused and imperfect, separated from God, and thus spiritually unassociated with Yahowah. Without the energy needed to survive, such souls cease to exist upon a person's Earthly demise.

This statement reveals an especially enriching contrast between the imperfect and perfect conjugations. In the imperfect, light will be associated with Yahowah forever, with the relationship enduring throughout time. But in the perfect conjugation, darkness will only exist for a finite period of time.

God's next statement is helpful in that it causes us to question the way we normally consider time. The order of things suggests looking at the creation account in reverse, from the Creator's perspective rather than our own. Yahowah has "the end of the day" preceding the "beginning of the day."

But there is more to it than that. "Evening, or end of the day," is represented by 'ereb—and that's where the fun begins. The three Hebrew letters which comprise 'ereb can be rendered five ways, several of which seem appropriate. Boqer, the word rendered as "morning," or "beginning of the day," has several potential meanings as well—all of which seem to fit.

"**And there was** (*wa hayah* – there exists with unfolding implications over time (qal imperfect)) **evening** (*'erab* / *'arab* – a period of darkness, a time of sadness and hopelessness, a discouraged state of foreign occupation, an era of ignorant commingling of and adherence to faiths and beliefs, a time for the adversary to intermix and of noxious swarms of Arab pests bartering and trading a great amount of something black, dominating commerce) **and there would be** (*wa hayah* – there also exists with unfolding implications over time (qal imperfect)) **morning** (*boqer* – tomorrow, the beginning of a new day, a time to be observant, perceptive, and judgmental, a time for consideration, a period to be attentive and respond appropriately, an extended stretch to be inquisitive and seek information in order to make a good decision) – **one day** (*yowm 'echad* – the first, a single, solitary, unique, and

individual day; from *'achad* – to go one way or the other)."
(*Bare'syth* / In the Beginning / Genesis 1:5)

Whether God intended to convey *'ereb* or *'arab*, the implications go well beyond evening and day one of creation. The Chosen People have endured a period of darkness, a time of hopelessness and despair, of "biblical" proportions. Indeed, there have been twenty-five centuries of foreign occupiers in the land of Yisra'el. Christians and Muslims have come to believe an irrational commingling of pagan myths as noxious swarms of Arab terrorists have sought to devour the Promised Land.

Boqer is the good news – the promise of a new day. There would be a brighter future, a new beginning for God's people. And today, as was the case in the time of Moseh and Dowd, we all have the opportunity to be observant, to seek the information Yahowah revealed and decide how to respond. With *boqer*, the perceptive and discerning can contemplate the merit of the Miqra' and make a good decision about God, aware of what He is offering and asking in return.

During this time of universal genesis, there would have been no shortage of darkness or light as energy was being transformed into matter, space, and time. Everything was mixing together and joining to form the interwoven fabric we call the cosmos. It was as pleasing to God as it is to us. But let us not forget, Bare'syth is also God's message to us, His pledge of fellowship, and His plan of salvation— one in which He explains His undertaking and exchange: our redemption.

Yahowah distinguished this day, and only this day, with a cardinal number – in this case *'echad | one*. It represents a quantitative measure of a singular solitary and yet unified day – the period when the universe and time began. All other creative days are presented in relation to each other, as they are called the "second, third, and fourth," respectively. *'Echad* means "one," not first.

Spiritually, day one is focused on introductions. Yahowah, who is One, tells us that He exists and that He is the reason we exist. God declares that He is creative and that words are causal and important. The Almighty further conveys that His nature can be equated to light.

Day one is also reminiscent of Passover, the first of seven *Miqra'ey* | Invitations to be Called Out and Meet with God which represent the path from the material realm to the spiritual. Yahowah's Spirit passed over the abyss, which was obscured in darkness, bringing light which would lead to life.

Historically, moving forward from creation and out of 'Eden, day one is symbolic of the first man created in Yahowah's image, and of his personal one-on-one relationship with the One who is Light and Spirit. It should not be surprising therefore, that including 'Adam's time in 'Eden, the first man lived nearly one thousand years – the length of the first millennia of human history.

Therefore, an Earth-based clock can be used to measure time back to the commencement of the sixth day of creation. At that point, the creative timeline is chronologically synced with recorded history – both of which began just shy of 6,000 years ago.

Scientifically, every nuance of Yahowah's testimony was accurate. The universe was created. It didn't always exist. It began with a Big Bang. God said, "Let there be light and light existed."

Consistent with God's accounting, light energy was transformed into matter in the formless void of space, one that was originally lifeless and very chaotic—during a time when physical laws were suspended. There was an inflationary period of rapid expansion, just as Yah affirms. It was in fact when time began.

Galactic formation commenced during the first relative day of this epoch with stars filling the darkness of space with the first rays of visible light. This occurred 300,000 years into an epoch which lasted 7,000,000,000 years (plus or minus 20%).

And yet, the initial phase of creation, at least from the perspective of the only eyewitness at the scene, lasted exactly one solitary day. And that is what this is all about – the Towrah is Yahowah's eyewitness account of how and why He created us.

𐤋𐤄𐤅𐤄𐤉

5

Raqya' | Matter & Space

An Orderly Expansion...

Applying the galactic unit of measure Yahowah inspired *Dowd* | David to use to quantify His creative timetable in the 19th *Mizmowr* | Psalm, we can deduce that the second cosmological epoch began approximately 7 billion years after creation and 7 billion years ago. That same formula suggests that the second day lasted around 3.5 billion years in Earth-time. Although, to keep it real and appreciate this evolution from energy to matter, the Earth, which is comprised of the heavier elements formed by the supernova explosions of dying stars, would not exist until the waning days of this initial period.

Scientifically, several rather important things occurred toward the end of the second cosmological day. Cosmologists believe that 4.8×10^9 (billion) years ago the star we call our sun was created as a second-generation luminary within the spiral galaxy we refer to as the Milky Way. Shortly thereafter, the Earth was formed, some 4.5 billion years in our past. Even the 3.8×10^9 terminus date is significant. It marks the time the steady influx of large asteroids ceased impacting our planet, facilitating the conditions that would immediately lead to life. But that is the subject of the third day.

In His initial statement describing the second creative era, Yahowah reveals something we have only just recently come to learn; H_2O is an abundant molecule in the interstellar clouds which serve as wombs for new stars and planets like our own.

"**God** (*wu 'elohym* – next, the Almighty) **said** (*'amar* – He spoke with a focus on the content to follow; He thought, intended, and declared that) **matter and space** (*raqya'* – a measure of the material within the vastness of space, the extended solid support of universal expansion; from *raqa'* – spreading out, expanding, and broadening of things forged and formed) **shall exist** (*hayah* – by choice, was and will be (qal imperfect jussive – since God is speaking of Himself in third person, it is His desire)) **in the midst of** (*ba tawek* – among and between, in relationship to) **the waters** (*maym* – source of inquiry and life and the fluid plasma state), **existing** (*hayah* – by choice, was and will be (qal imperfect jussive – a genuine expression of God's consistent and ongoing desire)) **dividing and separating** (*badal* – making a distinction between, to associate with or abandon, being selected or expelled, differentiating among and setting apart, choosing or withdrawing over an interval of time, to make a distinction and difference) **between things for the purpose of understanding** (*bayn* – connecting and dividing to perceive, consider, discern, discriminate, and respond, intelligently associating and dissociating to facilitate comprehension and provide insights, giving revelation deeper meaning in the midst) **of the waters** (*ha maym* – of the liquid which is common and essential to all life, serving as a source of inquiry) **in relation to** (*la* – toward, among, and concerning) **this source of inquiry and life** (*maym* – waters)." (*Bare'syth* / In the Beginning / Genesis 1:6)

The second day does not chronicle a creative act. According to Yahowah, and confirmed by science three millennia later, matter, space, and time were the product of light energy and the result of the Big Bang. "Matter and space" were derivatives of that which God called into existence on day one. By unleashing the appropriate amount of energy during the first "interval of time," our solar system was enabled in the second. And as is suggested by this passage, our sun and the Earth were literally born in the midst of molecular clouds composed of hydrogen and water vapor.

The Submillimeter Wave Astronomy Satellite has recently confirmed that water exists in great abundance in the translucent clouds where new stars are being born – as was the case at this moment in creation. This super-heated gas plays a major role in the chemistry of molecular clouds.

God was and remains correct in this depiction. Giant molecular clouds comprised largely of H_2 molecules, some a million times more massive than our sun and 150 light-years across, still serve as nurseries for star formation. Many can be seen with the naked eye in our own galaxy, as they cause the patchy appearance of the Milky Way by obscuring the light of the stars behind them. Hubble Space Telescope photographs of these nebulae are breath-taking in their beauty, including the Carina, Crab, Horsehead, Eagle, Mystic Mountain, Lagoon, Bubble, Butterfly, Spirograph, Ring, Veil, Hourglass, Ghost, Glowing Eye, Orion Nebula, and of course, the Pillars of Creation.

More recently we have detected these molecular clouds in distant galaxies through the presence of CO, carbon monoxide. This is telling because we are carbon-based lifeforms and oxygen transforms molecular hydrogen into H_2O. As the densest areas within these molecular clouds collapse from the gravitational effects, they begin to rotate. As is the case with a figure skater when she brings in her arms and legs, the more these nebulae clusters shrink in size, the faster they spin, flattening the cloud and concentrating its mass in the center, giving birth to a protostar and protoplanets.

Scientists witness this marvelous show when observing the birth of new stars in the constellation Taurus. And each new star is always found in or near the densest molecular clouds. And by this reckoning, our own galaxy, the Milky Way, is dying. The mass of free gas is declining, such that only seven new stars are formed annually.

Also interesting, we have discovered that our galaxy originally consisted of 77 percent hydrogen by mass, with the rest of the constituent matter, helium. But today, as a result of nuclear fusion, the Milky Way is filled with heavier elements, including carbon, of which our planet and bodies are comprised. As such, physically, we are a product of the stars.

This pronouncement goes on to highlight the process, emphasizing that there was further division and separation over time. The words God continues to select have far-ranging implications. Due to the complexity of the subject material, let's first view God's statement without amplification.

"God (*wa 'elohym*) **said** (*'amar*) **matter and space** (*raqya'*) **shall exist** (*hayah*) **in the midst of** (*ba tawek*) **the waters** (*maym*)**, existing** (*hayah*) **dividing and separating** (*badal*) **between things for the purpose of understanding** (*bayn*) **of the waters** (*ha maym*) **in relation to** (*la*) **this source of inquiry and life** (*maym*)**."** (*Bare'syth* / In the Beginning / Genesis 1:6)

Maym | waters is a fascinating concept because the *ym* ending makes the word plural, leaving us with just the ᴍ *mah*. In Hebrew, *ma* and *my* are interrogatives, telling us that there is a lot to ponder if we want to understand the role of water in our lives and the fluid state of creation. *Maym* is literally a source of inquiry and life. It addresses fluids overall and water in all three natural states, liquid, frozen, and gas, throughout its many manifestations: clouds, rain, lakes, rivers, and seas, steam, snow, and ice.

Maym, which is written ᴍᴧᴍ in Hebrew, is like *hayah* | ✷⊁✷, the basis of Yahowah's name, meaning "was, is, and will be," and is an eternal expression of existence. In Hebrew, ᴍᴧᴍ and ✷⊁✷ read the same from beginning to end as they do from their conclusion to their initiation. These are eternally evolving concepts, both as a result of Yahowah's outstretched hand.

Water is the third most prevalent molecule in the universe following hydrogen and helium. The human body is 60% water, with the heart and brain composed 75% of water. Without water, there is no life.

Water is the universal solvent and thus an essential ingredient for cleansing. Water is unique, in that it is the only substance which becomes less dense in a solid state, expanding when frozen. Had that not been the case, the Earth would not be habitable. Moreover, with water, we have a tangible expression of the vast difference between energy and matter, with steam being vastly more empowering than ice. And speaking of ice, solid water is incapable of acting as a lubricant for the molecular process of life – which is why it is central to our search to find other intelligent beings.

Astronomers have long held that water was a relative latecomer to the universe because they believed that any element heavier than helium had to have been formed in the cores of stars, and not during the Big Bang, itself. Since the earliest stars would have taken some time to form, mature, and die, it was presumed that it took billions of years for oxygen atoms to disperse throughout the universe and attach to hydrogen to produce the first interstellar H_2O.

New research published in Astrophysical Journal Letters by Tel Aviv University and Harvard University researchers reveals that the first reservoirs of water may have formed much earlier than previously thought – less than a billion years after the Big Bang when the universe was only 5 percent of its current age – approximately 700 million years old. According to the study, led by Ph.D. student Shmuel Bialy and his advisor Professor Amiel Sternberg of the Department of Astrophysics at TAU's

School of Physics and Astronomy, in collaboration with Dr. Abraham Loeb of Harvard's Astronomy Department, the timing of the formation of water in the universe has important implications for the question of when life itself originated.

"Our theoretical model predicts that significant amounts of water vapor could form in molecular clouds in young galaxies, even though these clouds bear thousands of times less oxygen than that in our own galaxy today," said Bialy, the lead author of the study.

For the purpose of the study, the researchers examined chemical reactions that led to the formation of water within the oxygen-poor environment of early molecular clouds. They found that, at temperatures greater than 80 degrees Fahrenheit, the formation process became very efficient, and in the gas phase, abundant water could form despite the relative lack of raw materials.

"The universe then was warmer than today and gas clouds were unable to cool effectively," said Prof. Sternberg. "Indeed the glow of the cosmic microwave background was hotter, and gas densities were higher," said Prof. Loeb, at the School of Physics and Astronomy at TAU.

"We found that it is possible to build up significant quantities of water in the gas phase without much enrichment in heavy elements," said Bialy. "In this current work, we calculated how much water could exist in the gas phase within molecular clouds that would form later generations of stars and planets. In future research, we intend to address questions such as how much water could have existed as interstellar ice, as in our own galaxy, and what fraction of all the water might actually be incorporated into newly-forming planetary systems."

This has been affirmed by the Herschel Space Observatory, launched on May 14, 2009 from French

Guyana by the European Space Agency. As the largest orbiting telescope ever built at the time, with a single mirror measuring 3.5 meters in diameter, its instruments provide spectroscopic capabilities in the 55 to 670 μm wavelength range, which is particularly effective in observing the massive amounts of molecular H_2O in space. It offered astronomers a unique opportunity to observe water throughout the universe unhampered by the Earth's moist atmosphere. And its initial findings, first reported in October 2011, revealed that water emission elucidates key episodes in stellar birth. Oceans of cold water vapor were discovered in the accretion discs of young stars. It served as an amazing corroboration of God's testimony.

Water is undoubtedly one of the most important molecules found in space. As a dominant form of oxygen, it is the most abundant element in the universe after hydrogen and helium. Water controls the chemistry of many other substances, whether in a gaseous or solid phase. It is a unique diagnostic of the warmer gas and the energetic processes that take place close to forming stars. It is responsible for keeping the gas at low temperatures because the cloud cools as line radiation escapes. These low temperatures, in turn, allow clouds to collapse to form stars.

The Herschel Space Observatory's primary objective was WISH (finding Water In Star-forming regions with Herschel). While the 3D mapping is complicated, WISH found a plethora of water in stellar nurseries. This fact was beautifully illustrated in the first water map of a forming star, as the water emission "lights up" in proximity to a protostar. Water is the primary catalyst for star formation, just as Yahowah disclosed 3,400 years prior to Herschel's deployment.

It was not until recently that the findings derived from the Herschel Space Observatory were published, affirming that an abundance of water was available for star and planet

192

formation – as is suggested here in Genesis. Some 50 signatories highlight the peer-reviewed April 2021 article in *Astronomy & Astrophysics*. Their research, entitled Water in Star-Forming Regions: Physics and Chemistry from Clouds to Disks as Probed by Herschel Spectroscopy, demonstrates that water continues to be a key component of the physics and chemistry of stellar nurseries. Providing the first confirmation of the Genesis account in 3,500 years, the opening line of the Abstract reads: "Water is a key molecule in the physics and chemistry of star and planet formation."

Also interesting, the Fourth Phase of Water was initially proposed by Dr. Gerald Pollack at the University of Washington. Under extreme pressure in small places, water is neither liquid, solid, nor gaseous, but appears to "tunnel." This suggests that tunneling water could travel through an impervious barrier and be present on both sides simultaneously. For this to occur, the oxygen and hydrogen atoms of the water must molecule delocalize, presenting all six symmetrical and equivalent positions at the same time. It revolutionizes our perceptions of water, how it moves and utilizes energy.

𐤔𐤉𐤔ᴶ

What follows serves as an introduction to the concepts of relativity and thermodynamics. There is also an insinuation that a relationship exists between energy and matter, including how one can be exchanged for the other. There is even a hint into the nature of spacetime as these physical properties existed during the formative era of our solar system.

Therefore, the only way to render the following statement in simpler terms would be to inadequately translate it.

"God acted and engaged in association with matter and space. He divided and separated relative things in space over an interval of time from the various fluids and forms of water relative to and in association with that which is interchanged in an orderly arrangement regarding the support for matter and the expanse of space.

So, these are the connections between things in space over the time of this source of inquiry regarding the existence of water relative to that which is distinct from and yet in proximity to matter and the expansion of space. Thereby it existed correctly verified and portrayed." (*Bare'syth* 1:7)

Amplified, the passage reveals:

"**God** (*wa 'elohym* – the Almighty) **acted and engaged** (*'asah* – expended considerable energy, caused to happen, made, gained and profited from, dealt with, ordained, fashioned, and brought about, preparing and producing (qal imperfect)) **in association with** (*'eth* – through the connection between) **matter and space** (*raqya'* – a measure of the material within the vastness of space, the extended solid support of universal expansion; from *raqa'* – spreading out, expanding, and broadening of things forged and formed).

He divided and separated (*badal* – He made a distinction between that which He would associate with or abandon, select or expel, distinguishing among and setting apart, choosing to desire or withdrawing from over an interval of time, to make a distinction and difference) **relative things in space over an interval of time** (*bayn* – in the midst He differentiated between them for the purpose of understanding, connecting and dividing to perceive, consider, discern, discriminate, and respond, intelligently associating and dissociating to facilitate comprehension and provide insights, giving revelation deeper meaning in

194

the midst) **from** (*min* – out of) **the fluid state and various forms of water** (*ha maym* – the common and essential source of creation and life, serving as a means of inquiry) **relative to** (*'asher* – demonstrating linkage and association, revealing the source and cause responsible for it, revealing the proper way, leading to the correct conclusion, while providing for the maximum benefit) **and in association with that which is interchanged in an orderly arrangement** (*tachath* – for the sake and purpose of establishing that which underlies everything, extending by exchanging one thing for another such that the undertaking and results are neither random nor chaotic) **regarding the support for matter and the expanse of space** (*la ha raqya'* – pertaining to the measure of the material within the vastness of space, the extended solid support of universal expansion; from *raqa'* – spreading out, expanding, and broadening of things forged and formed).

So (*wa*), **these are the connections between things in space over the time** (*bayn* – in the midst of things and between them for the purpose of understanding, connecting and dividing to perceive, consider, discern, discriminate, and respond, intelligently associating and disassociating to facilitate comprehension and provide insights, giving revelation deeper meaning in the midst) **of this fluid state and the source of inquiry regarding existence of water** (*ha maym* – pondering the various forms of liquid as the means to life) **relative to** (*'asher* – demonstrating linkage and association, revealing the source and cause responsible for it, revealing the proper way, leading to the correct conclusion, while providing for the maximum benefit) **that which is distinct from** (*min* – as an extension of the source and relative to the event, as part of and by reason of, revealing the substance from which something is made and as a fractional part of the whole, on account of and by means of) **and yet in proximity to** (*'al* – near, close to, around, toward, over and above, and spatially next to a determined location of the Almighty) **matter and the expansion of space** (*la ha raqya'* – concerning the measure of the material within the vastness of space, regarding the extended solid support of universal expansion; from *raqa'* – spreading out, expanding, and broadening of things forged and formed).

Thereby (*wa* – then and therefore), **it existed** (*hayah* – it was and will be (qal imperfect – actual and continuing as)) **correctly verified and portrayed** (*ken* – honestly reported and right regarding the sequence of events, factually conveying what is truthful and proper)." (*Bare'syth* / In the Beginning / Genesis 1:7)

Almighty God (*'elohym*) is mentioned once in this declaration. The concept of relativity (*'asher* and *bayn*) is presented four times, providing us with a frame of reference. The preparation, production, and composition of "*raqya'* – matter and space," and the "orderly arrangement of it, its sequence, source, and basis," is conveyed three times. By so doing, Yahowah disclosed which scientific methods humanity would need to develop to appreciate the creative process.

As for me, I am happy to be here and delighted to be in His presence. I appreciate this opportunity to be energized by His Spirit and enlightened by His Word. While I am not going to pretend that I have rendered every word as God intended or that I understand how all of this occurred, I am thrilled to have this opportunity.

'Asher, translated as "relative to," brought me to this place. Had *'asher* not been so consistently misrepresented in English Bibles, I would not have devoted the past twenty-two years of my life to these translations. *'Asher* not only demonstrates a linkage and association between things, but it also reveals the reason behind creation. *'Asher* "shows the proper way and leads to the right conclusion,

providing for the maximum benefit." *'Asher* draws our attention to the relationship God intended.

Bayn is a derivation of *byn*, a word I have come to appreciate because it describes the process I used to go from knowing to understanding. The verb explains that we should seek to find the relationships between the things we observe so that by making the proper connections we come to comprehend what we are witnessing. It is a little like the Dot to Dot puzzles I enjoyed as a child, where we are encouraged to connect the dots in the appropriate way such that a picture emerges out of what would otherwise appear random.

The second thing we must accomplish when seeking to find order in the apparent chaos of life, and then derive understanding amidst the confusion, is to have a filter, the ability to "*badal* – separate fact from fiction, distinguishing between right and wrong, and discerning what is beneficial and counterproductive." Relative to God, *badal* reveals that He has always sought to divide and separate, setting Himself and those He values apart from that which is common.

This leads us to the conclusion of this statement, where *ken* is used to explain that the process God has engaged in and presented as "verifiable and correct." It was all "honestly reported and right regarding the sequence of events, factually conveying what is truthful and proper."

Let's acknowledge what should now be obvious: recognizing that the process He deployed to create the universe is beyond our comprehension, Yahowah described the means we would need to deploy to understand how all of this applies to our relationship with Him. While day one was devoted to introductions, the second day is about understanding.

I will openly admit that scientifically, this is all rather complex. I recognize that time is relative and that matter is a derivative and diminished form of energy. And yet, the sheer size of it all, the forces at play, and the dimensions are beyond our comprehension.

Specifically, God is talking about separation, and these cosmic sources of repulsion exist within the realm of dark energy – something which along with dark matter comprise 96% of the fundamental nature of the universe. Our challenge is that we only know the effects, not the substance, of dark energy and dark matter. Worse, we do not possess the capacity to understand – not now, and probably not ever. An enormous source of repulsion exists to be sure, but it is outside our relative realm of reality. Therefore, no scientist can explain the actual processes at work in *Bare'syth* 1:7 – even today.

All we know for sure is that the focus of the second day is on the galactic expansion occurring within molecular clouds, differentiating matter and space in an orderly and verifiable fashion – something which is consistent with recent scientific discovery.

"And (*wa* – therefore) **God** (*'elohym* – the Almighty) **called out in an inviting and welcoming way** (*qara'* – He saw as appealing, pleasing, and alluring, issuing an invitation to read and recite about being called out while expecting a response regarding this greeting and meeting, designating and announcing (qal imperfect – creating an actual ongoing relationship between God and the heavens)) **to the expansion of matter in the vastness of space** (*la ha raqya'* – concerning the measure of the physical material within the expanding realm of the universe, regarding the extended solid support of cosmic expansion; from *raqa'* – spreading out, expanding, and broadening of things forged and formed) **of the heavens** (*shamaym* – of the universe in the uppermost portion of the sky above from the spiritual realm of God).

"And there was (*wa hayah* – there exists with unfolding implications over time (qal imperfect)) **evening** (*'erab* / *'arab* – a period of darkness, the mixing together of an interwoven fabric, the mingling and joining together of things, a nighttime of hopelessness during a discouraged state of foreign occupation, an era of ignorant commingling of and adherence to faiths and beliefs when the adversary will combine this with noxious swarms of Arab pests) **and there would be** (*wa hayah* – there also exists with unfolding implications over time (qal imperfect)) **morning** (*boqer* – tomorrow, the beginning of a new day, a time to be observant, perceptive, and judgmental, a time for consideration, a period to be attentive and respond appropriately, an extended stretch for being inquisitive and seeking information in order to make good decisions; from *baqar* – to seek, search, rendered as "e, consider, and reflect) – **the second day** (*yowm sheny* – the second in a sequence of days; from *shanah* – to repeat)." (*Bare'syth* / In the Beginning / Genesis 1:8)

Scientifically, our solar system was created during this period. It happened in the manner God has testified. Water was present and essential. There is an association between all things because relativity and time are linked. And distancing, the repulsive nature of dark energy, still lies at the heart of the effects we can observe.

Spiritually, two is the number denoting choice. The second day is focused on separation. We need to decide whose side we want to be on – the side of light or darkness. Are we going to remain mired in the realm of matter and space or are we going to relate to our Creator in such a way as to exist eternally with Him in *Shamaym*?

Likewise, from the perspective of our relationship with God, the second creative day is linked to the second *Mow'ed Miqra'*, or Invitation to be Called Out and Meet with God of *Matsah*, known as "Unleavened or UnYeasted Bread." Its purpose is to remove this naturally occurring fungus, which is symbolic of religion and governance, from the bread which represents our mortal souls. It is this separation which makes us acceptable to Yah while we are still in this physical realm.

Historically, the second millennium of human history, consistent with Yahowah's creative witness, was punctuated with the ultimate story of water separating mankind from life and from God. *Noach* | Noah was called out and separated from the midst of evil men, living in a wooden ark of protection designed by God while the waters rose and consumed those who chose the wrong side of the divide. If you want to live with Yahowah you will have to trust Him, too. Noach listened intently to God and then acted, engaging by doing what Yah had instructed. He and his family were saved and endured as a result. It has always been a rather simple, straightforward equation.

As an interesting note, we know for certain that a flood of Towrah-ical proportions occurred between four and five thousand years ago (around 2370 BCE) in the region where the men who were created in God's image (with a *neshamah* | conscience in addition to a *nepesh* | soul or consciousness) were said to have lived. Yahowah will explicitly demonstrate that 'Eden was at the headwaters of the Tigris and Euphrates Rivers, near the Black Sea, and that 'Adam's and Chawah's (Eve is the name of a pagan sun goddess) children ultimately formed the civilizations east and south of the Garden including Babylon, Assyria, and Sumer. Archeologists have found cities 200 to 500 feet below the current shores of the Black Sea, and a twelve-foot-thick layer of silt and mud was laid down at the same time in Mesopotamia, precisely when the oldest textual witness said the flood occurred. If you keep reading, you will discover an entire chapter dedicated to this event.

As evidence for the obvious, consider *Bare'syth* / Genesis 7:22. It speaks of the aftermath and purpose of the flood. But be forewarned, to appreciate Yahowah's insights, one has to correctly communicate what God actually revealed. English translations uniformly add three words which are not in the text, and they ignore three words which are actually there, then they inaccurately communicate the meaning of the words which remain.

"All (*kol*) **who were there with** (*'asher*) **a conscience** (*neshamah* – the ability to think, distinguishing between right and wrong, judging between good and bad, the capacity to process information and comprehend, indicative of cause and effect, inspiring and inflaming passions; from *nasham* – indicating that the *neshamah* is passed on through childbirth and is spiritually receptive) **from** (*min*) **an animating and continuously living** (*chay*) **spirit** (*ruwach*) **with its resentment and provocation** (*ba 'aph huw'* – in his anger and ill temper, with his improper self-confidence and haughtiness, in his wrath and hostility), **everyone** (*kol*) **in relation to** (*'asher*) **the dry land and resulting rubble** (*ba ha charabah* – among the areas desolated and depopulated), **died** (*muwth* – were killed)." (*Bare'syth* / Genesis 7:22)

The *neshamah* is that part of human nature that enables us to connect our souls to a spirit, either good or bad, and thus facilitates the capacity to distinguish between the two, to know right from wrong, good from bad, truth from deception, God from the Adversary. It serves as our conscience and is passed down through 'Adam and Chawah. Therefore, the only people Yahowah was interested in eliminating were those with a *neshamah* who had chosen to associate with the spirit of arrogance and provocation.

Also, so that you are not misled, the word translated as "earth" in reference to the flood in most Bibles, typically means "land, ground, realm, or region." When the account of Noah and the ark is translated to infer that every animal on the planet was aboard, that all *Homo sapiens* drowned, and that the whole Earth was submerged to the tops of the highest mountains, the translators are errantly conveying Yahowah's message and making a mockery of the Towrah. There was not remotely enough water in, on, and above the planet to reach the summit of Everest. But there was more than enough to accomplish what Yahowah claimed.

While we are on the subject of the deluge, when we rely on the Masoretic Text (prepared 1000 CE through 1550), the flood is dated to 2369 BCE. The *Septuagint* (prepared between 300 to 200 BCE) adds one hundred years to six generations between Shem and 'Abraham, and twenty years to a seventh – something confirmed by the Samaritan *Pentateuch* (prepared 400 to 600 BCE) in each case. This would place the flood closer to 2968 BCE – which is year 1000 Yah.

The reason for these textual discrepancies is actually very simple. Paleo-Hebrew used a horizontal line above an alpha-numerical representation to convey the one hundred's place numerically. Papyrus was woven such that the fibers formed horizontal ridges and indentations. With the ink and writing instruments of the day, and with the constant unfurling of scrolls, horizontal lines eventually become invisible in all but the best light. So, the scribes may have left out the one hundred's place in these six post-flood and pre-Abraham generations. And if not, then year 1000 Yah is marked by the year of Noach's birth.

𐤋𐤀𐤅𐤔

Now that our solar system has been formed, and our planet has had time to cool, the Earth was ready for the gathering of liquid water into oceans, the cradle of life. Using the formula we were given, we can safely conclude that the third cosmological day dawned sometime around 3.5 billion years ago. This corresponds to the time the fossil record tells us that plants first flourished in our planet's emerging seas.

God's testimony remains consistent with the evidence at our disposal...

"**The Almighty** (*wa 'elohym* – then God) **said** (*'amar* – communicated and exclaimed), **'The waters** (*ha maym* – the source of inquiry, existence, and life along with the various states of water) **will be gathered** (*qawah* – I have chosen to collect, establishing an expectation, eagerly longing for the anticipated result (nifal imperfect jussive – the waters receive and carry out the intended purpose and directive based upon the direction and will of God)) **from** (*min* – out of) **beneath** (*tachath* – parts of and under, even for the sake of) **the heavens** (*ha shamaym* – the abode of the stars, universe, and spiritual realm) **directed toward** (*'el* – in the direction of) **one special place** (*maqowm 'echad* – a singular site, spatial area, home, and dwelling for the existence of life; a compound of *ma* – to question and *quwm* – to take a stand and be established).'

Then (*wa*), **He wanted to see the solid ground appear** (*ra'ah ha yabeshah* – it became His will to reveal and expose the dry land on the surface of the earth (nifal imperfect jussive)).

Therefore (*wa* – then and accordingly) **it existed** (*hayah* – it was and will be (qal imperfect – actual and continuing as)) **verifiable and correct** (*ken* – honestly reported and right regarding the sequence of events, factually conveying what is truthful and proper)." (*Bare'syth* / In the Beginning / Genesis 1:9)

Scientists have struggled to explain the presence of such vast amounts of water on our blue planet. This has left many to postulate a theory that it was brought in through icy asteroid and comet impacts. However, even if distributed equally on a million comets with our planet in their trajectory, they would have to be so large, each would annihilate the Earth. The proof is rather simple. There are 326,000,000,000,000,000,000,000 (326 million trillion / 3.26 x 10^{20}) gallons of water on Earth. On average, these million comets would have to carry 3.26 x 10^{14} gallons of water, making each a staggering 45,000,000,000,000 cubic feet. This is 300 cubic miles – making each a planet-killer. Stephen Hawking even proposed such a ridiculous theory – evidently unwilling to do the math.

Suffice it to say, we humans are clueless as to how 326 million trillion gallons of water suddenly appeared on Earth. But we should not have been since Yahowah used *qawah* to explain...

"The waters (*ha maym*) **will be gathered** (*qawah* – I have chosen to collect, establishing an expectation, eagerly longing for the anticipated result) **from** (*min*) **beneath** (*tachath*) **the heavens** (*ha shamaym*) **directed toward** (*'el*) **one special place** (*maqowm 'echad*)**."**

Just as Yahowah commenced the creative process with a big bang, and then facilitated star formation in molecular clouds, He deliberately directed some of that water to our special place in the universe. And He did so between 3 and 4 billion years ago.

Yabeshah is used in this context to describe a natural condition which will, by design, become suitable for mankind. It is used in Genesis 8:7 and 8:14 to signify that, after cleansing the region of malignant souls, the land was restored in support of the Covenant. Then in keeping with the same theme, *yabeshah* appears in *Yahowsha'* / Joshua 2:10 to reveal that Yahowah created a path through the sea for the Children of Yisra'el to traverse as they walked away from Egypt to the Promised Land. God then provided a way across the *Yarden* | Jordan River into the land He had given to 'Abraham during the initiation of the Covenant in *Yahowsha'* / Joshua 4:3. This intent is transported into the future throughout *Yasha'yah* / Isaiah and used prophetically to describe how Yahowah will intervene on behalf of Yisra'el and Yahuwdah during the last days – restoring the relationship.

My favorite application of *yabeshah* is when Yahowah in *Yasha'yah* / Isaiah 40 quotes *Dowd's* | David's exceptional prose in the 22nd *Mizmowr* / Psalm comparing the mortality of man to the enduring nature of God. I share this to affirm that *yabeshah* reveals more about Yahowah's intent and interaction with humankind than it does dried dirt.

"And (*wa*) **God** (*'elohym* – the Almighty) **called out in an inviting and welcoming way** (*qara'* – He saw as appealing, pleasing, and alluring, issuing an invitation to read and recite about being called out while expecting a response regarding this greeting and meeting, designating and announcing (qal imperfect – creating an actual and ongoing relationship between God and the heavens)) **to the surface of the earth** (*la ha yabeshah* – on behalf of the land cleared of water, and thus dry, solid, and firm, therefore walkable) **as *'erets* | land** (*'erets* – the material realm comprised of the ground in a region of the earth).

And (*wa*) **regarding** (*la*) **the accumulation and beneficial expectation of the gathering together** (*miqawah* – the insights which can be derived by looking forward with confident anticipation and pondering the implications of this collection into a home suitable for living; a compound of *my* – to ponder the implications and *maqowm* – a place for living, a home or dwelling) **of the waters** (*ha maym* – the many phases of water providing the opportunity to ponder the consequence of life) **He called** (*qara'* – He welcomed as appealing, issuing an invitation to read and recite about being called out while expecting a response regarding this greeting and meeting, designating and announcing, assigning and naming (qal perfect – creating an actual but temporal, constrained in time, and short-lived relationship between God and the seas)) **seas**

205

(*yamym* – large bodies of water, especially in the West (serving as a metaphor for Gentiles)).

God (*wa 'elohym* – therefore the Almighty) **saw and considered** (*ra'ah* – inspected and perceived, viewed and revealed (qal imperfect)) **that indeed** (*ky* – by contrast to any other option and truthfully) **it was beneficial and good** (*towb* – appropriate, desirable, and agreeable, excellent and valuable, prosperous and productive)." (*Bare'syth* / In the Beginning / Genesis 1:10)

There is also more to *'erets* than "land, earth (as in ground, not the planet), region, realm, or territory." It addresses that which is "firm," and thus "material," contrasting it with space and light energy during the initiation of the creative process and was therefore translated as "material realm." *'Erets* is most often used to describe the land of *Yisra'el* | Israel. The designation "Promised Land" is from *'amar 'erets*, meaning "the land which is spoken about." It is therefore symbolic of *Yahuwdym* | Jews.

Ky | By contrast, the *yamym* | seas, especially in the West, are symbolic of *gowym* | gentiles. And this distinction makes the fact that Yahowah's welcoming invitation to *'erets*, representing Jews, as written in the imperfect conjugation, and thus ongoing throughout time, while His call to the *yamym*, indicative of Gentiles, was in the perfect conjugation – and thus short-lived.

This is an adroit declaration of what occurred on planet Earth at this time. Our world cooled to below the boiling point as volcanic activity began to wane. A more translucent atmosphere started to form as a result of diminished plumes of volcanic ash, but also as a consequence of a radically diminished asteroid bombardment. Water began to flow into the Earth's seas. These fortuitous conditions afforded an immediate opportunity for life.

What is interesting here is that, once again, nothing was created on this day. One thing simply flowed from another. The sequence Yahowah laid out was substantive, orderly, and rational. His words continue to sound more like a scientific text than the "religious" musings of primitive humans.

ו𐤉𐤅𐤉

Spiritually, the first half of the third day was devoted to gathering the beneficial and uniting nature of the "*maym* – waters" while preparing the "*yabeshah* – that which can be used to cross the divide." While *maym* is clearly water, *yabeshah* can be a bit of a mystery. It is usually translated as "dry *land*" even though there is no reference to "land, dirt, soil, ground, or earth" in the etymology of the word.

We highlighted some of the possibilities associated with this feminine noun where it first appeared. In addition to the cited references, it is used in *Yasha'yah* / Isaiah 44:3 to depict the Maternal Set-Apart Spirit being poured out upon the spiritually parched descendants of Ya'aqob at a still-future date. So, let's turn to that passage to see if Yasha'yah can convey the intent of *yabeshah* for us in the context of a message that is especially relevant to us.

The prophetic chapter opens with a creative flashback…

"So now, at this moment in time (*wa 'atah* – in concert with what follows in this discussion)**, listen** (*shama'* – choose to hear this pronouncement (qal imperative)) **Ya'aqob** (*Ya'aqob* – the Consequence of His Stance, serving as a synonym for Yisra'el)**, My coworker** (*'ebed 'any* – My associate)**, and Yisra'el** (*wa Yisra'el* – therefore those who engage and endure with God)**, whom I have chosen** (*bachar ba huw'* – whom I have selected, prefer, and desire, whom I examine and assess, and whom I appointed and will accept). (*Yasha'yah* / Isaiah 44:1)

This is what (*koh* – prompting your attention to the content which follows, thus) **Yahowah** (𐤉𐤄𐤅𐤄 – the pronunciation of *YaHoWaH* as guided by His *towrah* – teaching regarding His *hayah* – existence) **says** (*'amar* – declares and promises, expressing in words at this specific time (qal perfect)) **who engaged on your behalf** (*'asah 'atah* – who acted for you, working on your behalf to prepare you) **by creating you** (*wa yatsar 'atah* – fashioning and forming you) **from the womb** (*min beten*), **and who has and will help you** (*'azar 'atah* – and who will come to your aid, supporting you, increasing every aspect of your nature (qal imperfect energic nun active preterite – actually as a result of a genuine relationship and continually on an ongoing basis enthusiastically and emphatically, actively in the past and future has and will serve to help you)).

'**Do not fear or be distressed** (*'al yare'* – never be awed or afraid, do not be frightened or intimidated, and never respect any authority) **as My coworker** (*'ebed 'any* – as My associate and one who serves with Me), **Ya'aqob** (*Ya'aqob* – the Consequence of His Stance, serving as a synonym for Yisra'el), **the Upright One** (*yashuruwm* – the straightforward one who is approved and on the level) **whom I have appointed and find acceptable** (*bachar ba huw'* – whom I have selected, prefer, and desire, whom I examine and assess, and whom I have chosen). (*Yasha'yah* / Isaiah 44:2)

For indeed (*ky* – because it is certain), **I will pour out** (*yatsaq* – I will favor and anoint, I will wash and cleanse by dispensing (qal imperfect)) **water** (*maym* – that which is common to life and the universal solvent in all of its forms and sources) **upon** (*'al* – for and over) **the thirsty, flowing forth upon the parched** (*tsame'* – those desiring water), **as well as streams** (*wa nazal* – massive amounts of liquid water from cisterns to seas, gushing and flowing rivers running) **upon** (*'al* – over) **the desolate surface of the earth** (*yabeshah* – the dry land deprived of water, which was established to be firm and walkable; from *yabesh* – to become dry and withered).

I will pour out (*yatsaq* – I will favor and anoint, I will wash and cleanse by dispensing (qal imperfect first-person singular active – based upon a literal interpretation of an ongoing and genuine relationship God alone will actively engage for the benefit of Ya'aqob's descendants)) **My Spirit** (*ruwach 'any* – My identity and essential nature, My energetic source of enlightenment and empowerment, the breath of life from the heart and mind of God, the spirit of understanding and acceptance) **upon your descendants** (*'al zera' 'atah* – over your seed and before that which you have sown, for your offspring and extended family) **as My blessing** (*wa barakah 'any* – including My willingness to kneel down to lift you up, as My source of reconciliation, the gift of My covenant, in addition to a means of uplifting enrichment and empowerment; from *barak* – to kneel down in love and adoration to lift up and support as a present and gift, a contribution to prosperity and peace) **upon your descendants** (*'al zera' 'atah* – over your seed and before that which you have sown, toward and among your offspring and extended family).'" (*Yasha'yah* / Liberation and Salvation are from Yah / Isaiah 44:3)

When it comes to reinforcing the connections we have made between the Spirit and water, between water and life, and between *yabeshah* and parched souls, we have had our suppositions affirmed. In this case, *yabeshah* is used as a metaphor for receptive Yisra'elites – the descendants of Ya'aqob in advance of Yahowah's return who thirst for a spiritual awakening.

The purpose of Yahowah's Spirit is demonstrated through water – which is essential to life. What's more, the Spirit's place in the lives of Her children is that of a loving

209

Mother getting down on Her knees to raise Her child. *Barakah* depicts Yahowah serving humankind in this same way, and explicitly *Yisra'el* | Israel, as an adoring Father and Mother, interacting with, elevating and supporting, protecting and raising, the children of the descendants of Ya'aqob.

Yabeshah describes souls who, bereft of Yahowah's anointing Spirit (which is akin to His gift of living waters), are on the cusp of being restored. The passage has nothing to do with the ground, dry or otherwise.

There is something else said here which is as essential to our understanding as it is misunderstood. Since Yahowah's Spirit is being poured out upon Ya'aqob's descendants, and it is Ya'aqob's children who are being raised by God, Yahowah has not replaced them with Christians or Muslims. As such, the underlying supposition required to justify the existence of these, the world's most popular religions, is obliterated.

When we search the root of *yabeshah* we discover that *yabesh* means "withered and dried up" – in other words, "desolate or lifeless." In *Bamidbar* / Ponder the Word / Numbers 11:6 *yabesh* is used in connection with *nepesh* to indicate a wayward "soul is forsaken," and therefore "desolate of life." From a spiritual perspective, we can conclude that Yahowah selected *yabeshah* at the onset of His accounting of what occurred on creation's third day to convey that without His Spiritual anointing, without His cleansing, without His gift of living waters, our soul is parched, and therefore desolate and forsaken, destined to shrivel up and die. Had Yahowah simply intended to convey "dry land" He would have used a term other than *yabeshah*.

This spiritual insight is further evidenced in the word for "gathering," *qawah*, which means "to provide hope, to look forward with confidence to that which is good and beneficial, anticipating the future event in eager expectation of salvation and deliverance." Even the word for "place" is synonymous with our Savior. *Maqowm* is a "standing place where one lives," and therefore analogous to all of Yisra'el but especially Mount Mowryah's upright pole upon which Passover, the Doorway to Life, was fulfilled.

Further, the word for "appear" has redemption written all over it as well. *Ra'ah* means "to show oneself and become visible by way of illumination, to find delight through revelation, to be considered and provided for, aided and supported, and to be selected so as to be present with, meet and experience" God.

Since Yah could have chosen more mundane terms, but didn't, it's incumbent upon us to explore the reasons for His salvation references within the *Bare'syth* timeline. Personally, I think the answer is obvious: there are three accounts embedded in the Genesis witness. This is the story of creation, salvation, and human history. As such, the six-plus-one pattern presented in *Bare'syth*, and reaffirmed in countless other places, serves as the foundation of Yahowah's prophetic timeline, especially as it relates to the fall and restoration of man.

Before we return to God's narrative and decipher the events depicted on the second half of the third creative day, let's complete Yahowah's prophetic announcement in *Yasha'yah* / Isaiah. God wants us to know that His Spirit will fulfill this *Bare'syth* prophecy by providing the anointing gift of cleansing waters to "*Yahuwdym* – the Beloved of Yah."

"**This one** (*zeh*) **will consistently and genuinely say** (*'amar* – will literally and continually express in words, actually declaring throughout time (qal imperfect active)), **'I am for** (*la 'any* – I respect and therefore am approaching and drawing near) **Yahowah** (*YaHoWaH* – an accurate presentation of the name of *'elowah* – God as guided by His *towrah* – instructions regarding His *hayah* – existence).' **Then** (*wa*)**, another** (zeh) **will summon and call upon** (*qara' ba* – will call out, welcoming, reading and reciting, announcing and proclaiming (qal imperfect active)) **the name** (*shem* – the personal and proper designation) **of Ya'aqob** (*Ya'aqob* – to surpass and reward as a consequence, to grasp hold and embed one's heels and thus walk without wavering, serving as a synonym for Yisra'el).

The next (*wa zeh*) **will write** (*kathab* – will inscribe) **Yahowah** (*Yahowah* – a transliteration of 𐤉𐤄𐤅𐤄, our *'elowah* – God as directed in His *towrah* – teaching regarding His *hayah* – existence) **with his hand** (*yad huw' la*) **along with** (*wa ba*) **the name** (*shem*) *Yisra'el* | **Israel** (*Yisra'el* – One who Engages and Endures with God, having been liberated and empowered by the Almighty: Israel), **using the designation honorably as a surname** (*kanah* – bestowing it as a title while demonstrating a commitment to be rooted in the land)." (*Yasha'yah* / Liberation and Salvation are from Yah / Isaiah 44:5)

It is being said now, today, and written for the first time in thousands of years: "I am for Yahowah." Soon hundreds will become thousands as Yahowah's Chosen People, Yisra'el, come to embrace their relationship with Ya'aqob and the Covenant. They will embody what Yisra'el represents: Individuals who Engage and Endure with God. They will wear both names honorably.

And that means that there will be no rabbis or religious Jews present on this day because they are vehemently opposed to Yahowah's name. It is a mistake that will cost them their lives.

Be aware, those who endure will be declaring and writing Yahowah's name – not "Jesus," "Christ," "the Lord," "Allah," or "HaShem." Further, the only other acceptable name on the list was Ya'aqob – the father of Yisra'el. And that would exclude the founding fathers and heroes of every other nation or creed. Moreover, these declarations are definitive, not only because this is occurring at the end of the day, but also because in the next statement, Yahowah removes any possibility that there is salvation by any other name.

"**Thus** (*koh* – at this time and in this manner) **declares** (*'amar* – emphatically states, expressing at this moment (qal perfect)) **Yahowah** (*Yahowah* – the proper pronunciation of YaHoWaH, our *'elowah* – God as directed in His *ToWRaH* – teaching regarding His *HaYaH* – existence and our *ShaLoWM* – restoration)**, the King** (*melek* – the One to carefully consider and respond to thoughtfully because He reigns over and leads by counseling and advising) **of Yisra'el** (*Yisra'el* – Individuals who are Liberated and Empowered by God; from *'ysh* – people, *sarah* – who engage and endure, with *'el* – the Almighty) **and his Redeemer** (*wa ga'al huw'* – in addition to the One who delivers him from slavery, oppression, and subjugation by mankind (qal participle active))**, Yahowah** (*Yahowah* – written as directed by His *towrah* – teaching regarding His *hayah* – existence) **of the vast array of spiritual implements** (*tsaba'* – of heavenly messengers who serve and assist),

'**I am the first** (*'any ri'shown* – I was prior to time, I am the beginning and before everything, I am the uppermost limit) **and I am the last** (*wa 'any 'acharown* – I am the future and I will be there in the end)**. There is none besides Me** (*wa min bal'ady 'any 'ayn* – so apart from Me and with Me as the lone exception, there is no other Divine being, disassociated from all others)**.'**" (*Yasha'yah* / Liberation and Salvation are from Yah / Isaiah 44:6)

As kings are wont to do, Yahowah offered His crown to His beloved Son, Dowd, who reigned with distinction

3,000 years ago and served with compassion 1,000 years thereafter. He will inherit the role of leading by counseling and advising Yisra'el from his Father, who will return him to sovereignty to shepherd their flock.

Redemption is a very special form of salvation. To be redeemed is to be acquired through an exchange – offering something of value for the life of another. Yahowah accomplished this, by allowing His Son, Dowd, to suffer the consequence of us having been mistaken and missing the way, as the Passover Lamb. Then Dowd paid the penalty for our religious and political rebellion on UnYeasted Bread – perfecting us in the process of delivering our souls from harm's way.

God then asks a probing question followed by a provocative challenge the religious seem incapable of processing...

"'**Who can be compared to Me** (*wa my kemow 'any* – therefore, who, posing a question, is like Me, even similar to Me)**? Let him issue an invitation and declare it** (*qara'* – let him announce his name, summon his people, call them out, meet with them, and fulfill the *miqra'ey* (qal imperfect jussive – have him actually express his will on an ongoing basis, be consistent and genuine in his pronouncements and greetings, especially invitations to meet)).

Let him convey an informative and cogent message and conspicuously declare his purpose (*wa nagad huw'* – of his own initiative, let him demonstrate his existence, announce an explanation, propose a plan, and be effective, provide a show-and-tell or put up or shut up regarding him or it (hifil imperfect jussive – demonstrating third-person initiative on an ongoing basis whereby the subject actually interacts with those to whom he is communicating)).

Take a position, make the necessary preparations, arrange the proposition in an orderly fashion, and place this information before Me (*wa 'arak huw' la 'any –*

propose an organized and thoughtful reply which is sensible and consistent, then lay it all out in a reasonable fashion with regard to Me (qal imperfect jussive)) **since** (*min* – because) **I placed Mine out openly for examination before** (*sym* – I set My explanation of cause and effect in a place where the information could be examined and questioned by appointing and preserving, even naming on a written document (qal infinitive construct active – genuinely connected and bound to these people, literally and actually acting without being constrained by time)) **My people** (*'any 'am* – My nation and family) **a long time ago** (*'owlam* – back in antiquity and covering eternity).

Furthermore (*wa* – in addition), **provide some guidance to show the way** (*'asher* – lead by revealing the correct path to receive the benefits of the relationship) **by having him on his own initiative prove his existence by emphatically stating an enlightening and convincing message which is conspicuously declared revealing his purpose** (*wa nagad huw'* – of his or its own accord, let him or it demonstrate his relevance by announcing an explanation, proposing a plan, and being effective, providing a show-and-tell, putting up or shutting up (hifil imperfect jussive – demonstrating third-person initiative on an ongoing basis whereby the subject actually interacts with those to whom he or it is communicating)) **by coming to them** (*bow' la hem* – by arriving and returning to them, coming and going, leading and directing them, while concerned about them, approaching them in an inclusive manner (qal imperfect – in an actual and ongoing basis on behalf of the relationship)).'" (*Yasha'yah* / Liberation and Salvation are from Yah / Isaiah 44:7)

Men have made a multitude of gods, but one God made all men. He is incomparable, set apart, and unique. To compare Yahowah to Jesus, Allah, Shiva, the Lord,

Divine Providence, Mother Earth, or Nature is ignorant and insulting.

Yahowah alone met with His creation. And He, explaining the means He would use to redeem His people in His previous statement, issues *"qara'* – an invitation to be called out and meet with Him as a result of Dowd having fulfilled the Miqra'ey."

Having done what He said He would do for Yisra'el, Yahowah chides the religious, telling them to have their gods put up or shut up. He is in this position and has earned this right because Yahowah *"nagad* – has conspicuously conveyed an enlightening and coherent, edifying and persuasive message." Having "proposed and fulfilled His plan, He proved His existence and demonstrated His effectiveness." By comparison, religious scriptures are mythical stories composed by men which are unproven, contradictory, irrational, and thus ineffective. Considering our options, why do only one in a million choose the real God instead of the fake ones?

Yahowah tells the religious, "Get your act together, think it through, and give Me your best shot." *'Arak* lays it all out for us. For man's gods to have any merit, the religious should be able to *'arak*: take a position, then no matter how much time is required, prepare a cogent, rational response, be accurate with the evidence cited, orderly and consistent with the arguments, and systematic in the approach, laying everything out openly in a reasonable manner. While that has never been done and cannot be done in support of any religious divinity without misrepresenting the facts, misappropriating the effects, and making assertions that are both irrational and contradictory, the best man can do is infinitely inferior to anything Yahowah has said or done. If this were a contest, it would be like pitting an eighty-year-old stuttering shepherd wielding a stick against the most powerful empire on Earth, eight-year-old David with a stone against the

216

towering hulk of Goliath with, javelin, shield and sword, or tiny little Israel defending itself against a billion Muslims.

Yahowah has "*sym* – placed His explanation out in plain view to be openly examined and questioned, preserving it through written documentation in conjunction with" His people. He did so long ago. And we are the beneficiaries – reading what He revealed about our distant past and near future.

𐤉𐤄𐤅𐤄

6

Ma'owr | Luminaries

The Greater and Lesser Lights...

The 4.6% of the universe which is knowable is comprised of hundred quadrillion vigintillion atoms. That is in the range of 10^{80} fundamental elements. Of these, half are molecules, comprised of two or more atoms. However, less than one in a quadrillion vigintillion of those atoms are found supporting life – and yet, here on Earth it abounds.

Since we have covered a lot of ground, and expended considerable energy and space, let's review where we have been before considering the culmination of the third day...

"In (*ba*) the beginning, at the start of time and the initiation of the process of existence (*re'shyth*), the Almighty (*'elohym*), for accompaniment and association (*'eth*), created, conceiving and causing a new existence (*bara'*) of the spiritual world and heavens (*ha shamaym*) and (*wa*) alongside (*'eth*) the material realm (*ha 'erets*). (*Bare'syth* / Genesis 1:1)

And (*wa*) the material realm (*ha 'erets*) existed for a finite period of time (*hayah*) formless and without shape, lacking organization (*tohuw*), a disorderly, chaotic, and empty space (*wa bohuw*), dark, hidden, obscure, and unknowable (*wa choshek*) in proximity to (*'al*) the presence (*paneh*) of the vast, inexhaustible power and inaccessible, mysterious energy of the big bang (*tahowm*).

Then (*wa*), the *Ruwach* | Spirit (*ruwach*) of the Almighty (*'elohym*) hovered over and quickly

218

administered to, supervising (*rachaph 'al*) the appearance (*paneh*) of the fluid state (*maym*). (*Bare'syth* / Genesis 1:2)

In addition (*wa*), God (*'elohym*) said (*'amar*), 'Let there continuously be (*hayah*) light (*'owr*) and (*wa*) light (*'owr*) exists (*hayah*).' (*Bare'syth* / Genesis 1:3)

And so (*wa*), the Almighty (*'elohym*) saw (*ra'ah*) that the association with (*'eth*) the light (*ha 'owr*) was truly (*ky*) good, beneficial and productive, having desirable and positive qualities (*towb*).

God (*wa 'elohym*) caused the ongoing separation (*badal*) between (*bayn*) the light (*ha 'owr*) and (*wa* – in addition to being) making understanding possible through this connection with (*bayn*) the darkness (*ha choshek*). (*Bare'syth* / Genesis 1:4)

The Almighty (*wa 'elohym*) accordingly (*la*) called out in a welcoming way and proclaimed (*qara'*) the continuous nature of the approaching light (*la ha 'owr*) day (*yowm*). And concerning (*wa la*) the darkness concealing and mystifying by way of ignorance and confusion with the absence of light (*ha chosek*) He called its limited existence (*qara'*) night (*laylah*).

Then, there was (*wa hayah*) evening, a period of darkness, a time of sadness and hopelessness, a discouraged state of foreign occupation, an era of ignorant commingling of and adherence to faiths and beliefs (*'erab* / *'arab*) and there would be (*wa hayah*) morning, the beginning of a new day, a time to be observant, perceptive, and judgmental, a time for consideration, a period to be attentive and respond appropriately (*boqer*) – one day (*yowm 'echad*). (*Bare'syth* / Genesis 1:5)

God (*wa 'elohym*) said (*'amar*) matter and space, the extended solid support of universal expansion (*raqya'*) **shall exist** (*hayah*) **in the midst of** (*ba tawek*) **the fluid conditions and water as a source of inquiry and life** (*maym*)**, existing** (*hayah*) **dividing and separating** (*badal*) **between things for the purpose of understanding** (*bayn*) **water** (*ha maym*) **in relation to** (*la* – toward, among, and concerning) **this fluid state as this source of inquiry and life** (*maym*)**.** (*Bare'syth* / Genesis 1:6)

The Almighty (*wa 'elohym*) **acted and engaged, expending considerable energy** (*'asah*) **in association with** (*'eth*) **matter and space, the measure of the material within the vastness of the universe which was expanding** (*raqya'*)**.**

He divided and separated, making a distinction between (*badal*) **relative things in space over an interval of time** (*bayn*) **from** (*min*) **the various forms of water** (*ha maym*) **relative to** (*'asher*) **and in association with that which is interchanged in an orderly arrangement for the sake and purpose of establishing that which underlies everything** (*tachat*) **regarding the support for matter and the expanse of space** (*la ha raqya'*)**.**

So (*wa*)**, these are the connections between things in space over the time** (*bayn*) **of this source of inquiry regarding existence and life among the waters** (*ha maym*) **relative to** (*'asher*) **that which is distinct from** (*min*) **and yet in proximity to** (*'al*) **matter and the expansion of space** (*la ha raqya'*)**. Thereby** (*wa*) **it existed** (*hayah*) **correctly verified and portrayed** (*ken*)**.** (*Bare'syth* / Genesis 1:7)

Then (*wa*)**, God** (*'elohym*) **called out in an inviting and welcoming way** (*qara'*) **to the expansion of matter in the vastness of space** (*la ha raqya'*) **of the heavens** (*shamaym*)**. And there was** (*wa hayah*) **evening, a period of darkness, the mixing together of an interwoven fabric, the mingling and joining together of things**

(*'erab* / *'arab*) **and there would be** (*wa hayah*) **morning, the beginning of a new day, a time to be observant, perceptive, and judgmental** (*boqer*) **– the second day** (*yowm sheny*). (*Bare'syth* / Genesis 1:8)

The Almighty (*wa 'elohym*) **said** (*'amar*), **'The waters** (*ha maym*) **will be gathered** (*qawah*) **from** (*min*) **beneath** (*tachath*) **the heavens** (*ha shamaym*) **directed toward** (*'el*) **one special place** (*maqowm 'echad*).'

Then (*wa*), **He wanted to see the solid ground appear, exposing the surface of the earth** (*ra'ah ha yabeshah*). **Therefore** (*wa*) **it existed** (*hayah*) **verifiable and correct** (*ken*). (*Bare'syth* / Genesis 1:9)

And (*wa*) **God** (*'elohym*) **called out in an inviting and welcoming way** (*qara'*) **to the surface of the earth** (*la ha yabeshah*) **as *'erets* | land** (*'erets*). **Then** (*wa*), **regarding** (*la*) **the accumulation and beneficial expectation of the gathering together of insights which can be derived by looking forward with confident anticipation and pondering the implications of this collection into a home suitable for living** (*miqawah*) **of the many phases of water** (*ha maym*) **He called** (*qara'*) **seas** (*yamym*).

And God (*wa 'elohym*) **saw and considered** (*ra'ah*) **that indeed** (*ky*) **it was beneficial and good** (*towb*)." (*Bare'syth* / Genesis 1:10)

Picking up now where we left off in the midst of the third creative *yowm* | day, we find plant life flourishing at Yahowah's direction…

"And God (*'elohym* – the Almighty) **said** (*'amar* – stated with ongoing consequences (qal imperfect)), **'Let the land produce plants such that the vegetation grows** (*dasha ha 'erets dashe'* – let the ground sprout green growth, bringing forth a proliferation of plant life on earth (hifil imperfect jussive – God is causing the plants to grow on a continual basis as an expression of His will)), **with shimmering green plants** (*'eseb* – verdant vegetation, herbs and grasses which glisten) **reproducing by spreading seeds** (*zera' zera'* – dispersing and evolving by scattering seeds which conceive new growth and yield an extended offspring through this genetic process of reproduction) **in successive generations** (*pary* – being fruitful, producing a harvest of first fruits)**, trees** (*'ets* – leafy plants with wooden trunks and branches) **producing** (*'asah* – making, being productive, engaging in the process, expending energy to bear) **the fruit** (*pery* – a productive result, the capacity to conceive the next generation, the seeds) **of their species of a living organism** (*myn huw'* – after their kind, of their type, category, and characteristic evolving from a partitioning of the original gene pool; from an unused root meaning to portion out) **relative to** (*'asher* – which is beneficial in relationship to, even the correct way for) **their seed** (*zera' huw'* – their ability to spread out, take root, be productive, and grow) **for its kind** (*ba huw'* – with it) **over** (*'al* – upon) **the earth** (*ha 'erets* – the land and ground).'

And it became so through this sequence of events (*wa hayah ken* – it was so, correct and verifiable)**."** (*Bare'syth* / In the Beginning / Genesis 1:11)

It would have been beautiful to behold: "*dasha ha 'erets dashe'* – the land producing plants, the vegetation growing, bringing forth a proliferation of life on earth" with "*'eseb* – shimmering green plants, herbs and grasses glistening." They "*zera' zera'* – reproduced by spreading seeds, dispersing them and evolving" "*pary* – throughout successive generations by being fruitful." The "*'ets* – trees" "*'asah* – bore" the fruit "*myn huw'* – of their species of a living organism after their kind."

In this statement, Yahowah revealed something most people do not fully appreciate. While conceiving life was an exceptional accomplishment, even more complicated than creating a universe in which it could thrive, doing so in such a way that life would be able to reproduce and proliferate was equally, if not more, challenging. It was something that God accomplished by inventing seeds, which would not only take root in the presence of soil and water but which would carry the unique genetic code of each species with them. It was a design element to encourage reproduction that He would incorporate into His conception of animals through sperm.

Interestingly, *dashen*, a derivative of *dasha'*, means "to anoint," symbolic of the Messiah Dowd and of what happens to us when we are immersed in the Set-Apart Spirit. It is one of the most telling terms in the beloved 23rd Psalm – a Mizmowr we celebrate in the concluding chapter of *Coming Home* Volume Two. The language of salvation continues to permeate every word of this revelation: from living and anointing to being born anew, from the firstfruits harvest and being part of an extended family, to being God's offspring, eternally existing and established because of what occurred through this sequence of events.

The third day is the spiritual story of "*Bikuwrym* – FirstFruits," also known as Firstborn Children. The third *Miqra'* is symbolic of temporal life transitioning to life everlasting. Once created, the souls of those who act upon Yahowah's advice shall never be extinguished. If we capitalize on the merciful gift of Passover and UnYeasted Bread, we become the "*bikuwr* – firstborn children" of God.

But this is also the story of parentage. If we want to live forever, we have to be born anew into Yahowah's Family. That is why the third day is presented in two parts. Life initially flows from the living waters and then from God's Maternal Spirit.

Scientifically speaking, the word "create" was not used on this day. With a little direction, the system

Yahowah had composed facilitated what happened naturally. The creation was the product of inputting the precise amount of energy required for the desired result based on the most complex, multi-variable equation ever conceived.

Based upon what we have learned from relativity and the natural spiral measurement standards ascribed by the prophets, cosmologically the third day of Yahowah's testimony begins when the evidence dictates: 3.5 billion years ago. Fossil finds from around the world attest that life began at this precise moment.

Consistent with Yahowah's testimony, the instant the smoke dissipated, and the Earth cooled allowing liquid water to appear, the simplest organic lifeforms sprouted forth in great abundance. And they "reproduced after their kind" making the Earth green. This cosmic epoch would last nearly two billion years, concluding around 1.75 billion years before our era. It was then that our atmosphere began to show the benefits of plants converting carbon dioxide into breathable oxygen.

While it was not his intent, Elso Barghoorn was the first paleontologist to validate Yahowah's testimony. He discovered bacteria and algae fossils in rocks dating to 3.5 billion years ago – coterminous with the time liquid water first appeared and gathered in seas and lakes. The most prolific example is found in the greenstone belt of southwestern Greenland. It is there that we have found confirmation that the surface temperatures of our planet first fell below the boiling point of water (100° C) 3.5×10^9 (billion) years ago. The lower layer of sedimentary rocks in this region contains organic materials, demonstrating the emergence of life at precisely this time. Sediments from the Warrawona region in northwestern Australia, dating to 3.5×10^9 years ago, record a shallow marine environment containing the fossils of filamentous cyanobacterium. They are procaryotes similar to modern Nostoc cyanobacteria.

Procaryote microfossils of Archaeopheroides barbertonensis are also found in Swaziland's Fig-Tree formation dating to this period.

As a result of these findings, biologists recognize that the first lifeforms on Earth did not emerge following 2 to 3 billion years of random interactions as previously thought – and as Darwin's evolutionary model requires. Life emerged concurrently with the appearance of liquid water. This realization is exceedingly important because these facts completely disprove the theory of macroevolution. And yet, most scientists are unwilling to admit it or take the next logical step.

Harvard University biology professor, and Nobel laureate, George Wald, is one of those still living in the past and desperately clinging to a disproven theory rather than embracing the Creator. He wrote these words which were published in, and later refuted by, *Scientific American*: "However improbable we regard the start of all life, or any of the steps which it involves, given enough time it will almost certainly happen at least once. And for life as we know it...once may be enough. Time is in fact the hero of the plot. The time with which we have to deal is of the order of two billion years. What we regard as impossible on the basis of human experience is meaningless here. Given so much time the 'impossible' becomes the possible, the possible probable, and the probable virtually certain. One has only to wait: time itself performs the miracles." The hero of his plot and the basis of his leap of faith proved to be false, rendering his conclusion erroneous.

This "time makes the improbable certain" position was promulgated for decades by leading biologists and is still taught today, but it is untrue. *Scientific American* admitted as much in a special 1979 publication called *Life: Origin and Evolution*. It was their first and only retraction of a Nobel laureate's writings...

"Although stimulating, this article probably represents one of the very few times in his professional life when Wald has been wrong. Examine his main thesis and see. Can time form a biological cell by waiting for chance combinations of organic compounds? Dr. Harold Morowitz, a biophysicist at Yale, studied the application of thermodynamics within living organisms at the conception of life for fifty years. In his book, *Energy Flow in Biology*, he computed that merely to create a bacterium would require more time than the Universe might ever see if chance combinations of its molecules were the only driving force."

The "driving force" who resolved the problem of "chance combinations," making life certain and abundant, did so by creating the three-dimensional language known as DNA. He has a name, and we find it within the Creation account which has never been retracted.

Also, if I may interject, while George Wald was ethnically Jewish, he was among the first to denounce circumcision. He was wrong about that, too.

Be aware, the argument against macroevolution being made by the retraction in *Scientific American* was not just that there was insufficient time. Now that we understand the infrastructure of biological systems (something of which Darwin was unaware), we know that life's mechanisms are way too complicated and interdependent to have emerged through random chance rather than purposeful design. Further, the most significant problem for evolutionists is that beneficial mutations (leading to more complex systems where information is gained and the lifeform is enhanced) are so uncommon, and so enormously overwhelmed by detrimental alterations in propensity (those which lose or corrupt genetic information), that macroevolution is not just "improbable," it is rationally and mathematically impossible. Plants and animals degrade over time. And beyond modest adaptations, they seldom evolve. They are consistently and systematically degraded by genetic mutations. Therefore, since the vast majority of genetic alterations are counterproductive, and often deadly, without an intervening force capable of manipulating the code, given enough time, life would evolve itself out of existence.

According to Professor Morowitz, not only was the possibility that life formed through random chance interactions of inorganic materials mathematically incalculable to the point of being beyond reason within the size and age of the entire universe, constrained to the Earth's relative size and bereft of billions of years, the improbable scheme was diminished to an absurdity – less rational even than religious beliefs, here on Earth. And that is for the first lifeform to emerge – which was not nearly enough. For life to succeed, the inaugural plant would have had to locate a source of food, process that fortuitous source of energy in a way that was productive rather than destructive, and then find a way to reproduce itself.

If the first generation of life failed to accomplish any of these enormously complex and improbable tasks, life would need more than 14 billion years and the entire universe to have even the remotest chance of starting all over again. That is why Fred Hoyle, the famed British astronomer, has said that the spontaneous emergence of a single-cell organism from random couplings of chemicals was about as likely as the assemblage of a 747 jet by a tornado whirling through a junkyard. Frankly, the odds are not nearly that good. Not even remotely.

Even Morowitz, the man who used thermodynamics to falsify Wald's claims, was unable to accept where they inevitably led. In 1983 he testified in McLean v. Arkansas, a case that successfully challenged a state law mandating the teaching of creation science in public schools, calling it "somewhat deceptive." He would claim that the propensity of things to become less ordered over time, as is the dictate of the 2nd Law of Thermodynamics, could be ignored with the input of energy. What he failed to mention is that, while life requires a source of energy, almost every form of energy is lethal to life. He was simply unwilling to acknowledge that it was God who introduced, organized, and orchestrated an appropriate source and amount of energy for this purpose.

Aware of these facts, why are so many scientists still lying to us and to themselves? Why do the smartest people cling to the most foolish and disproven notions? Why have they abandoned evidence and reason with regard to the origins of life? Creation has become their god, and science has become their religion. And now, having been indoctrinated in Progressive institutions, scientists are losing the capacity to be rational.

It clearly was not Yahowah's fault that mankind, in seeking to disassociate God from the conception of life, has neglected the fact that reproduction is by design...

"Then, the earth (*wa ha 'erets* – the material realm, the land, region, and ground)**, as a result of this input, continually brought forth** (*yatsa'* – produced, disseminated, and spread (hifil imperfect – God brought this effect about, influencing plant life such that it would continue to spread out and grow)) **a shimmering and verdant variation of vegetation and plant life** (*dashe' 'eseb* – green plants which would proliferate and grow)**, reproducing by spreading the seeds** (*zera' zera'* – dispersing and evolving by scattering seeds which conceive new growth and yield an extended offspring) **of their species of a living organism** (*la myn huw'* – after their kind, of their type, category, and characteristic evolving from a partitioning of the original gene pool; from an unused root meaning to portion out).

And (*wa*) **the trees** (*'ets* – the leafy plants with wooden trunks and branches) **produced** (*'asah* – made,

228

were also productive, engaging in the process, expending energy to bear) **the fruit** (*pery* – a productive result, the capacity to conceive the next generation, the seeds) **which, to advance the beneficial aspects of this relationship** (*'asher* – which to encourage the desired result and a proliferation of meaningful life), **was their seed** (*zera' huw'* – their means to reproduction) **for the advancement of their species** (*ba huw' la myn* – in their approach to advance their type and kind).

And God (*wa 'elohym* – therefore, the Almighty) **saw** (*ra'ah* – looked at it, perceived, and viewed (qal imperfect)) **that indeed it was** (*ky* – that in contrast to any other approach, it was exceptionally and truly) **good** (*towb* – beautiful and beneficial, productive and pleasing, suitable and desirable, enjoyable and valuable, appropriate and agreeable)." (*Bare'syth* / In the Beginning / Genesis 1:12)

The emergence of life is only the second time the Creator has expressed satisfaction with His creation. He was also pleased by the onset of light. And indeed, His Light still leads to life.

Yahowah's concluding comment on the benefit of having established the conditions necessary for life to emerge and reproduce, proliferating around the world, was rather understated. But nonetheless, He just said: Life is good.

"And there was (*wa hayah* – there exists with unfolding implications over time (qal imperfect)) **evening** (*'erab* / *'arab* – a period of darkness, the mixing together of an interwoven fabric, the mingling and joining together of things, a nighttime of hopelessness during a discouraged state of foreign occupation, an era of ignorant commingling of and adherence to faiths and beliefs when the adversary will combine this with noxious swarms of Arab pests) **and there would be** (*wa hayah* – there also exists with unfolding implications over time (qal imperfect)) **morning** (*boqer* – tomorrow, the beginning of a new day, a time to be observant, perceptive, and judgmental, a time for consideration, a period to be attentive and respond appropriately, an extended stretch for being inquisitive and seeking information in order to make good decisions; from *baqar* – to seek, search, rendered as "e, consider, and reflect) – **the third day** (*yowm shalyshy* – the third in a sequence of days; from *shalowsh* – three)." (*Bare'syth* / In the Beginning / Genesis 1:13)

Three is Yahowah's second favorite number. It represents family, especially His Family. It is comprised of our Heavenly Father, our Spiritual Mother – Yah's Maternal manifestation – and the Son of God, Yah's beloved, *Dowd* | David. He represents Yahowah's Firstborn and is the living manifestation of the Covenant.

Therefore, historically, it should not be surprising that Yahowah established His human family at the beginning of the third millennium of the human era. 'Abraham left Mesopotamia – the Babylon of false religions – married Sarah and entered the Promised Land. 'Abraham, whose God-given name means "Merciful Father," formed a "*beryth* – familial covenant relationship" with Yahowah, was the father of *Yitschaq* / Isaac / Laughter, remained faithful, and ultimately became the patriarch of the chosen people, a family which would serve as God's witnesses— a family whose seed would ultimately save us.

At the conclusion of the third day of human history, Yahowah chose to adopt His favorite son: *Dowd* / the Beloved / David. It was the best of times.

𐤋𐤅𐤄𐤉

230

Having completed the third day, Yahowah's most important creation was about to be manifested: He was a Father enjoying His relationship with His Son. We have reached the dawn of the fourth millennium of human development. It is the year 1,750,000,000 BCE cosmologically. Spiritually, this day predicts the events which would unfold during man's fourth millennia: Yahowah's year 3000 to 4000, an epoch which corresponds to 968 BCE through 33 CE – with Dowd playing the starring role from Cornerstone of the Home to the Lamb opening the Door. (968 BCE to 33 CE represents 1,000 years because the Roman Catholics were not thoughtful enough to include the year 0 on their Gregorian calendar.)

"**God** (*wa 'elohym* – the Almighty) **said** (*'amar* – declared, expressing in words)**, 'There shall be** (*hayah* – let there exist (qal imperfect jussive)) **lights** (*ma'owr* – luminaries, sources of illumination; a compound of *ma* – to ponder the implications of *'owr* – light) **in the expanse** (*ba raqya'* – within the spreading out of the matter and space) **of the heavens** (*shamaym* – beyond the sky and atmosphere) **to understand the separation between** (*badal bayn* – to distinguish the divide and discern what it means to be set apart, to ascertain the means to inclusion or cause of expulsion, to appreciate how to be included or be disassociated between) **the daylight** (*ha yowm* – the reckoning of time when there is light) **as it is distinct from** (*wa bayn* – differentiated from) **the darkness of the night** (*ha laylah* – the period of substantially diminished light, a wanting of illumination)**.**

For a time, they will exist (*wa hayah* – they will be (qal perfect)) **as symbols and signs** (*la 'owth* – for the purpose of signals concerning distinguishing words to be recognized and remembered, non-verbal representations which have meaning, providing indications, illustrations, examples, and proof as metaphors which make something more clearly known when evaluating recompense and reward; from *'uwth* – a means to be seen agreeing, providing consent) **and for the appointed meeting times of the feasts** (*wa la mow'ed* – concerning the designated periods which are related to others for a specific purpose authorized by the authority, directly associated with the Miqra'ey by Yahowah and thus descriptive of the seven celebrations of the set-apart festival feasts; from *ya'ad* – to meet on an appointed schedule)**, as well as** (*wa*) **for days** (*yowm* – the reckoning of time when there is light, the seven 24-hour periods of a week) **and for years** (*wa shanah* – the complete cycle of the seasons, a solar year which is a measure of age and the renewal of life)**."** (*Bare'syth* / In the Beginning / Genesis 1:14)

Ma'owr encourages us to ponder the implications of light, differentiating it from the surrounding darkness. And just as the moon, planets, and stars represent tiny specks of light in the vast expanse of the night sky, in our world and throughout time, an infinitesimal percentage of people reflect Yah's light.

And yet, without light, there is no life, and without darkness, no death. This makes it essential for us to *bayn* | understand the difference between them.

When words like *'owth* and *mow'ed* are inadequately translated as "signs" and "seasons" respectively in most English Bibles, the profoundly important message contained in the passage is squandered. Accurately communicated, these two sentences convey that the *Mow'ed Miqra'ey* – the Invitations to be Called Out and Meet at the Designated Times for the Renewing Testimony – can be known, timed, and better understood through the distinction that is being made here on the fourth day between daylight and darkness.

It is through the *Mow'ed* | Appointed Meeting Times that we approach Yahowah. They are "wondrous signs

232

which convey an important message" from our Creator. Understand the *Mow'ed Miqra'ey* and you will understand the means God went through to restore our relationship with Him. They not only demonstrate Yahowah's commitment to His plan of salvation, but they also reveal the very framework of time itself from beginning to end.

This is why the fourth day commences with *Dowd* | David representing the Cornerstone of the Covenant Home. He is Yahowah's Shepherd, and as His most brilliant Son, he became Messiah and King. Then this formative era concludes with Dowd serving as the Passover Lamb. The *Mashyach* | Messiah wrote the words at the dawn of this era that he would fulfill during Chag Matsah as the sun set in *Yaruwshalaim* | the Source of Guidance regarding Reconciliation.

Failing to appreciate the merit of the seven annual *Mow'ed Miqra'ey*, clerics and laity alike have been deceived into believing that salvation, to the extent it exists, is either a product of religious faith or laborious works. Blinded by their beliefs and rules, they are as manipulative of Yahowah's calendar as they are prone to misappropriate His purpose. They remain unaware of the means He has provided to reconcile our relationship with Him, why He did so or with whom. And they do not know that it is now possible to date almost every significant event from the Garden and back into 'Eden – past, present, and future. The fulfillments of the Mow'ed Miqra'ey are the hallmarks of time.

When we lose track of the significance and symbolism of Yahowah's *Mow'ed Miqra'ey* of *Pesach* | Passover, *Matsah* | UnYeasted Bread, *Bikuwrym* | Firstborn Children, *Shabuw'ah* | Seven Shabats, *Taruw'ah* | Trumpets, *Kipurym* | Reconciliations, and *Sukah* | Shelters, we become lost and blind, stumbling in the dark without a map. When we replace Yahowah's Festival Feasts with Purim, Rosh Hashanah, or Hannukah, New Year's or St.

233

Valentine's Days, Lent, Good Friday, Easter Sunday, Halloween, or Christmas, we squander our opportunity to live with the Light.

The *Mow'ed Miqra'ey* embody Yahowah's seven-step plan of redemption and reconciliation, while also providing the Covenant's benefits. Since they establish the "days and years" upon which redemptive history and prophecy unfold, there are very few things as important as knowing that they "*hayah 'owth* – exist as symbols, signs, and signals, distinguished by the words written about them to help us remember" the "*mow'ed* – appointed and assigned meeting times presented within the eternal witness and restoring testimony." Between the moon and the sun, we can ascertain the intended days each year for us to meet with our Maker.

As we have grown to expect, there is a direct and profound correlation between the description of the fourth creative day and the fulfillment of the first three Mow'ed Miqra'ey – Pesach, Matsah, and Bikuwrym – each of which was fulfilled in year 4000 Yah. Dowd, as the Passover Lamb, opened the Doorway to Life at this time in 33 CE. Dowd's soul then fulfilled UnYeasted Bread the following day, unleavening our souls of the fungus of religion and politics. Released from She'owl, Dowd's soul was reunited with the Set-Apart Spirit on Firstborn Children, facilitating the adoption of the Covenant Family. At this time, God's children were enriched and empowered in keeping with the promised benefits of the *Beryth* | Covenant.

Most especially, the fourth *Miqra'* – that of Seven Shabats or the Promise of Seven – is on display on this, the fourth day. While the first three Called-Out Assembly Meetings depict the means to our redemption and restoration, the fourth appointment is an open invitation whereby everyone can witness the benefit of having chosen to rely on the solution Yahowah has provided by way of

Pesach, *Matsah*, and *Bikuwrym*. On *Shabuw'ah*, the Covenant's children are immersed in Yahowah's Light, separated from the world, enriched, enlightened, and empowered, in addition to being emancipated during the Ingathering so that we can come out of the darkness into the light. In this regard, *Dowd* | David is God's most illustrative example. He loved the light and wrote the lyrics which lead us all to this place and then he returned to make it all possible.

This opportunity to become part of Yahowah's Family, and this distinction and determination, are highlighted by "*badal bayn* – to distinguish and discern what it means to be set apart, to ascertain the means to be included or expelled" from the *Beryth* | Covenant. God wants us "*badal bayn* – to comprehend the divide by separating" light from darkness.

Essential to this understanding is the fact that the "*ma'owr* – sources of light which we are encouraged to contemplate and evaluate" "*wa hayah la 'owth* – will exist for a period of time" as "*la 'owth* – non-verbal representations which have meaning, providing indications, illustrations, and examples, even proof regarding how to approach, serving as metaphors which make this more clearly known, especially when evaluating our recompense or reward." In this light, the root of *'owth* is *'uwth*, which is "a means to be seen as agreeing, where we provide our consent" regarding Yahowah's provisions during the Mow'ed.

Returning to the scientific aspects of His witness we discover that calibrated to the Creator's clock, the fourth day dawned around 1.75 billion years ago and closed just 875 million years in our past. During this period Yahowah said that the sun, moon, and stars became signs, which is to say that they became visible. He did not say that He created the sun, moon, or stars on the fourth day, because that had already occurred on the second. Disingenuous

235

atheists have lamely attacked the Torah's creation account based upon this false premise, creating a straw man whereby the emergence of plant life preceded the creation of the sun, but that is a religious and logical fallacy.

Scientists have recently discovered that during the epoch referenced by the fourth day of creation, the Earth's atmosphere, formally smoggy and barely translucent, became transparent. Photosynthesis occurring within the vegetation which was conceived and disseminated on the third day consumed much of the carbon dioxide in the air and produced an oxygen-rich atmosphere, setting the stage for the emergence of higher-functioning oxygen-dependent animals. But it took a long time, three billion years to be precise (all of the second and third day cosmologically), for plants to produce sufficient oxygen to fuel more complex animal lifeforms. That is why there is no mention of them living at this time. Animal life would not explode onto the scene until the fifth day, cosmologically speaking.

In recognition that Yahowah's explanation of His intent regarding the fourth day draws its sense of purpose from the opening statement, let's set what follows into that context…

"God (*wa 'elohym*) said, expressing in words (*'amar*), 'There shall be (*hayah*) lights whose implications should be pondered (*ma'owr*) in the expanse (*ba raqya'*) of the heavens (*shamaym*) to better understand the separation between (*badal bayn*) the daylight, this time of reckoning when there is light (*ha yowm*) because it is distinct from (*wa bayn*) the darkness of the night where there is limited light (*ha laylah*).

For a time, they will exist (*wa hayah*) as symbols and signs, as non-verbal representations which make the approach more clearly known, providing indications advising one's consent when evaluating recompense and reward (*la 'owth*) regarding the

appointed meeting times of the feasts (*wa la mow 'ed*), **as well as** (*wa*) **for days when there is light** (*yowm*) **and for years, the cycle of the seasons, renewal of life, and measure of time** (*wa shanah*). (*Bare'syth* 1:14)

Therefore, let them exist for a time (*wa hayah* – accordingly, let them be for a finite period (qal perfect)) **as sources of illumination** (*la ma'owr* – for lights and luminaries to approach, a means to enlightenment to draw near; a compound of *ma* – to ponder the implications of *'owr* – light) **in the expanse** (*ba raqya'* – within the spreading out of the matter and space) **of the heavens** (*ha shamaym* – beyond the sky and atmosphere) **to provide light** (*la 'owr* – to illuminate and approach, to brighten and enlighten) **upon** (*'al* – for and over) **the earth** (*ha 'erets* – the land).'

And therefore (*wa*), **it continued to exist like this thereafter based upon what preceded it** (*hayah ken* – it came to be true within this sequence of events (qal imperfect)). (*Bare'syth* 1:15)

God (*wa 'elohym* – so the Almighty) **engaged to appoint for this particular task** (*'asah* – to function in this manner He endeavored to serve by assigning and deploying (qal imperfect)) **both** (*'eth shanaym* – the two) **of these substantial and empowering sources of illumination** (*ha ma'owr ha gadowl* – these important and massive luminaries and large, growth-enabling lights) – **with the greater** (*'eth ha gadowl* – with the most important and massive, the older and larger, the more enormous in magnitude and intensity, the mighty and distinguished; from *gadal* – to enable growth and to magnify, doing great things by empowering) **luminary** (*ha ma'owr* – the source of illumination and light) **becoming prominent and clearly known as the influence over** (*memshalah* – to govern and empower, to effect and control; from *mashal* – to serve as a proverb, as a means to compare and understand what is being represented by this parable and

237

picture being painted with words to describe) **the daylight hours** (*ha yowm* – the daytime and warm period) **and** (*wa*) **with the lesser** (*'eth ha qatan* – with the diminished and less significant, the more easily understood and younger chronologically, even the less important; from *quwt* – loathed, opposed, abhorred, and detested as a source of grieving) **luminary** (*ma'owr* – light to be questioned) **becoming known and prominent as the influence over** (*la memshalah* – to empower, to effect control over; from *mashal* – to serve as a proverb, as a means to compare and understand what is being represented by this parable and picture being painted with words to describe the effect of) **the night** (*ha laylah* – the scarcity of light, the comparative darkness, ignorance as a result of failing to observe) **along with the heavenly powers** (*wa 'eth ha kowkab* – in addition to the stars and spiritual luminaries). (*Bare'syth* 1:16)

The **Almighty** (*wa 'elohym* – accordingly and in addition, God) **caused them to be placed there for this purpose** (*nathan 'eth hem* – bestowed and assigned them for this opportunity and task (qal imperfect)) **in the expanse** (*ba raqya'* – within the spreading out of the matter and space) **of the heavens** (*ha shamaym* – beyond the sky and atmosphere and in the spiritual realm) **to provide light** (*la 'owr* – to illuminate, to brighten and enlighten the approach) **upon** (*'al* – for and over) **the land** (*ha 'erets* – the earth). (*Bare'syth* 1:17)

And **therefore** (*wa la*), **they will function as proverbs** (*mashal* – as parables to tell a revealing story in a memorable way) **with the daylight** (*ba ha yowm* – in the daytime and warm period) **and in the time of darkness** (*wa ha laylah* – without as much light, the ignorance for failing to be observant) **providing a contrast to appreciate the difference between** (*wa la badal bayn* – to distinguish and discern what it means to be set apart, to ascertain the means to inclusion or cause of expulsion, to appreciate how to be included or be disassociated between) **the light** (*ha 'owr* – the source of enlightenment, instruction, life, and brilliance guidance) **and comprehend being separated from the darkness** (*wa bayn ha choshek* – to realize the difference between obscurity, blackness, concealment and confusion; the diminishment of light from ignorance by failing to be observant).

God (*wa 'elohym* – therefore the Almighty) **saw** (*ra'ah* – perceived and considered, regarded and distinguished) **that indeed** (*ky* – that this contrast and differentiation) **it was good** (*towb* – it was useful and agreeable, valuable and appropriate, productive and beneficial)." (*Bare'syth* / In the Beginning / Genesis 1:18)

Yahowah's seven annual *Mow'ed* | Appointed Meeting Times are set using the sun and the moon. They are annual events whose dates each year are established based on the timing of the first and seventh new moons. The greater and lesser lights, therefore, enable us to meet with God on the appropriate days each year. Further, this was all incorporated into the discussion of the fourth day because the first three Mow'ed were fulfilled at the conclusion of the fourth millennium of human history in year 4000 Yah (33 CE) during the second of Dowd's three lives.

Beyond this realization, Yahowah wants us to understand that life and death are determined based on light and darkness. God enlightens us during the day and *ha Satan* | the Adversary beguiles at night – in the absence of sufficient light. And it is not that there is no light at night, but that it is insufficient, making the ignorant more susceptible to being misled.

In this regard, the Adversary, *ha satan* in Hebrew, as a fallen messenger, is still luminous, albeit in "abhorrent and detestable opposition" to Light. Acquiescing to his authority and control leads mankind away from God and to the lightless enclosure known as *She'owl* | Hell.

But that is not the point I think Yahowah is making because both the greater and lesser luminaries, Father and Son, are sources of illumination, both enlighten and draw us closer to God. Moreover, Yahowah appointed both sources of light, with each serving a specific purpose, one distinct from the other.

If we consider the lives of the most enlightening men in human history, they would include *Moseh* | Moses and *Dowd* | David – the authors of the Towrah and Psalms. However, only one of them is relevant at the conclusions of the 3rd and 4th millennia, and that is *ha Mashyach Dowd*, the Son of God and King. Second only in brilliance to Yahowah – he became the greatest luminary in human history when he did as he had foretold.

Reinforcing this realization, upon his return and the restoration of his kingdom in 2033, Yahowah says that Dowd will be as brilliant as the sun and that he will appear as if he were God. He is the most brilliant orator among men and the greatest thinker when it comes to knowing God. And while these conclusions may seem extreme to you at this point in Yahowah's story, rest assured that by the time we have completed our review of the *Mizmowr* / Psalms in *Coming Home*, it will be as obvious as are the Towrah and its Covenant.

Should you have been tainted, as I once was, by the mythology of Christianity, and wonder if there was any role for the misnomer "Jesus," the answer is no. Dowd was the focus of the Prophets and he authored at least a hundred Psalms and thirty Proverbs which address what he would achieve. By contrast, there is no reliable witness to a single word the Christian substitute conveyed in the language he would have spoken should he have existed. Even within the mythology written about him, there is no record of him

240

writing so much as a single word. So, it should be obvious: when it comes to being enlightened, Dowd is a far greater luminary than the mythical misnomer.

But what about the negative connotations of *quwt*, the root of *qatan* | the lesser light? And that is the interesting part because the Towrah's audience, *Yahuwdym* | Jews, have been opposed to the realization that *Dowd* | David is the Son of God, the returning Messiah, as well as the Passover Lamb. And without the Lamb of God opening the Door to Life, there is only darkness and death. In fact, it is out of the darkness of religious and political ignorance that Dowd serves us – which is how the lesser light is cast in this presentation.

It also proves that God has no ego. He would prefer to celebrate the life of His Son, Dowd, than boast about His role in fulfilling the Mow'ed Miqra'ey. More than anything, Yahowah is a devoted and loving Father.

In life, Dowd's lyrics proclaim that we can choose to love Yah and to be set apart unto Him, or we can elect to be ruled by men under the influence of the Adversary. And this is why the religious are expelled, either losing their soul or having it endure an eternity in darkness. Our very existence is purposed by this choice, making these words worthy of our consideration. It is a spiritual choice with a direct influence on our status and fate.

Once again, with all of this rhetoric, God neither said nor inferred that He created the sun or moon on the fourth day. Instead, He engaged such that they would serve His purpose and ours. The sun and moon would become parables, conveying a message we would be wise to ponder and comprehend – especially as they serve as metaphors for Dowd's lives and lyrics, accolades and achievements.

In this regard, the "*gadowl*" light was presented as "the most important" and as the one "promoting growth in a way that would be empowering." By contrast, the "*qatan*"

241

luminary was "considered less important and insignificant." With the Shepherd, we grow and with the Lamb we live.

By using *mashal* | proverbs, Yahowah is reinforcing the realization that this discussion has been part of a revealing story, one that would be easy for us to understand. It is about the difference between an abundance of light and very little of it.

Historically, in accordance with the *'owth* | symbolism of the "*Mow'ed Miqra'ey* – Invitations to Meet" with God, the "*gadowl* – magnificent, mighty, important, and distinguished individual, the magnified, great, and powerful luminary able to make and do great things" appeared right on schedule during the commencement of the fourth millennium of man, which began on 968 BCE with the revelation of the 89th Mizmowr serving as Dowd's Song. It ended one thousand years later in 33 CE with Dowd returning to fulfill Pesach and Matsah on behalf of Bikuwrym.

The year of Dowd's second arrival, when errantly attributed to the misnomer "Jesus," is broadly believed by biblical scholars to be 4 BCE. This is because the imposter known as Matthew claimed that it occurred during the reign of King Herod. However, he was neither present nor inspired. Having never met Dowd, "Matthew" would plagiarize his Gospel a century thereafter.

The scholarly extrapolation is based upon an erroneous interpretation of Josephus' recording of an eclipse (which turned out to be only partial) on March 13, 4 BCE, "shortly before Herod died." There are a number of problems with this accounting in addition to the fact that Josephus, while infinitely more reliable than 'Matthew,' was still a traitor who shouldn't be trusted. More to the point, the only total eclipse visible in the region during this period actually occurred on January 1, 1 CE on the Julian calendar.

This duly noted, I'm not sure it matters since 'Matthew's' rhetoric isn't credible. But nonetheless, should Dowd's second appearance have coincided with the *Miqra'* of *Sukah* in the Fall of 2 BCE, he would have been 33 when he fulfilled Passover in 33 CE.

Returning to the Genesis timeline, the *Mashyach* | Messiah arrived prior to the conclusion of *Bare'syth's* fourth day to fulfill the prophecy. This period would have commenced in 968 BCE and ended in 33 CE. To appreciate the timing of this epoch, it is instructive to know that the 1st era began in 3968 BCE with 'Adam's and Chawah's (Eve is the name of a pagan goddess) expulsion from 'Eden. The 2nd millennium of man began in 2968 BCE with Yahowah approaching *Noach* | Noah in advance of the flood. The 3rd one-thousand-year human epoch started in 1968 BCE with Yahowah affirming the Covenant with 'Abraham on Mount Mowryah. The 4th era of human history commenced in 968 BCE with Dowd being heralded as the Cornerstone of Yahowah's Home on Mount Mowryah. It concluded in 33 CE with Dowd returning to fulfill *Pesach*, *Matsah*, and *Bikuwrym* in year 4000 Yah.

The next thousand years may have been man's darkest with the birth of Judaism, Christianity, and Islam. The 6th got underway in 1033 CE when the *Bamidbar* / Numbers' 5 test for infidelity caused the waters under where the Temple had once stood to be poisoned. It will conclude as the 7th begins in 2033 with Father's and Son's fulfillment of *Yowm Kipurym* and *Sukah* in year 6000 Yah.

While there are six one-thousand-year epochs leading to the seventh, just as there are six Mow'ed leading to the seventh, where we Camp Out with God, Yah's plan unfurls in increments of forty Yowbel years – or in 2,000-year increments. Forty *Yowbel* | Redemptive Years separate

243

'Adam's expulsion from the Garden to the initiation of the Covenant with 'Abraham. And exactly forty Yowbel separate the establishment of the Covenant from the fulfillment of the means to provide its benefits through the first three *Mow'ed Miqra'ey*.

In this light, 33 CE (Year 4000 Yah) was the only year during this period of time in which Passover began on Thursday at sundown. This allowed Dowd to celebrate the meal with his Father on Thursday evening after sunset while at the same time serving as the Passover Lamb on Friday before sundown – which was still the 14th of 'Abyb from the Towrah's perspective. It is also a perfect match for what Dowd, as *Gabry'el* | God's Most Competent and Courageous Man, foretold would transpire when addressing Daniel. He arrived right on schedule, four days prior to Passover, 'Abyb 10, Monday, March 30th, 33 CE.

As we have discovered by dissecting *Bare'syth*, each creative day ends with a benediction. In them, time is reversed. Dusk precedes dawn. Yahowah wants us to look at the creation account from His perspective, looking forward in time, not ours, looking back.

"And there was (*wa hayah* – there exists with unfolding implications over time (qal imperfect)) **evening** (*'erab* / *'arab* – a period of darkness, the mixing together of an interwoven fabric, the mingling and joining together of things, a nighttime of hopelessness during a discouraged state of foreign occupation, an era of ignorant commingling of and adherence to faiths and beliefs when the adversary will combine this with noxious swarms of Arab pests) **and there would be** (*wa hayah* – there also exists with unfolding implications over time (qal imperfect)) **morning** (*boqer* – tomorrow, the beginning of a new day, a time to be observant, perceptive, and judgmental, a time for consideration, a period to be attentive and respond appropriately, an extended stretch for being inquisitive and seeking information in order to make good decisions; from *baqar* – to seek, search, rendered as "e, consider, and reflect) – **the fourth day** (*yowm rabyi'y* – the fourth in a sequence of days; from *raba'* – to be square)." (*Bare'syth* / In the Beginning / Genesis 1:19)

More than any day, the fourth epoch of creation serves as a lesson to me. Fifteen years ago, around 2005, I invested a month trying to reconcile its accounting with the observable evidence. While researching Islam, I considered a number of scholarly tomes written by atheists. In one, the author tried to be evenhanded, assaulting the biblical creation account with the same tenacity he did Allah's laughable tale. The atheist's point of attack was twofold. First, he said that astronomy and the fossil record prove that the universe and the Earth are billions of years old, not six thousand years. Since I saw *yowm* as being a period of time, I wasn't troubled by this. But then he claimed that the fourth day was out of order because the plants created on the third day could not survive without the sun. That was a problem.

While the atheist's position was based upon a misrepresentation of the *Bare'syth* / Genesis testimony, I did not recognize it at the time as I had not yet come to appreciate the errant status of English translations. Not comfortable with the thought God could be wrong, I immersed myself in scholarly commentaries on Genesis. Over the course of that study, I came to see the stories of creation and the flood as prehistory. They became symbolic revelations, focused more on salvation than creation – on *why* God created and flooded rather than *how* or *when* He did these things.

The fourth day, I reckoned, was purposely set out of place, specifically designed to tell us when the Messiah would arrive. I saw the plan of six plus one revealed in the creation account as providing a framework with which we could evaluate history – as it represented the six plus one millennia of mankind following the fall of 'Adam.

But when my sons chose to become mechanical engineers and biochemists, going on to Cambridge one summer to study relativity under one of Stephen Hawking's protégés, my perspective was broadened. Both sons demonstrated a proclivity for relativity over quantum mechanics. One of their favorite conversational topics became the unification of Yahowah's teachings with observed reality. Their insights were brilliant. But try as they would, their Dad was too dense to appreciate Einstein.

Cognizant of the majesty of Yahowah's Word, the biochemist did his best to enlighten Dad, albeit chuckling under his breath. Fortunately, about this time I stumbled upon a *Scientific American* issue dedicated entirely to the ongoing debate between quantum theory and relativity, and I became the beneficiary of a book on relativity edited by Hawking. Better still, a friend loaned me his copy of Gerald Schroeder's *The Science of God*. Little by little I started to understand. Yet that was not enough. It was only when I was encouraged to translate the Towrah and Prophets directly from the Hebrew, and reflect on what God had actually revealed, that I came to appreciate just how right and wrong I had been.

I was wrong because I had sold God short. Scientifically, the six days of creation are perfectly accurate in time, sequence, and substance. Moreover, while the creation account provides a human historical framework, it is much more than just six millennia plus one. Each day is correlated to man's existence as it is recorded both independently and prophetically. *Bare'syth* / Genesis provides the framework upon which the time of man flows. And while I recognized that the message embedded in the fourth and seventh days provided significant insights into Yahowah's plan, I have come to see that each day contains a redemptive lesson.

Unfortunately, a decade ago, back in 2013 when I had previously edited *Yada Yahowah*, I did not yet realize that

Dowd was not only the Messiah and Shepherd, the King of Kings and Son of God, he was also the Passover Lamb. Therefore, I did not know that the lesser and greater luminaries were Father and Son.

The moral of the story is God is really smart, and I am not nearly as bright. Yahowah is perfect and I make mistakes. Please keep that in mind as you consider my commentary. It is designed so that you pause and reflect on what God has revealed. I do it so that you are afforded the opportunity to see many of the insights I have garnered along the way.

By exploring and sharing related passages we are able to connect the dots, forming a more complete picture which broadens our perspective. But never lose sight of the fact that I am learning and discovering right along with you.

Most often, I do not know what the next passage is going to reveal until we jump into the middle of it and allow the Spirit to guide us. Sometimes, I do not even know the next passage we are going to consider before we are directed to it. I believe that one of the reasons I was encouraged to embark on this task was because I recognized that I was unqualified. That, in turn, made me reliant.

And it was words such as these which brought me to this place…

"God (*'elohym*) explained (*'amar*), 'Let the land produce plants such that the vegetation grows (*dasha ha 'erets dashe'*), verdant vegetation (*'eseb*) reproducing by spreading seeds, evolving and conceiving new growth through this genetic process of reproduction (*zera' zera'*) in successive generations (*pary*), trees (*'ets*) producing (*'asah*) the fruit (*pery*) of their species of a living organism (*myn huw'*) relative to (*'asher*) their seed (*zera' huw'*) for its kind (*ba huw'*) over (*'al*) the earth (*ha 'erets*).'

And it became so through this sequence of events (*wa hayah ken*). (*Bare'syth* / Genesis 1:11)

"Then, the earth (*wa ha 'erets*) as a result of this input continually brought forth (*yatsa'*) a shimmering and verdant variation of vegetation and plant life (*dashe' 'eseb*), reproducing by spreading the seeds (*zera' zera'*) of their type and characteristic, evolving from a partitioning of the original gene pool (*la myn huw'*).

And (*wa*) the trees, the leafy plants with wooden trunks and branches (*'ets*), produced (*'asah*) the fruit (*pery*) which, to advance the beneficial aspects of this relationship (*'asher*), was their seed (*zera' huw'*) for the advancement of their species (*ba huw' la myn*).

And the Almighty (*wa 'elohym*) saw (*ra'ah*) that indeed it was (*ky*) good, productive and pleasing, suitable and desirable (*towb*). (*Bare'syth* / Genesis 1:12)

And there was (*wa hayah*) evening, the mingling and joining together of things (*'erab* / *'arab*) and there would be (*wa hayah*) morning, the beginning of a new day (*boqer*) – the third day (*yowm shalyshy*). (*Bare'syth* / Genesis 1:13)

God (*wa 'elohym*) said, expressing in words (*'amar*), 'There shall be (*hayah*) lights whose implications should be pondered (*ma'owr*) in the expanse (*ba raqya'*) of the heavens (*shamaym*) to better understand the separation between (*badal bayn*) the daylight, this time of reckoning when there is light (*ha yowm*) because it is distinct from (*wa bayn*) the darkness of the night where there is limited light (*ha laylah*).

For a time, they will exist (*wa hayah*) as symbols and signs, as non-verbal representations which make the approach more clearly known, providing indications advising one's consent when evaluating

248

recompense and reward (*la 'owth*) **regarding the appointed meeting times of the feasts** (*wa la mow 'ed*), **as well as** (*wa*) **for days when there is light** (*yowm*) **and for years, the cycle of the seasons, renewal of life, and measure of time** (*wa shanah*). (*Bare'syth* / Genesis 1:14)

Therefore, let them exist for a time (*wa hayah*) **as sources of illumination** (*la ma'owr*) **in the expanse** (*ba raqya'*) **of the heavens** (*ha shamaym*) **to provide light** (*la 'owr*) **upon** (*'al*) **the earth** (*ha 'erets*). **And therefore** (*wa*), **it continued to exist like this thereafter based upon what preceded it** (*hayah ken*). (*Bare'syth* / Genesis 1:15)

God (*wa 'elohym*) **engaged to appoint for this particular task** (*'asah*) **both** (*'eth shanaym*) **of these substantial and empowering sources of illumination** (*ha ma'owr ha gadowl*), **with the older, the most important, intense, and distinguished** (*'eth ha gadowl*) **luminary** (*ha ma'owr*) **becoming prominent and clearly known as the influence over** (*memshalah*) **the daylight hours** (*ha yowm*) **and** (*wa*) **with the lesser, the less significant, albeit more easily understood, the younger chronologically and diminished relationally, the abhorred** (*'eth ha qatan*) **luminary** (*ma'owr* – light to be questioned) **becoming known and prominent as the influence over** (*la memshalah*) **the night** (*ha laylah*) **along with the heavenly powers** (*wa 'eth ha kowkab*). (*Bare'syth* / Genesis 1:16)

The Almighty (*wa 'elohym*) **caused them to be placed there for this purpose** (*nathan 'eth hem*) **in the expanse** (*ba raqya'*) **of the heavens** (*ha shamaym*) **to provide light** (*la 'owr*) **upon** (*'al*) **the land** (*ha 'erets*). (*Bare'syth* / Genesis 1:17)

And therefore (*wa la*), **they will function as proverbs** (*mashal*) **with the daylight** (*ba ha yowm*) **and in the time of darkness** (*wa ha laylah*) **providing a contrast to appreciate the difference between** (*wa la*

249

badal) **the light** (*ha 'owr*) **and comprehend being separated from the darkness** (*wa bayn ha choshek*)**.**

God (*wa 'elohym*) **saw** (*ra'ah*) **that indeed** (*ky*) **it was good, appropriate, productive, and beneficial** (*towb*)**.** (*Bare'syth* / Genesis 1:18)

And there was (*wa hayah*) **evening, the mingling and joining together of things** (*'erab* / *'arab*) **and there would be** (*wa hayah*) **morning, the beginning of a new dawn** (*boqer*) **– the fourth day** (*yowm rabyi'y*)**."** (*Bare'syth* / Genesis 1:19)

ﭏﭏﭏﭏﭏ

250

7

Chay | Life

Emergence of Consciousness...

According to what can be deduced from the Towrah and relativity, the fifth day dawned approximately 880 million years ago and closed 440,000,000 years in our past. At this time, God's testimony reveals that animal life flourished. It began in the sea.

"**Then** (*wa*), **God** (*'elohym* – the Almighty) **said** (*'amar* – spoke and declared), '**The waters** (*ha maym* – the forms of water to ponder as the source of life; the plural form of the interrogative – to inquire and question) **by design will literally and continuously conceive an innumerable abundance** (*sharats* – will actually swarm with a multiplicity of living entities, swimming and scurrying about while evolving, growing, and reproducing (qal imperfect jussive)) **of creatures creeping, wiggling, crawling, and swarming around** (*sherets* – a proliferation of sea creatures, bacteria, fish, insects, amphibians, reptiles, and rodents) **as living** (*chay* – animated and alive, animal life, active, nourished, sustainable, and reproducing; from *chayah* – to live and remain alive, sustaining, nourishing, and reproducing) **souls** (*nepesh* – consciousness, the ability to observe one's environment and respond, the breath of life)**...**" (*Bare'syth* / In the Beginning / Genesis 1:20)

God created the proper environment and recipe for life and then gave His creation a free hand to evolve and grow – just as He has with us when it comes to engaging in a relationship with Him. According to His testimony, life is formulaic, calculated upon the composition of energy and matter formulated on day one. It was guided from there by language. And on this day, that language would be DNA – the programming code of life. Once these things were accomplished, nature, like man, was free to run its course.

In this declaration, we learn that a *nepesh* | soul, or consciousness, is not unique or distinctive to man. All animals have one, even insects. ('Adam was also given a *neshamah* | conscience, something we'll investigate later.) According to Yahowah, and corroborated by science, animals and insects were initially conceived in water. In our genesis, we are all alike, composed of the elements of the earth and born in the seas. Even today, our bodies are 60% water as adults and 75% during the first six months of life. Our brains are 80-85% water, while our kidneys, heart, lungs, and liver are 70-75% water. Water enables cellular structure, function, and metabolism, carries nutrients and oxygen to our cells while facilitating biochemical reactions, protects our sensitive tissues, regulates our temperature, facilitates waste removal, and cushions our joints. Water molecules not only surround DNA in an ordered fashion to support its characteristic double-helix conformation but without being immersed in water, our cells would be incapable of following the careful and explicit instructions encoded by the DNA.

It should be noted that while consciousness is the determining factor between animal and plant life, there are no serious scientific studies designed to ascertain its nature. We recognize that it exists and that it is fundamental to animal life, but we are clueless as to what it is, how it works, where it comes from during conception, or where it goes upon death. And yet, Yahowah discussed it openly, directly associating *nepesh* | consciousness with the emergence of animal life. However, unlike the *Ruwach* | Spirit, a *nepesh* | soul is not inherently immortal.

Also interesting, *nepesh*, as the breath of life, appears to carry Divine qualities. God may have quite literally breathed an aspect of His nature into His creation – causing animals to exist as living beings with the ability to be observant and responsive.

Speaking of life, while Yahowah's statement is wholly inconsistent with macroevolution, the notion that life started with a single bacterium and then systematically evolved into ever more complex animals over billions of years by random chance. It is consistent with the fossil record. Animal life was the product of design, and it was conceived in innumerable abundance from the beginning. Moreover, it was designed to move about, to evolve, to nourish itself, to grow, and to reproduce from the onset. In this regard, Yahowah's position is the antithesis of that promoted by liberal societal architects who seek to rise above their Creator by negating His existence, and yet, it is Yahowah who is correct in this regard.

The word for life, *chay*, is interesting in that it is from *chayah* – and thus bears the name of its Author. Further, it differs by only a single letter from *hayah*, which is the basis of Yahowah's name – meaning "to exist."

Bare'syth / Genesis 1:20 concludes with: "**...in addition to** (*wa* – along with and then) **winged creatures which can fly** (*'owph 'uwph* – animals that can fly including insects, flying reptiles and mammals, and birds) **above the earth** (*'al ha 'erets* – over the land) **before the presence** (*'al paneh* – in closer proximity to the face and appearance) **of the expanse of space** (*raqya'* – the vastness of the sky) **in the sky** (*ha shamaym* – in the heavens)."

I do not think that this is about bugs or birds. While bugs would have emerged along with the other creeping, wiggling, crawling, and swarming critters, they are not approaching the heavens. And yes, birds can soar high above the Earth, but why use *raqya'* | the expanse of space

253

in addition to *shamaym*, which can be anything from the sky to the universe, from the heavens to the spiritual realm? So perhaps, this is Yahowah's way of encouraging the most capable animal, one not yet conceived, to consider life beyond the Earth. Indeed, as we are elevated in dimensions, the Covenant's children will travel effortlessly from the spiritual realm throughout the universe. And in this regard, Yahowah frequently refers to Himself as a bird protecting His chicks.

With the 21ˢᵗ verse of *Bare'syth* / Genesis God uses *bara'*, the Hebrew term for "create," again. It is only the second time. Scientifically, it is significant that the first word following *bara'* is "large reptiles," better known by its Greek derivative, "dinosaurs." Spiritually, it is an admonition to be leery of serpents, God's metaphor for demons.

"Thereby (*wa***) God (***'elohym***) created, shaped, and fashioned (***bara'*** – caused something unique to occur, conceiving something new and unheralded, making it out of the existing elements (qal imperfect)) accordingly, the great dinosaurs and mighty, monstrous reptiles (***'eth gadowl ha tanyn*** – massive reptilian lizards, impressive appearing creatures, very large marine, amphibian, and land animals, from an unused root meaning to elongate) along with all life with a soul (***wa 'eth kol nepesh ha chay*** – in addition to all living animals with consciousness) who move about (***ramas*** – who have mobility, differentiating animals from plants) for their benefit (***'asher*** – to their advantage and to form relationships) to proliferate (***sharats*** – which are found in great abundance and are innumerable, living and moving together) from the waters (***min ha maym*** – out of the source of life and many sources of water) according to their kind (***la myn hem*** – from their species and type, groups of living organisms descended from similar ancestral gene pool), and (***wa***) every (***'eth kol***) winged creature which can fly (***'owph kanaph*** –**

animals with wings that can fly including insects, flying reptiles and mammals, and birds) **according to its species** (*la myn hem* – from its kind and type, its group of living organisms descended from a similar genes).

God saw (*wa ra'ah 'elohym* – the Almighty observed, witnessed, viewed, and perceived (qal imperfect)) **that indeed, it was** (*ky* – truly it was) **appropriate, beautiful, and productive** (*towb* – good, agreeable, excellent, enjoyable, valuable, and beneficial)." (*Bare'syth* / In the Beginning / Genesis 1:21)

The animals conceived during this day were all by design. God "*bara'* – caused something unique to occur, conceiving something unheralded" – intelligent life. It was reality reflecting the imagination of its inspiration.

One of the reasons we know that "*gadowl tanyn*" means "giant reptiles" or "mighty lizards," and thus "dinosaurs," and not "serpent" is because the common Hebrew word for snake is *nachash*. In his first miracle, one designed to bolster Moseh's fledgling confidence, he tossed his staff to the ground, and it turned into a *nachash* – snake. But later, when Moses appeared before Pharaoh with his brother, and Aaron cast down a rod before the arrogant dictator, it was transformed into a *tanyn* | fearsome reptile. Aligned with the Adversary, Pharaoh's sorcerers and religious charlatans performed a similar feat, with *tanyn* | crocodiles now menacing the stage. The Greek derived "*deinos saurus* / dinosaur / terrible lizard" and the Hebrew "*gadowl tanyn* / mighty reptile" are therefore synonymous – although Yahowah's depiction is not a pejorative. There was nothing "terrible" about a brontosaurus.

If we pause a moment and ponder the implications, this is actually pretty funny. For the better part of a century, paleontologists have mocked creationists, condemning their god for having failed to mention beasts as prolific and majestic as dinosaurs. And yet, contemporaneous with their creation, Yahowah named them – the only species named thus far.

The reference to "*myn* – species" on this day is consistent with current biological science as well. What we perceive as new lifeforms actually represent a partitioning of the original gene pool, not a mutation. And that is because mutations lead to a loss of information rather than a gain. Yahowah was right and so was His creation, Darwin – at least as it relates to subtle changes within species. Further, all evidence suggests that animal life emerged from water consistent with Yahowah's 3,500-year-old witness.

Myn defines "a group of living organisms descended from similar genes." It is a derivation of *min*, which means "from, out of, or according to." The lone difference is the hand | ᴗ | *Yowd* of Yahowah between the waters | ᴍ | *Mem* and seed and sperm of new life | ᴺ | *Nun*. The letters tell the story.

It is a crime that evolution has been pitted against creation. Many aspects of evolution are true, especially in the sense that animals reproduce after their kind. But a duck and a beaver doe not a platypus make. Fruit flies have been bred infinitum – and never once has a unicorn emerged. After countless billions of trillions of attempts, a fruit fly has yet to conceive a house fly, much less a bee or bird. Evolution from organic matter to plant life, from plants to bacteria, and from single-cell animals to lions, tigers, and bears is not remotely plausible.

I suspect that one of the reasons so many people are confused by all of this is because, heretofore, Bible translations have run the gamut from bad to worse. *Gadowl tanyn* were not "sea serpents" or "great sea monsters" and *nepesh* means "soul or consciousness," not "living." As a result, they remain unaware of Yahowah's depiction of dinosaurs or that all animals have souls or consciousness. And even when the connection between language, consciousness, and life is manifest they seem incapable of attributing either DNA or souls to intelligent design – much less to God. Nonetheless, DNA is a language and even if science could get the formula correct, cobbling together what God created, no one has ever been able to ascertain the composition, design, or operation of animal consciousness.

Animals are differentiated from plants in that they "*ramas* – have mobility, moving about." And unlike vegetation, animals can observe their environment, consider what they have experienced, and then respond appropriately. This is all for their "*'asher* – benefit," especially when animals elect to "*'asher* – travel together."

Further, and as Yahowah has stated, it is one thing to have the wherewithal to conceive life; it is another altogether to design creatures which can replicate and grow, producing tremendous variation to keep it all so very interesting.

God was obviously enjoying Himself, having fun…

"The Almighty (*wa 'elohym*) **adored and blessed that which was associated with them** (*barak 'eth hem* – knelt down to greet and commend them and lift them up, invoking Divine favor while expecting a favorable result (piel imperfect)), **saying** (*la 'amar* – approaching to instruct, speaking and intending), **'Be fruitful, flourish** (*parah* – choose to be productive, produce offspring in abundance, and conceive future generations (qal imperative)), **thrive, and multiply** (*rabah* – become many, abundant, and numerous, increasing).

Fill (*wa male'* – fulfill and accomplish, providing a sufficient quantity to replenish) **the waters** (*ha 'eth maym* – the sources of inquiry; from *ma* – to ponder and question and *ym* – the pluralistic nature of) **in the seas** (*ba ha yamym*

– within the oceans). **Also** (*wa*) **let flying creatures** (*'owph* – everything which flies, including birds) **become numerous** (*rabah* – increase in number and size, thriving and proliferating) **upon the earth** (*ba ha 'erets* – in the land and realm).'" (*Bare'syth* / In the Beginning / Genesis 1:22)

Let it be known: Yahowah is pro-life. That is now undeniable. We also know that Yahowah is pro-choice. However, I did not expect Him to be so vocal about this aspect of His nature and intent this early on. And yet, after conveying numerous verbs in the jussive volitional mood as an expression of freewill and desire, He is immediately attributing the imperative mood – expressing volition in the second person – to animal reproduction. And in fact, most animals choose their mates.

It was an extraordinary time...

"And there was (*wa hayah* – there exists with unfolding implications over time (qal imperfect)) **evening** (*'erab* / *'arab* – a period of darkness, the mixing together of an interwoven fabric, the mingling and joining together of things, a nighttime of hopelessness during a discouraged state of foreign occupation, an era of ignorant commingling of and adherence to faiths and beliefs when the adversary will combine this with noxious swarms of Arab pests) **and there would be** (*wa hayah* – there also exists with unfolding implications over time (qal imperfect)) **morning** (*boqer* – tomorrow, the beginning of a new day, a time to be observant, perceptive, and judgmental, a time for consideration, a period to be attentive and respond appropriately, an extended stretch for being inquisitive and seeking information in order to make good decisions; from *baqar* – to seek, search, rendered as "e, consider, and reflect) – **the fifth day** (*yowm chamyshy* – the fifth in a sequence of days)." (*Bare'syth* / In the Beginning / Genesis 1:23)

The *Bare'syth* / In the Beginning / Genesis account of this era fits with the fossil record. Each of the 34 phyla, or basic body plans that comprise the full spectrum of animal life, burst onto the scene in their entirety during the Cambrian Explosion – 544 million years ago – well within Yahowah's timeline of 880 to 440 million years BCE. Not a single new phylum has emerged since. These findings are completely incompatible with macroevolution, of eons of time changing inorganic minerals into humans.

To be fair, over 99.9% of the more than two million animal types past and present can be categorized within ten of the thirty-four phyla. They are Annelida (17,000 species / 3 groups of segmented worms found in the oceans, freshwater, and damp soils), Arthropoda (1,100,000 species / 5 groups of crustaceans, shrimp, insects, arachnids, scorpions, centipedes, millipedes, and trilobites), Bryozoa (20,000 species / small aquatic animals living in colonies like corals), Chordata (60,000+ species / vertebrates, amphibians, reptiles, and, more recently, mammals, dinosaurs, frogs, birds, snakes, and lastly, humans), Cnidaria (11,000 species / jellyfish), Echinodermata (20,000 species / starfish), Mollusca (112,000 species / mollusks and snails), Nematoda (1,000,000 species / roundworms), Platyhelminthes (25,000 species / tapeworms, flatworms, and other parasites), and Porifera (5,000 species / sponges).

And while it is a detail, it is an insightful one. Insects, fish, amphibians, reptiles, and birds made Yahowah's fifth-day list – mammals did not. The fossil record reveals that while insects, fish, amphibians, reptiles, and birds all came into being just over 500 million years ago, the first mammal would not exist for another 250 million years. That is why Yahowah spoke of them on the sixth day. Scientifically, Yahowah's accounting remains precisely accurate in substance, sequence, and duration.

It should be noted that Darwin had no explanation for the Cambrian Explosion. It was contrary to his theory, and he knew it, but could not reconcile it with his views on evolution. The evidence simply does not support macroevolution.

Thermodynamics, the most basic of the natural laws governing physics, dictates that without an outside influence, an engaged, intelligent, and purposeful Creator, our planet's environment and the life it spawned would have regressed, not progressed – going from order to disorder. Genetically, random mutations do not add complexity; they diminish it. Information is lost, not gained.

And then there is the matter of sex. To reproduce, animals must mate. In most species, males and female perform complementary roles in gestation, nurturing, and protection. To think that this happened by chance, at the onset of each new animal form, and similarly for all animal types, is akin to believing in fairy tales.

Moreover, animal biology is sustained through the interworking of countless interconnected, mutually reliant, and astonishingly complex machines. They each have a source of energy, a mission, and a means to replicate themselves. And they all work harmoniously together based upon a language not unlike a very sophisticated, multidimensional, computer code. Had any of this been known in the late 19th century, Darwin's theory of evolution would have been stillborn.

Spiritually, there is profound truth encapsulated in the message of the fifth day. The first living *nepesh* | souls were born of water, not Spirit. God used water-conceived life to alert us to the fact that our souls must be anointed in His Spirit, His breath of life, to live life free as a bird in heaven.

Taruw'ah, known as Trumpets, is the fifth of seven *Mow'ed Miqra'*. It is a day called out for us to shout for joy and to signal a warning. The joyous news is that the first three Called-Out Assembly Meetings present Yahowah's plan of reconciliation. The warning is that animals abound in this creation account, and the mightiest of them will corrupt God's Word to lead as many people as possible astray. In His *Qara'* / Invitations to be Called Out / Leviticus depiction of *Taruw'ah*, Yahowah even tells us that the message is one of "inheritance" and that it is a "calling out," not unlike God calling His creation out of the water, telling them to be fruitful and multiply.

From a historical perspective, the souls created on this day were surrounded by mighty beasts, satanic deceptions of the worst possible kind. Death and dying became the counterpart of birth and living. That is why God reminds us twice during the fifth day that living souls reproduce after their kind. A society immersed in religious poison will breed dysfunctional and demonic souls.

In this historical context, look at the barbaric and terrorist rise of Christianity and Islam as well as the Dark Ages. This era was plagued by the stifling religions conceived by Paul and Muhammad.

Historically, the fifth millennium of man after the fall of 'Adam was our worst. Religions multiplied: Paul and Roman Christianity, Akiba's and Maimonides' Rabbinic Judaism, and Muhammad's and Satan's Islam – plaguing the world and damning countless souls. Man endured the plagues of death. Rather than following Yahowah's instructions in His Towrah and flourishing, almost every soul listened to the serpentine men instead. Evil begat evil from 33 to 1033CE. While the fifth millennium opened in glory and with promise it closed in darkness and despair. Spiritually, five is the number of confusion (6/man without

1/God = 5), which is why the five-pointed star, or pentagram, is the most prevalent occult symbol.

ᛘᛉᛘᛚ

Six is the number of man who was created on the sixth day. The object of creation, humanity, was the last thing God formed. But before He got to us, the Creator offered this narrative on life...

"And next (*wa*), **God** (*'elohym* – the Almighty) **said** (*'amar* – exclaimed), 'Let the earth proceed to bring forth** (*yatsa' ha 'erets* – God wanted the material realm to be continuously productive and deliver (hifil imperfect jussive)) **living** (*chay* – animated life, biological existence with) **souls** (*nepesh* – consciousness capable of observing and responding) **with unique characteristics** (*la myn hy'* – each special while derived from the similar genes), **wild animals** (*bahemah* – mammals) **and reptiles as creatures capable of moving about** (*wa remes* – beings noted for their agility and mobility) **and other lifeforms** (*wa chayah* – in addition to other animals) **for the land** (*ha 'erets*) **from their different species** (*la myn hy'*).' **And it was so** (*wa hayah ken* – it occurred just that way)." (*Bare'syth* / In the Beginning / Genesis 1:24)

It is the Earth which is being productive, doing exactly what it was designed to accomplish – supporting life. The magnificence and dignity of life were now on display, from fish and birds to reptiles to mammals.

"So (*wa*), **the Almighty** (*'elohym*) **engaged with** (*'asah 'eth* – acted and caused, expending considerable effort to create (qal imperfect)) **the animals of the earth** (*chayah ha 'erets* – the living creatures and lifeforms of the material realm) **based upon their nature and type** (*la myn hy'* – approaching based upon what made each unique and

262

special), **including with the mammals and wild animals** (*wa 'eth ha bahemah* – even with the domesticated animals (often transliterated *bahemah*)) **predicated on their distinguishing characteristics** (*la myn hy'*)**, as well as with all of the reptiles that moved** (*wa 'eth kol remes* – with all of the lifeforms that had mobility) **on the ground** (*'adamah* – soil, earthen land) **approaching the various species** (*la myn hy'*)**.**

And God saw, witnessed, and considered (*wa 'elohym ra'ah* – the Almighty viewed and perceived, delighting in) **that it was truly** (*ky* – that it was actually and exceptionally) **beneficial, appropriate, and good** (*towb* – pleasing, beautiful, and worth celebrating)**."** (*Bare'syth* / In the Beginning / Genesis 1:25)

God created all of this for His enjoyment. That is why we find Him engaging in the process. He approached the animals He had created based on their distinguishing characteristics. Having conceived DNA, Yahowah rearranged the letters such that they would result in a wondrous variation of size, shape, and color. It was, indeed, beautiful.

This is the third time that Yahowah has affirmed His status as not only the Creator but also as a witness. That is important because the fourteen-billion-year timeline from beginning to end is predicated upon His relative proximity to creation – i.e., being a witness.

Cosmologically, the sixth day began 440 million years ago and it, unlike the other epochs of time, has yet to conclude. I say this because the seventh day, the Millennial Shabat celebration, does not commence until the *Miqra'* of *Sukah* | Shelters in the fall of 2033. We are still living in this era.

Scientifically, we know that this was the time mammals were first conceived – around two hundred million years ago. The first *Homo sapiens* walked the Earth a scant 600,000 years before us.

Throughout this creative process, Yahowah has used language to conceive, influence, and communicate. Words are the medium of thought and creativity. Language is the means to enlightenment and to build a relationship. The Word is how God communes with us. In that light, let's consider what comes next.

"Then (*wa* – next), **Almighty God** (*'elohym* – the Mighty One) **said** (*'amar* – spoke, declared, and informed (qal imperfect – genuinely, relationally, and actually on an ongoing basis)), **'We are genuinely going to engage to bring about** (*'asah* – We will actually and relationally act to create out of existing materials (qal stem – denoting a relationship which is genuine and should be interpreted literally, imperfect conjugation – denoting something that this engagement will be ongoing and continuous with unfolding implications, first person, plural))**..."**

Yahowah said "we" rather than "I" because God is our Heavenly Father, the *"re'syth* – Head of the Family." And as we know based upon His declaration during day one, God's feminine nature was represented by the *"Ruwach Qodesh* – Set-Apart Spirit," who serves as our Spiritual Mother. She is responsible for our spiritual birth, purifying us, and then adorning us in a Garment of Light. Just as Yahowah's parental nature had worked harmoniously in creating the universe, it would naturally engage together to conceive life.

'Asah means "to act and to engage." Yahowah uses it throughout His testimony to describe His interactions with humankind through the Covenant. Relationships are only meaningful when both parties engage, and here we find God doing His part. The grammar is telling too, with the qal and imperfect revealing that this relationship would be genuine and enduring.

All other lifeforms were described as either "*dasha* – sprouting, shooting forth greenery, being productive, living and growing," "*bara'* – being created and shaped, causing something new to happen," or "*yatsa 'chay nepesh* – proceeding to come forth via the delivery of a living soul." But not this time. By using *'asah*, which conveys the idea of "actually doing the work necessary to accomplish the required task," He would be "forming mankind out of existing materials." This is to suggest that 'Adam was not the first human but instead the first man with whom God "*'asah* – engaged."

We were conceived for this purpose, designed to *'asah* | to act upon and engage in a genuine and continual relationship with our Creator. And now we know that God initiated contact.

To facilitate this end, and unlike all other lifeforms, we were given freewill and a conscience to exercise it. This is the basis of choice and a requirement for love. It also means that man is held responsible for his decisions.

"...*'Adam* | a man (*'adam* – a person named 'Adam, a human being) in our image and our example (*ba tselem 'anachnuw* – in our likeness and resemblance, with our pattern and model, similar to us but in three dimensions to represent us; from an unused root meaning shade), similar to a blueprint of ourselves (*ka damuwth 'anachnuw* – consistent with our manner, patterned after us, comparable to a builder's draft, graphic representation, and plan designed by ourselves; from *damah* – to be like, to resemble, to be comparable in imagination and thinking).'" (*Bare'syth* / In the Beginning / Genesis 1:26)

'Adam is one of several Hebrew words for mankind. Others include *'ysh*, which is masculine singular for "individual," *'enowsh* which speaks to our "mortality," and *gibowr*, our potential as a "man who is a strong, moral, and

influential leader." Therefore, by using *'Adam,* God is addressing this man and his descendants.

Reinforcing this point, *'Adam* is most always specific. It is typically preceded by the definite article, *ha* | the, suggesting that it is a title. This was one of the few exceptions, where *'Adam* was not prefixed by *ha* – and that is perhaps because it was intended as a name.

This is a subtle way of telling us that 'Adam was a specific individual, a unique creation. That's important because the scientific and prophetic evidence confirms that 'Adam wasn't the only human. So, we need to pay close attention to ascertain what made this particular man unique.

The same word vocalized *'adem* means "ruddy red in color." This may be an ode to Dowd, Yahowah's beloved Son, who was said to have been *'adem.* The same letters pronounced *'odem* denote a "precious stone," typically a "ruby" – a potentially humbling thought when we consider the blood which was shed by the Rock of our Salvation. In the feminine, *'adamah* is "ground, as in the surface of the earth," the "soil, dust, and dirt" including the "material of which earth is comprised." This may suggest that 'Adam, and thus mankind, was made out of the elements of the earth. That is interesting because the earth is stardust – comprised of the residue of first-generation stars. And that would make us the product of light.

Tselem appears 16 times in the Towrah and prophets – five of those say that God created man in His image. It is most often used "to represent a two- or three-dimensional painted or sculptured representation of something." Just as our shadow is a two-dimensional representation of our three-dimensional bodies cast by a source of light, we are 3D shadows of our 7D God.

I knew a woman once who preferred using "like" to love in defining relationships. If she really, really liked someone she said that she "like liked" him. That is what Yahowah is saying here with *ka damuwth* since both words mean "like."

In this case, God conceived man *"ka damuwth –* similar to a blueprint" of Himself. Our design is "consistent with and patterned after" our Maker as if we were a "graphic representation" of Yahowah. And that is to say that we are like God but in fewer dimensions, just as a blueprint is a two-dimensional plan for a home. And from its root, *damah*, we also resemble God in imagination and thinking.

The evidence is pervasive. Just as a mirror reflects our image and a shadow represents our shape in one less dimension, we were fashioned to resemble God, but in fewer dimensions. He is eternal in time, the fourth dimension. We are not. But we can be. And that is the purpose of this message. We were fashioned from the Builder's sketch as a representation of the Tabernacle of God that we are designed to become.

But there is so much more: for Yahowah to commune with us, for Him to grow through experiencing our relationships with Him, we have to be somewhat similar and substantially comparable. Let me share an example. We cannot have a relationship with an ant – as worthy, productive, strong, and industrious as ants seem to be. Their nature and intellect are too far beneath us. We have no means to communicate with, much less love, ants. And since these are God's primary objectives related to the conception of *'Adam*, this line of reasoning reveals that we must be more comparable to Yahowah than humans are to ants. Our nature must be a diminished version of Yahowah's nature. God is like us because we are like God.

By telling us that we were made in His image, not once but four times, it is obvious that Yahowah does not want us to worship Him. He wants us to sit down beside Him, to walk with Him, to be at ease and converse with Him, to love Him; not fear Him. While He is our God, He wants to be our Father.

That said, man is not God, no matter how desperately some men want to be. God is greater than we are in every conceivable way. We are simply His shadow – diminished in dimensions, light, life, knowledge, judgment, authority, and power.

The Towrah will remind us twice more that we were "created in God's image, resemblance, likeness, pattern, and model" – God's "shadow" if you will. Either Yahowah is forgetful and verbose – which is unlikely in the context of His creative testimony, salvation story, and prophetic human history – or this point is so important He wanted to make certain we would not miss it.

We are like God. God is like us. The reason is hard to miss: God wants to have a close, personal relationship with us. That is the purpose of all of this.

Yahowah wanted us to appreciate our place in His world...

"And let him demonstrate his influence (*wa radah* – let him guide and direct, showing control and leadership (qal imperfect jussive – as a reflection of his freewill, let man choose to actually and consistently demonstrate his influence)) **with the fish of the sea** (*ba dagah ha yam*) **and with the birds of the air** (*wa ba 'owph ha shamaym*), **as well as with the wild animals** (*wa ba ha bahemah*), **all within the entire realm** (*wa ba kol ha 'erets*) **with every creature which moves about** (*ba kol ha remes ha remes*) **on the ground** (*'al ha 'erets*)."** (*Bare'syth* / In the Beginning / Genesis 1:26)

While the lexicons support existing English translations by rendering *radad* "dominion," the preposition which follows is *ba*, which means "with," not "over." Further, since *radad* is more appropriately translated as "influence, lead, and guide, demonstrating leadership and control," since these things are more *tselem*, *ka*, and *damuwth* Yahowah, and because they are better suited for "*ba* – with," it becomes hard to justify the predilection for "dominion over." Further, God made this our choice, and freewill is as incompatible with dominion as it is with submission.

If we are reading this correctly, God wants us to engage with animals as He has, appreciating what makes them so valuable and beautiful. We have been given the opportunity to demonstrate that we are indeed like God and can be responsible, reflecting His love of life.

Should you have questioned my conclusion that "us" and "we" in the previous statements referred to Yahowah's masculine and feminine natures, and that God fulfills the roles of Heavenly Father and Spiritual Mother, please consider the following...

"So (*wa* – in addition) **God** (*'elohym* – the Almighty) **created** (*bara'* – conceived and brought into existence, designed and fashioned (qal imperfect)) *'Adam* | **the man for association** (*'eth ha 'adam* – this person named 'Adam accordingly) **in His image and pattern** (*ba tselem huw'* – in a manner resembling Him as an example and model).

In the image (*ba tselem* – in the likeness and resemblance, pattern and model, in three dimensions) **of the Almighty** (*'elohym* – of God), **He created** (*bara'* – conceived, invented, and brought into existence, designed and fashioned (qal perfect)) **him** (*'eth huw'*).

Male (*zakar* – as a child to remember, a son worth mentioning, and a boy whose name is renowned) **and female** (*naqebah* – as a girl and woman; the feminine of *naqab* – speaking anatomically of a hole to bore), **He brought them into existence to be together** (*bara' 'eth hem* – He conceived and created, fashioned and formed them for association)." (*Bare'syth* / In the Beginning / Genesis 1:27)

Since God created humankind in His image with both a masculine and feminine nature, it means that Yahowah manifests a paternal and maternal persona. In the context of the Covenant Family, God is our Heavenly Father and Spiritual Mother. It is the aforementioned *Ruwach Qodesh* | Set-Apart Spirit in the more nurturing role. In this regard, it is worth noting that Yahowah, with the *ah* ending, is a feminine name.

This is not to suggest that Yahowah is a sexual being, although He is clearly the inspiration behind this marvelous invention. This would also explain why God was not concerned with Dowd's inherent love of women, or that he had eighteen lovers, including eight wives. Apart from incest and pedophilia, bestiality and rape, God does not much care what we do sexually. Moreover, as a rebuff to Roman Catholics and evangelical Christians, Yahowah did not actually rebuke homosexuality. That myth is a product of inaccurate translations – one we will correct in subsequent books. Even His admonitions against adultery and harlots are there to encourage fidelity in the Covenant relationship.

With *'eth* we can translate it or ignore it depending upon whether or not it adds to our understanding by reinforcing an aspect of the relationship Yahowah envisions. Here it seems to suggest that men and women were created to enjoy a relationship with one another and with God.

The realization that Yahowah, by His own admission, has male and female characteristics is shocking to most people. And yet, there is no other informed or rational way to interpret these words and letters.

This all serves to complete Yahowah's familial metaphor. We, humans, were made like God, male and female, so that we would naturally come to appreciate God's purpose. As a result, men and women have fallen in love, bonded in marriage, built homes, and raised families. This in turn has caused us to experience the things God enjoys: communication, affection, the birth of children, their growth, nurturing, protection, relationship, trust, reliance, and especially sacrificial love.

The bottom line is we have the capacity to understand the kind of relationship Yah wants to develop with us, and the means to it, because God created it within us. Keep in mind, the Covenant itself is a marriage vow and a familial relationship. Even the root of the Hebrew word which forms the basis of "*beryth* – Covenant," *beyth*, means "family and home." It is further evidence that we were created to become part of Yahowah's Family and live within God's Home.

What comes next is a surprise, except for those who see God as a devoted and loving father...

"**Thereafter** (*wa*), **God** (*'elohym*) **knelt down in love to lift them up** (*barak 'eth hem* – adored and blessed them, got down on His knees to greet them while extolling their virtues (piel imperfect)), **saying to them** (*wa 'amar la hem* – encouraging them), '**Be productive** (*parah* – flourish and be industrious, increase abundantly) **and grow, becoming increasingly great** (*wa rabah* – become boundless and numerous, being enlarged, reaching a very high point).

Choose to be satisfied and prosper (*wa male'* – opt to live a fulfilling life (qal imperative – genuinely of your own freewill be fulfilled)) **within the material realm** (*'eth ha 'erets*) **and overcome it** (*wa kebes hy'* – tread upon it reliant upon the lamb).

And let him choose to demonstrate his influence (*wa radah* – let him guide and direct, showing control and leadership (qal imperfect jussive – as a reflection of his freewill, let man choose to actually and consistently

271

demonstrate his influence)) **with the fish of the sea** (*ba dagah ha yam*) **and with the birds of the air** (*wa ba 'owph ha shamaym*), **as well as with the wild animals** (*wa ba ha bahemah*), **all within the entire realm** (*wa ba kol ha 'erets*) **with every creature which moves about** (*ba kol ha remes ha remes*) **on the ground** (*'al ha 'erets*).'" (*Bare'syth* / In the Beginning / Genesis 1:28)

The primary meaning of *barak* is "to kneel down in adoration, to greet, to lift up and bless." It is the first thing God did after creating *'Adam* and it speaks volumes about His nature, character, and especially His purpose. Yah is willing to come down to our level to relate to us just like a father chooses to get down on his knees to look his children in the eyes.

Yahowah's ultimate demonstration of love occurred when He supported His Son's decision to serve as the Passover Lamb and then made it possible for Dowd's soul to carry our guilt into She'owl on UnYeasted Bread, thereby lifting us up, blessing us with the benefits of the Covenant. No greater love can be demonstrated than this, that God's beloved sacrificed so much for his family.

Parah and *rabah* demonstrate Yahowah's intent for the Covenant's children. He wants us to reciprocate His love because, when we do, not only does God's Family grow, we individually increase, becoming more than we are. We become enlarged, growing from three dimensions to at least four, and I suspect seven. By being reborn from above in His Spirit we become like God in yet another way – eternal. Similarly, *male'* speaks of living a fulfilling life, satisfied by our choices.

Spiritually, the lesson of the sixth day is reflected in Yahowah's selection of words. *'Adam* was made like God so the model for His love has been established. This day, therefore, provides the insights which underlie the fifth Instruction since God has revealed that He has masculine and feminine characteristics, making Yahowah the Mother and Father we should value if we want our days prolonged.

The sixth day is also representative of the sixth *Mow'ed Miqra'*. But most miss it; just as they miss the fact Yahowah is both our Heavenly Father and Spiritual Mother. In the chapter devoted to a proper translation of *Yowm Kipurym*, the Day of Reconciliations, we will discover that Yahowah is calling us to come into the presence of the feminine aspects of the light so that we might come to camp out with Him in His Home.

Historically, man's sixth millennia dawned almost as horridly as it will conclude. It started with the Catholic Crusades and Inquisition. And while the Reformation was a step in the right direction, it did not go nearly far enough, and as a result, we have squandered its lessons.

In this, mankind's final millennium, the religion of man was conceived. Adam Weishaupt, brewing a poisonous concoction of Mystery Babylon, Rabbinic Kabbalah, and Jesuit Catholicism, conceived Socialist Secular Humanism, which Karl Marx developed into Communism – and thus began the march toward the Master/Slave Fascist state known as the New World Order. Today, his religion permeates the globe and controls American politics. Collectively, under the guise of Socialist Secular Humanism, more people were murdered during the last century than during all of human history combined. Thinking ourselves wise, we have worshiped fools.

Scientifically, Yahowah's testimony regarding this day is consistent with the evidence. This is when mammals first tread the Earth. Man is an animal – one who arrived very late on the scene.

𐤉𐤄𐤅𐤄

By way of review, day one focused on God's Spirit and on Light, something 'Adam experienced directly and intimately in the Garden. And yet all around him, just outside 'Eden's walls, was "*tohuw, bohuw* and *chosek*— destructiveness, death and separation" – something 'Adam would also come to know after his fall. Day one of man's history, where a day is a thousand years, dawns with God who is one, initiating a one-on-one, one-thousand-year relationship with the first man created in His image. Here we learn that God, who is named "Yahowah," is the source of our existence. He equated Himself to light, He called light into being, and is like light in that He exists in the eternal now. And He invites us to join Him there.

Two is the number of choice so it stands to reason that the second millennia of man, like the creation account, was all about separation and water. The flood separated the lone family who chose God from those who did not. The deluge occurred in the midst of this era, 2968 to 1968 BCE – right when Yahowah told us it would.

Three is the number of family – father, mother, and child. And so, it was that throughout mankind's third one-thousand-year era we humans multiplied prodigiously as did our civilizations. It was during the third millennium after the expulsion from the Garden, and deliverance from the Ark that God established His Covenant with 'Abraham, Sarah, and Yitschaq, who in turn created the ultimate human family.

Acting out a dress rehearsal for the fulfillment of Passover, 'Abraham (whose name means Merciful Father) was asked to take his son Yitschaq (whose name means Laughter) to Mount Mowryah (meaning to Revere Yahowah) in 1968 BCE, the very year the third millennium of human history began. A thousand years later, at the close of the third era and the dawn of the fourth, on that same mountain, in 968 BCE, Dowd was presented as the Cornerstone of Yahowah's Home. Exactly 1,000 years later, in 33 CE, also on Mowryah, Dowd would return to serve as the Passover Lamb as the first three Mow'ed Miqra'ey were fulfilled by Father and Son – enabling the benefits of the Covenant.

The seminal events in human history from a redemptive perspective occur every forty *Yowbel* | Yah's Lamb is God (errantly rendered Jubilee). This fifty-year celebration of Yahowah's means to enable the Covenant's benefits and reconcile His relationship with His people (presented in *Qara'* / Called Out / Leviticus 25) is based upon the formula of *Shabuw'ah* – seven times seven years plus one. During a Yowbel year, slaves are freed, debts are forgiven, and we return to share the land – all symbolic of God's redemptive plan.

So that you do not miss what should be obvious, the last set of forty "fifties" will conclude on the *Mow'ed Miqra'* of *Sukah* / Shelters in 2033. Yahowah, faithful to His prophetic promise, after returning five days earlier on *Yowm Kipurym* | Reconciliations, will, in conjunction with Dowd, remove religion and politics, militarism and conspiracies, from the world – prolonging and protecting the life He cherishes, while returning Earth to 'Eden.

Historically, the thousand-year epoch beginning in 33 CE and ending in 1033 was among our worst. The world witnessed the rise of Judaism and Christianity, followed seven hundred years later by Islam and with it a flood of terror lasting to this day. During these Dark Ages, mankind was also plagued as never before by the stifling religion of Christianity. The fifth millennium gave rise to Rabbinic Judaism with the creation of the Babylonian Talmud. Written in 500 CE, man's oral law was steeped in the counterfeit of Mystery Babylon. It grew into Qabalah – the mysticism of universal religion. And it did not take long for these satanic imposters to consume their creators and devour the faithful.

In the sixth millennium mysticism and philosophy would give rise to the Illuminati, Freemasonry, Communism, Nazism, Socialist Secular Humanism, world wars, and universal jihad – the very doctrines that have murdered men and women by the hundreds of millions. And yet, with a litany of failures, economic collapse, deprivation of freedoms, intrusive surveillance, overcrowded prisons, an onslaught of refugees, cities in ruins, and streets stained in blood, politicians the world over have doubled down on their tyranny, depriving billions of their liberty and livelihoods to combat a virus far less lethal than their draconian response. And rising in the ashes is an even more destructive force pursuing class warfare while masquerading under the false premise of racial injustice.

These relatively few years which remain between now and Dowd's return to lead and protect God's people will be hellish. The world is in freefall, accelerating its inevitable demise in a death spiral. It is devolving before our very eyes. There is no hope for your country or community, only for yourself and those you love.

In the Towrah, six is the number of man. And so, it would be that the sixth millennium showcased the errant ways of humankind. As a result, this era will terminate even more horridly than it commenced. Years 1033 through 2033 CE underscore the ugliness of Catholic Crusades and Inquisition. While the Reformation made Yahowah's Word available to the masses and reduced the influence of the Catholic Church, the Protestants brought too much ugly baggage with them and were ultimately no better. Even worse, Jews would wrap themselves, their nation and religion in a six-pointed star during this era – one whose inspiration would come from a false messiah.

In mankind's final millennium, the religion of man, Socialist Secular Humanism, has become the national religion of Russia, China, and most of Europe. Even in

America, politics, the media, and academia became slaves to political correctness – man's replacement moral code. As a result, we stopped being judgmental, and with that, we ceased to be just, civil, moral, and rational.

Soon it will be all over. In the next 10 years (between 2023 and 2033), we will poison and scorch our planet, killing as many as six billion people in horrible wars – with the chaos beginning with Muslims striking Israel. As the era of man comes to a climactic close, humankind will come within an hour of destroying the Earth, eliminating choice and life. We are in for a rough ride. The road ahead is dark and serpentine for the preponderance of people.

Apart from God, we humans are a conniving lot, devious, destructive, self-serving, vicious, and cruel. Blind to Yahowah's Towrah, the man of science is the sum of his existence. There is nothing more.

But for those who choose to know Yahowah, to value Him, to join His Family on His terms, the seventh day will be long and glorious. On it, God observed and celebrated what He had achieved and so shall we. Those who survive the upcoming Time of Ya'aqob's Troubles will enter the Millennial Kingdom. One thousand years of great joy await.

In this regard, the seventh day is symbolic of the seventh *Mow'ed Miqra'*. It is the culmination of all things, of God and man forming a relationship and living together as a Family. *Sukah* | Camping Out is the result of the first six *Miqra'ey* | Invitations to be Called Out and Meet with God.

ᛤᎩᛤﬞ

The first use of *hineh* | pay very close attention in the Towrah is a teaching moment. The very first thing

Yahowah did after conceiving 'Adam was provide some guidance and instruction, also known as *towrah*...

"**Then, God said** (*wa 'elohym 'amar*), '**Behold** (*hineh* – look up now and pay attention to this part of the narrative, consider how the details in this discussion paint a picture), '**I have provided for you and given to you** (*nathan la 'atah 'eth* – I have constituted and offered you accordingly (qal perfect – literally, albeit for a limited time)) **every plant yielding seeds** (*kol 'eseb zera' zera'* – all vegetation capable of reproducing and propagating the species with seeds) **which, for the enjoyment of the relationship** (*'asher* – to receive the benefits of the correct approach) **appears on the surface** (*'al paneh* – is present upon) **of this entire realm** (*kol ha 'erets* – upon the earth and throughout all the material realm) **along with every one of the trees** (*wa 'eth kol 'ets*) **which beneficially** (*'asher* – to reveal the proper way to the relationship) **has fruit on the tree** (*ba huw' pery 'ets*) **to sow its seeds** (*zera' zera'* – to propagate the species).

They shall continually exist (*hayah* – they will always be (qal imperfect)) **for you** (*la 'atem*) **to consider as food** (*la 'aklah* – to consume for nourishment).' (*Bare'syth* / In the Beginning / Genesis 1:29)

'**And regarding every living creature** (*wa la kol chayah* – then concerning all animals) **of the realm** (*ha 'erets* – the earth), **as well as every bird** (*wa la kol 'owph*) **of the sky** (*ha shamaym*), **and all else** (*wa kol*) **that moves around** (*ramas*) **on the ground** (*'al ha 'erets*) **with which is** (*'asher ba huw'* – relationally and beneficially) **a living consciousness** (*nepesh chay* – a soul which is alive), **including all healthy vegetation and green plants** (*'eth kol yereq 'eseb*), **they should be considered edible** (*la 'aklah* – may be consumed as food).'

And it occurred as such (*wa hayah ken* – it came to be likewise and verifiable)." (*Bare'syth* / In the Beginning / Genesis 1:30)

Everything was on the menu. Yahowah was not restrictive in any way. 'Adam was free to eat fruits and vegetables, fowl and flesh. Therefore, when we find God advising us what not to eat later on in the Towrah, we ought to be mindful of this fact. The logical conclusion is that our Heavenly Father knew that there was nothing in the Garden which would harm 'Adam, as it was a perfect place. But then later, as humankind was exposed to the world as we know it, His advice was to be more careful – avoiding eating animals that were unsafe.

This duly noted, our Maker mentioned meat once and plants thrice, suggesting a healthy diet. He is also on record acknowledging that our brains function best on protein, which is why animals, and specifically birds, were recommended. And while not explicitly stated, since Yah and 'Adam camped out together, it is likely that God introduced His son to fire.

"Almighty God (*wa 'elohym*) **saw** (*ra'ah* – witnessed and recognized, observed and perceived (qal imperfect)) **everything** (*'eth kol*) **which to reveal the way to the benefits of the relationship and to get the most out of life** (*'asher* – which lead to the correct, albeit narrow path to walk to be genuinely happy) **could be beheld** (*wa hineh* – paid close attention to, looked at and noticed), **and it was exceedingly good, tremendously pleasing, and abundantly productive** (*towb ma'od* – extremely beautiful, altogether beneficial, and highly entertaining).

That was (*wa hayah* – there exists with unfolding implications over time (qal imperfect)) **evening** (*'erab* / *'arab* – a period of darkness, the mixing together of an interwoven fabric, the mingling and joining together of things, a nighttime of hopelessness during a discouraged state of foreign occupation, an era of ignorant commingling of and adherence to faiths and beliefs when the adversary will combine this with noxious swarms of Arab pests) **and there would be** (*wa hayah* – there also exists with unfolding implications over time (qal imperfect)) **morning** (*boqer* – tomorrow, the beginning of a new day, a time to be observant, perceptive, and judgmental, a time for consideration, a period to be attentive and respond appropriately, an extended stretch for being inquisitive and seeking information in order to make good decisions; from *baqar* – to seek, search, rendered as "e, consider, and reflect) – **the sixth day** (*yowm ha shishy* – the sixth in a sequence of days)." (*Bare'syth* / In the Beginning / Genesis 1:31)

It was "*towb ma'od* – exceedingly good, tremendously pleasing, and abundantly productive, extremely beautiful, altogether beneficial, and highly entertaining." Yahowah's recognition is important because, in a matter of years, He will be taking His children back to this place of *towb ma'od*. He thought it was marvelous, as shall we.

Here once again for our benefit and nourishment are the words our God shared at the conclusion of *Bare'syth* / Genesis One.

"Then (*wa*), **God** (*'elohym*) **said** (*'amar*), **'The waters to ponder as the source of life** (*ha maym*) **by design will literally and continuously conceive an innumerable abundance** (*sharats*) **of creatures creeping, wiggling, crawling, and swarming around with a proliferation of sea creatures from bacteria to fish, including insects, amphibians, and reptiles** (*sherets*) **as living** (*chay*) **souls with consciousness** (*nepesh*), **in addition to** (*wa*) **winged creature which can fly** (*'owph 'uwph*) **above the earth** (*'al ha 'erets*) **before the presence** (*'al paneh*) **of the expanse of space** (*raqya'*) **in the sky** (*ha shamaym*).'** (*Bare'syth* / Genesis 1:20)

Thereby (*wa*) God (*'elohym*) conceived and created something new and unheralded (*bara'*) such as the great dinosaurs and mighty, monstrous reptiles (*'eth gadowl ha tanyn*) along with all life with a soul (*wa 'eth kol nepesh ha chay*) who move about (*ramas*) for their benefit (*'asher*) to proliferate (*sharats*) from the waters (*min ha maym*) according to their kind (*la myn hem*), and (*wa*) every (*'eth kol*) winged creature which can fly (*'owph kanaph*) according to its species (*la myn hem*).

God saw (*wa ra'ah 'elohym*) that indeed, it was (*ky*) appropriate, beautiful, and productive (*towb*). (*Bare'syth* / Genesis 1:21)

The Almighty (*wa 'elohym*) adored and blessed that which was associated with them (*barak 'eth hem*), saying (*la 'amar*), 'Be fruitful, flourish (*parah*), thrive, and multiply (*rabah*). Fill (*wa male'*) the waters (*ha 'eth maym*) in the seas (*ba ha yamym*). Also (*wa*) let flying creatures (*'owph*) become numerous (*rabah*) upon the earth (*ba ha 'erets*).' (*Bare'syth* / Genesis 1:22)

And there was with unfolding implications (*wa hayah*), evening, a period of darkness mingling and joining together of things leading to a discouraged state of foreign occupation and of an ignorant commingling of and adherence to faiths and beliefs (*'erab* / *'arab*) and there would be (*wa hayah*) morning, a time to be observant and judgmental, a time for consideration to respond appropriately (*boqer*) – the fifth day (*yowm chamyshy*). (*Bare'syth* / Genesis 1:23)

Next (*wa*), God (*'elohym*) explained (*'amar*), 'Let the earth proceed to bring forth (*yatsa' ha 'erets*) living (*chay*) souls (*nepesh*) with unique characteristics (*la myn hy'*), wild animals (*bahemah*) and reptiles as creatures capable of moving about (*wa remes*) and other lifeforms (*wa chayah*) for the land (*ha 'erets*) from their different

281

species (*la myn hy '*).' And it was so (*wa hayah ken*). (*Bare'syth* / Genesis 1:24)

Then (*wa*), the Almighty (*'elohym*) engaged with (*'asah 'eth*) the animals of the earth (*chayah ha 'erets*) based upon their nature and type (*la myn hy '*), including with the mammals and wild animals (*wa 'eth ha bahemah*) predicated on their distinguishing characteristics (*la myn hy '*), as well as with all of the reptiles that moved (*wa 'eth kol remes*) on the ground (*'adamah*), approaching the various species (*la myn hy '*).

God saw, witnessed, and considered (*wa 'elohym ra'ah*) that was truly (*ky*) beneficial, appropriate, and good (*towb*). (*Bare'syth* / Genesis 1:25)

Then (*wa*), Almighty God (*'elohym*) said (*'amar*), 'We are genuinely going to engage to bring about (*'asah*) **'Adam | a man** (*'adam*) **in our image and our example** (*ba tselem 'anachnuw*), as if he were a blueprint of ourselves and patterned after us (*ka damuwth 'anachnuw*).

And let him demonstrate his influence (*wa radah*) with the fish of the sea (*ba dagah ha yam*) and with the birds of the air (*wa ba 'owph ha shamaym*), as well as with the wild animals (*wa ba ha bahemah*), all within the entire realm (*wa ba kol ha 'erets*) with every creature which moves about (*ba kol ha remes ha remes*) on the ground (*'al ha 'erets*).' (*Bare'syth* / Genesis 1:26)

So (*wa*) God (*'elohym*) conceived and created, designed and fashioned (*bara'*) **'Adam | the man for association** (*'eth ha 'adam*) in His image and pattern (*ba tselem huw '*).

In the image (*ba tselem*) of the Almighty (*'elohym*) He created (*bara'*) him (*'eth huw '*). As a male child to remember, a son worth mentioning (*zakar*), and a female, as a woman (*naqebah*), He brought them into existence to be together (*bara' 'eth hem*). (*Bare'syth* / Genesis 1:27)

Thereafter (*wa*), **God** (*'elohym*) **knelt down in love to lift them up** (*barak 'eth hem*), **saying to them** (*wa 'amar la hem*), **'Be productive and industrious** (*parah*), **and grow, becoming increasingly great, enlarged and boundless** (*wa rabah*).

Choose to be satisfied and prosper, living a fulfilling life (*wa male'*) **within the material realm** (*'eth ha 'erets*) **and overcome it** (*wa kebesh hy'*).

And let him choose to demonstrate his influence (*wa radah*) **with the fish of the sea** (*ba dagah ha yam*) **and with the birds of the air** (*wa ba 'owph ha shamaym*), **as well as with the wild animals** (*wa ba ha bahemah*), **all within the entire realm** (*wa ba kol ha 'erets*) **with every creature which moves about** (*ba kol ha remes ha remes*) **on the ground** (*'al ha 'erets*).' (*Bare'syth* / Genesis 1:28)

Then, God said (*wa 'elohym 'amar*), **'Behold, look up now and pay attention to this part of the narrative** (*hineh*), **'I have provided for you and given to you** (*nathan la 'atah 'eth*) **every plant yielding seeds, all vegetation capable of reproducing and propagating the species** (*kol 'eseb zera' zera'*) **which, for the enjoyment of the relationship** (*'asher*), **appears on the surface** (*'al paneh*) **of this entire realm** (*kol ha 'erets*) **along with every one of the trees** (*wa 'eth kol 'ets*) **which beneficially** (*'asher*) **has fruit on the tree** (*ba huw' pery 'ets*) **to sow its seeds** (*zera' zera'*).

They shall continually exist (*hayah*) **for you** (*la 'atem*) **to consider as food** (*la 'aklah*). (*Bare'syth* / Genesis 1:29)

And regarding every living creature (*wa la kol chayah*) **of the realm** (*ha 'erets* – the earth), **as well as every bird** (*wa la kol 'owph*) **of the sky** (*ha shamaym*), and all else (*wa kol*) that moves around (*ramas*) on the ground (*'al ha 'erets*) with which is (*'asher ba huw'*) a living consciousness (*nepesh chay*), including all healthy vegetation and green plants (*'eth kol yereq 'eseb*), they can be considered edible (*la 'aklah*).'

And it occurred as such (*wa hayah ken*).' (*Bare'syth* / Genesis 1:30)

Almighty God (*wa 'elohym*) witnessed and recognized, observed and perceived (*ra'ah*) everything (*'eth kol*) to reveal the way to the joyous relationship and to get the most out of life which (*'asher*) could be beheld (*wa hineh*) and it was exceedingly good, tremendously pleasing, abundantly productive, and highly entertaining (*towb ma'od*).

With unfolding implications over time, that was (*wa hayah*) evening, the blending together of things, a nighttime of discouragement from foreign occupation, an era of ignorant commingling of and adherence to faiths (*'erab* / *'arab*) and there would be (*wa hayah*) morning, the dawning of a new day, a time to be observant, perceptive, and judgmental (*boqer*) – the sixth day (*yowm ha shishy*)." (*Bare'syth* / In the Beginning / Genesis 1:31)

ᛨᛉᛉᛡ

8

Shabat | Seventh Day

The Plan is Unfurled...

A picture is beginning to form. By opening the second chapter of Yahowah's first book, we discover an interwoven tapestry whose threads comprise the fabric of life: revelation, reconciliation, and relationship.

God begins by revealing that His words take precedence over everything. He underscores the importance of light, associating it with His nature and purpose. As He telescopes in and out of space and time. He explains our tenuous and yet tremendously important place in the universe He created for fellowship. God reveals that He is the Architect of life, of consciousness and conscience.

By thoughtfully contemplating our genesis, we are afforded an undeniable treasure: Yahowah created us in His image because He enjoys the camaraderie of close personal relationships. Our Heavenly Father's preferred association is predicated upon home and family, upon a man and a woman becoming husband and wife, father and mother, coming together in love to conceive and raise children.

We have also witnessed the establishment of an essential pattern – one from which God will never vary. Yahowah's foundational formula is six plus one equals seven. Within this model, we witness seven creative epochs, seven thousand years of relationship history, and the seven-part plan which serves as the basis for our adoption into Yah's Covenant and entry into Heaven. With it, the seven essential dates which form Yahowah's prophetic calendar mark the flow of history.

Central to this line of thought, the Sabbath, or Seventh Day, was set apart to reflect upon God's promises. The *shabat* is the day of promise, a special day to experience Yahowah's love for us. It is a time for us to celebrate the realization that He got down on His knees to lift us up, greeting us as His children, and sharing His knowledge and advice with us to make our lives more satisfying and complete.

With these things in mind, let's pick up the story of our genesis and the reasons behind it by opening the second chapter of *Bare'syth* / Genesis. And as we do, let's remain mindful that Yahowah's explanation is explicitly worded to convey God's thinking behind the implications of the *Shabat* | Seventh Day and how we should be observing it.

"Thereby (*wa* – here and now)**, the universe and the spiritual realm** (*ha shamaym* – the heavens) **as well as the material realm and earth** (*ha 'erets* – the land, ground, and matter) **were being completed** (*kalah* – were prepared and would conclude as intended, being accomplished as designed (pual imperfect – the ongoing influence on the *shamaym*, *'erets,* and *tsaba'* would be passive with unfolding consequences over time)) **including all** (*wa kol* – the entirety of) **their spiritual messengers and heavenly implements** (*tsaba' hem* – the host of God's envoys arranged in a command and control regimen)**."** (*Bare'syth* / In the Beginning / Genesis 2:1)

Yahowah has infused the universe with His power and sparked the life within it by speaking both into existence, thereby revealing the merit of His words. It was the perfect blend of design and serendipity, of planning for an infinite number of random outcomes, allowing for freewill, and yet, remain on a prescribed schedule. That schedule would remain six days of input, influence, and guidance followed by a seventh, where the results would be experienced and celebrated.

Kalah is based on *kol*, and it means "everything had been prepared and was being completed as planned." In the pual imperfect, we find that Yahowah would not have to actively intervene with His creation for it to all play out and accomplish its purpose over time.

This provides a clue which prompts us to ponder something profound. Based upon what I know of science and towrah, before time and space began, God calculated the precise amount of energy required and provided the guidance necessary to achieve the specific outcome He desired. The result of this multivariable equation was a universe with six dimensions, one capable of supporting a lifeform that would mirror the Creator's nature, one in which life would be temporal but could be eternal, one in which God's timeline of six plus one creative days would transpire over the course of seven millennia, and one where freewill would remain sacrosanct. It was a calculation so complex, and with so many variables, all of man's computers combined could not ascertain the formula, much less process the data.

The reasons for this are quite simple. The purpose of creation is reflected in its formula. Yahowah introduced Himself as the lone architect and builder on day one. He created 'Adam in His image on the sixth day, suggesting that this number would represent mankind. Alone, God lived a life void of loving relationships, an existence deprived of the growth freewill associations provide. So, He conceived and created a universe capable of supporting a creature designed to fulfill that need. That matrix was intended to bring man and God together by adding six to one, and thus achieving perfection: the celebration of the promise of seven.

This realization suggests that Yahowah is both inventive and a mathematician. Every element of revelation, reconciliation, and relationship relates to aspects of His pattern of six plus one. No matter the question, if the answer is important, it is seven.

There is yet another profound implication associated with *kalah* considering the imperfect conjugation. It is used to address actions and activities which are ongoing and is the opposite of the perfect conjugation which conveys a completed act. Therefore, the spiritual and material realms were neither "finished" nor "completed" with nothing left to do or achieve but instead "were being completed." They "were prepared and would be concluded as intended" and thus "were being accomplished as designed." This and what follows are of great importance because it has been wrongly assumed by the religious that the Shabat is a time for being idle because God was done and thus rested. It is not true. As a result, the implications on how we ought to observe the Shabat change.

My understanding is that the Shabat is something to be experienced and celebrated for what was planned and is now underway and ongoing. It is a time to reflect on the past such that we can more fully appreciate the present involvement of God and capitalize upon our very active, future relationship with Him. If I am correct, and the grammar is supportive of this conclusion, it provides a fundamental shift in our understanding of the Seventh Day and of the Instruction Yahowah would inscribe in stone regarding the Shabat.

The next most misunderstood word in this passage may be *tsaba'*. It is translated as "hosts" eighty-five percent of the nearly five hundred times it is found in the Torah, Prophets, and Psalms. "War, army, and battle" comprise the residual renderings. I don't think one person in a million knows why "host" was selected or what this choice implies.

The word is defined by scholars to mean "military congregation or a large fighting unit, a division of an army." If we were to extrapolate superficially based upon this rather human line of thought, it would imply that Yahowah has competitors and that He either requires defending or covets conquest. After all, conquest, defense, and control are the sole purposes of militaries. But since the notion of multiple rival gods is in complete conflict with His testimony and with reason, and since by definition, a Creator with sufficient energy to produce our universe isn't short on power, there must be another reason for God selecting a militaristic term.

That is not to say that there is not a battle being waged. There is one to be sure. It is a spiritual battle for your soul. We will delve further into this in subsequent chapters: *'Eden* – Joy, and *'Adam* – *Man,* and *'Ishah* – Woman. I share this now because there is some merit to the "fighting" aspects of *tsaba',* at least when seen through a lens focused upon the forces which are battling for your love or your submission.

Towrah, when seen as a whole fabric, suggests that Yahowah's *mal'ak,* or spiritual messengers, the "heavenly host" in this context, exist in a command-and-control regime without freewill. In this way, the beings we errantly call "angels" are just like soldiers in America's military, where a single refusal to obey a superior officer results in the subordinate being banished from the corps, being incarcerated, or losing their life, depending upon the severity of the rebellion.

The "*mal'ak* – spiritual representatives" serve as Yah's workforce. They are His messengers, envoys, and implements. Without them, and without the Set-Apart Spirit, Yahowah's interactions with His creation would be severely handicapped due to the difference in dimensions.

Our focus on *tsaba'*, representing the "vast array of spiritual messengers and heavenly implements," known as *mal'ak*, individually, was shared with us for two significant reasons. First, with *kalah* | being completed, written as an ongoing action, the means Yahowah would use to engage over time would be through the *tsaba'*. We have, thereby, learned something of their role in all of this and how God uses them.

The second reason is to enlighten the observant such that we are able to more fully explain the use of *mala'kah* in the next statement. The Hebrew word *mala'kah*, as the feminine of *mal'ak*, is used to speak of the "work done and message conveyed by heaven's Maternal influence." While *mal'ak* is a masculine noun, the concluding 𐤄 | hey, as is the case with 𐤄𐤅𐤄𐤉 | Yahowah and 𐤄𐤓𐤅𐤕 | Towrah, makes 𐤊𐤀𐤋𐤌 | *mal'ak* masculine and 𐤄𐤊𐤀𐤋𐤌 | *mala'kah* feminine.

Continuing to address the *mal'ak*, they are not compensated, so it would be inappropriate to consider them employees. They aren't equals, so they are not partners. There is no indication of mutual affection, so they aren't part of a loving relationship. They cannot procreate, so they are not family. I think it would be fair to consider them "tools engaged in the work of God." This changes appreciably in subtle ways in the transition from mal'ak to *mala'kah*.

The *mal'ak* who comprise the "*tsaba'* – spiritual implements and heavenly messengers," more popularly known as "angels" (by foolishly transliterating *aggelos*, the Greek word for messenger out of the Christian New Testament), are greater than we mortals in that they are eternal in time and have a greater capacity to travel within the dimensions of space. They are also comprised of substantially more energy than we are, making them more effective implements. As a result, these spiritual beings are considerably more knowledgeable and powerful than humans. But without the capacity to choose freely, they would be incapable of love and severely diminished in creativity and causality, as these things are dependent upon freewill.

Please consider this example: short of breaking, which would be a singular act of rebellion, a shovel has no option but to dig when and where the user dictates. That does not mean that a shovel is not valued or useful, only that it has no freewill and thus no ability to be creative on its own initiative. Yahowah's spiritual messengers are like this because they do what they are told. Even demons, rather than create, counterfeit to confuse and commingle to confound.

Therefore, while mortal, comparatively powerless, and trapped in time, we are vastly superior to the heavenly host when it comes to those things which are born of choice: creativity, causality, communion, and compassion. These, not surprisingly, are the hallmarks of God, which is why He said that we were created in His image.

There are insights related to these conclusions I do not want you to miss. The first deals with eternity. Immortal, the spiritual messengers or envoys whom we errantly call "angels" cannot be killed, even by God. That is why Yahowah created She'owl as a prison for Heylel ben Shachar, better known as Satan (a transliteration of *satan*, the Hebrew word for adversary), and for any other *mal'ak* who rebelled with him. She'owl is a lightless place, where time is eternal but there is no freedom of mobility or escape. This is where he, the other rebellious *mal'ak*, and all human souls who associate with and serve these demons will be incarcerated. Their mental anguish will be the result of enduring eternal consciousness cognizant of their mistake in judgment.

Souls born in Yahowah's Spirit will also become immortal, but they will spend their eternity with their

Heavenly Father rather than with "*ha Satan* – the Adversary." The preponderance of souls will make neither connection, and they will therefore remain mortal. For them, there will be nothing beyond death. These three choices and three destinations are further developed in the "*She'owl* – Questioning Separation" and "*Ruwach* – Spirit" chapters of the *'Azab* | Separation volume of *Yada Yahowah*.

Second, choice is an exceptionally valuable gift, one that many never come to appreciate. Without freewill, love is impossible. Love requires the option not to love. That is to say, we have been given the authority to reject or to ignore God. Further, since love cannot be compelled, the choice not to love must be compelling—or at the very least credible and persuasive.

That in turn is the reason God created a division of spiritual beings who were capable of rebelling, but yet possessed very limited creative capabilities. Rebellious, and thus fallen messengers, now demons, function in this role – one which God not only foresaw but which was actually necessary. They serve to make the choices to reject or ignore God plausible. They do so by using the only means they know: submission based upon concealment, corruption, and counterfeiting. More on this in a moment.

Remember, the *tsaba'* is a command-and-control construct, similar in operational structure to most militaries. For an interesting perspective on this, consider the fact that the institution falsely credited for preserving freedom, the United States military, is among the least free institutions on Earth.

Outside of the military, submission is most commonly manifest in politicized religions. It is why Catholicism prior to the Reformation was submit or die. Heretics were silenced, removed from society, tortured, and then killed. It is why "Islam" is the Arabic word for submission – a religion so intolerant of criticism, anyone daring to do so earns an avalanche of death threats. It is why the religion of man, Socialist Secular Humanism, manifests itself in dictatorial regimes devoid of freedom – places where the leaders control everything, even who lives and dies. Communism and Catholicism represent humankind's most adversarial institutions with regard to knowing and loving God. They are the most opposed to choice, especially an informed, judgmental exercise of freewill which is counter to their objectives.

While religions provide compelling counterfeits – dogmas that distance man from God by hiding, altering, and replacing the truth – it was essential from Yahowah's perspective that the *mal'ak* not be creative. Should Satan have been able to conceive anything beyond "not God," beyond concealing aspects of God's message, beyond corrupting God's instructions, and/or beyond counterfeiting God's symbols, the Adversary and his minions would have conceived schemes capable of completely hiding the Divine Writ, of convincing most everyone that Satan, Heylel ben Shachar, was God. And Satan would have become sufficiently oppressive to essentially constrain the exercise of freewill.

This is why the Adversary's schemes are all concealments, counterfeits, and corruptions of Yahowah's creativity, nothing more. At their core, Rabbinic Judaism, Roman Catholicism, Protestant Christianity, Muhammadan Islam, and to some degree Communism are variations of the politicized religious schemes first deployed in Sumer, Babylon, Assyria, and Egypt. Their common denominator is a mirror-image reversal, or backward portrayal, of Yahowah's relational plan. Freedom to choose is replaced by submission and obedience. Therefore, it should not be a surprise that religion is based upon the Latin word, "religare," meaning "to bind." We will find countless insights into this beast in our long walk through Yahowah's Word.

In this regard, the Hebrew word most often translated as "to save," *yasha'*, is more about freedom and liberation than salvation. Yahowah is the original and ultimate proponent of all things free, from His Towrah to His Covenant, from His Invitations to His Home.

I realize that this is a lot to extrapolate from the Hebrew words, *tsaba'*, *mala'kah,* and *mal'ak*, but I am confident that Yahowah used the first of these terms because He wants us to understand the nature of spirits, the importance of freewill, and the consequence of concealing, corrupting, and counterfeiting His purpose and plan. They are also vital because, apart from His *Ruwach Qodesh* | Set-Apart Spirit, these spiritual implements are the most effective way for Yahowah to interact with us – especially to protect us.

This is because a seven-dimensional being cannot enter a three-dimensional space. Just as Walt Disney interacted with his creation, Mickey Mouse, using drawing implements, Yah engages in lesser dimensions using spiritual implements. Therefore, to bridge the gap between the seven dimensions and the three dimensions known to us here on Earth, Yahowah conceived and deployed the full quotient of *tsaba'*.

Returning to *Bare'syth* | Genesis, Yahowah said of His ongoing involvement with His creation...

"**Therefore** (*wa*), **in** (*ba* – with) **the seventh** (*ha sheby'iy* – from *sheba'* – seven, solemn promise, or oath which fulfills and satisfies, the basis of the *shabat* – Sabbath) **day** (*yowm* – a measure of time from sunset to the following sundown), **God** (*'elohym* – the Almighty) **was and would be completing** (*kalah* – was finishing and would be accomplishing and concluding as He determined over time to fulfill (piel imperfect – the ongoing

294

relationship with and influence over the *mala'kah* would be active and ongoing regarding)) **His work pertaining to the Maternal aspects of His message** (*mala'kah huw'* – His expenditure of feminine energy and His maternal occupation (a feminine noun), from *mal'ak* – the mission of the heavenly messenger and spiritual representative of God), **which by way of this relationship** (*'asher* – by making a connection regarding the way to get the most out of life) **He had engaged in and would accomplish over a finite time** (*'asah* – He had prepared and acted upon and would fashion and produce in a moment in time, completed in the past, present, and or future (qal perfect – a genuine relationship existed in the past and could manifest again in the future for a limited duration of time between the *mala'kah* and what God sought and seeks to accomplish)).

So (*wa*), **He was observant and would be experiencing the Shabat** (*shabat* – He was reflecting upon the promise of seven and would continuously be experiencing the result of the oath and of seven which enriches; from *shaba'* – solemn promise and oath of seven which fulfills and satisfies while abundantly enriching (qal imperfect – He was actually and will be continually experiencing the oath associated with seven)) **during** (*ba*) **the seventh** (*ha shaby'iy* – the solemn promise of seven which fulfills and satisfies those who listen and are observant of the role of the seventh) **day** (*ha yowm* – time rendered from sunset-to-sunset) **because of** (*min* – as a result of) **all** (*kol*) **of His Divine endeavors as the Spiritual Messenger** (*mala'kah huw'* – of His Maternal message as conveyed through the prescribed work of the Spirit, His expenditure of energy pertaining to the focus of His feminine attributes and accomplishments, Her occupation and business (a feminine noun), from *mal'ak* – the mission of the heavenly messenger and spiritual representative of God) **which, to show the benefits of the relationship** (*'asher* – by making a connection regarding the correct path to walk to live a joyous life), **He had**

engaged and accomplished at the prescribed time (*'asah* – He had acted upon and would benefit from, He had prepared, fashioned, and produced by causing and creating during a finite period (qal perfect – He had actually done and achieved during this time))**.**" (*Bare'syth* / In the Beginning / Genesis 2:2)

There is no way to overestimate the importance of *shaby'iy*, from *sheba'* | seven, from Yahowah's perspective. That is especially true as it relates to it being the sum of six (the number of man) plus one (the number of God) combining to equal seven. When they are joined, God's purpose is achieved. When one is subtracted from the other, both God and man are diminished.

Before we ponder the full import of Yah's essential formula, let's defuse the bombshell laden in the last sentence. Man apart from God is diminished to nothingness. For those estranged from Yahowah, death is the end of life. The souls of those who perish unknown to God, of those who do not know or rely upon Yahowah and His seven-part restorative plan, will be diminished to nothingness, meaning that their consciousness will cease to exist.

According to the Word, such souls do not live forever in either heaven (*shamaym* – the spiritual abode of God) or hell (actually *She'owl*, which is the place of questioning). Therefore, it is precisely accurate, and in complete harmony with the Towrah to say that man apart from God is diminished.

It is also accurate to say that God apart from man is reduced. Unless God intended to grow through human relationships, there would be no reason to create mankind or the universe. In the same way, we become greater through the experiences and conversations we share with our spouses and children, God grows. Seven is greater than one. To be deprived of loving, familial relationships diminishes our Creator. There is no other viable explanation for why we exist. Growth is an essential element of life. And the Author of both is God.

The idea of God growing is such an uncommon concept, let's contemplate Yahowah's perspective on it…

"I will grow and thrive (*wa rabah* – I will be substantially increased) **with** (*'eth* – alongside) **your offspring** (*zera'* – seed) **in connection with** (*ka* – corresponding to) **the highest and most illuminated** (*kowkab* – light emanating from stars in the loftiness of) **heaven** (*shamaym* – the spiritual realm). **And I will give** (*nathan* – I will bestow and deliver as a gift) **to** (*la*) **your offspring** (*zera'*) **everything** (*kol*) **associated with** (*'eth*) **the realm** (*ha 'erets* – the land) **of God** (*'el*). **Also** (*wa*) **all** (*kol*) **people from every race and place** (*gowym* – gentile individuals) **on the earth** (*'erets*) **will be blessed with favorable circumstances** (*barak* – they will be greeted and adored) **through** (*ba* – with and because of) **your offspring** (*zera'* – seed)."** (*Bare'syth* / In the Beginning / Genesis 26:4)

While it may sound like an oversimplification, Yahowah's plan is based on the formula: six plus one equals seven. Some of the most obvious examples are: six days of creation with the seventh being a day of reflection. There have been six millennia of human history since 'Adam's and Chawah's ouster from the Garden and there will be one final Millennial Sabbath where mankind lives in the presence of God. There are six annual celebratory *Mow'ed Miqra'ey* or Invitations to be Called Out and Meet, which step-by-step lead to the seventh, Sukah, which is camping out with God. These seven days, set apart from all others, foretell and depict the means and timing of our reconciliation.

Every seventh year the land was to rest or lie fallow as prescribed by the Sabbatical Year. Then, every seven times seven years plus one, people and property are to be restored, as depicted in the *Yowbel*, or Year of Yah's Lamb. There are six sidelights and one central flame in the *Manowrah* | Menorah. It is one of the few objects in which Yahowah not only personally ordained the design, but also placed in His Home.

There are seven visits in corporeal form by Yahowah, six for revelation and the Covenant (all in our past) and one for reconciliation (in our not-too-distant future). They include One: "God walked in the Garden with 'Adam – the first man with a *neshamah* | conscience. (*Bare'syth* / Genesis 3:8) Two: "Yahowah appeared to 'Abraham" in the form of a "*'ysh* | individual *natsab* | standing upright." God talked, walked, and ate with him throughout the time the *beryth* | covenant relationship was being initiated. (Bare'syth 17 and 18) Three: In a meeting which included a wrestling match with Satan, Ya'aqob was renamed *Yisra'el*. (Bare'syth 32) Four: God met several times with Moseh prior to and during the forty-day revelation of His *Towrah* | Teaching. (Shemowth 24) Five: Yahowah appears to Yahowsha' in human form before the Battle of Jericho as is revealed in Yahowsha' 5:13-15. Six, God revealed Himself, speaking to *Shamuw'el* | Samuel near the Ark of the Covenant in *Shiloh* five times. The passage reveals: "Yahowah came, stood, and spoke to Samuel…appearing so as to be seen, revealing and disclosing Himself as the Word of Yahowah." (*Shamuw'el* / 1 Samuel 3) And Seven: Yahowah will return with *Dowd* | David, fulfilling the Towrah's remaining prophetic promises on *Yowm Kipurym* | the Day of Reconciliations in 2033. (Bare'syth 1, Qara' 23-25, Dany'el 9, and Howsha' 6)

Continuing to explore God's fascination with seven, Yahowah is depicted devoting seven Spirits to enlighten and embolden the Choter. The seven spirits are listed in *Yasha'yah* / Isaiah 11:1-2 as: Yahowah, Wisdom,

Understanding, Counsel, Power, Knowledge, and Respect. In the same order, the seven metaphors are: 1) Yahowah is Light, 2) Wisdom is nurtured by the Bread of Life, 3) Understanding comes from the Upright Pillar, 4) Counsel is provided by the Living Waters of the Set-Apart Spirit, 5) the Mighty One is the Rock of our Salvation, 6) the Truth and the Word are equivalent, and 7) Life is associated with the Set-Apart Family.

Even the Time of Ya'aqob's Troubles, that horrible culmination of man's and Satan's influence on Earth, is seven years long. So the bottom line is: if you want to understand Yahowah's timeline, you need to think in terms of six plus one – man plus God – equaling perfection, represented by seven. This formula encapsulates Yahowah's solemn oath and promise to His creation: Man in addition to God is perfect.

Before we leave the *Bare'syth* / Genesis 2:2 passage, there are three additional words deserving of closer scrutiny. It is interesting to note that *kalah,* translated as "completed," has two meanings which, apart from the Towrah, would be unrelated. In Bare'syth 2:1, *kalah* is conveyed as "were determined complete, were prepared and concluded as intended and accomplished as designed." Here, in Bare'syth 2:2, it was used to convey the idea that God "*kalah* – was and would be completing" the "*mala'kah* – Maternal and Spiritual aspects of His mission." Both times, *kalah* was conveyed in the imperfect, making the accomplishments ongoing.

The implication that Yahowah did not do any work on the seventh day, therefore, remains errant. Affirming the connotations of the ongoing nature of the conjugation, *kalah* speaks of "completing," not "ceasing." Further, there is very little evidence to suggest that *shabat* should be translated as "rest." Based upon "*sheba'* – seven," it more adroitly conveys the idea that a "promise has been made which is a sworn oath" – one which God intends to fulfill.

We are reintroduced to *mala'kah*. It isn't among the ordinary Hebrew words for work. These include *ma'aseh* (appearing 235 times plus 23 additional times as part of Ma'aseyah), *'abodah* (appearing 140 times), *'abad / 'ebed* (appearing 987 times), and *'asah* (which is used 2,633 times). Every scholastic etymological tome acknowledges that *mala'kah* is a cognate of *mal'ak*, but hardly anyone attempts to deduce its meaning from this obvious connection. That is remarkable since *mal'ak* is the Hebrew word that Bibles errantly render "angel" but which actually means: "spiritual messenger, heavenly representative, ambassador, envoy, or theophany – an implement serving God."

While most *mal'ak* are servants, tools if you will, within the heavenly host, the most acclaimed messenger, representative, and manifestation of God is the *Ruwach Qodesh* | Set-Apart Spirit. She is the embodiment of *mala'kah* – the feminine and Maternal manifestation of God's work.

In this regard, *mala'kah* should be understood in association with the feminine aspects of *mal'ak*. That is why I translated it: "His work, especially the Maternal aspects of His message" and then "His Divine endeavors as the Spiritual Messenger." To disassociate *mala'kah* from *mal'ak* is as disingenuous as failing to acknowledge its feminine characteristics.

Understanding *mal'ak*'s connection to the Set-Apart Spirit puts much of Yahowah's plan of reconciliation and renewal into focus. It explains the real significance of the Sabbath, of UnYeasted Bread, of Firstborn Children, and of the Promise of Seven, even Trumpets and Reconciliations. This is God's work. The result is the redemption and reconciliation of Yisra'el. So rest assured, we will deal with the consequence of *mal'ak* and its relationship to *mala'kah* many more times as we walk through Yah's Word.

300

Yahowah used both *mala'kah* and *'asah* twice in this statement. He did this so that we might reflect upon the differences between them – especially in the context of the Sabbath. *'Asah*, which means "to act upon something" or "to engage in it," is used throughout the Towrah for what will come to represent our ordinary work, while *mala'kah* will represent God's. The Sabbath is set apart for us to reflect upon what He has done for us.

Particularly revealing, with *kalah* scribed in the piel imperfect, and with it now referencing *mala'kah*, unlike the previous time which was scribed in the pual, where the ongoing interactions with the spiritual and material realms were to be passive, God is now seen actively engaging with the *mala'kah*. And that is as it should be since the *mala'kah* represents Yahowah's feminine and Maternal nature. The *mala'kah*, as the Set-Apart Spirit, is the force behind the enlightenment of men like *Dowd* | David and the fulfillment of the *Mow'ed Miqra'ey*, particularly Matsah, Bikuwrym, Shabuw'ah, and Taruw'ah.

Further, since " *'asah* – had engaged in and would accomplish over a finite time" was written in the qal perfect, we must realize that Yahowah's involvement in the past with the Spirit to guide universal development, and His future intervention with 'Adam, Noach, 'Abraham, Yitschaq, Ya'aqob, Moseh, Yahowsha', Shamuw'el, Dowd, Yasha'yah, and His Choter, would be time-constrained engagements. Similarly, Her conveyance and liberation of Dowd's soul to fulfill Matsah and enable Bikuwrym, then independently honor God's promises centuries later during the Ingatherings of Shabuw'ah and Taruw'ah, would all be one-and-done events.

Said another way, Yahowah will always be actively celebrating Shabat, and continuously working through His Ruwach Qodesh, but will never recreate this universe nor fulfill the Miqra'ey more than once. In fact, the Mow'edym of Matsah, Shabuw'ah, Taruw'ah, and Sukah will all be fulfilled during the Shabat, which is when Yahowah does His best work.

There are many, equally valid, ways to transliterate the Hebrew verb, "*shabat* – observe and experience the *Shabat*." Should you be checking, it is listed as *Strong's* H7673 and appears 71 times. These pronunciations include: *sabat, shabat, sabath, shabath, sabbat, shabbat, sabbath, shabbath, Sabat, Shabat, Sabath, Shabath, Sabbat, Shabbat, Sabbath,* and *Shabbath.* But what is important here, and what is not subject to alternative approaches, is that *shabat* was written as a verb in the third person, masculine, singular qal imperfect. This affirms that "He (speaking of Yahowah) would continue to actually experience and genuinely celebrate the Sabbath." We should do the same.

Since it has been ingrained in us to consider "the Sabbath" to be a proper noun, a title, or name no less, it is somewhat difficult to recognize that it is actually a verb conveying the idea of "God shabating." In this light, the reason many lexicons render "*shabat* – to observe the Sabbath," rather than "to cease," is because they, unlike most Bible translators, recognize the association of *shabat* with two of the Towrah's most important verbs: "*shama'* – to listen" (appearing 1159 times (*Strong's* H8085)) and "*shamar* – to closely examine and carefully consider" (appearing 468 times (*Strong's* H8104)).

Moreover, if God had wanted to say that "He rested" as opposed to "He observed the Shabat," He would have used "*nuwach* – rest," as in "relaxed after having settled His affairs." If He intended to say "ceased," He would have used *batal* (*Strong's* H989), which also conveys "stopped." There are a number of other Hebrew words to say stopped such as: *satham, shasam, saker,* and *'atsar.*

The "ceased" connotation of *shabat* is derived in part from an inadequate rendering of *nuwach* as simply "rested," as opposed to "settled," in *Shemowth* / Exodus 20:11. There, *nuwach* communicates the idea that the Sabbath is the day Yahowah "settled" us in His Home by "settling" our debt as well as the conflicts which have separated us from Him. And because He has done this work on our behalf, we can rest, reflect, and rely upon Him.

In this regard, *nuwach* is the basis of *Noach's* | Noah's name. His survival was anything but restful. However, by listening to Yahowah and then doing what God asked, the Ark settled safely, saving everyone aboard.

In our quest to know what it means "to Sabbat," there is a Hebrew noun, "*shabat* – Sabbath" (*Strong's* H7676), which is represented in the text by the same three letters. And while we are told that it is based upon the verb form, all that means is that the Shabat is actionable.

There is another vocalization of the word which appears sparingly, albeit with different definitions. *Sebeth*, used on three occasions, is translated as "loss of time" and "still." And *sebeth* is found an additional four times and is rendered as "seat." So, it's obvious that we have to look elsewhere to learn how "to Sabbat."

Since this is the first time the word *shabat* appears in the Towrah, we can take our clues from the context. Yahowah was completing His presentation of how He spoke the universe and life into existence. Therefore, on the Shabat, we may want to listen to what our Creator has to say. It is also used in conjunction with God's *mala'kah*, where the work and message are ongoing.

Interwoven into His *Bare'syth* / Genesis testimony, Yahowah predicted the future history of humankind by way of a broad outline and revealed the broad strokes of His plan to reconcile mankind back into fellowship with Him. Therefore, on the Shabat, we can celebrate together by observing the rest of His testimony.

Beyond the insights related to "observing the Sabbath" which can be drawn from the context, there are some obvious word associations that I am confident God would like us to contemplate. In *Bare'syth* / Genesis 2:2, Yahowah has set "*shabat* – observing the Sabbath" between two references to "*ha sheby'iy yowm* – the seventh day." By doing so, He has reinforced two things. The Shabat is to be observed on the seventh day of the week, not the first as is the practice of Christians, or the sixth as with Muslims. Further *shabat* and *sheby'iy* – Shabat and seventh – are closely related etymologically and conceptually.

To observe the Shabat is to closely observe the meaning of seven throughout the Towrah. And in this light, *sheba'* (*Strong's* H7651 (found 394 times)), the Hebrew word for "seven" and *shabat* are very closely related. Shabat can, therefore, be best understood within the context of "*sheba'* – seven" rather than "*nuwach* – to settle and rest."

The most telling of Yahowah's application of seven is played out in His seven *Mow'ed Miqra'ey*. They represent God's promise to do His "*mala'kah* – spiritual work and deliver His heavenly message" to save mankind. So, since Yahowah's *mala'kah* has been directly associated with "*shabat* – observing the Sabbath" in Bare'syth 2:2, we should acknowledge this promise on this day.

Speaking of acknowledging God's promise as part of "*shabat* – observing the Shabat," *shaba'* (*Strong's* H7650) is used 187 times in towrah to convey: "making a vow and issuing a promise." This is not a coincidence.

Similarly, *shaba'* (*Strong's* H7646) means "to satisfy and fulfill" a prediction and oath. This then unifies "*shabat* – experiencing the Shabat" with Yahowah's "*mala'kah* – spiritual and Maternal work of delivering His heavenly message" with the fulfillment of these seven *Mow'ed Miqra'ey*. These Invitations to be Called Out and Meet with God represent the most important fulfillments in the Towrah and Prophets.

Therefore, "*shabat* – to observe, experience, and celebrate the Shabat" encourages us to ponder each of the following word associations:

One... *ha Shabat* – the Shabat, which is the more common noun version of the verb: is to be spent "*shabat* – observing the Sabbath." The name defines its purpose.

Two... *Sheby'iy* – seventh: tells us to make the seventh day special, setting it apart from all others as a day to reflect upon Yahowah's testimony and celebrate His promises.

Three... *Sheba'* – seven: encourages us to realize that every important aspect of Yahowah's plan is based upon this number. It is a formula which reveals that God (who is one) in addition to man (who was created on the sixth day) equates to perfection (*sheba'* – seven). This is most adroitly embodied within the *Mow'ed Miqra'* of *Sukah* where, after approaching through six steps, we are afforded the opportunity to camp out with Yahowah.

Four... *Shaba'* – to satisfy and fulfill: inspires us to recognize that Yahowah satisfied the problem of religion and politics, settling our debts through the ransom He paid and by the "*mala'kah* – spiritual work done by His Heavenly Maternal Messenger and Spirit," especially upon "*Matsah* – UnYeasted Bread," and "*Bikuwrym* – Firstborn Children," and will do so on "*Shabuw'ah* – the Promise of Seven."

Five... *Shaba'* – a vow, oath, and promise: lies at the heart of God's message to mankind. The Towrah represents Yahowah's vow to establish a "*beryth* – familial covenant relationship" with humankind and His "*shaba'* – promise" to save us from ourselves.

Six... *Shama'* – listen: to Yahowah's voice on the Shabat by reciting the Towrah, Prophets, and Psalms. It is

305

what Dowd did in preparation for writing the Mizmowr and Mashal and then serving as the Passover Lamb.

Seven... *Shamar* – observe: what God has written to us in His Towrah on the Shabat, closely examining and carefully considering His prophetic testimony.

Additionally, *shabar* is "to contemplate favorably." *Shib'ah* is the "satisfactory fulfillment of an oath or promise." And *shaber* means "to interpret and explain the meaning or significance of a communication."

Collectively then, the second chapter of Yahowah's genesis testimony begins:

"Thereby (*wa***), the universe and the spiritual realm (***ha shamaym***) as well as the material realm and the earth (***ha 'erets***) were being completed, prepared such that they would conclude as intended, everything accomplished as designed (***kalah***) including all (***wa kol***) the spiritual messengers and heavenly implements (***tsaba' hem***).** (*Bare'syth* / Genesis 2:1)

Therefore (*wa***), during (***ba***) the seventh (***ha shabyi'y***) day (***yowm***), God (***'elohym***) was completing and accomplishing, as He was determined to fulfill (***kalah***) His work pertaining to the Maternal aspects of His message, His expenditure of feminine energy and His Maternal work (***mala'kah huw'***), which by way of this relationship (***'asher***), He had engaged in and would accomplish (***'asah***).**

So (*wa***), He was observing the Shabat, celebrating the promise of seven and reflecting on that which would be abundantly satisfying (***shabat***) during (***ba***) the seventh (***ha shabyi'y***) day (***ha yowm***) because of (***min***) all (***kol***) of His Divine endeavors as the Heavenly Messenger, the communication through the effort of the Spirit (***mala'kah huw'***) which, to show the benefits of the relationship (***'asher*** – by making a connection regarding**

306

the correct path to walk to live a joyous life), **He had engaged in and would accomplish** (*'asah*)." (*Bare'syth* / In the Beginning / Genesis 2:2)

ᛯᛦᚤᛯ

Christians ignore the Divine connection to the Sabbath, and Jews make a troublesome game of it, while Muslims use it to practice jihad. And yet, there is no denying that the seventh day means a great deal to our Creator. This is a hard concept to swallow for those besmirching it, torturing themselves on it, or using it to terrorize others...

"**As a result** (*wa* – then, therefore), **Almighty God** (*'elohym*) **blessed and adored** (*barak* – knelt down and lowered Himself to greet and extol (piel imperfect – with this stem and conjugation, the seventh becomes a time for our ongoing benefit and approval)) **His association with** (*'eth*) **the seventh** (*ha shabyi'y* – solemn promise which fulfills and satisfies those who listen and are observant of the role of seven with their lives abundantly enriched) **day** (*yowm*), **and** (*wa*) **He set it apart** (*qodesh* – He separated it from others to purify by means of it, making it uncommon, unique, and special) **because indeed** (*ky* – surely and truthfully) **during and with it** (*ba 'eth huw'*) **He observed the Shabat** (*shabat* – He celebrated the promise to enrich and satisfy in accord with seven; from *shaba'* – solemn promise and oath which fulfills and satisfies by resolving debts and settling us in His home (qal perfect – literally and actually, completely and totally, at some point in time)) **on account of** (*min*) **all** (*kol*) **His heavenly endeavors as the Spiritual Messenger** (*mala'kah* – of His Maternal message as conveyed through the prescribed work of the Spirit, His expenditure of energy pertaining to the focus of His feminine attributes and accomplishments (a feminine noun), from *mal'ak* – the mission of the heavenly messenger and spiritual representative of God) **which, to show the benefits of the relationship** (*'asher* – by making a connection regarding the correct path to walk to live a joyous life), **He, Almighty God, had conceived and created** (*bara' 'elohym* – God had caused to exist, formed and fashioned, introducing into existence (qal perfect)), **prepared and produced** (*la 'asah* – acted upon and engaged in, accomplished and done (qal infinitive – a verbal noun, which can intensify the action))." (*Bare'syth* / In the Beginning / Genesis 2:3)

In all of the world, throughout the entirety of human history, there is only one credible source of Divine revelation. And His testimony is unambiguous: the *Shabat* – the seventh day – is the time Yahowah has chosen to bless those He adores. Those who bow down and worship their god on Sundays, or who prostrate themselves on Fridays, have upended God's approach while rejecting His preference.

To appreciate the Covenant, we must become comfortable with and accept, even celebrate, the realization that Yahowah, as our Heavenly Father, wants to "*barak* – get down on His knees to lift us up in love." At the same time, we must reject the insidious and insulting notion that God wants us to bow down and worship Him.

Since the Covenant is His Home and Family, to enter we must also accept Yahowah's timing and approach. And that means that we should also come to adore the Shabat, "*qodesh* – setting this day apart from all others" such that it becomes a special time in our relationship.

Qodesh, which means "set apart," and thus "uncommon and special," is among the most telling words in Yahowah's *towrah* | teaching. Everything that is important to God is *qodesh*, including: the *Ruwach Qodesh* | Set-Apart Spirit. The *Shabat* is *qodesh* as are: Yahowah's name, the *Miqra'ey* | Invitations to be Called Out and Meet, the *Beryth* | Covenant Family, the *Towrah* | Guidance and Teaching, *Yahuwdym* | Beloved of Yah, *Yisra'el* | Individuals who Engage and Endure with God, *Yaruwshalaim* | Source of Reconciliation, *Mowryah* | to Revere Yah, *Tsyown* | Signs Posted Along the Way, and even *Dowd* | the Beloved Son of God. Further, it is the Mashyach Dowd, the King of Kings, the *Qodesh* | Set-Apart One of Yisra'el, and our Shepherd who will return to usher in the Millennial Shabat on the Sabbath celebration of Sukah, the seventh Called-Out Assembly, in 2033 CE.

To be set apart is to be uncommon. And since the most common of human institutions are politics, patriotism, militarism, religion, and conspiracies, to be *qodesh* we must separate ourselves from these things if we want to be included in God's Covenant Family. The very things that men and women are most prone to align themselves with are the things which exclude a relationship with God.

Yahowah has reinforced His example. He is not only actively observing the Shabat, this time He has accompanied it with a blessing, demonstrating His love for this day. If you want to be set apart unto God, set it apart to be with God.

It is well past time for honesty, to be forthright and blunt. In the shadow of Yahowah's assessment of the *Shabat* | Seventh Day, especially if you are a *Yahuwd* | a Jew but also if you are a *Gowy* | a Gentile, 99.9999% of people, past and present, are either misled or mistaken about God. With regard to the Sunday Worshipers, the wannabe apostle Paul, who was born as *Sha'uwl* | Question Him, and who was proclaimed in the Prophets as the "Plague of Death," the author of fourteen New Testament books, the subject of Acts, and the inspiration behind Mark, Luke, and Matthew, was, by his own admission, demon-possessed. The religion of Christianity was the result, inspired by Satan, to discredit and degrade, to delegitimize and destroy, to malign and murder Jews. In its appalling attempt to invert the truth, the overwhelming preponderance of the Christian New Testament became disreputable and dishonest, even delusional and despicable – conclusions I will prove beyond any doubt throughout these books, most especially in *Twistianity*, *Observations*, and *Coming Home*.

God did not replace Jews with Gentiles, Dowd with "Jesus," His Covenant with a Church, His Towrah and Prophets with mindless and mercurial rabbinical or Christian drivel, His Miqra'ey with delusional pagan holidays, a relationship with a religion, or the Shabat with Sunday. If you are a Jew, do not seek accommodation with this Anti-Semitic institution in the hope of peace. If you are a Gentile, run from it.

Addressing those who prostrate themselves to Allah on Fridays, Muhammad, by his own admission, was also demon-possessed. Inspired by Satan, his Quran is not only the most Anti-Semitic book ever written, it is the dumbest. What Satan began with Paul and the Sunday Worshipers, the Adversary sought to complete with the sexual pervert and terrorist Muhammad and his religion *Islam* | Submission. Second only to Christianity, it too has been a plague upon the Chosen People.

Addressing those who have corrupted the Shabat, upending it from a day of love, a day of blessings, and a day of active reflection and engagement in the Covenant with their paralyzing rules, Rabbinic Jews have done greater harm to themselves and their people than Christianity and Islam combined. May it be said unequivocally: God Damn Religion!

Should you be taken aback by such testimony, be assured, not only is what I'm telling you true, indeed rationally irrefutable, Yahowah's assessment of these men and their religions is far less accommodating. We ought not respect what God abhors.

Returning to the Towrah's Instruction, this is now the fourth time that Yahowah has directly associated His celebration of the Shabat with His *"mala'kah* – spiritual engagement through the Maternal manifestation of His nature."* And it would be so because She separated us from the devious nature of the plague of religion on the *Mow'ed Miqra'* of *Matsah* | UnYeasted Bread on a Sabbath in 33 CE – removing this deplorable fungus from our souls.

Bare'syth / Genesis 2:3 is the third of 330 times *barak* is used throughout the Towrah and Prophets. The first occurrence was in Genesis 1:22 where, after creating animals with *nepesh* | souls on the fifth day, God: **"adored and blessed them by kneeling down to greet them and lift them up** (*barak*), **saying: "Be productive and flourish, conceiving life in abundance."** Therefore, *barak* is tied to something God does out of love which is instrumental to life.

The second occurrence of *barak* is directly attributed to mankind. Five statements later, in *Bare'syth* / Genesis 1:27-28, we find: **"So God created 'Adam in His image, in the image of God, He created him. Male and female, He created them. And God knelt down next to them** (*barak* – adoring and blessing them, greeting them in love and lifting them up), **saying to them, 'Be fruitful and become even greater.'"** Since *barak* is the first thing Yahowah does after creating man, it tells us that He loves us and that His first priority is to come down to our level to greet us and raise us up to Him, making us exceedingly great.

While we were made in the image of God, in the shade of God so to speak, *barak* provides the means to increase our dimensions and enlightenment sufficiently to be substantially more like Him – to become enriched and empowered. The source of Yahowah's love stems from His willingness to diminish Himself to elevate us. This is the essence of the plan of salvation that God incorporated into the *Mow'ed Miqra'ey*, and which He fulfilled through the Set-Apart Spirit. He allowed His Beloved Son's soul to descend into *She'owl* to redeem His children. The Upright One bent down so that we could stand upright with Him.

Continuing with Yahowah's testimony, God revealed:

"**These are** (*'el-leh* – in close proximity to provide perspective, here are) **the written records of the birth and genealogy** (*towledowt* – the inscribed account of the conception of a family line along with the story, the proceedings and results) **of the heavens and earth** (*shamaym wa ha 'erets* – of the spiritual and material realms) **when they were created** (*ba bara' hem* – during their genesis when they came into existence (nifal infinitive – the subject carries out and then receives the benefits associated with creation in a demonstrative and definitive way as a verbal noun)) **in the day** (*ba ha yowm* – during the time) **Yahowah** (𐤄𐤅𐤄𐤉 – a transliteration of *YaHoWaH* as instructed in His *towrah* – teaching regarding His *hayah* – existence) **acted and engaged as God to prepare and produce** (*'asah 'elohym* – Almighty made, fashioned and formed (qal infinitive)) **the material realm** (*'erets* – matter and the earth) **and the spiritual realm** (*wa shamaym* – the universe)." (*Bare'syth* / In the Beginning / Genesis 2:4)

Now that the universe had been created, the Creator introduced Himself by name for the first time. God's name is Yahowah. In the original pictographic alphabet, it was written 𐤄𐤅𐤄𐤉. Reading from right to left, we find Yahowah reaching down and out to us with an open, welcoming hand. It is extended on behalf of two individuals, both of whom are standing up, reaching up, and looking toward Him. The two unbowed individuals are indicative of 'Abraham and Sarah, the father and mother of the Covenant Family. Between them is a tent peg, symbolic of securing and enlarging a home while connecting and augmenting the inhabitants.

These insights are always relevant, but no more so than when Yahowah makes the connection between His name and "*towledowt* – the written records and the inscribed account of the conception of the family along with its story, the proceedings and the results."

This means that God's name isn't God, Lord, Ba'al, Amen Ra, Osiris, Isis, Zeus, Jupiter, Jesus, Christ, Jehovah, Apollo, Allah, Shiva, Buddha, or HaShem. God has a name, and now you know it.

His name is so important, so relevant to knowing Him, so essential to our salvation, Yahowah will inscribe it in His Towrah, Naby', wa Mizmowr 7000 times. It's obvious He wants us to know it and to use it.

Yahowah called His written account of creation's history a genealogical record. By inference then, this is the story of the birth of the cosmos. It is also the future history of the generations of man.

By reflecting on the genealogy of creation, we noticed that something occurred during each creative era which was prophetic of man's future history as it would play out in one-thousand-year intervals. There was also an element to each day that represented a significant aspect of God's plan of redemption.

Streamlined for easier reading and better retention, here are Yahowah's final statements on the creative process…

"As a result (*wa*), Almighty God (*'elohym*) blessed and adored, lowering Himself to greet and provide benefits (*barak*) relative to His association with (*'eth*) the seventh abundantly enriching and satisfying (*ha shabyi'y*) day (*yowm*).

313

He set it apart as special, making it unique and uncommon (*wa qodesh*) because indeed (*ky*) during it (*ba 'eth huw'*) He observed the Shabat, celebrating and experiencing the promise of seven (*shabat*) on account of (*min*) all (*kol*) His Spiritual endeavors as the Maternal manifestation of the message (*mala'kah*) which, to show the benefits of the relationship (*'asher*), He, Almighty God, had conceived and created (*bara' 'elohym*), prepared and produced (*la 'asah*). (*Bare'syth* / Genesis 2:3)

In close proximity, and to provide perspective, here are (*'el-leh*) the written records of the birth and genealogy, the inscribed account of the conception of the family line along with the story (*towledowt*) of the heavens and earth (*shamaym wa ha 'erets*) when they were created (*ba bara' hem*) in the day (*ba ha yowm*) Yahowah (𐤉𐤄𐤅𐤄) acted and engaged as God to prepare and produce (*'asah 'elohym*) the material realm (*'erets*) and the spiritual realm (*wa shamaym*)." (*Bare'syth* / Genesis 2:4)

It is the most important story ever told. Without this story, there would be no other stories to tell.

𐤉𐤄𐤅𐤄

It's interesting that *Bare'syth* / Genesis 5:5 tells us: "**All the days** (*kol ha yowmym*) **which by relationship** (*'asher*) **'Adam** (*'Adam*) **was restored to life** (*chayah* – remained alive after being renewed, continued to live once revived, was spared, saved, and preserved) **were** (*hayah* – existed as) **nine hundred and thirty years, and he died** (*wa muwth huw'*)."

Since 'Adam represents the first thousand years of mankind's history, as well as our restoration to life by way

314

of a personal one-on-one relationship with God, this statement suggests that 'Adam lived five or six decades with Yahowah in the perfection of the Garden before the Adversary was allowed to slither in and corrupt God's Word. Yahowah has a penchant for the number seven.

According to the corroborating genealogical testimony preserved in the *Septuagint* (prepared as early as 250 BCE) and Samaritan *Pentateuch* (perhaps dating to around 125 BCE (of which there are some 6,000 differences with the Masoretic Text, 2,000 of which are supported by the *Septuagint*)), 'Adam's expulsion from the Garden occurred in 3968 BCE, year 0 Yah on God's calendar.

Two is the number of choice. The second day in the creation account predicted that this era would be about separation and water. And so, it would be: the flood separated the lone family who chose God from those who did not. In 2968 BCE Noach was born and later afforded the opportunity to save his family and avoid the ensuing deluge which occurred during this era, commencing with a massive asteroid impact right when Yahowah told us it would occur.

This is evidenced by Burckle's discovery of an eighteen-mile-wide crater 12,500 feet below the surface of the Indian Ocean near Madagascar, whose impact occurred 4,400 years ago. It produced a 600-foot-high tsunami that flooded Mesopotamia all the way up to the Black Sea. It inundated the region where men with a conscience had come to be belligerent toward God. The message is that listening to Yahowah and acting upon His guidance prepares our souls to live with Him.

Regarding this choice to accept or reject God's testimony, the acclaimed historian Arnold Toynbee, in his twelve-volume *Study of History*, written between 1934 and 1961, described the rise, flower, and decline of 26 cultures from Egypt, Greece and Rome to Polynesia and Peru. After

315

stating that "Civilizations die from suicide, not by murder," (destroying themselves from within) the British historian queried: "So what does the universe look like?" He answered, "It looks as if everything were on the move either toward its Creator or away from Him.... The course of human history consists of a series of encounters...in which each man, woman, or child...is challenged by God to make the choice between doing His will and refusing to do it. When Man refuses, he [accepts] the consequences." While I would have changed that to more accurately read "to make the choice between listening to God and acting upon His instructions," Toynbee was correct.

The third day represents the time life burst forth on planet Earth – flourishing, reproducing, and growing. Not surprisingly, three is the number of family – father, mother, and child: the cradle of human life. Historically, during mankind's third one-thousand-year era, we humans multiplied prodigiously as did our civilizations. So, right on schedule, exactly one thousand years later, in 1968 BCE (year 2000 Yah), after 'Abraham left Babylon, the world's religious center and lone superpower, and en route to the Promised Land, Yahowah established His Covenant relationship with him. It was ratified on Mount *Mowryah* | Revere Yah – the most important place on Earth. In the years which followed, 'Abraham sowed the seeds of the Covenant Family.

For the next forty *Yowbel* (meaning Yahowah's Lamb is God), which is 2,000 years, man's history from Yahowah's perspective and His redemptive plan are one. They are embodied in the *Miqra'ey, Beryth,* and *Towrah.* As we shall discover in the next several chapters, father and son, 'Abraham and Yitschaq, acted out a dress rehearsal for the fulfillment of Passover in year 4000 Yah, the very year the third millennium of human history began.

A thousand years thereafter, and four years after the conclusion of his first of three lives, Dowd was commemorated in the 89th Mizmowr as the living embodiment of the Covenant, becoming the cornerstone of God's Home on Mowryah as construction commenced in year 3000 Yah / 968 BCE. Exactly 1,000 years later, in 33 CE, at the close of the fourth millennium, also on *Mowryah*, Dowd became the *Pesach 'Ayil | Passover Lamb* as Father and Son fulfilled the first of four Miqra'ey that year.

From a redemptive perspective, the seminal events in human history occur every forty *Yowbel* Years. These multiples of forty, fifty-year segments of time, depicted as "seven times seven years plus one," determine the years Yahowah engages to restore His relationship with us. Forty is the number of completion, especially as it relates to a time of testing. And the *Yowbel* is symbolic of Yahowah, our God, forgiving our debts and setting us free from human oppression. The *Yowbel* foreshadow the restoration provided by Dowd and the Set-Apart Spirit during Chag Matsah.

While nothing was created on the fourth day, it remains the longest narrative because it foretells the fulfillment of the first three *Mow'ed*, each enabling the benefits of the Covenant. It is the day the work of the greater and lesser lights, Father and Son, Yahowah and Dowd, became visible to us as a sign of the Covenant. A child was born and a son was provided to guide us Home.

In the final year of man's fourth millennium, in the *Yowbel* year 4000 Yah / 33 CE, Dowd honored the words he had written about himself enduring Roman crucifixion as the Passover Lamb on the Miqra' of Pesach, opening the doorway to life on the *Mow'ed*. The following day, on the *Miqra'* of *Matsah*, a Sabbath, Dowd's soul carried the guilt of every Covenant member into She'owl, depositing it there to make us appear perfect in God's eyes. Reunited with the Ruwach Qodesh, Yahowah honored the promise

317

of Firstborn Children the next day with His Firstborn, facilitating our adoption into the Covenant Family.

The fourth Invitation to be Called Out and Meet with Yahowah, the Feast of Seven Shabats, or *Shabuw'ah*, will be fulfilled on the appointed day, the Shabat of May 22nd at sunset, in 2026, at the commencement of the Time of Israel's Troubles and seven years prior to the Messiah's return. The prophetic significance of the fourth day of creation is thereby honored.

In the fifth creative day, the first mortal *nepesh* | souls were conceived of water, helping us understand that our souls must be cleansed to grow. On this day, Yahowah told us that "great serpents" would "move about...producing after their kind." From a historical perspective, the souls created on this day were surrounded by them – satanic deceptions of the worst kind: religions. That is why, from a redemptive perspective, God reminded us twice during the fifth day that living souls reproduce after their kind. A society drenched in religion will breed deception, death, and damnation.

The marker for the initiation of year 5000 Yah (1033 CE) is obscure because it is not especially relevant, even to those who closely observe the Towrah and seek to correlate its timeline with human history. But nonetheless, in 1033 CE, the waters beneath where the Temple had once stood, and now beneath Islamic trophies, were poisoned. This may have served as a fulfillment of the *Bamidbar* / In the Wilderness / Numbers' 5 prophecy whereby the world was declared "unfaithful." There was a resounding divorce decree. If nothing else, it is a reminder that God prefers divorce over remaining in a loveless relationship. And that is something to think about.

From the Towrah's perspective, six is the number of man, and so it was that on this day man was conceived. From the perspective of Yahowah's relationship plan, we have reached the object of restoration. That is why we were told in the words which precede the introduction of 'Adam that: "renewed and restored life exists upright and established." We discovered that "'Adam was fashioned in God's image, after His likeness." More importantly, the Towrah reveals: "And God knelt down next to them, adoring and blessing them, greeting them in love and lifting them up, saying to them, 'Be fruitful and flourish, be productive and increase, becoming exceedingly great.'" When we are restored to life, we become like our Creator. So spiritually, the sixth era is about transforming man into the image of God so that we can live upright in His presence during the seventh day.

Historically, the sixth millennium dawned deluged in the errant ways of humankind. It will terminate with a seven-year tribulation of our making: the Time of Ya'aqob's Troubles. During this period, the religion of man was conceived and then it devoured liberty and livelihoods. Many of man's best lies – Catholicism and other forms of Christianity, Rabbinic Judaism and Qabalah, Islam and Nazism, even Communism – were mixed together to create a toxic brew. Today, Woke Progressives as the prodigy of the Socialist Secular Humanist religion permeate the globe, becoming the only acceptable belief system in American politics, the media, and academia – even in the sciences. Those duped by this deadly decree have murdered over two hundred million souls during the last century alone. We have turned ourselves into gods and become foolish and deadly.

Soon the era of mortal man will be over. The seventh day begins on a Sabbath, the *Mow'ed Miqra'* of *Sukah* | Shelters in 2033 (year 6000 Yah). Those who come home to Yah and survive the Time of Ya'aqob's Troubles will enter the Millennial Kingdom. They will get to camp out with God for one thousand years, living on an Earth

319

restored to the status of the Garden of 'Eden until year 7000 Yah. Then, there will be a new beginning.

Such is the genealogical history of mankind from conception to perfection. It is the story of six plus one.

Bringing it all together, one (3968-2968 BCE) is about God who is one creating a one-on-one relationship with the first man. Two (2968-1968 BCE) is the presentation of choice, choosing the Ark or the deluge brought on by mankind's delusions of grandeur. Three (1968-968 BCE) is the story of family, and so 'Abraham established what would become the Covenant Family in the third millennium of man. Four (968 BCE-33 CE) completes the time of testing and the arrival of the greater light at its inception and the lesser light at the twilight of the fourth millennial epoch as we transition from Dowd's first life to his second, from Shepherd to Lamb, from a united Yisra'el to a world united against Yahuwdym. Five (33-1033 CE) designates the time of the great serpent and, consequently, the era of religious confusion. Six (1033-2033 CE) is the time of man, the time that gave rise to Socialist Secular Humanism and its replacement moral code, Political Correctness, where being judgmental has become a sin. This has led to injustice, immorality, irrational opinions, deceit, destruction, and death on an unparalleled scale. Seven (2033-3033 CE) is the *shabat*, the time man and God will come together, our debts settled so that we can settle down with Him and camp out for a thousand years.

In light of Yahowah's focus on seven and the Sabbath, if you are a Roman Catholic, Orthodox Christian, Protestant, or Evangelical attending Sunday Worship services at the behest of a pastor or priest, believing that you are doing something good that is pleasing to God, sorry, but you are dead wrong. Yahowah doesn't want to be worshiped, as worship has no place in a familial relationship. Remember *barak*: God bowed down so He could lift us up. And Sunday is "the Lord's Day," where

Bel and Ba'al, Ra and Zeus, Jupiter and Satan are worshiped – the day virtually all wannabe gods want mankind to bow down before them.

The Catholic Church, misguided by Paul, became so anti-Semitic and anti-Towrah, so pro-sun-god worship and pro-religion, they made it a crime punishable by death to observe the Sabbath, mandating that all things required on that day be transferred to the "Lord's Day, Sunday." While they were at it, they also made it a capital offense to gather on any of Yahowah's seven *Mow'ed Miqra'ey* in accordance with His Towrah instructions. The Invitations to be Called Out and Meet with God of Passover, UnYeasted Bread, Firstborn Children, Seven Shabats, Trumpets, Reconciliations, and Shelters were replaced with Satanic substitutes, like: New Year's Day, Lent, Good Friday, Easter Sunday, the Assumption of Mary, Halloween, and Christmas. Even today, almost all Orthodox, Protestant, and Evangelical congregations follow their pagan example. Ignoring Yahowah's *Mow'ed Miqra'ey*, they have become a "Church" – a place to go in, not out, which borrows its name from Circe, a Greek and, later, Germanic sun goddess. And then there is the unGodly devotion to Purim, Rosh Hashanah, and Hannukah by Jews who have forgotten Matsah and Taruw'ah while inverting the purpose of Kipurym.

𐤉𐤄𐤅𐤄

You may think that one day is as good as any other. You may believe that God is not troubled by the details and does not mind men exchanging His plan for one of their own. You may consider the Sunday substitute less significant than what is in your heart, your intent and purpose. You may justify Sunday by reasoning that since so many religious folks observe it, it can't be contrary to

God. But if you do, your god isn't the Spirit who inspired the Towrah.

Unaware of the redemptive significance of the Passover Lamb or the special Shabat of UnYeasted Bread, you may think that Sunday worship is justified because the supposed "resurrection" of a corruptible body was somehow more significant than Yahowah's plan of salvation. Unaware that the only eyewitness testimony regarding what actually occurred was composed by *Dowd* | David a thousand years in advance of his fulfillment of Chag Matsah, you may think that the body of the Passover Lamb, rather than incinerated, was resurrected. You might even believe that nothing worth noting occurred during UnYeasted Bread.

Indoctrinated by religion, and confused by Pauline Doctrine, you might think that the "Church" has been given the authority to establish doctrine, even to change God's instructions as its clergy sees fit. You may be so lost as to suppose that there is no rhyme or reason to the Towrah, or that it is no more rational than the religions spawned to negate it. For you, the notion that it contains a mathematical equation that defines God's purpose, His timeline and His plan, may well be unfathomable.

If so, Hosea 4:6 was written for you.

"**'My people** (*'am 'any* – My nation and family) **have destroyed themselves and they will perish** (*damah* – they have cut themselves off and will succumb for a time, they have ruined themselves and are devastated (niphal perfect – they have actively participated in their own demise and will perish as a result of their actions for a duration of time)) **because of** (*min* – from) **a lack of understanding** (*bely ha da'ath* – corrupted information, inadequate knowledge, and deficient discernment being without perception by negating observation and avoiding instruction).

322

Indeed, because (*ky* – truthfully as a result and as a consequence) you (*'atah*) have refused, avoided, and even rejected (*ma'as* – have spurned and despised, literally limited an association with and loathed, showing an aversion to (qal perfect – the avoidance was complete and the rejection was literal)) knowledge and instruction (*da'ath* – information and discernment and therefore understanding, being observant and discriminating, informed and rational), so then (*wa* – therefore) I will continuously reject and actually avoid you (*ma'as 'atah* – I will literally and consistently avoid you and disassociate from you, will rebuff you, limiting any association with you, showing an aversion to you (qal imperfect – actually, literally, and continuously refuse to allow with unfolding consequences over time)) from approaching Me and acting like priests and ministers (*min kahan la 'any* – from serving as counselors or clerics in association with Me and from adorning oneself and dressing up as if they were a priest (piel infinitive – as a verbal, and thus demonstrable noun, *kahan* is speaking of men who claim to be serving God, especially when acting in the role of mediators, revealing that they have brought this on themselves and will be banned as a result of what they have done to keep others from approaching God)).

Since (*wa* – because) you have continually ignored (*shakach* – you have consistently overlooked and literally forgotten, you have lost sight of the significance of and responded improperly to (qal imperfect – actually, consistently, literally, and continuously failing to consider)) the Towrah (*Towrah* – the Source of Instruction and Teaching, Guidance and Direction; derived from: *tow* – signed, written, and enduring, *towrah* – way of treating people, *tuwr* – giving us the means to explore, to seek, to find, and to choose, *yarah* – the source of instruction, teaching, guidance, and direction that flows from God, which *tuwb* – provides answers to facilitate our restoration and return, even our response and reply to that which is *towb* – good, pleasing, beneficial, favorable, healing, and right, and that which causes us to be loved, become acceptable, and to endure, *tahowr* and *tohorah* – purifying and cleansing us, thereby *towr* – providing us with the opportunity to change our attitude, thinking, and direction) **of your God** (*'elohym 'atah*), **I also** (*'any gam* – therefore, I) **will consistently overlook and no longer be mindful of** (*shakah* – I will ignore and forget about, viewing as less significant, and for an ongoing period no longer remembering or responding to (qal imperfect)) **your children** (*ben 'atah* – your sons, your offspring and descendants).'" (*Howsha'* / Salvation / Hosea 4:6)

Ignorance is not bliss. It is deadly, not only for oneself, but for one's children. When we reject the Towrah we are neglecting our primary responsibility toward our children.

Those who either advocate or justify the abolition of the Towrah destroy themselves, making their souls totally unacceptable to God. "I just didn't know" isn't an excuse. Nor is: "Everybody else was doing it." The truth is available. All you have to do is "*shabat* – celebrate the Shabat by reflecting upon" what God had to say – especially as it relates to His plan for settling our debts so we could settle down with Him.

Our celebration of the Covenant on the Shabat is a time to fully experience all the relationship has to offer. This is why it is the preeminent Instruction among the seven on the second of the two tablets. One day would not be just as good as another. The model God established regarding time and redemption is emblazoned on every reference to the seventh day.

When Yahowah etched the Ten Statements in stone with His own hand, He reiterated the formula…

INTRODUCTION

"**Moseh** (*wa Mosheh* – the One who Draws Out) **invited** (*qara' 'el* – summoned and welcomed, meeting with and calling out to for the purpose of reading and reciting (qal imperfect – establishing a genuine relationship with ongoing implications)) **all of** (*kol*) **Yisra'el** (*Yisra'el* – Individuals who Engage and Endure with God).

He said to them (*wa 'amar 'el hem* – he spoke on behalf of God to them), **'Choose to listen** (*shama'* – opt to hear) **this day** (*ha yowm* – at this time [from 4QDeut]), **Yisra'el** (*Yisra'el*), **to the clearly communicated prescriptions which have been engraved** (*'eth ha choq* – to the thoughts which are inscribed offering an allotment and share, to that which is carved in stone to cut us into the relationship) **along with the means to exercise good judgment and resolve disputes** (*wa ha mishpat* – as well as to the way to question the who, what, where, why, and how of being judgmental so as to be vindicated; from *ma* – to question and *shaphat* – to judge and decide), **which, to show the correct and beneficial way** (*'asher* – which to reveal the path to walk to get the most out of life and this relationship), **I am communicating** (*'any dabar* – I am conveying using written and spoken words (qal participle)) **in your hearing** (*ba 'ozen 'atah* – for your ears) **this day** (*ha yowm*).

You should choose of your own volition to learn about them (*wa lamed 'eth hem* – you should want to gather in this information and respond appropriately, instructing others what you have been taught regarding them (qal perfect consecutive)), **closely examining and carefully considering them** (*wa shamar la hem* – observing them under the auspices of freewill, becoming aware of, contemplating, and then celebrating them (qal perfect consecutive)) **so as to act upon them** (*la 'asah hem* – such that you engage and approach with them (qal infinitive construct)). (*Dabarym* / Deuteronomy 5:1)

Yahowah (𐤉𐤄𐤅𐤄), **our God** (*'elohym 'anachnuw*), **has cut** (*karat* – has made and established, creating through separating (qal perfect)) **a Covenant** (*beryth* – a family-oriented relationship, a mutually beneficial and binding contract) **with us** (*'im 'anachnuw*) **in Choreb** (*ba Choreb* – in the desolation of the desert along a knife-shaped section of stone). (*Dabarym* 5:2)

Yahowah (𐤉𐤄𐤅𐤄) **cut** (*karat* – made and established through separation (qal perfect)) **this Covenant** (*'eth ha beryth ha zo'th* – this specific relationship agreement as a unique family-oriented compact) **for us** (*'eth 'anachnuw*) **instead of our fathers** (*lo' 'eth 'aby 'anachnuw* – because it could not have been exactly the same with our forefathers), **for those of us here today** (*'anachnuw' 'el leh poh yowm* – for those of us in this place at this time) – **indeed for all of us who are alive now** (*ky kol 'anachnuw chay* – for all living among us [from 4QDeut]). (*Dabarym* 5:3)

Appearing before us and in our very presence (*paneh ba paneh* – His personal existence and identity directed toward us), **Yahowah** (𐤉𐤄𐤅𐤄) **spoke** (*dabar* – communicated using words, conversing (piel perfect)) **with you** (*'im 'atem* – in your company, engaged in a relationship with you) **at the mountain** (*ba ha har* – within the ridgeline) **out of the midst** (*min tawek* – from the middle) **of the fire** (*ha 'esh*). (*Dabarym* 5:4)

And (*wa* – so then [from 4QDeut]) **I was present, standing** (*'anoky 'amad* – I stood, accounted for, appointed and sustained, enduring (qal participle)), **discerning insights while making the connections necessary to better appreciate** (*bayn* – receiving the revelation while deducing its meaning so as to respond properly in connection to) **Yahowah** (𐤉𐤄𐤅𐤄) **for you, such that you would understand** (*wa bayn 'atem* – and also so that you would more fully comprehend) **Him in this moment and throughout time** (*ba ha 'eth ha huw'* – now and later, especially at the right moment in time) **by conspicuously providing this information to you in a straightforward manner, declaring and expounding upon** (*la nagad la 'atah* – announcing and making publicly known right in front of you, reporting in plain sight to you (hifil infinitive construct)) **the words** (*ha dabarym* – the statements and accounts [plural in 1QDeut]) **of Yahowah** (𐤉𐤄𐤅𐤄), **your God** (*'elohym 'atah* – your Mighty One [from 1QDeut]). (*Dabarym 5:5*)

And yet (*ky* – but by contrast, indeed), **you, rather than respect and revere the profound and awesome appearance of the fire, at that moment, you might have been frightened by the presence of the flames** (*yare' min paneh ha 'esh* – you could have been nervous and anxious, a bit timid to face the glowing light and energy (qal perfect)).

And so (*wa*), **you have not ascended** (*'alah* – you have not climbed or gone up (qal perfect)) **into the mountain** (*ba ha har*) **for the declaration of this statement** (*la 'amar* (qal infinitive))." (*Dabarym* / Words 5:5)

TABLET ONE

"'**I am** (*'anky*) **Yahowah** (𐤉𐤄𐤅𐤄 – YaHoWaH; from *y-hayah* – I was, I am, and I will always be), **your God** (*'elohym 'atah* – your shepherd, a ram among the sheep, the doorway to an expansive and abundant life for those who are engaged, standing up, reaching up, and looking up), **who relationally and beneficially** (*'asher* – who to show the correct and narrow path to get the most out of life) **brought you out and delivered you** (*yatsa' 'atah* – descended to serve you individually in this moment in time, extending Myself to guide you such that you would respond to Me, becoming more like Me in the process (hifil perfect – at this moment God engaged in such a way that

327

we were empowered to come out)) **away from the realm**
(*min 'erets* – out of the land) **of the crucibles of Egypt**
(*mitsraym* – the smelting furnace, serving as a metaphor for
the crucibles of political, religious, economic, and military
oppression), **out of the house** (*min beyth* – from the place)
of slavery and servitude (*'ebed* – of bondage and working
for one's salvation, of being under the control of
government authorities and religious officials). (*Dabarym*
5:6)

Quite literally, you will not continually exist with
(*lo' hayah la 'atah* – you shall not be, neither function nor
exist, drawing near if you negate the basis of your existence
(qal imperfect – continually and literally)) **other** (*'acher* –
someone else's, different, extra, another, or additional)
gods (*'elohym*) **over and above** (*'al* – elevated beyond, in
proximity to or near, before, or in addition to) **My presence**
(*paneh 'any* – My appearance or face, My proximity or
identity). (*Dabarym* 5:7)

You should not continue to act on behalf of or
associate yourself with (*lo' 'asah la 'atah* – you should
not make a practice of attending to nor doing anything with,
you should not conceive, celebrate, nor work near (qal
imperfect – conveying a literal interpretation of ongoing
actions with unfolding consequences)) **a religious image**
or object of worship (*pesel* – a shaped, sculpted, carved,
cast, chiseled, or designed icon or idol associated with the
divine, a depiction of a god), **or any** (*wa kol* – a variation
of a [*wa* is from 4QDeut]) **visual or formed**
representation of something (*tamunah* – likeness,
appearance, idiom, association, or appearance, in a shape
or form which resembles and attempts to establish a
relationship by way of a substitution), **which by**
association is (*'asher*) **in** (*ba*) **the heavens above** (*ha*
shamaym min ma'al), **or** (*wa*) **is related to that which is**
(*'asher*) **on** (*ba*) **the earth** (*ha 'erets*) **below** (*min tachath*),
or (*wa*) **found in connection** (*'asher*) **with** (*ba*) **the waters**

(*ha maym*) **beneath the land** (*min tachath la ha 'erets*). (*Dabarym* 5:8)

You should not speak about them on your own initiative nor make a practice of bowing down and worshiping them (*lo' chawah la hem* – you should not continue to promote their message nor display their words because such uncoerced and ongoing verbal declarations and announcements will influence you, you should not religiously prostrate yourself in obeisance and homage to them, show any allegiance to them, nor habitually make confessions (hitpael imperfect jussive – acting without any compulsion, habitually or continually responding to the will of the religious influences)).

And (*wa*) **you should not habitually serve them nor compel anyone to worship them** (*lo' 'abad hem* – you should not labor in their cause nor make a career of working as their ministers, you should not submit to them nor encourage anyone else to do so (hofal imperfect – you should not make a habit of compelling anyone to act or serve on their behalf)).

For, indeed (*ky* – emphasizing this point), **I** (*'anky*), **Yahowah** (𐤉𐤅𐤄𐤅), **your God** (*'elohy 'atah*), **am a fiercely protective and emotionally devoted God, a steadfastly loyal and jealous God** (*qana' 'el* – a God who is desirous of exclusivity in a deeply loving and committed relationship, a God who is defensive of those He zealously loves), **actually counting and reckoning** (*paqad* – literally taking stock of and genuinely recording (qal participle – a descriptive verb with literal implications)) **the perversity of twisting and distorting** (*'awon* – the depravity of perverting and manipulating, deviating from the way) **of the fathers** (*'ab* – of parents) **onto** (*'al*) **the children** (*ben* – sons) **to** (*'el* – unto [from 4QDeut]) **the third and the fourth generations** (*shileshym wa 'al ribea'*) **of those who are averse to Me** (*sane' 'any* – of those who are openly hostile and detest Me, who strive

329

maliciously against Me, shunning Me (qal participle – serving as a literal and vivid depiction as a verbal adjective)). (*Dabarym* 5:9)

However, I act and engage to prepare, perform, and produce (*'asah* – I actively effect and appoint, offering and celebrating, even demonstrating by doing what is required to deliver (qal participle)) **loyal and devoted love, unfailing mercy, unearned favor, and genuine kindness** (*chesed* – actual forgiveness, steadfast appreciation, and an affectionate relationship) **on behalf of** (*la'*) **thousands** (*'elephym*) **who move toward Me and love Me** (*la 'ahab 'any* – who form a close and affectionate, loving and friendly, familial relationship with Me) **and also** (*wa*) **who approach Me by closely observing and carefully considering** (*la shamar* – who enter My presence by becoming observant, thoroughly examining and thoughtfully evaluating (qal participle)) **My instructions and directions, My terms and conditions** (*mitswah 'any* – the verbal and written stipulations which uphold My Covenant, My authoritative guidelines which serve as prescriptions for My relationship agreement; a compound of *ma* – to ponder the who, what, why, when, where, and how questions regarding God's *tsawah* – authorized and authoritative communications). (*Dabarym* 5:10)

You should not continue to deceive, nor should you tolerate or support delusions (*lo' nasha'* – you should not habitually deploy or advance clever ideas to enrich yourself by indebting others, and you should avoid beguiling people by consistently promoting that which causes them to miss the way by forgetting something (qal imperfect)) **associated with** (*'eth* – through or by way of the) **the name and reputation** (*shem* – the renown and proper designation) **of Yahowah** (𐤉𐤄𐤅𐤄), **your God** (*'elohym*), **thereby negating the value of My name by advancing worthless and lifeless deceptions** (*la ha showa'* (errantly transliterated *shav'*) – deploying that which advances

330

dishonesty, nullifying one's existence, leading to emptiness and nothingness, lifeless lies which are ineffectual, futile, and ruinous).

For, indeed (*ky* – because), **Yahowah** (𐤉𐤄𐤅𐤄) **will not forgive or leave unpunished** (*lo' naqah* – as an ongoing admonition unconstrained by time, He will not purify nor pardon, He will not acquit nor free from guilt, He will not exempt from judgment or sentencing, nor will He consider innocent nor release (piel imperfect)) **those who** (*'eth 'asher* – in association with others) **consistently deceive, actually beguile, and habitually delude, promoting or accepting foolish notions which negate** (*nasha'* – religiously using deception to continually mislead, lifting up and advancing a clever, albeit dishonest, ruse in (qal imperfect)) **an association with** (*'eth* – through) **His name** (*shem* – renown, reputation, and proper designation) **such that it diminishes its value, including ineffectual lies which lead to lifelessness, nullifying one's existence** (*la ha showa'* – devastating deceptions which destroy, leading to emptiness, worthlessness, and nothingness, deceiving in a ruinous manner).'" (*Dabarym* / Words 5:11)

TABLET TWO

"**'Observe** (*shamar* – closely examine and carefully consider (qal infinitive absolute)) **that which is associated with the day of the Shabat** (*'eth ha yowm ha shabat* – the purpose of the seventh day, the period of reflection at the end of the week, reminiscent of the promise of settling debts so we can settle down by observing the oath in association with this means to satisfy and enrich; from *shaba'* – fulfilling and satisfying the promise of seven to abundantly empower and enrich) **so as to keep it set apart** (*la qadash huw'* – such that it remains separate and distinct unto Him for purifying and cleansing and thus special to approach Him (piel infinitive – Yahowah is engaged in dramatic fashion and acts in response to our willingness to set this day apart)), **consistent with its purpose which is to show the way to the benefits of the relationship as** (*ka 'asher* – for the express reason of its comparative symbolism which is designed to reveal the correct and straightforward path to walk to get the greatest joy out of life as) **Yahowah** (𐤉𐤅𐤄𐤅), **your God** (*'elohy 'atah*), **instructed you** (*tsawah 'atah* – directed you (piel perfect)). (*Dabarym* 5:12)

Six (*shesh* – that which is bleached white or adorned in fine linen) **days** (*yowmym* – periods of time) **you should actually and continuously work** (*'abad* – you should engage in ongoing labor, working for oneself or for another, expending the energy to be productive at your job (qal stem – denoting a literal interpretation and imperfect conjugation – speaking of that which is ongoing)), **and** (*wa*) **choose to act, engaging in** (*'asah* – express your freewill to prepare and accomplish what you can do at that time, capitalizing upon and advancing, doing and profiting from (qal perfect consecutive – addressing a genuine relationship in which the actions have been accomplished at some point in time under the auspices of freewill)) **all** (*kol* – the entirety of) **your service as a heavenly messenger** (*mala'kah 'atah* – your usefulness communicating as a Divine implement, working on behalf of the feminine manifestation of the Spiritual Messenger, making informative announcements as a witness on God's behalf; feminine of *mal'ak* – beings created to represent and serve God as messengers). (*Dabarym* 5:13)

But (*wa*) **the seventh** (*sheby'iy* – the solemn promise which fulfills and satisfies, abundantly enriching those who listen and are observant of the role of the seventh; from *shaba'* – to take an oath and make a sworn promise to fulfill, completely satisfying, providing an abundance of enriching benefits) **day** (*yowm* – period of time), **the**

Shabat (*ha shabat* – the seventh day, the period of reflection at the end of the week, reminiscent of the promise of settling debts so we can settle down by observing the oath of association; from *shaba'* – fulfilling and satisfying the promise of seven to abundantly empower and enrich), **is to approach** (*la* – is for drawing near, associating with and moving toward) **Yahowah** (𐤉𐤄𐤅𐤄), **your God** (*'elohym*).

On it (*'al hy'* – during it [from 4QDeut]), **you should not continuously engage in** (*lo' 'asah* – you should not habitually act out, consistently preparing or producing, nor should you try to actually fashion, accomplish, or constantly do (qal stem imperfect conjugation)) **any part of** (*kol*) **the service of God's Representative and Messenger** (*mala'kah* – endeavors of the Heavenly Envoy, serving as a witness; feminine of *mal'ak* – the ministry and mission of the Divine Implement, the endeavors and labor of God's spiritual manifestation and presence, the Maternal Counselor) **yourself** (*'atah*), **your son** (*ben*), **your daughter** (*bat*), **your male and female servants and staff** (*'ebed wa 'amah* – your employees and those men and women who work for and with you), **your means of production** (*behemah* – your animals and beasts of burden) **as well as** (*wa*) **those visitors** (*ger* – foreigners) **who relationally** (*'asher*) **are in your home or on your property** (*ba sha'ar* – are inside your doors or gates; from *sha'ar* – to think and be reasonable), **so that** (*lama'an* – for the reason, intent, and purpose) **your male and female employees** (*'ebed wa 'amah* – your staff and servants, those men and women who work for and with you), **as well as you** (*kamow 'atah* – like you, similarly and simultaneously along with you) **may be restored spiritually** (*nuwach* – may be reenergized spiritually; from *ruwach* – spirit (qal imperfect)). (*Dabarym* 5:14)

In addition (*wa*), **you should remember** (*zakar* – call to mind, recollect, mention, and proclaim (qal perfect)) that indeed (*ky*), **you were** (*hayah* – you existed as (qal perfect)) **a slave** (*'ebed* – a servant owned by another) **in the land** (*ba 'erets* – in the realm and country) **of the crucibles of Egypt** (*Mitsraym* – the pressure and hostility of religious and governmental oppression, and military and economic subjugation) **when** (*wa* – then) **Yahowah** (𐤉𐤄𐤅𐤄), **your God** (*'elohy 'atah*), **brought you out** (*yatsa' 'atah* – descended and extended Himself, came forth to lead and deliver you, taking you (hifil imperfect)) **from there** (*min sham | shem* – out of and away from that place called by this name and having that reputation) **with** (*ba* – by and in) **a resolutely firm, powerful and protective** (*chazaq* – very strong and influential, extraordinarily capable and intensely prepared, passionate and encouraging, assertive and steadfast) **hand** (*yad* – ability to accomplish the mission, a *yad* – the first letter in Yah's name which as an open hand reaching down and out, defining Yah's role in our lives), **and with** (*wa ba*) **the sacrificial lamb, the productive arm shepherding the flock** (*zarowa'* – the prevailing and effective nature, the strength, resolve, and overall ability of this remarkably important and impactful individual of action who, as a leader and fighter is engaged as a shepherd among his sheep, who is fruitful in his ways, accomplishing the mission, especially when sowing the seeds of truth while denoting and advancing the purpose of the arm of God, of His shepherd and sacrificial lamb) **having been extended** (*natah* – having been reached out and outstretched).

For this reason (*'al ken* – upon these grounds above all others, it is right that), **Yahowah** (𐤉𐤄𐤅𐤄), **your God** (*'elohy 'atah*), **instructed you** (*tsawah 'atah* – directed you (piel perfect)) **to approach by observing** (*la shamar* – to move toward and draw near, by closely examining and carefully considering (qal infinitive construct – a literal descriptive verb and actionable noun) [from 1QDeut]) **that which is associated with the day** (*'eth yowm*) **of the Shabat** (*ha shabat* – the seventh day, the period of reflection at the end of the week to observe the oath of association; from *shaba'* – fulfilling and satisfying the promise of seven to abundantly empower and enrich) **so that it is set apart and special** (*'eth qodesh* – so that it is uncommon, cleansing, and perfecting [from 1QDeut]). (*Dabarym* 5:15)

For (*ky*) **in six** (*shesh* – symbolic of mankind being bleached white and purified on the sixth) **days** (*yowmym*), **Yahowah** (𐤉𐤄𐤅𐤄) **acted and engaged, preparing and producing everything associated with completing** (*'asah* – totally fashioning, instituting, advancing, accomplishing, doing, celebrating, and attending to the full extent of (qal stem perfect conjugation)) **the heavens** (*'eth ha shamaym* – the spiritual realm) **and the earth** (*wa ha 'erets* – the material world), **as well as the waters** (*wa ha yam*) **and all** (*kol* – everything) **which relationally** (*'asher*) **is in them** (*ba hem*).

And then (*wa*), **He became completely settled spiritually** (*nuwach* – He resolved every remaining issue, satisfying and conciliating by way of the Spirit (*nuwach* is related to *ruwach* – spirit)) **during** (*ba*) **the Almighty's seventh** (*ha sheby'iy 'al* – God's solemn promise which fulfills and satisfies those who listen and are observant of the role of the oath of the seventh) **day** (*yowm*).

Therefore (*ken* – consequently, this is true and correct), **Yahowah** (𐤉𐤄𐤅𐤄) **blessed and adored** (*barak* – knelt down and lowered Himself, offering a greeting along with an opportunity to meet, favoring (piel perfect)) **everything associated with this day** (*'eth ha yowm*), **the Shabat** (*ha shabat* – the seventh day, the period of reflection at the end of the week, reminiscent of the promise of settling debts so we can settle down by observing the oath of association which abundantly satisfies, empowers, and enriches), **setting it apart** (*qodesh* – separating it from that which is common, ordinary, and popular, making it special)."' (*Dabarym* 5:15-6 from 1QDeut4)

Yahowah's instruction was unambiguous and authoritative. So, what do you suppose the motivation was for the imperial edict Constantine's propagandist, pseudo-historian, and Church father, Eusebius, recorded in 321 CE? "All things whatsoever that it was the duty to do on the Sabbath, these we have transferred to the Lord's Day." Emperor Constantine, credited by many as the founder of Roman Catholicism, called Sunday *"Sol Invictus Mithras"*—"The day of the Unconquerable Sun, Mithras." Under penalty of death, he decreed that all within his empire must cease work on Sun-Day to honor the sun god.

Did Constantine, at Eusebius' urging, do this because he and the newly empowered clerics were illiterate and thus ignorant? Was this exchange just a colossal blunder, one born out of confusion rather than intent? Or did Constantine issue this order at Eusebius' behest because they rejected Yahowah's revelation in favor of Paul's endorsement of the Roman Empire?

Changing the day is obviously and unambiguously in direct conflict with God's intent. So, I ask you, why did corrupting Yahowah's purpose become a life-and-death issue to General Constantine and the first Catholics? Why does every priest and virtually every pastor replicate their repudiation of Yahowah's instruction every Sunday morning? Why does anyone show up? Are people so lost, so ignorant and indoctrinated, that they can no longer differentiate between right and wrong, good and bad, religion or relationship, the first versus the seventh?

By virtue of the fact you are reading this, you are not part of the problem. You already know that the reason we are encouraged not to do Yahowah's work on the Sabbath, the seventh day, is because it is set apart as the day God knelt down, lowering Himself in love to lift us up. You

336

understand that this is why the seven *Mow'ed Miqra'ey* | Invitations to be Called Out and Meet with God are special, representing the seven essential steps in Yahowah's plan of adoption and reconciliation. You understand that they are prophetic of the work Yahowah will do and has done on our behalf.

Yahowah's instruction regarding this day was as we had surmised. He wants us to "*shamar* – be observant, closely examining and carefully considering" "'*eth ha yowm ha shabat* – that which is associated with the purpose of the seventh day, including its means to satisfy and enrich." He was clear, in that He wants us to "*la qadash huw'* – keep it set apart such that it remains separate and distinct unto Him." And this time, Yah added one of my favorite words, to tell us that our celebration of the Shabat should be "*ka 'asher* – consistent with its purpose which is to show the way to the benefits of the relationship." And then so that we would not be confused and wrongly attribute this day to an ethnicity or religious entity, "Yahowah our God" said that this "*tsawah* – instruction" came directly from Him.

In recognition that the six plus one days of creation are prophetic of six thousand years of human toil followed by a thousand years of "shabating," I see the following as revealing that the time remaining to share Yahowah's message is dwindling. We are fast approaching year 6000 Yah and the commencement of the Millennial Shabat: **"'Six days you may actually work and choose to act, engaging to accomplish what you can do during that time, capitalizing upon and advancing all of your services as a heavenly messenger, including your usefulness communicating as a Divine implement, because the seventh day, the Shabat, is to approach Yahowah, your God.'"**

During His definitive explanation of the purpose of the Shabat, Yahowah asks us to remember that we were once slaves to men, oppressed and subjugated by the religious and political. Having freed us from such men and their institutions, God defines the Shabat as a day of liberation, of deliverance from the ways of man. And that is what makes it "*qodesh* – set apart and separated from that which is common."

The surprise for many in this part of Yah's depiction is the use of *zarowa'*. We will discover that there are three of them – the first of whom was Moseh. He was asked to "*zarowa'* – shepherd the flock and sow the seeds of truth." The second was Yahowah's beloved Shepherd, the Mashyach Dowd, the productive and protective arm of God, the most important and impactful individual in human history. He was also the "sacrificial lamb" who volunteered to fulfill Pesach. And the third serves as his Herald, as someone sowing the seeds of reconciliation such that they may take root and grow. The ability to recognize and identify each will eventually loom large, as it is the key to unveiling several remarkable prophecies.

Beyond this realization, by using *chazaq* | firm and capable in conjunction with *yad* | hand and *natah* | to reach out, Yahowah is helping us better understand the outstretched yad / ﬞ / hand in His name. He has chosen to work through men like Moseh, Dowd, and Yada because it is against His nature to serve alone.

When we reach the statement in Dabarym 5:15, we are reminded that these are Yahowah's instructions on how to approach Him. They focus, as they did at the beginning, on being "*shamar* – observant." The path to God on this day is open to those who "closely examine and carefully consider" His Towrah's Guidance.

Yahowah concludes His dissertation on the Shabat, and how it is to be observed with these words: "**'And then (*wa*), He became completely settled, resolving every remaining issue spiritually (*nuwach*) as part of (*ba*) the**

Almighty's solemn promise to fulfill and satisfy those who listen and are observant regarding the role of the oath of the seventh (*ha sheby'iy 'al*) day (*yowm*). Therefore (*ken*), Yahowah (𐤅𐤄𐤅𐤉) blessed and adored, kneeling down in love to lift up (*barak*) everything associated with this day (*'eth ha yowm*), the Shabat (*ha shabat*), setting it apart and making it special (*qodesh*).'" (*Dabarym* 5:15-16)

According to the etymological tools at our disposal, *nuwach* wasn't so much about "resting," as in the absence of movement, but instead used to convey the idea that God's mind was completely settled, having achieved exactly what He had intended. By extension, *nuwach* speaks of "security," and thus of "victory and salvation."

This is confirmed in *Bare'syth* / Genesis 2:15. There, Yahowah "*nuwach* | safely settles 'Adam in the Garden." Then in Bare'syth 8:4, we discover that the Ark "*nuwach* | settled safely upon the mountains of Ararat" after the flood. It is even used in conjunction with Yahowsha' and the Ark of the Covenant: **"And it shall come to be similar to the soles of the feet of the priests who are lifting up and bearing the Ark of Yahowah, the Upright Pillar of all the Land, *nuwach* | settle securely and victoriously in the waters of the *Yarden* | Jordan. The waters of the Yarden shall be cut, and the waters will descend from above, and shall be present, taking a stand as one unified barrier."** (*Yahowsha'* / Yah Saves / Joshua 3:13)

Therefore, *nuwach* tells us that the Shabat is the time Yahowah settles on the means to achieve our eternal safety, our victory over death. It is the time God resolved the religious and political plagues which have separated us by settling our debts so that we could settle down with Him. Therefore, those who observe the Shabat as our celebration of the Covenant relationship will be settled in our Heavenly Father's Home.

339

Beyond this, it is important to note that "Yahowah *'barak* – descended, knelt down in love, diminishing Himself, to bless' [us on] the Shabat." It is the very day His Beloved's soul descended to *She'owl* bearing the burden of our guilt. This represents the single most important day in the history of the universe: the Shabat of the *Mow'ed Miqra'* of *Matsah* in 4000 Yah, 33 CE – a day forgotten by Christians and Jews.

The second most important Shabat is still on our horizon: *Sukah*, the seventh *Mow'ed Miqra'*, which will be fulfilled on a Shabat in year 6000 Yah, 2033 CE, ushering in the Millennial Shabat – a time when God will bless the Earth with His presence.

"Yahowah *'qodesh shabat yowm* – set the Shabat day apart, separating the Shabat from all other days, making the seventh day devoted to separation, cleansing, and purifying'" our souls.

Having read the Word, and having come to know God, I am certain that Yahowah's position on the Shabat remains unchanged. While Yah's Instructions serve many purposes, they are as vital today as they were when He etched them in stone. Observing them makes us happier and more productive, prolonging our days unto eternity in the Promised Land, according to Dabarym 4:40. They exist so that we might learn from them, suggesting that there is profound truth beneath the plain reading. Observing them is one of the ways we demonstrate our respect and reverence for Yahowah based on the preamble in Dabarym 10:12.

According to God, His Towrah instructions serve as the answer to the most important question ever asked…

"So then (*'attah* – from this time forth), **Yisra'el** (individuals who live with and are empowered by God), **what** (*mah*) **will Yahowah** (𐤉𐤄𐤅𐤄), **your God** (*'elohym*), **ask** (*sha'al* – look for, question and earnestly request) **from**

you (*min 'im* – as part of our association and relationship)?'" (*Dabarym* / Deuteronomy 10:12)

The answer is:

"**Surely** (*ky* – indeed, truthfully), **if** (*'im*) **you revere and respect** (*yare'* – highly value) **Yahowah** (*YaHoWaH* – an accurate presentation of the name of *'elowah* – God as guided by His *towrah* – instructions regarding His *hayah* – existence), **your God** (*'elohym*), **you will walk** (*halak* – you will proceed) **in** (*ba*) **all** (*kol*) **His ways** (*derek*).

As a result, you will come to love (*wa 'ahab* – you will befriend and adore Him in a familial sense, developing a close, affectionate relationship with) **Him, choosing to serve with** (*'aba' 'eth*) **Yahowah** (ⵈⵖⵈⵀⵍ), **your God** (*'elohym*), **with regard to** (*ba*) **all of your thinking and decisions** (*kol lebab* – the entirety of your best judgment, inclinations, motivations, and thoughts) **and with all your soul** (*wa kol nepesh 'atah* – your entire consciousness).

You should closely observe (*shamar* – you ought to examine and carefully consider, treasuring and celebrating), **accordingly,** (*'eth*) **the terms and conditions of the relationship** (*mitswah* – the authoritative directions and instructions of the agreement which are mutually binding) **of Yahowah** (*Yahowah* - written as directed by His *towrah* – teaching regarding His *hayah* – existence), **and also** (*wa*) **the clearly communicated prescriptions** (*chuqah* – that which has been engraved in stone describing what one should do) **which relationally are for the benefit of the relationship** (*'asher* – which to so show the way to get the most out of life) **I** (*'anky*) **have instructed and directed you** (*tsawah*) **today** (*yowm*) **for** (*la*) **your benefit** (*towb* – to make you pleasing, valuable, and agreeable, prosperous, beautiful, and happy)." (*Dabarym* / Words / Deuteronomy 10:12-13)

God wants man to love Him or, at the very least, respect and befriend Him. This is the sole reason we were created. He even tells us that paying attention to His prescriptions is for our own good – and that would include observing the Shabat.

So, I don't suppose Yahowah is pleased with religious clerics and their congregations for having negated His Statements, effectively showing that they do not respect Him or His advice. And while we have focused on the First of Seven Instructions Yahowah etched in stone on the second of two tablets, because this has been God's focus, religious types have routinely rejected the first three statements on the initial tablet as well. And while secularists make a mockery of the last six instructions, we'll deal with them later.

In that I have shared them with you, let's leave this chapter devoted to the Shabat by carefully considering the three statements Yahowah etched on the first of the two tablets. The first Statement, or Instruction for living, introduces God by name. Yet, there isn't a single Christian or Jewish congregation of significance to be found anywhere in the world that consistently proclaims Yahowah's name. And most do not even know it.

Yahowah revealed that He is our liberator and that He is devoted to our freedom. As such, the notion of submitting to and obeying a Lord is preposterous. Most importantly, Yahowah saved us from ourselves, from being subjugated and oppressed by religions and governments. As such, we can live with Him or die without Him.

"'I am Yahowah, your God (a ram among the sheep and your shepherd, your doorway to an expansive abundant life), who relationally and beneficially to show the correct and narrow path to get the most out of this beneficial relationship brought you out and delivered you, descending to serve you by doing everything which was required to lead those who respond away from the land of Egypt and the realm of

the crucibles of political, religious, economic, and military oppression, out of the house of slavery, that place of worship and servitude, of bondage and working for one's salvation, and of government authority and religious officials.

You shall not actually or continually exist with other, different or additional, gods over and above My presence.'"

In the Second Statement Yahowah asks us to avoid religious imagery and worship. Yet Christian churches display carved statues of "Mary" as the "Mother of God and Queen of Heaven," in addition to graven images of "Jesus Christ" as a dead god on a stick. Knowing they were in violation of the Second Statement, for centuries the Roman Catholic Church actually removed it from God's list, dividing the tenth into two parts to keep the total unchanged.

"'You should not continue to associate yourself with nor make a practice of attending to, you should not engage on behalf of a religious image, object of worship, or any representation of any god, nor visual representation of something which is in the heavens above, including the sun, moon, planets, and stars, or which is on the earth below, or which is in the waters beneath the land.

You should not speak about them on your own initiative nor make a practice of bowing down and worshiping them. You should not promote their message on your own accord nor display their words because such uncoerced and ongoing verbal declarations will influence you. You should not worship them, especially if not compelled or forced, and you should not serve them nor encourage anyone to be passionate about them.

Do not work or labor in their cause nor make a career of serving as their ministers, nor inspire anyone else to do so.

For, indeed, I, Yahowah, your God, am a fiercely protective, steadfastly loyal, and jealous God, a God who is desirous of exclusivity in a deeply devoted relationship.

I consider and reckon the perversity of twisting and distorting, and the depravity of perverting and manipulating, deviating from the way, of the fathers upon the children up to the third and the fourth generations of those who are openly hostile and adverse toward Me, striving maliciously against Me while shunning Me.

And yet, I will genuinely act and engage to literally prepare, perform, and produce loyal and devoted love, unfailing mercy, unearned favor, and genuine kindness, even forgiveness, developing an affectionate relationship on behalf of thousands who move toward Me and love Me, forming a close and familial relationship with Me, caring enough to know Me, and also who approach Me by closely observing and carefully considering My instructions, the terms and conditions which uphold My Covenant.'"

Fathers corrupt their children by leading them astray. It is one of many reasons we should recognize that the Father we should honor in the fifth statement is our Heavenly Father rather than the ones who have misled us.

Yahowah is merciful and loving, but not universally so. His kindness is directed toward the thousands who closely examine and carefully consider the terms and conditions of His Covenant. It is a seldom considered realization, but thousands among billions is just one in a million. Heaven will be an uncrowded and surprisingly unpopular place.

With catastrophic consequences, every Jewish and Christian denomination has edited the Third Statement such that it reinforces their abuse of the First. Yet in it, at least properly translated, Yahowah actually condemned this deceitful tactic.

No matter how many hundreds of millions of Bibles, placards, and statuary say otherwise, Yahowah did not write: "You shall not take the name of the Lord, thy God, in vain." Not even close. He wrote…

"'You should not continue to deceive, beguiling people by promoting delusions regarding the name and reputation of Yahowah, your God, thereby advancing worthless deceptions and devastating dishonesty, nullifying one's existence.

For, indeed, Yahowah will not forgive nor exempt from judgment an individual who consistently deceives using religious duplicity to mislead, advancing dishonest ruses to forget His name because these lies lead to lifelessness.'"

Why is it that Jews avoid speaking Yahowah's name as if it were a deadly curse? Why did the Roman Catholic Church ban its use? They actually did this very thing on June 29, 2008, in a letter from the Vatican's top liturgical body, the Congregation for Divine Worship and Sacraments, to Catholic Bishops' Conferences worldwide. This directive prohibiting the inclusion of Yahowah's name from any aspect of Roman Catholicism was issued by Pope Benedict XVI.

Why do Jews and Christians call God "the LORD," "HaShem," "'Adonai," "Jesus," or "Christ," when none of these is His name? How is it that Jews and Christians alike have been beguiled into believing that this "Commandment" condemns saying "God Damn" when in fact, they are damning themselves for interpreting Yahowah's instruction that way? As ironic as it may seem,

345

their substitution of names and misrepresentation of words violated the very Statement they were corrupting.

Let's listen to what Moseh said in His presentation on the Statements and Instructions...

"**In association with** ('eth – when accompanying and associated with, to be in accord with and concerning) **Yahowah** (𐤉𐤄𐤅𐤄 – the pronunciation of *YaHoWaH* as guided by His *towrah* – teaching regarding His *hayah* – existence)**, your God** ('*elohym* '*atah*)**, you should show respect for Him by serving alongside Him** (*yare*' '*eth huw*' '*abad* – you should genuinely and consistently revere Him and be inspired by Him, showing concern regarding Him by working with Him, affording Him the status He deserves, continually cognizant of His awesome nature, while expending considerable energy and intensity engaging beside Him).

And with regard to Him (*wa ba huw*' – therefore, unto Him)**, stay close and remain in an intimate relationship** (*dabaq* – be closely associated, join and cling to, pursue and stick together, holding fast and staying with, being steadfast and faithful).

Then, with His name (*wa ba shem huw*' – in His personal and proper designation and reputation)**, you should affirm the truth as a witness** (*shaba*' – promise to do what is right, confirming the relevance of seven). (*Dabarym* / Deuteronomy 10:20)

He is your source of positive and empowering words and your acclaimed reputation (*huw*' *tahilah* '*atah* – He is the source of your commendation and thanksgiving, your laudable qualities and magnificent blessings, your renown and the manifestation of your power; from *halal*, meaning that which radiates light; from *halal* – to shine, to be brilliant, and to radiate light).

He is your God (*wa huw' 'elohym 'atah*) **who relationally and beneficially** (*'asher* – who has led, showing the correct steps to follow to get the most out of life) **acted and engaged with you to prepare and produce** (*'asah 'eth 'atah* – worked in concert with you to do, fashioning, accomplishing, instituting, and performing for you (qal perfect)) **with regard to these many great** (*'eth ha gadowl* – numerous magnificent and distinguished, important and extensive; from *gadal* – empowering, magnifying, and growth-promoting) **and** (*wa*) **tremendously awesome** (*'eth ha yare'* – awe-inspiring and astonishing, worthy of respect and honorable) **things that, for your benefit, you have witnessed with your eyes** (*ha 'elleh 'asher ra'ah 'ayn 'atah* – which to reveal the correct path to walk to get the most out of life you were visually shown (qal perfect))." (*Dabarym* / Words / Deuteronomy 10:21)

We tangibly demonstrate our respect for Yahowah when we engage and work along with Him for the betterment of mankind and the Covenant relationship. I am inspired to serve with Him.

In this way, respect is reciprocal and reciprocated. God appreciates those who engage on behalf of His testimony and people. Recognizing our relative capabilities, Yahowah is thrilled when we endeavor to serve with Him, even though our contribution to the relationship and mission will always be less robust than His own. There are so few who are willing that God makes the most of every opportunity.

Our purpose in life is to engage in an intimate relationship with Yahowah, as if He is our Father, learn from Him, and then attend to the needs of His Family. With nearly seven million words written thus far on twenty thousand pages in thirty-five books, that is the essence of what I have tried to convey.

In Yahowah's name, and with His name, we should devote ourselves to affirming His truth as credible witnesses. His words are resolutely positive and absolutely empowering. Whatever contribution I may have made and acclaim I may have achieved as a result over the past score of years are solely attributable to His laudable qualities. Even a flimsy stem grafted into a productive branch can produce fruit.

Yahowah has engaged on behalf of His children and will do so again. And each time, past and future, He will do so in concert with us, and for our benefit.

The Covenant is not an entitlement nor a God-given right. Entry into Yahowah's Family is afforded to those who choose to benefit from what you are witnessing.

Sadly, many clerics and most theologians hold a contrarian position. The Talmud, for example, serves to transfer authority from God to man. Rabbis, holding a manmade title derived from *rabah*, meaning "exceedingly great and enlarged, reaching a very high status," claim that service to them, to a group of religious men without mention in Towrah, is the highest calling – one which leads to redemption. The Talmud further claims that failure to serve these self-exalted men leads to exile from the community of Yisra'el. Since this conflicts with the Word, either Yahowah or the Jewish religious leaders are disingenuous.

It is worth noting that *shaba'*, translated as "affirming the truth as a witness," vocalized above as *sheba'*, is the Hebrew word for "seven." And in this regard, *shaber* means "to interpret and explain the meaning or significance of a communication." Along with "*shabat* – the day to reflect on God's promise to liberate us from human oppression on the seventh day," we quickly discover that all these words and concepts are related, elucidating the meaning and purpose of the Shabat.

This brings us to an important and yet misunderstood word. *Yare'* can mean "fear and terrify" or it can mean "revere and respect, to see as awesome and inspiring." Both definitions are equally valid. So, each time the word appears, it is incumbent upon the translator to choose the definition most in keeping with the intent of the message portrayed in the Towrah.

In support of prior religious dictates, English translators universally render *yare'* "fear," even though that definition is most often in conflict with the context of the discussion and with God's nature and purpose. But that should not be surprising; these same religious clerics replaced Yahowah's name with Satan's title, "Lord," in this passage and elsewhere.

I have rendered *yare'* "revere and respect" for three reasons. First, this statement, like the previous one, is about love and close personal relationships. Respect and reverence are not only compatible with this kind of intimacy, they are baseline requirements. Second, since one should never approach or love someone they are afraid of, rendering *yare'* "fear" is obviously a mistake.

And third, Yahowah said that fearing Him was a manmade tradition. God inspired *Yasha'yah* / Salvation and Deliverance are from Yahowah / Isaiah to write:

"Then (*wa*), **Yahowah** (*YaHoWaH* – an accurate presentation of the name of *'elowah* – God as guided by His *towrah* – instructions regarding His *hayah* – existence [from 1QIsa]) **said** (*'amar* – stated and declared (qal imperfect)), **'Indeed** (*ky* – emphasizing this point), **forasmuch as** (*ya'an* – since with intent, and on account of this reason, because) **these people** (*ha 'am ha zeh* – the nation and clans) **approach Me** (*nagash 'any* – present themselves before Me and confront Me) **with their mouths, and with their lip service** (*ba peh huw' wa ba sapah huw'* – language that is ironic, statements which

349

depict a false sense of light in deep shadows and utter gloom, words which vainly seek approval), **putting on airs** (*kabad* – pretending to be somebody special, acting in a pretentious way), **they avoid exercising good judgment and distance themselves** (*wa rachaq leb huw'* – wandered away spiritually, emotionally, and intellectually, allowing their hearts to become distant) **from Me** (*min 'any*).

And their fear (*wa yira'th hem* – their sense of dread and distress (qal infinitive active)) **of Me** (*'eth 'any* – regarding Me) **exists** (*hayah* – is and occurs (qal imperfect)) **as a condition** (*mitswah* – an authoritative directive, prescription, and directive) **of men** (*'iyshym* – of individuals and mankind) **which is taught** (*lamad* – is part of their instruction and training, even indoctrination (pual passive participle – these individuals suffer the effect passively and yet demonstrably as a verbal adjective)).'"* (*Yasha'yah* / Freedom and Salvation are from Yah / Isaiah 29:13)

Fearing God makes religions tick. It is how they control the masses. They use it to influence donations. It makes them powerful. People want to be protected from a fearsome deity. And they will do almost anything to avoid such a spirit's wrath. It is why the Quran's most telling verse says: "Those who fear will obey." Perhaps that is why Islam means "submission."

The *beryth* is a familial relationship, one that thrives upon respect. Man was conceived for this purpose. And that is the reason we turned to this passage, as it unmasks a grotesque translation error. Since you cannot love what you fear, it is obvious that *yare'* should be translated as "revere and/or respect" when used in reference to God.

In *Dabarym* / Deuteronomy, He taught us that He loves us and wants us to love Him in return. The fear of God is a manmade corruption, a human invention, a stifling and deadly abomination which causes men to cower in the face of religion.

This verse is instructive of something else. It represents one of the 132 times the Masoretes actually removed Yahowah's name from His testimony and replaced it with *'adonay* – a noun typically translated as "Lord." Fortunately, the Dead Sea Scrolls correctly preserve Yahowah's signature in the text. "Lord" is Ba'al's title; it is what *ba'al* means; it is what Satan craves. Lord is neither God's name nor His title. Although, Satan's sun-god manifestation, Adonis, seemed pleased with it.

The reason I bring the textual error to your attention during this discussion of seven and the *Shabat* is because, when you add the number of times Yahowah's name has been retained in His Word (6,868) to the number of times we know it was replaced by rabbis (132), we get yet another confirmation of Yahowah's affinity for seven. Do you suppose that it's just a coincidence that Yahowah included His name in the Torah, Prophets, and Psalms exactly 7,000 times?

Make no mistake. The removal of God's name from His Word is the result of religion, of man controlling men by recreating God in their own image. Rabbis insist on calling their god "*HaShem* – the Name," and aggressively denigrate anyone who says or writes "Yahowah."

Religion is nothing more than lip service, a worthless flicker of artificial light in an ocean of gloom – of half-truths which have whitewashed and covered over the Divine writ. They are based upon concealment (removing Yahowah's name for example), corruption (justifying Sunday over the Sabbath or the Talmud over the Towrah as another), counterfeit (substituting Passover for Easter or Rosh Hashanah for Taruw'ah), and replacement (Gentiles for Jews and the Church for Israel). Yahowah is not buying it. He knows the difference between real and fake, the truth and a counterfeit, even if men do not.

There are billions of Christians (most of whom are Catholics) who believe that their Church is authorized to establish doctrine as an ongoing part of revelation. And while there is no justification for their position, and plenty of statements which condemn this view, the claim becomes especially beguiling and lethal because most religious edicts conflict with and contradict God's testimony, changing or misrepresenting what He has said. Their position falls like a house of cards in the slightest breeze. If the Word of God cannot be trusted, then God cannot be trusted. If the Word of God is not reliable, God is not reliable. If God's teachings do not stand the test of time, then they are incapable of extending our time. If God's Word was for a different people in a different place, then it has no value to us today.

More to the point, an organization that routinely contradicts the Divine writ upon which it claims to be based is irrefutably false – as are its teachings. Two things which contradict one another cannot both be true.

ᛧᛉᚥᛉᚱ